THE ENGLISH-SPEAKING CARIBBEAN

CARIBBEAN

a bibliography of bibliographies

A
Reference
Publication
in
Latin American
Studies

William V. Jackson
Editor

THE ENGLISH-SPEAKING CARIBBEAN

a bibliography of bibliographies

ALMA JORDAN *and* BARBARA COMISSIONG

G.K. HALL & CO.

70 LINCOLN STREET, BOSTON, MASS.

Library of Congress Cataloging in Publication Data

Jordan Alma.
  The English-speaking Caribbean.

  (Reference publications in Latin American studies)
  Includes indexes.
    1. Bibliography—Bibliography—Caribbean Area.
  2. Caribbean Area—Bibliography.   3.   West Indies,
  British—Bibliography.   I.   Title.   II.   Series.
  Z1595.J67   1984   [F2161]   016.0169729   84-16823
  ISBN 0-8161-8607-3

This publication is printed on permanent/durable acid-free paper
MANUFACTURED IN THE UNITED STATES OF AMERICA

Contents

The Authors vii

Preface ix

Acknowledgments xxi

Location Symbols xxiii

THE ENGLISH-SPEAKING CARIBBEAN 1

    Bibliography of Bibliographies 1
    Bibliography, General--Library Catalogues 7
    Bibliography, Regional 18
    Bibliography, National 20
    Bibliography, General 22
    Agriculture 108
    Anthropology 125
    Archaeology 128
    Architecture 129
    Art 129
    Biography 129
    Biology 141
    Botany 143
    Commerce and Trade 145
    Communication 145
    Criminology. 148
    Dance 149
    Description and Travel 149
    Economics 151
    Education 158
    Ethnic Groups 164
    Ethnography 168
    Ethnology 169

Ethnomusicology 174
Folklore 176
Forestry 180
Geography 182
Geology 185
History 190
Housing and Planning 218
Industrial Relations 218
Industry and Technology 219
International Relations 226
Language and Linguistics 228
Law 234
Librarianship 256
Literature 257
Medicine 278
Music 282
Natural Resources 283
Numismatics 284
Oceanography 285
Philately 285
Political Sociology 286
Politics and Government 287
Population 300
Psychology 303
Race Relations 304
Regional Co-operation and Integration 306
Religion 311
Science 315
Slavery and Slave Trade 317
Social and Economic Conditions 320
Social and Economic Development 329
Social Sciences 334
Sociology 345
Spiritualism 345
Statistics 346
Tourism 347
Transportation 348
Volcanoes 348
Women 349
Youth and Adolescence 351
Zoology 352

Name Index 355

Subject Index 385

The Authors

Alma Jordan is University Librarian at the University of the West Indies and stationed at the St. Augustine campus in Trinidad and Tobago. She was a founding member and first President of the Association of Caribbean University Research and Institutional Libraries (ACURIL) and is also a Past President of the Seminar on the Acquisition of Latin American Library Materials (SALALM). Her doctoral dissertation on library co-operation in the Caribbean was published in 1970 by Scarecrow Press. She has edited the Proceedings of the first two ACURIL conferences published by the American Library Association in 1973 entitled Research library cooperation in the Caribbean and published several articles on Caribbean libraries and librarianship.

Barbara Comissiong is Deputy Librarian at the St. Augustine Campus of the University of the West Indies in Trinidad and Tobago. She has been involved in bibliographic projects at the university library and published a Preliminary Index to Chairmen of Trinidad and Tobago Commissions of Enquiry. She has also published a Select Bibliography of Women Writers in the Eastern Caribbean (excluding Guyana) in World Literature Written in English.

Preface

Origins

This bibliography of bibliographies of and on the English-speaking territories of the Caribbean has been in the making for several years. More than ten years ago in the course of our efforts to serve researchers on Caribbean topics, we began to observe an upsurge in the number of bibliographies covering the Caribbean area, in whole or in part. Several related factors had also come to our attention over the years. Among these were:

1) the increasing pursuit of research on the Caribbean within and outside the region and the conflicting absence of organized bibliographic control in support of such studies

2) the relative wealth of sources, especially in-house and ad hoc compilations by libraries and individual researchers in response to specific enquiries or research needs, as well as for special occasions, such as documenting an exhibition; although of potential value to research most of these remain virtually unknown outside the institutions where they originated

3) the unsystematic and incomplete nature of many existing compilations in relation to arrangement, subject coverage, content, and bibliographic form and therefore difficulty of access to complete information

4) the extent of duplication in coverage and repetition of some themes with an obvious neglect of others.

In this setting the need for a comprehensive subject listing to rationalize these piecemeal and partly unpublished efforts in the field of Caribbean bibliography was obvious. It is against this background that this compilation was conceived and undertaken. At that time there were no national bibliographies and the main regional bibliography--Current Caribbean Bibliography, which is now dormant-- suffered from increasing delays. Few published sources of information

on Caribbean bibilography as a whole existed and although this
pattern has since begun to improve, with one regional and four
national bibliographies in regular publication, the other factors
identifying this need continue to prevail; indeed, many of them have
been accentuated with the passage of time.

Objectives

In this undertaking we therefore set out to follow in the path
set by our predecessors in the compilation of major bibliographies of
this nature. In the tradition of Besterman, whose monumental and
landmark World Bibliography of Bibliographies still stands out, and
Gropp, whose Bibliography of Latin American bibliographies comes
nearer to home, we aim, on a still narrower plane, at providing as
comprehensive a list as possible of the known bibliographies of all
kinds--general and special, national and regional, retrospective and
current, on the English-speaking Caribbean.

The bibliography is designed to guide and assist researchers on
Caribbean topics in the task of identifying published and unpublished
works relevant to their fields of interest and held by libraries
within or outside the region. It aims not only at making information
on existing sources more readily accessible and widely known but also
at emphasizing the research potential in the field of Caribbean
Studies and, indirectly, at highlighting areas of least coverage as a
guide to more systematic bibliographic work on this area in the
future.

Further, it is our hope that this effort may promote more
constructive interaction between experts in their several fields and
librarians who attempt to provide support services in anticipation of
their needs. By publishing information on a wealth of available
sources some improvement in resources may follow wherever Caribbean-
centred research is being conducted since building library resources
is a natural adjunct of such research.

Previous Bibliographies

There is no comparable bibliography of Caribbean bibliographies
but all major bibliographies of the Caribbean published in recent
years include useful (though short) sections on bibliographies.
Notable among these is Lambros Comitas' Caribbeana, two editions of
which have appeared in the last decade. Standard works such as
Besterman's World Bibliography of Bibliographies, Gropp's Bibliography of Bibliographies of Latin America and the Caribbean, and the
supplements to this work all include some references to Caribbean
bibliographies which are traceable in some cases through the indexes.

Noteworthy attempts at listing bibliographies on the area have
also been made continuously by the Bibliography Committees of two
Library Associations--SALALM--the Seminar on the Acquisition of Latin
American Library Materials and ACURIL--the Association of Caribbean
University, Research and Institutional Libraries. After annual
compilations by the Bibliography Committee from 1973 to 1975 ACURIL
agreed to merge its own file of references for the English-speaking
areas with this compilation in order to avoid duplication of effort.
The SALALM Bibliography Committee has continued to prepare annual
listings including references to Caribbean items as part of its wider
scope, and latterly both author and subject indexes have been provided.
Work in progress is included in these SALALM listings and they are
being regularly edited for publication as supplements to the Gropp
bibliography; two of these supplements have appeared so far.

The wealth of bibliographic activity in and on the English-
speaking Caribbean is best attested to by Irene Zimmerman's[1] paper
on the subject at ACURIL 1 (1969) and by Valerie Bloomfield's[2] paper
for SALALM XXIV (1979) ten years later. It is hoped that this
comprehensive compilation in a single source appropriately culminates
these years of widespread activity in the field.

Scope

The bibliography covers bibliographies produced up to April 1981
about the lands and peoples of the former British Caribbean terri-
tories, both island and mainland. These include: Anguilla, Antigua,
Bahamas, Barbados, Barbuda, Belize, Bermuda, British Virgin Islands,
Cayman Islands, Dominica, Grenada, Guyana, Jamaica, Montserrat, St.
Kitts-Nevis, St. Lucia, St. Vincent, Turks and Caicos Islands, and
Trinidad and Tobago. Nowadays they are most conveniently referred to
as the English-speaking Caribbean. The U.S. Virgin Islands (St.
Thomas and St. Croix), which should also be embraced by the latter
description are not, however, included; they have had no British
affiliation and were not part of the Federation of the West Indies
which lasted from 1958 to 1962.

Previous sub-groupings such as the Windward Islands (Dominica,
Grenada, St. Lucia, and St. Vincent) and the Leeward Islands
(Antigua, Montserrat, St. Kitts, and Nevis-Anguilla) are reflected
in the bibliography. So too are many of the other group names, such
as the Associated States, which have been applied to the smaller
states of the Eastern Caribbean. Many of these territories have
become independent in very recent times and increasing interest in
pursuing serious study on them is already evident.

The delimitation of a bibliography of this nature is a practical
necessity that poses unavoidable problems. The Caribbean, while
subject to many definitions and distinctions in different contexts,
is nonetheless an integrated unit in many respects. Inevitably,

therefore, some items listed in this bibliography include the Dutch and/or Spanish (and occasionally Frency) speaking territories as well as the English-speaking. In order to cover Guyana adequately, for example, some titles are listed that are otherwise exclusively on the Netherlands Antilles or the French Caribbean. Moreover, some or all of these Caribbean territories are often included as parts of Latin America so that a number of items are cited which have this wider coverage as well. The problem arises also in reverse in that items on Latin America in several sources checked, which may well include the Caribbean islands, could not always be so identified, and they often had to be omitted unless they were seen and their scope verified. Even in cases where they are included, the extent of such coverage can vary widely and difficult decisions were posed.

Further problems of this kind arose in the case of publications on the British Commonwealth where coverage of these former British colonies also varies. Although basically aiming at exhaustive listing of all relevant bibliographies we drew the line at listings on wider areas for which Caribbean coverage was very slight and inconsequential.

The work includes both brief and substantial bibliographies, whether unpublished, privately issued, appearing in conference proceedings, or otherwise published as separate items. It also includes lists appearing in journals, unlike Besterman, but like Gropp who provided these in a separate work. Titles identified as most relevant were fully searched, while a number of other scattered journal references were brought to light in the course of our searches in other sources. Bibliographies provided in books were included only where it was considered that they were significant either by their scholarly nature, extensive and important listings, or their useful addition to an otherwise poor subject coverage. Although more substantial than some brief in-house compilations which have been listed, bibliographies as parts of books which have not been included are more easily traced and, therefore, any references they include are less likely to be missed. In a few cases independent biblio-graphies (even by a different author), or wide-ranging background bibliographies were found to accompany books with narrower subject titles, and these were included. Such inclusions, which may seem arbitrary at first, were based on careful decisions related to our main purpose in time-saving assistance to researchers and librarians serving them. Some listings located on library files, even in photo-copy rather than originals, were of unspecified origin and often undated, but in keeping with the criteria outlined above these were included.

Excluded are publishers' and booksellers' catalogues with a few rare exceptions based on the above criteria; with the exceptions already noted, routine bibliographies in books are excluded, as are foreign language sources except where these happened to come to our attention through one of the sources listed. The catalogues of outstanding library collections with relevant and specialized holdings are, however, included. Lists, catalogues, and other descriptions of manuscript and other archival material and of non-book material such as maps, films, phonograph records, etc., are all included as research material. Bibliographies appearing in the many unpublished theses on Caribbean topics were not included but many lists of such theses themselves appear in the bibliography.

Several in-house compilations known to be in progress or on cards awaiting final editing were excluded, partly because it was uncertain when and how they would be taken forward, and partly because access to these could not be guaranteed. The number of such items in progress of which we became aware further attests to the wealth of potential research aids and the continuing concern and enthusiasm of many in this regard.

Methodology and Sources

The assembling of entries for this compilation was approached in several ways to ensure as full a coverage as possible within the defined limits.

1. First, a circular letter was addressed to all major libraries (public, special and university) in the region explaining our purpose and requesting items produced or held by them as well as any others of which they were aware. A few letter responses with lists of references, especially to in-house bibliographies, were received.
2. Second, the holdings of major libraries in the region were checked on different occasions up to 1981. The three campus libraries of the University of the West Indies and the University of Guyana were fully covered as was the Institute of Jamaica (now the National Library of Jamaica) through its published catalogue.

    In the case of the Central Library of Trinidad and Tobago its bibliography correspondence files were checked and entries prepared directly from all the typescript, photocopy, or mimeographed lists located.
3. The holdings of three major libraries outside the Caribbean were checked as follows: Foreign and Commonwealth Office Library, London; Institute of Commonwealth Studies, University of London; and Research Institute for the Study of Man, New York.
4. A full list of relevant published sources was drawn up and systematically checked.

In a sense all the items of the bibliography itself served as sources. Two special side-effects of this process should be noted. First, many sources led to a chain of new entries as new bibliographies cited in one source often led to further new references when they were in turn located for consultation. Truly, "of the making making of bibliographies there is no end"![3] Many such secondary source citations unfortunately have remained unseen; while these additions contribute to further comprehensiveness and are in that context most welcome, there is a second (and potentially dangerous) side-effect against which it was impossible to take precaution without full knowledge in each case. This is the repetition of mistakes appearing in such secondary sources, which could be gravely misleading.

Two examples of incorrect citations which might well have been repeated here (were they not so recognized) should serve to illustrate this danger. In Besterman's deservedly renowned World Bibliography of Bibliographies, located under the heading Anguilla is a French title referring not to the island Anguilla but to "l'anguille" (the eel) and a second equally unlikely English title on the electric eel. Similarly in the same work listed under Dominica are titles referring both to the Spanish-speaking Dominican Republic and the English-speaking island (now the Republic) of Dominica. Besterman himself makes reference to secondhand and untrustworthy sources and to the inevitable mistakes and omissions which can plague the unwitting bibliographer.

In some cases the citations for unseen works in two (or even more) sources are in conflict on the exact form of a title or on other bibliographic details and the older more contemporary work has been quoted by choice.

Thus, although the bibliography draws on many sources and on the resources of many libraries, both within and outside the Caribbean region, it is largely based on items which were seen and examined by one of us, both to evaluate appropriateness and to prepare an annotation. Notwithstanding this general intention, some items, either submitted by the ACURIL Bibliography Committee, or for which references otherwise came to hand, could not be obtained and remain unannotated.

Apart from the general assessment of bibliographies in books for possible inclusion as described before, no attempt has been made to evaluate the usefulness of items included. Instead, the approximate number of entries is frequently given (even for unnumbered bibliographies) as a basic guide; descriptive annotations include the style of arrangement, extent of indexes, where these are provided, and generally give some indication of the length,

scope, and context of the compilation so that its worth and
relevance to a particular need can be assessed by the potential
user.

While every effort has been made to list all the relevant
bibliographies which have come to our attention it is certain that
some omissions will nonetheless be identified. We would welcome
notification of such additions for future supplements. In spite of
our efforts to verify each entry, it is also certain that errors
and other discrepancies will be discovered. We are painfully aware
of the pitfalls of many kinds which stalk the bibliographer and no
compilation can be immune from them.

Style of Entries

The style used for entries conforms with the International
Standard Bibliographic Description for Monographs ISBD(M), Serials
ISBD(S), and the revised Anglo-American Cataloguing Rules (AACR II)
which were published while the bibliography was in preparation.
Minor variations from the latter, however, occur. All items are
listed alphabetically under author but corporate bodies (institutions) have been used in preference to individuals whenever the
former have been clearly associated with, or responsible in some
way for the publication. In such cases the names of individual
compilers and authors appear both in the body of the entry and in
the name index, as does the institution name. It should be noted
that:

> 1) The AACR II provides for six possible areas or
> parts for each entry. These are: (1) title and
> statement of responsibility (2) edition (3) publi-
> cation (4) physical description (5) series (6)
> notes. Each of these areas is separated from the
> other by a —.

> 2) In this work each entry begins with an author state-
> ment (surname first) which is followed by the title
> of the work in a separate line and then by a slash
> mark / before the author is repeated in the exact
> style of the title page. A period and dash separate
> this statement of responsibility or authorship area

from the edition area and also from the publication area which follows. The physical description area is the last which appears consistently.

3) The major differences from former bibliographic style therefore arise in the repetition of the authorship (i.e., statement of responsibility for the work) after the title, and in the style of punctuation.

4) The following entry illustrates the style which has been adopted by identifying typical features.

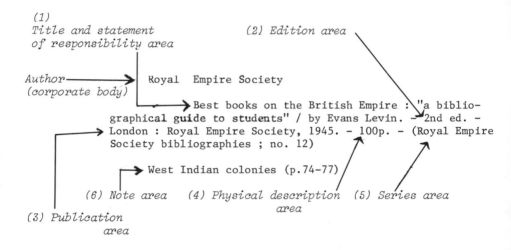

(1)
Title and statement   *(2) Edition area*
of responsibility area

Author
(corporate body)

Royal   Empire Society

Best books on the British Empire : "a biblio-graphical guide to students" / by Evans Levin. - 2nd ed. - London : Royal Empire Society, 1945. - 100p. - (Royal Empire Society bibliographies ; no. 12)

West Indian colonies (p.74-77)

(6) Note area   *(4) Physical description*   *(5) Series area*
                                    area
(3) Publication
        area

Arrangement

Individually numbered entries are arranged alphabetically by author, under broad subjects, with form and country subdivisions in the style of Besterman and Gropp.

Under each subject a section with works covering the area in general precedes sections on the countries individually or in groups in alphabetical order. A country approach is therefore available through this basic arrangement. In addition, two indexes are provided; the first by name and the second by subject.

Name Index

The name index includes all the names of individuals and corporate bodies associated in some way with the publications listed. The names of libraries and other repositories cited as the sources of material listed in a given bibliography are included in this index as are those of journals and other serials cited in the entries. An asterisk is used to identify all serial titles in the name index which actually include some of the bibliographies listed in this work, or the relevant reference numbers are asterisked where necessary. The listings for government bodies omit the country and are entered directly under the names of Ministries and Departments with "see" references as appropriate.

Subject Index

A specific subject index is provided to ensure proper subject access to all significant aspects of the works listed. This is a necessary complement to the basic subject arrangement under broad headings, similar to those used by Gropp. Although this arrangement was selected with ease of access for the researcher in mind its limited choice of one subject heading is seldom fully satisfactory and it can never suffice for multidisciplinary works. Moreover, composite subject coverage, a common feature in many general bibliographies, serves to compound the problem. The specific subject index affords a satisfactory solution.

Thus a general bibliography on Saba, Montserrat, and St. Kitts-Nevis-Anguilla listed in the general section under the Leeward Islands would include subject index entries for the specific islands of the Leewards which fall within the scope of the bibliography-- Montserrat and St. Kitts-Nevis-Anguilla--and second for the subjects history, geography, literature, natural resources, and social and economic conditions which all appear in the annotation. The subject entries in this case are subdivided under Leeward Islands since the bibliography is a three-leaf in-house compilation and the entries on any subject for a particular island would not warrant further subdivision by island.

Where country names have changed general references carry the name which applied at the time of publication but the current name is used for subdivisions under all subject references. Thus a group of general references will be found for British Guiana and British Honduras as well as under their current names, Guyana and Belize respectively, but only the latter names will be found under subjects.

In order to avoid undue repetition of index entries specific subjects which are broken down by country are not repeated under the country itself. Instead each country entry is followed by the reference "see also under specific subjects." Several form headings are included in the index and these are subdivided by country, facilitating a panoramic view of listings for maps, newspapers, government publications, periodicals, and serials among others. An exception was made for four form headings--bibliographic essays, dissertations, doctoral theses, and student project reports; these were subdivided both by country and by subject in order to highlight the range of projects and listings available.

Location

The compilation is based first on the holdings of the St. Augustine campus library of the University of the West Indies and second on those of other research libraries, mainly within the Caribbean region, but also outside of it.

One Caribbean library location is provided for most entries. Works located only through libraries abroad or through other bibliographies and catalogues are so identified in lieu of a location. In the latter case the relevant work, when also listed in the bibliography, is cited by reference number followed by the relevant item number or page in that work. Thus Ref. no. 9 (item no. 102) refers to item 102 in Gropp's Bibliography of Latin American Bibliographies which is fully listed here at reference no. 9. A list of sources used and not cited in this bibliography follows.

Benjamin
    Benjamin, Joel. [A preliminary bibliography on Guyana] / Joel
       Benjamin. - [S.l.] : [s.n.], [1980]. - [Unpaged]. - Typescript

    Reference occurs in his Bibliography of Guyana : an outline
    survey. - p.313-325 In Windward, Leeward and Main see full entry
    next page (Notes) to be quoted after Mary / Valerie Bloomfield

Bloomfield
    Bloomfield, Valerie. Research survey : Caribbean acquisitions . -
       p.86-100 In Caribbean Studies. - Vol.13, no.4 (Jan. 1974).

BNB
    British National Bibliography. London : British Library,
       Bibliographic Services Division, 1950-

CBI
    Cumulative Book Index ; a world list of books in the English
       language. - New York : H.W. Wilson Co., 1898-

Choice
    Choice. Middletown, Conn. : Association of College and
       Research Libraries, 1964-

LAR
  Library Association Record. London : Library Association, 1899–

SARRA
  Sage Race Relations Abstracts. London : [Institute of Race
    Relations], Sage Publications, 1975–

Wasserman
  Wasserman, Paul. Library bibliographies and indexes : a subject
    guide to resource material available from libraries, infor-
    mation centers, library schools and library associations in
    the United States and Canada / Paul Wasserman. – Detroit : Gale
    Research, 1975. – 301p.

Notes

1. Irene Zimmerman, "Cooperative bibliographic and indexing projects
    in the Caribbean area," in Research library cooperation in the
    Caribbean: Papers of the first and second meetings of the
    Association of Caribbean University and Research Libraries, ed.
    Alma Jordan (Chicago : American Library Association, 1972), pp.
    36–59.

2. Valerie Bloomfield, "The bibliography of the English-speaking
    Caribbean Islands," to cite on page xvii. In Windward, Leeward
    and Main pp. 285–311 . – op.cit. (Madison, Wisc.: SALALM
    Secretariat, 1980), pp. 285–311.

3. Theodore Besterman, A world bibliography of bibliographies, 4th
    ed. (Lausanne : Societas Bibliographica, 1966).

Acknowledgments

We are deeply indebted to many individuals, institutions and organizations for their kind co-operation, encouragement and support. Our thanks go especially to the University of the West Indies, our employers, for the two successive sabbatical leave periods which enabled us to devote intensive work periods to advancing the initial work to near completion; to our many colleagues, librarians and non-librarians, throughout the Caribbean region and beyond, who assisted us by providing material and/or references, patiently checking points of detail, chasing references, answering our letters of enquiry, and in a few cases providing annotations; and to the ACURIL Executive Council of 1978 and the members of the Bibliography Committee at that time who sanctioned the incorporation of some entries they had gathered for a similar purpose. Finally we wish to pay tribute to the skill and patience of the typists who labored over the draft during preparatory stages. Any work of this kind owes its existence also to the co-operation and assistance given by many others, too numerous to be individually named, but indispensable.

Location Symbols

BL	British Library
BPL	Barbados Public Library
BU	Brandeis University
CADEC–B	Christian Action for Development in the Caribbean – Barbados
CARDI–T	Caribbean Agricultural Research and Development Institute – Trinidad
CBS	Commonwealth Bureau of Soils, Hertfordshire, England
CB–T	Central Bank of Trinidad and Tobago
CARIRI	Caribbean Industrial Research Institute, Trinidad
CCS	Caribbean Community Secretariat
CLE–T	Council of Legal Education (Hugh Wooding Law School) Trinidad
ECLA–T	Economic Commission for Latin America, Office for the Caribbean, Trinidad
FCO	Foreign and Commonwealth Office, London
GSL	Guyana Science Library
HLBC	Hispanic and Luso Brazilian Council, London (Canning House Library)
ICS	Institute of Commonwealth Studies, University of London
IDC–T	Industrial Development Corporation – Trinidad
IDRC	International Development Research Centre Library, Ottawa, Canada
IIR–T	Institute of International Relations, UWI – Trinidad
ILAS	Institute of Latin American Studies, University of London
LC	Library of Congress, Washington D.C.
LTCL	Land Tenure Center Library, University of Wisconsin, Madison
MF–T	Ministry of Finance, Trinidad and Tobago
NLG	National Library of Guyana
NLJ	National Library of Jamaica (formerly Institute of Jamaica)
NYPL	New York Public Library
OAS	Organization of American States Library, Washington, D.C.
RCS	Royal Commonwealth Society, London
RIS	Research Institute for the Study of Man, New York
TCL	Central Library of Trinidad and Tobago
TLL	Supreme Court Library, Trinidad
TU	University of Texas, Austin

TUN	Tulane University (New Orleans)
UF	University of Florida, Gainesville
UG	University of Guyana
UM	University of Miami
UT	University of Toronto, Canada
UWI-B	University of the West Indies, Cave Hill, Barbados
UWI-J	University of the West Indies, Mona, Jamaica
UWI-LL	University of the West Indies, Law Library, Cave Hill, Barbados
UWI-T	University of the West Indies, St. Augustine, Trinidad

The English-Speaking Caribbean

BIBLIOGRAPHY OF BIBLIOGRAPHIES

1 Asociación de Bibliotecas Universitarias y de Investigación
del Caribe (ACURIL). Comité de Bibliografía
Bibliografiás del Caribe / compilada por el Comité ... . -
Presentada a la V Conferencia de la Asociación ... , Miami,
Florida, 1973. - Miami, Fla. : ACURIL, 1973. - 15, 5p.
Mimeographed

This was the first such compilation of the Bibliography
Committee of ACURIL under the Chairmanship of María Elena
Argüello de Cardona. This and later lists are arranged by
country within the ACURIL Caribbean area scope sometimes
including French, Spanish, Dutch and English-speaking territories
within and bordering the Caribbean sea. This first list includes
a separate 5-page bibliography of new acquisitions lists
received at the Caribbean Regional Library.

UWI-T

2 Asociación de Bibliotecas Universitarias y de Investigación
del Caribe (ACURIL). Comité Central de Bibliografía
Bibliografía de bibliografías del Caribe / compilada por
el Comité ... . - Presentada a la VI Conferencia de la
Asociación ... , St. Thomas, U.S. Virgin Islands, 1972. - St.
Thomas, U.S. Virgin Islands : ACURIL, 1974. - 23p.
Mimeographed

Committee Chairman: María Elena Argüello de Cardona.
Over 200 entries are provided.

UWI-T

3 Asociación de Bibliotecas Universitarias y de Investigación
del Caribe (ACURIL) . Comité Central de Bibliografía
Bibliografía de bibliografías del Cariba (Versión
Preliminar) sometide a la VII Conferencia de la Asociación ...,

1

Willemstad, Curaçao ... 1975. - San Juan, Puerto Rico :
ACURIL, 1975. - 209p.
    Mimeographed

    Committee Chairman: Arabia Teresa Cova. Over 1,900
entries are provided.

UWI-T

4   BESTERMAN, THEODORE
    A world bibliography of bibliographies and of bibliographi-
cal catalogues, calendars, abstracts, digests, indexes and the
like / by Theodore Besterman. - 4th ed. ... - Lausanne :
Societas Bibliographica, 1965-66. - 5v.

    117,000 items arranged under about 16,000 headings and
sub-headings with an author index. Entries under Caribbean Region
and individual countries of the English-speaking Caribbean.

UWI-T

5   Bibliographic index: a cumulative bibliography of biblio-
    graphies / edited by Dorothy Charles and Ben Joseph. - 1937- . -
    New York : The H.W. Wilson Company, 1937-

    Published semi-annually with bound cumulation and permanent
cumulative volume. Alphabetical subject arrangement. Entries
appear under Caribbean region, West Indies and individual
countries.

UWI-T

6   A bibliography of bibliographies on the West Indies. - p.655-
    658
    In A bibliography of the negro in Africa and America /
    compiled by Monroe N. Work. - New York : Argosy-Antiquarian
    Ltd., 1965

    Over 40 references including archival and manuscript
records and published library catalogues.

UWI-T

7   CHANG, HENRY C.
    A selected annotated bibliography of Caribbean biblio-
graphies in English / by Henry C. Chang. - St. Thomas, U.S.
Virgin Islands : The Caribbean Research Institute, College
of the Virgin Islands, 1975. - 54p.

    101 annotated entries arranged alphabetically by author
with subject and title indexes. Includes some references on the
wider Caribbean area - Costa Rica, Venezuela, etc. Gives one or
more of five library locations for each entry, two in the Virgin
Islands and three in the U.S., including the Library of Congress.

UWI-T

8   CORDEIRO, DANIEL R.
        A bibliography of Latin American bibliographies : social
    sciences and humanities supplementing the original works by
    Arthur E. Gropp / edited by Daniel Raposo Cordeiro. - Vol.1. -
    Metuchen, N.J. : Scarecrow Press, 1979. - 272p.

        Lists 1,750 items in social sciences and humanities
    covering 1969 to 1974 (monographs) and 1966 to 1974 (journal
    articles). 36 broad headings are used and author and subject
    indexes are provided. A second supplement to Gropp (Ref.no.9).
                                                            OAS

9   GROPP, ARTHUR E.
        A bibliography of Latin American bibliographies / compiled
    by Arthur E. Gropp. - Metuchen, N.J. : Scarecrow Press, 1968. -
    ix, 515p.

        An updating of the 2nd edition of C.K. Jones' similar and
    pioneering work (Ref.no.20) with some works on the West Indies
    included. Arranged by subject with country sub-divisions under
    each, and a detailed index to the 7,210 entries. Sources are
    cited where the works listed are not obtainable at the Columbus
    Memorial Library or the Library of Congress.
                                                            UWI-T

10   GROPP, ARTHUR E.
        A bibliography of Latin American bibliographies : Supple-
    ment [1965-1969] / by Arthur E. Gropp. - Metuchen, N.J. :
    Scarecrow Press, 1971. - xiii, 277p.

        Includes references to 64 bibliographical journals not
    cited in the previous edition.
                                                            UWI-T

11   GROPP, ARTHUR E.
        A bibliography of Latin American bibliographies published
    in periodicals / by Arthur E. Gropp. - Metuchen, N.J. : Scare-
    crow Press, 1976. - 2v.

        A companion work to the author's major bibliography (Ref.
    no.9) and its supplement (Ref.no.10) with references to monographic
    bibliographies. Includes references to short bibliographies
    accompanying periodical articles as well as articles which are
    themselves bibliographies. Arrangement is similar to the work for
    monographs and is similarly indexed.
                                                            UWI-T

12   Guyana. National Library
        Bibliographies on Guyana [published up to 1971] / National
    Library. - Georgetown : National Library, 1972. - 2 leaves.
        Typescript
                                                            NLG

13 Guyana. National Library
      Bibliographies relating to Guyana available at the National
    Library, Georgetown. - [Georgetown, Guyana : National Library],
    1977. - 19 leaves
      Typescript

NLG

14 Guyana. Public Free Library
      Bibliographies on or including Guyana available at the
    Public Free Library, Georgetown. - Georgetown : Public Free
    Library, 1971. - 7 leaves
      Typescript

NLG

15 Handbook of Latin American Studies / prepared by a number of
    scholars. - No.1 (1935)- . - Gainesville, Fla. : University of
    Florida Press, 1936-
      Annual
      Edited by / Lewis Hanke

      The early numbers of the Handbook were prepared under the
auspices of such groups as the Committee on Latin American Studies
of the American Council of Learned Societies, the National Research
Council, the Social Science Research Council and the American
Council of Education. From no.11 (1945) the Library of Congress
was responsible for its preparation. Imprints have also varied.
Entries are listed under broad subject headings alphabetically
arranged. Within the subject groups items are listed by region
and then by country. The regions covered include the Caribbean
area. From vol.27 (1965) the Handbook is in two parts -
Humanities and Social Sciences.

UWI-T

16 Institute of Jamaica. West India Reference Library
      A bibliography of bibliography on the West Indies /
    compiled by Ursula Raymond. - [Kingston, Jamaica] : Institute
    of Jamaica, West India Reference Library, 1957. - 14 leaves
      Typescript

      The bibliography is based on material in the West India
Reference Library of the Institute of Jamaica. Includes
sections on maps, subject bibliographies and bibliographies of
official records. No index.

UWI-T

17 RICHARDS, JUDITH E.
      Bibliographical aids for building reference collections on
    the British Caribbean / Judith E. Richards. - Working paper
    no.13 submitted for the Seminar on the Acquisition of Latin

American Library Materials (SALALM) ... 12th, Los Angeles,
California, 1967. - p.3-32
    In Final report and working papers [of the Seminar]. -
Washington, D.C. : Pan American Union, 1968. - Vol.2

    Paper divided into three main sections: (1) General
bibliographies which include material on the British West Indies;
(2) Regional bibliographies dealing with the area as a whole; (3)
Subject bibliographies and specialized material such as archives,
maps, theses, etc.

UWI-T

18   Seminar on the Acquisition of Latin American Library Materials.
     Sub-Committee on Reporting Bibliographic Activities
         A report of [on] bibliographic activities [1965-] with a
     selected list of recent Latin American bibliographies / Sub-
     Committee [on] Reporting Bibliographic Activities
         In Final report and working papers [of the Seminar]. -
     Washington, D.C. : OAS General Secretariat, 1966-
         Later issued as: Bibliography of Latin American biblio-
     graphies, 1975-

    Begun in this form in 1965 and compiled successively by
Carl Deal, Herman Cline (1966-68), and the latter with Daniel
Raposo Cordeiro (1969), Gayle Watson (1971), Haydée Piedracueva
(1972-74) and Daniel Raposo Cordeiro (1975-76) as chairmen or
coordinators of a committee effort, these lists have varied in
title and imprint; some include an introductory essay and
annotations and list work reportedly in progress. Caribbean
material has always been included, with a separate supplement for
this purpose in 1972 only compiled by Alma Jordan and Barbara
Comissiong. The arrangement has also varied from broad subject
sub-divisions and separate listings of library catalogs, indexes,
national, trade and personal bibliographies with numbered entries,
author and country indexes to a simple alphabetical author
listing.

UWI-T

19   TOOMEY, ALICE F.
         A world bibliography of bibliographies 1964-1974 : a list
     of works represented by Library of Congress printed catalog
     cards; a decennial supplement to Theodore Besterman, A world
     bibliography of bibliographies / compiled by Alice Toomey. -
     Totowa, N.J. : Rowman & Littlefield, 1977. - 2v. (1,166p.)

    Arranged alphabetically by author or title under subject
headings or sub-headings, e.g., Caribbean literature, Caribbean
area, West Indians, West Indies, West Indian literature. No
index.

UWI-T

20   United States. Library of Congress. Hispanic Foundation
         A bibliography of Latin American bibliographies / by C.K.
     Jones. - 2nd ed. - Washington : U.S. Government Printing
     Office, 1942. - 311p.

         First published in 1922. Arranged by country including a
     section on the West Indies with only a few works of interest to
     the English-speaking territories although the heading indicates
     Spanish West Indies. Some brief annotations and an index
     provided.

                                                                UWI-T

21   University of Guyana. Library
         A select list of bibliographies relating to Guyana and the
     Caribbean, and arranged according to the International Standard
     Bibliographic Description (ISBD)/University of Guyana Library.
     - [Georgetown, Guyana : University of Guyana Library], [1974].
     - 3 leaves
         Mimeographed

                                                                   UG

22   University of the West Indies (Mona). Library
         Select list of major bibliographic works on the West Indies
     in the University of the West Indies Library / by William
     Gocking; Appendix II of Working paper no. 25, submitted for
     the Seminar on the Acquisition of Latin American Library
     Materials (SALALM) ... 12th, Los Angeles, California, 1967. -
     p.172-179
         In Final report and working papers [of the Seminar]. -
     Washington, D.C. : Pan American Union, 1968. - Vol.2.

         Cards reproduced from the Mona Library's special West
     Indies collection catalogue.

                                                                UWI-T

23   University of the West Indies (St. Augustine). Library
         A list of bibliographies relating to nineteenth and
     twentieth century British West Indian history / U.W.I.
     Library. - [St. Augustine, Trinidad : The University of the
     West Indies Library], 1975. - 3 leaves
         Mimeographed

         Includes general bibliographies and works relating to
     Trinidad and Tobago and Barbados. Material listed is located in
     the library's collection.

                                                                UWI-T

24   University of the West Indies (St. Augustine). Library
         A select list of Caribbean bibliographies in the social
     sciences / U.W.I. Library. - St. Augustine, Trinidad : U.W.I.
     Library, 1977. - 6p. - (Library instruction teaching aid ;
     no.4)

An annotated list sub-divided by country within 81 broad
sections - W.I. national bibliographies, indexes to journals,
general bibliographies of the Caribbean, bibliographies on
federation, on individual territories and guides to sources.

UWI-T

BIBLIOGRAPHY, GENERAL -- LIBRARY CATALOGUES

25 American Geographical Society (New York)
        Research catalog / American Geographical Society. - Boston :
    G.K. Hall, 1962. - 15v. (xx, 10,436p.)
        First supplement. - 1972
        Vol.6 : Regional numbers 11-16 : Mexico, Central America,
    Bermuda and West Indies, South America.

        Photographic reproduction of the card catalogue of all
    books, periodical articles [pamphlets] and maps received by the
    Society since 1923. Country arrangement includes Bermuda (12a),
    Bahamas (12b), Jamaica & the Caymans (12d) and all the Lesser
    Antilles (12h). Cards are arranged within these broad regional
    headings by subject using a systematic classification with cards
    for the same region and topic arranged in chronological order,
    the latest first.

UWI-J

26 Barbados Public Library
        [Card catalog file of the West Indian collection of the
    Bridgetown Public Library. - Bridgetown, Barbados : Public
    Library, 1964]
        Microfilm

UF

27 Boston College. Library
        Catalogue of books, manuscripts, etc. in the Caribbeana
    Section (specializing in Jamaicana) of the N.M. Williams
    Memorial Ethnological Collection / Boston College Library. -
    Boston : Boston College Library, 1932. - 133p.

        Listing "specializes in Jamaicana" but includes other
    Caribbean countries arranged by area.

RIS

28 Boston Public Library
        Biblioteca Barbadiensis : a catalog of materials relating
    to Barbados, 1650-1860 in the Boston Public Library. - Boston,
    Mass. : Boston Public Library, 1968. - iv, 27p.

A listing arranged by date of imprint of Boston Public
Library holdings on Barbados, including some items not found in
Sabin or Cundall. Printed materials, manuscripts and maps are
listed separately with an index of names, subjects and titles, and
an index of donors and former owners.

UWI-T

29 Brooklyn Public Library
A list of books on the West Indies and the Bermuda Islands
in the Brooklyn Public Library. - Brooklyn, [N.Y.] : Public
Library, 1904. - 12p.

Ref.no.9
Item no.51

30 CUNDALL, FRANK
Bibliographia Jamaicensis : a list of Jamaica books and
pamphlets, magazine articles, newspapers, and maps, most of
which are in the library of the Institute of Jamaica / by
Frank Cundall. - Kingston, Jamaica : The Institute of
Jamaica, 1902. - 83p.
Also in 1971 reprint edition / by Burt Franklin.

An earlier list appeared in 1895 entitled Bibliotheca
Jamaicensis. This list is arranged chronologically under subject
headings. Books and pamphlets are listed separately from
articles, newspapers and maps. An author index is provided.

UWI-T

31 CUNDALL, FRANK
Bibliotheca Jamaicensis : some account of the principal
works on Jamaica in the Library of the Institute / by Frank
Cundall. - Kingston, Jamaica : The Institute of Jamaica, 1895.
- 38p.
Reprinted from : The Handbook of Jamaica for 1895

A selection of 167 of the 700 volumes held by the library
on Jamaica including pamphlets, this is the first of the
published catalogues of the Institute. It is arranged chronologically under such headings as (1) General History, (2) Aspects
of History including slavery, maroons, churches, (3) Descriptive
Accounts, (4) Natural History and Fiction.

UWI-J

32 CUNDALL, FRANK
Supplement to Bibliographia Jamaicensis / by Frank Cundall.
- Kingston, Jamaica : The Institute of Jamaica, 1908. - 38p.

668 numbered entries in chronological order within subject
groups, updating the catalogue of the Institute's holdings on
Jamaica (Ref.no.41). Includes magazine articles in a separate
section and a name index.

UWI-J

33   Fisk University. Library
        Dictionary catalog of the Negro Collection of Fisk Univer-
     sity Library (Nashville). - Boston : G.K. Hall, 1974. - 6v.
     (2,719p.)

        "Contains material dating from the 18th century, with the
     bulk of its holdings representing the 19th century to the present.
     As curator of the collection for many years, Arthur A. Schomburg
     assembled works of black history and literature from America,
     Africa and the West Indies ... The Negro Collection contains
     theses, sheet music, microfilm, recordings, clippings, photo-
     graphs, reports, oral history tapes and many other items ... The
     major portion of the collection is arranged according to the Dewey
     Decimal Classification System, but items added in recent years are
     arranged by the Library of Congress System." - G.K. Hall and Co.
     Printed Book Catalogs 1978/1979.

                                                                UWI-J

34   Florida Technological University. Library
        Bryant West Indies Collection : a bibliography / Florida
     Technological University Library, Orlando, Florida. - Orlando,
     Fla. : Florida Technological University Library, 1978. - 79p.
     - (Library bibliography series ; no.6)

        The collection consists of "printed materials, works of
     art and artifacts" held from the William Bryant Foundation. The
     indexed bibliography serves as a guide to the books, serial
     publications and periodical articles in the collection and
     consists of approximately 1,000 files dating from 1709 to the
     present arranged in alphabetical author order.

                                                                UWI-T

35   Great Britain. Foreign and Commonwealth Office. Overseas
     Development Administration. British Development Division in
     the Caribbean. Library
        A catalogue of West Indian publications available in the
     library ... - Bridgetown, Barbados : British Development
     Division in the Caribbean, Overseas Development Administration,
     Foreign and Commonwealth Office, 1970. - 147p.
        Mimeographed
        First list of additions. - 1971
        Second list of additions. - 1971

        This catalogue represents half of the total library
     catalogue and includes all West Indian holdings arranged by
     territory and within each by subject. Universal Decimal Classi-
     fication numbers are used for subject headings and indexes to
     these numbers are provided alphabetically by territory and
     numerically to territories and subjects.

                                                                UWI-T

36   Great Britain. Colonial Office. Library
       Catalogue of the Colonial Office Library (Foreign and
     Commonwealth Office). - Boston : G.K. Hall, 1964. - 15v.
     (10,653p.)
         First supplement (1963-Aug. 1967). - 1967. - 1v (894p.)
         Second supplement (Sept. 1967-Apr. 1971). - 1973. - 2v.
     (1,217p.)

       Pre-1950 accessions in three volumes with separate
     alphabetical author and subject sequences. Post-1950 accessions
     in author and title, subject and classified (by Library of
     Congress) sequences. Includes most types of materials held by
     the library with imprint dates from the middle of the 17th
     century. Extensive holdings on the West Indies, pre- and post-
     independence.

                                                           UWI-T

37   Great Britain. Foreign and Commonwealth Office
       Foreign and Commonwealth Office : accessions to the
     library. - Boston : G.K. Hall, 1979. - 4v. (557; 542; 550;
     540p.)

       The catalogue lists accessions for the period May 1971-
     June 1977. It is in two sequences, alphabetical author and
     title, and is classified by the Library of Congress scheme.
     Previous accessions are listed in the Catalogue of the Colonial
     Office Library (Ref.no.36) as well as in the Catalogue of the
     Foreign Office Library, 1926-1968 (1972) and the Catalogue of
     the Printed Books in the Library of the Foreign Office (1926).
                                                           UWI-T

38   Hispanic Council (London)
       Canning House Library [catalogue] / Hispanic Council. -
     Boston : G.K. Hall, 1967. - 4v. (2,288p.)
         First supplement. - 1973. - 1v. (627p.)

       Catalogue of the Hispanic Council and Luso-Brazilian
     Council headquarters library with material concerning Latin
     America, Spain and Portugal to promote relations between these
     and the British Commonwealth. Two sequences, author and subject,
     are provided. The library also publishes an accessions list
     regularly (Ref.no.192).

                                                           UWI-T

39   Howard University. Library
       Dictionary catalog of the Arthur B. Spingarn collection of
     Negro authors / Howard University. - Boston : G.K. Hall, 1970.
     - 2v. (1,460p.)

       Entries appear under individual countries with subject
     sub-divisions.
                                                           UWI-T

40   Institute of Jamaica
        Books on Jamaica in the Library of the Institute ;
     excerpted from the Catalogue of the books in the Library of
     the Institute of Jamaica with a supplement containing the
     titles of those works which have been added while the
     Catalogue was passing through the press. - Kingston, Jamaica :
     The Institute of Jamaica [1894?]. - p.157-165, i-iiip.

        Arranged under authors and titles. Supplement covers works
     acquired between 27 July 1893 and 23 November 1894.
                                                             UWI-J

41   Institute of Jamaica
        Catalogue of the books in the Library of the Institute of
     Jamaica ; arranged under authors' names and under titles. -
     Kingston, Jamaica : The Institute of Jamaica, 1895. - 350p.
        First supplement. - 1915. - 78p.
        Second supplement. - 1919. - 66p.
                                                             UWI-J

42   Institute of Jamaica. West India Reference Library
        The catalogue of the West India Reference Library. -
     Millwood, N.Y. : Kraus International, 1980. - 6v. (4,349p.)
        Contents : Part 1. Catalogue of authors and titles. - 3v.
     - Part 2. Catalogue of subjects. - 3v.

        This Institute became the National Library of Jamaica in
     April 1979. The catalogue lists printed works on the West Indies
     from the year 1547 and is the fourth in a series of catalogues of
     the Institute's holdings; Frank Cundall was responsible for the
     three previous listings (Ref.nos.30, 31, 32). Subject emphases
     are history, literature, description and travel and social and
     economic conditions. Coverage includes all islands of the former
     British Caribbean, Belize, Guyana, U.S. possessions in the region,
     the Spanish, Dutch and French-speaking islands and the countries
     bordering the Caribbean.
                                                             UWI-J

43   International Monetary Fund and World Bank. Joint Bank-Fund
     Library
        The developing areas : a classed bibliography of the Joint
     Bank-Fund Library, Washington, D.C. - Boston : G.K. Hall, 1976.
     - 3v. (1,797p.)
        Vol. 1 : Latin America and the Caribbean. - xiv, 548p.

        Only forty percent of the material is represented.
     Includes Belize, Bermuda, British West Indies, Bahamas, Jamaica,
     Leeward Islands, Windward Islands, Trinidad and Tobago and
     Guyana. The entries are classified by the Dewey Decimal system
     within each country arrangement. There is a brief index to

countries, an alphabetical index to the classification system and
a guide to the subject classification system.

UWI-T

44   John Rylands University Library (Manchester)
        [Catalogue of the anti-slavery collection and subject
        index]. - [Manchester : John Rylands University Library]
        [197-?]. - xv, 35p.

        Alphabetical author (or title) listing with shelf numbers
and a subject index. Includes several references to works on
Jamaica and a few on other West Indian territories.

UWI-T

45   A London bibliography of the social sciences ; being the
        subject catalogue of the British Library of Political and
        Economic Science, at the School of Economics, the Goldsmiths'
        Library of Economic Literature at the University of London, the
        Libraries of the Royal Statistical Society and the Royal
        Anthropological Institute, and certain special collections at
        University College, London and elsewhere / compiled under the
        direction of B.M. Headicar and C. Fuller. - Vol. 1 (1929) - .
        - London : The London School of Economics and Political
        Science, 1931-

        Original four-volume subject catalogue using subject
headings in an alphabetical arrangement with several supplementary
volumes updating the extensive holdings of the group of London
libraries specializing in the field. Entries for the West Indies
and individual territories are included under these place names
as well as in subdivisions under such subjects as coffee trade,
education and finance. Includes early works and many items of
wider interest.

UWI-T

46   New York Public Library
        List of works in the New York Public Library relating to
        the West Indies. - New York : [New York Public Library], 1912.
        - iv, 392p.
        Reprinted from: The New York Public Library bulletin,
        vol. 16, no.1,3-8, (Jan.-Aug. 1912).

        The list is arranged as follows: - Bibliography, general
description, works relating to the individual islands and
colonies of Great Britain and other foreign countries.

UWI-J

47   New York Public Library. Reference Department
        Dictionary catalog of the history of the Americas / New
        York Public Library, Reference Department. - Boston : G.K.
        Hall, 1961. - 28v.

12

First supplement. - 1973. - 9v.

The substantial combined collections of the Astor Library,
James Lenox and George Bancroft Libraries which have become the
American history collection of the New York Public Library
include many works on the discovery and early history of the West
Indies as part of the Americas. Cards reproduced from the
catalogue are arranged in alphabetical dictionary order with
authors and subject headings in one sequence. Several entries
are to be found under country headings for the West Indian
islands as well as under the general headings for West Indies.

UWI-J

48 New York Public Library. Schomburg Collection
        Dictionary catalog of the Schomburg Collection of negro
    literature and history ; the New York Public Library. - Boston :
    G.K. Hall, 1962. - 9v. (8,474p.)
        First supplement. - 1967. - 2v.(1,769p.)
        Second supplement. - 1967. - 4v.(2,694p.)
        Supplements to the catalogue appear annually in: Biblio-
    graphic guide to black studies (Ref.no.176).

This "record of the experience of peoples of African
descent throughout the world" includes substantial material on
and from the West Indies. Entries under authors, titles and
subject headings for individual islands and groups as well as
subjects such as ethnology, slavery, etc. sub-divided by country
or area.   UWI-T

49 Puerto Rico. Inter-American University Library (San Germán)
        Caribbean bibliography / Inter-American University
    Library. - [San Germán, Puerto Rico : Inter-American
    University], [1971]. - 40, 6p.

Submitted at the third ACURIL Conference (Caracas) as a
separate, this is a listing of the holdings of the San Germán
Campus Library. The arrangement is by country and a brief
section on British territories includes Antigua, Barbados,
Dominica, the Bahama Islands and Guyana. The major holdings are
for the non-English-speaking areas, chiefly Puerto Rico, the
Dominican Republic and Haiti.

UWI-T

50 Royal Commonwealth Society. Library
        The manuscript catalogue of the library of the Royal
    Commonwealth Society. - London : Mansell, 1975. - 199p.

Consists of 600 entries, many fully annotated, arranged
geographically. Comprises hand-written documents, typescripts,
original drawings, paintings and maps, photographs, photostats,
collections of photographic prints of special historical

significance or biographical interest, printed books with very
substantial annotations or original illustrations or maps
inserted. Section on the Americas contains West Indian items
under headings - Caribbean Islands (p.131-144), Bermuda (p.144),
Belize (British Honduras) (p.145-149) and Guyana (p.149).
     Supplements to the volumes appear in the Society's Library
Notes, new series, no.217 (January-March 1976) and no.225
(January-March 1978).

UWI-T

51 Royal Commonwealth Society. Library
        Subject catalogue of the Royal Commonwealth Society,
    London. - Boston : G.K. Hall, 1971. - 7v.
        Vol.5 : The Americas. - 713p.
        This was formerly the Royal Empire Society with a
    published catalogue in 4 vols. (Ref.nos.52-53)

        Includes entries for periodical articles and chapters in
books as well as separately published material. Arranged by
subjects within each country and under each subject heading
entries are chronological with serial publications at the end.
West Indies (p.540-590), Bermuda (p.598-606), Bahamas (p.606-
611), Barbados (p. 611-617), Jamaica (p.617-644), Leeward
Islands (p.645-652), Trinidad and Tobago (p.653-670), Windward
Islands (p.671-680), British Honduras (p.680-687), Guyana (p.687-
708).

UWI-T

52 Royal Empire Society. Library
        Subject catalogue of the library ... formerly Royal
    Colonial Institute / by Evans Lewin. - London : The Royal
    Society, 1932. - 4v.
        Vol.3 : Canada, New Foundland, West Indies, Colonial
    America. - 822p.

        British West Indies (p.503-546), Jamaica (p.552-571),
Bahamas (p.572-575), Barbados (p.575-581), Leeward Islands (p.581-
587), Windward Islands (p.598-603), British Honduras (p.603-
607), Trinidad and Tobago (p.588-598), British Guiana (p.608-
631), Bermuda (p.631-634).

UWI-T

53 Royal Empire Society. Library
        Subject catalogue of the library of the Royal Empire
    Society / by Evans Lewin; with a new introduction by Donald
    H. Simpson. - London : Dawsons for the Royal Commonwealth
    Society, 1967. - 4v.
        Vol.3 : Canada, New Foundland, West Indies, Colonial
    America. - 822p.

14

First published in 1932 (Ref.no.52). Formerly the Royal
Colonial Institute Library. Sections similar to earlier edition.
                                                            UWI-T

54 STEVENS, HENRY
        Catalogue of the Mexican, Spanish American and West Indian
    books in the library of the British Museum at Christmas 1856 /
    Henry Stevens. - [S.1. : s.n.], 1856. - 62p.

        1,000 references.

                                                       Ref.no.4
                                                     Vol.1, p.343

55 STEVENS, HENRY
        Catalogue of the Mexican, Spanish American and West Indian
    books in the library of the British Museum / Henry Stevens. -
    [S.1. : s.n.], 1859. - 62p.

        950 references.

                                                       Ref.no.4
                                                    Vol.3, p.5081

56 Trinidad and Tobago. Historical Society (South Section).
    Library
        Archaeological : the Caribbean (as at May 23, 1976) /
    Historical Society Library. - [Pointe-à-Pierre, Trinidad] :
    Trinidad and Tobago Historical Society (South Section), Library,
    [1977]. - 4 leaves
        Mimeographed

        Holdings of the library listed under country to which works
    pertain (including most of the islands of the wider Caribbean
    area) with periodicals and general works listed first. Over 20
    items - reports, notes, manuscripts and published papers - listed
    for Trinidad and Tobago.
                                                            UWI-T

56a Tulane University. Latin American Library
        Catalog of the Latin American Library of the Tulane
    University Library, New Orleans. - Boston : G.K. Hall, 1970. -
    9v. (7,422p.)
        First supplement. - 1973. - 2v. (1,618p.)
        Second supplement. - 1975. - 2v. (1,571p.)

                                                              TUN

57 United States. Virgin Islands. Bureau of Libraries and
    Museums
        Catalog of microfilms available in the Von Scholten
    Collection of the St. Thomas Public Library ... including the
    holdings of the Library of the College of the Virgin Islands. -
    3rd ed. - St. Thomas, Virgin Islands : Bureau of Libraries and

Museums, Department of Conservation and Cultural Affairs,
1970. - 108p.

An expansion and updating of two previous editions (1967
and 1969) including material of Caribbean interest and origins.
Alphabetical listing of main headings including journal titles is
followed by listings grouped under such mixed form and subject
headings as architecture, archives, diaries, M.A. theses, newspapers, history. Substantial section with doctoral dissertations
on Caribbean topics.

UWI-T

58   University of Florida. Libraries
          Catalog of the Latin American collection, University of
     Florida Libraries. - Boston: G.K. Hall, 1973. - 13v.   (9,599p.)
          First supplement. - 1980. - 7v. (4,354p.)

The "catalogue covers a collection of approximately
120,000 volumes of books, pamphlets, periodicals and government
documents. It is a dictionary catalogue with author, title,
subject and added entries in one sequence. All works, including
periodicals are represented by at least one entry and there are
analytics for most series." The collection specializes in
Caribbean materials - official documents and statistical publications. Blanket order programmes achieved comprehensive
coverage of W.I. publications from 1967.

UWI-J

59   University of London. Institute of Education
          Catalogue of the Collection of Education in Tropical Areas
     / Institute of Education. - Boston : G.K. Hall, 1964. - 3v.
          Vol.1. Author catalogue. - Vol.2. Regional catalogue. -
     Vol.3. Subject catalogue

Ref.no.19
Vol.1, p. 342

60   University of London. Institute of Education
          Catalogue of the Comparative Education Library. - Boston :
     G.K. Hall, 1971. - 6v. (3,669p.)
          First supplement. - 1974. - 3v. (1,667p.)

Merger of the Catalogue of the Collection of Education in
Tropical Areas with the collection of the Institute's Department
of Comparative Education. Lists materials on education and allied
subjects. Catalogue is in three sections:- author/title, country
and subject.

Ref.no.19
Vol.1, p.342

61 University of Sussex. Centre for Multi-racial Studies,
    Barbados
        West Indian section of the Moore Collection / Centre for
    Multi-racial Studies. - [Barbados : Centre for Multi-racial
    Studies], 1960. - 48, 29p.
        Xerox copy
        List one and supplement

                                                                 UWI-B

62 University of Texas. Library
        Catalog of the Latin American Collection of the University
    of Texas Library (Austin). - Boston : G.K. Hall, 1969. - 31v.
    (22,854p.)
        First supplement. - 1971. - 5v. (3,561p.)
        Second supplement. - 1973. - 3v. (2,014p.)
        Third supplement. - 1975. - 8v. (6,254p.)
        Fourth supplement. - 1977. - 3v. (1,968p.)
        Continued by: Ref.no.176a.

    "Includes an extensive collection of manuscripts. The
catalog is a dictionary catalog of authors, titles and subjects
for books, pamphlets, periodicals, newspapers and microfilm."

                                                                    TU

63 University of the West Indies (Cave Hill). Library
        Caribbeana in the University Centre Library, Antigua /
    compiled by Jessica Wellum. - Cave Hill, Barbados : U.W.I.
    Library, 1970. - 28p.

    298 entries arranged alphabetically by author within such
broad subject groups as history, religion, folklore, literature,
economics, agriculture in random order. Country sub-divisions
are provided for history and literature.

                                                                 UWI-T

64 University of the West Indies (Cave Hill). Library
        Check-list of items in the West Indian collection at 30th
    June, 1971 / U.W.I. Library. - Cave Hill, Barbados : U.W.I.
    Library, 1971. - 55p.
        Mimeographed

    Lists books by or about West Indians and the West Indies,
not restricted to but biased towards the English-speaking
territories. Arranged by the broad classes of the Library of
Congress Classification and alphabetically by author within each
class or group.

                                                                 UWI-T

65   University of the West Indies (St. Augustine). Library
        Catalogue of the Imperial College of Tropical Agriculture,
     University of the West Indies, Trinidad. - Boston : G.K. Hall,
     1975. - 8v.

        The College collection specializes in tropical agriculture
     but items of general West Indian interest are also held.
     Arranged by author (including corporate headings) in (vols.1-3)
     and by title or subject in the Title and Classified Section
     (vols.4-8). There is a separate subject index in vol.8, a
     catalogue of theses and reports accepted by the ICTA, with
     author and subject approaches, a periodicals catalogue and an
     index to the journal, Tropical Agriculture, vol.1 (1924) - vol.37
     (1960).

                                                            UWI-T

66   West India Committee
        Catalogue of the library of the West India Committee -
     London : West India Committee, 1941. - iv, 125p.

        A list of holdings to 1940 arranged under subject
     headings - agriculture, natural history, law, sugar, etc. with
     further sub-divisions under each. The collection includes a
     wealth of pamphlets dealing with slavery and emancipation contro-
     versy and with the sugar industry. Few geographical sub-divisions
     and no index.

                                                            UWI-T

67   [West Indian collections of the Trinidad Public Library (Knox
     Street Library and Belmont Branch) and the Central Library]. -
     Port-of-Spain, Trinidad : [s.n.], 1960
        Microfilm copy

                                                               UF

                        BIBLIOGRAPHY, REGIONAL

68   The Caricom bibliography / Caribbean Community Secretariat
     Library. - Vol.1 (1977) - . - Georgetown, Guyana : Caribbean
     Community Secretariat Library, 1977-
        Annual

        The bibliography aims to list all material currently
     published in the Caribbean Community (CARICOM) member countries.
     The material listed is compiled from the national bibliographies
     of Barbados, Guyana, Jamaica and Trinidad and Tobago along with
     entries from the territories not yet producing national biblio-
     graphies submitted to the Caricom Secretariat through the
     National Bibliographical Centres of the above mentioned countries.

                                18

It is arranged in two parts – classified subject section and
alphabetical author/title/series index.

UWI-T

69   Current bibliography
        In Caribbean studies. – Vol.1 (1961/62)– . – Rio Piedras,
     Puerto Rico : University of Puerto Rico, Institute of Caribbean
     Studies, 1961–
        Quarterly

        Lists books, pamphlets and periodical articles of interest
to Caribbeanists under country. Items in all subject fields,
except the natural sciences, are included and geographical
coverage is of the Antilles and circum-Caribbean region.

UWI-T

70   Current Caribbean bibliography : an alphabetical list of
     publications issued in the Caribbean territories of France,
     Great Britain, the Netherlands and the United States /
     Caribbean Commission. – Vol.1 (1951)– . – Port-of-Spain:
     Caribbean Commission, 1951–
        Annual
        Vol.1 (1951)–vol.8 (1958) – Title in English and French.
     Vol.8 (1958) published: Hato Rey, Puerto Rico : Caribbean
     Commission, 1961. Vols.9–11, Parts 1 and 2 (1959–1961)
     published: Hato Rey, Puerto Rico : Caribbean Organization,
     1964 and 1968. Vols.12–14 (1962–1964)–vol.23 (1973) published:
     San Juan, Puerto Rico : Caribbean Regional Library, 1976.   From
     vols.9–11 title in English, Spanish and French. No sub-title.

        Publication follows the vicissitudes of the Commission
which moved to Puerto Rico, became the Caribbean Organization and
was finally dissolved. Its library was taken over by the government of Puerto Rico and publication of the bibliography continued
irregularly and it is now dormant. The publication originally
gave no classification numbers but listed periodicals, newspapers
and government serials of the region separately and carried feature
articles of a bibliographic nature. From vol.9 arrangement was
by the Universal Decimal Classification with an alphabetical index
of authors and subjects. A cooperative effort with input from
several libraries and librarians in the region edited and produced
centrally.

UWI-T

71   Current Caribbean bibliography : supplement / Caribbean
     Regional Library. – No.1 (Jan.1967) – No.12 (Dec.1970). – Hato
     Rey, Puerto Rico : Caribbean Economic Development Corporation,
     Caribbean Regional Library, 1967–1970
        Monthly

Formerly issued as: Selective list of recent additions to
the library. Publication lapsed and was subsequently reintroduced
monthly from 1969 but suspended after 1970 while annual cumulations continued to vol.23 (1973) (Ref.no.70).

UWI-T

BIBLIOGRAPHY, NATIONAL

Barbados

72 The National bibliography of Barbados : a subject list of books
received in the Public Library in compliance with legal
deposit laws ; and of books of Barbadian authorship printed
abroad / Barbados Public Library. - Vol.1, no.1 (1975)- . -
Bridgetown : Barbados Public Library, 1975-
Quarterly with annual cumulations

A classified subject section lists all new works published
in Barbados and works by Barbadians published abroad. Items are
classified by Dewey Decimal Classification. An alphabetical
author/title/series index is provided. Statutory instruments,
bills, single acts and parliamentary debates are listed in a
separate section. Earlier issues of the bibliography contained
items from St. Lucia and St. Vincent but this ceased on the
publication of the Caricom Bibliography (Ref.no.68).

UWI-T

Guyana

73 Guyanese national bibliography : a subject list of new books
printed in the Republic of Guyana, based on the books
deposited at the National Library ... . - Georgetown, Guyana :
National Library, 1973-
Quarterly with annual cumulations

Excludes pamphlets under five pages and certain government
publications such as acts, bills, gazettes and restricted items.
Listing in the order of the Dewey Decimal Classification, 16th
edition with full author, title and subject indexes and a list of
publishers.

UWI-T

Jamaica

74 Institute of Jamaica
       The Jamaica national bibliography 1964-1974 / Institute of
    Jamaica. - Millwood, N.Y. : Kraus International Publications,
    1980

        Only complete cumulation of publications in the field of
    Jamaican life and culture for the period covered. Serves as a
    union list of the holdings of the Institute of Jamaica, the
    Jamaica Library Service and the University of the West Indies at
    Mona. More than 3,300 entries arranged according to subject,
    comprising books, pamphlets, articles, extracts, government
    publications, microfilms, maps and manuscripts. Library locations
    given. Includes lists of the Jamaican periodicals in the
    libraries' holdings, arranged alphabetically by title and by
    subject. Comprehensive author and title index. Also covers works
    about Jamaica and works by Jamaican authors published elsewhere.
                                                              UWI-T

75 Institute of Jamaica. West India Reference Library
       Jamaican national bibliography, 1964-1970 ; cumulation /
    compiled by Rosalie Williams. - Kingston : Institute of Jamaica,
    West India Reference Library, 1973. - iii, 322p.

        Arranged by broad subject groups, such as arts and social
    sciences, within sections by form - books and pamphlets, manu-
    scripts and maps. A list of periodicals is given (p.208-231) and
    a full name index. Includes location symbols for three libraries
    but no classification numbers.
                                                              UWI-T

76 Jamaican national bibliography : a subject list of Jamaican
    material received in the West India Reference Library,
    Institute of Jamaica ... . - Vol.1, no.1 (Jan./Mar.1975)- . -
    Kingston, Jamaica : West India Reference Library, Institute of
    Jamaica, 1975-
       Quarterly

        "Arranged by Dewey Decimal Classification 18th edition,
    and catalogued according to the British Text of the Anglo-
    American Cataloguing Rules (1967) and the International Standard
    Bibliographic Description for Monographs and Serials." Includes
    a full author, title and series index and a list of Jamaican
    publishers.
                                                              UWI-T

Trinidad and Tobago

77   Trinidad and Tobago national bibliography ; a subject list of
     material published and printed in Trinidad and Tobago,
     classified according to the Dewey Decimal Classification, 18th
     edition, catalogued according to the British text of the
     Anglo-American Cataloguing Rules, 1967, and the International
     Standard Bibliographic Description for Monographs and Serials
     / U.W.I. Library and Central Library of Trinidad and Tobago. -
     Vol.1, nos.1 and 2 (Jan.-June 1975)- . - St. Augustine,
     Trinidad: University of the West Indies Library and Central
     Library of Trinidad and Tobago, 1975-
          Quarterly with annual cumulations

          A joint publication of the two libraries under the
     direction of a national editorial board. A full author/title/
     series index and a list of publishers with addresses are
     provided.

                                                         UWI-T

                        BIBLIOGRAPHY, GENERAL

78   BARHAM, A.
          Bibliography of the Caribbean / by A. Barham. - [Mona,
     U.W.I. : ISER], [1965]. - 1v. (various pagings)
          Mimeographed

          Includes journal articles among entries under the following
     headings:- Politics and Government; Sociology; Economic Studies;
     Anthropology; Linguistics; Folklore. Later supplemented by
     Rodney (Ref.no.789).

                                                         UWI-T

78a BECK, JANE C.
          To Windward of the land : the occult world of Alexander
     Charles / Jane C. Beck. - Bloomington; London : Indiana
     University Press, 1979. - xlix, 309p.
          Bibliography: p.281-290

          Alphabetical author listing of items on folklore, folk
     medicine, medicinal plants, obeah and social and economic
     conditions. Includes numerous articles in periodicals.

                                                         UWI-T

79   Bibliography of the English-speaking Caribbean : books,
     articles and reviews in English from the arts, humanities and
     social sciences. - Vol.1, nos.1 and 2 (1979)- . - [S.l.] :
     Robert J. Neymeyer, 1979-

                              22

Semi-annual

Bibliography is an ongoing serial listing published works
in English from North America, Europe and the Caribbean in the
arts, humanities and social sciences. Travel guides, cook books,
school text books, juvenile literature, popular fiction and works
not relating to the region are excluded. This double issue
consists of 589 items arranged under subjects such as tourism,
travel and description, archaeology, history, migration and West
Indian life overseas, culture and creative arts, religion,
language and linguistics and literature.

                                                          UWI-T

80 BLOOMFIELD, VALERIE
        Bibliography of the English-speaking Caribbean islands /
    Valerie Bloomfield. - p.297-311
        In Windward, Leeward and Main : Caribbean studies and
    library resources; Final report and working papers of the
    Twenty-fourth Seminar on the Acquisition of Latin American
    Library Materials, University of California, Los Angeles. -
    Madison, Wis. : SALALM Secretariat, 1980.

        The bibliography is an appendix to the paper.

                                                          UWI-T

81 BLUME, HELMUT
        Die westindischen Inseln / Helmut Blume. - Braunschweig :
    Georg Westermann, Verlag, 1968. - 352p.
        Bibliography: p.307-345

        Bibliography includes separate sections on sea studies,
    climate, plant and animal kingdom, discovery, political and
    economic development and political geography as well as sections
    on individual islands and groups of islands - British Leeward and
    Windward Islands, Barbados, Trinidad and Tobago.

                                                          UWI-T

82 BRATHWAITE, EDWARD KAMAU
        Our ancestral heritage : a bibliography of the English-
    speaking Caribbean ... / compiled by Edward Kamau Brathwaite. -
    Kingston, Jamaica : The Literary Committee of Carifesta '76,
    1976. - 194p.
        Mimeographed
        First draft edition

        The first of two volumes listing works on the Caribbean
    background, the Amerindians, Europe, the Europeans and their
    structural contribution, Africa and Africans in the New World.
    Partly annotated.

                                                          UWI-T

83   Brown University. John Carter Brown Library
         The British West Indies : an exhibition of books, maps and
     prints opened ... May 12, 1961 / John Carter Brown Library. -
     Providence, R.I. : The Library, 1961. - [16p.]

                                                              ICS

84   California State University, Los Angeles. Latin American
     Studies Center
         Black Latin America : a bibliography / Latin American
     Studies Center. - Los Angeles : Latin American Studies Center,
     California State University, 1977. - 74p. - (Latin American
     bibliography series ; 5)

         Includes British, French and Dutch West Indies.
                                                         Ref.no.18
                                                              1978

85   Caribbean Commission. Central Secretariat
         A catalogue of Caribbean Commission publications, 1957 /
     Central Secretariat. - Port of Spain : [Caribbean Commission,
     Central Secretariat], 1957. - 25p.

                                                         Ref.no.3

86   Caribbean Commission. Central Secretariat. Research Branch
         Agriculture, fisheries and forestry, building, engineering,
     technology, medicine and public health, natural sciences,
     social sciences / Caribbean Commission Central Secretariat. -
     Port of Spain, Trinidad : Caribbean Commission, Central
     Secretariat, 1949. - 296, 40, 65, 37, 82p.
         Yearbook of Caribbean research : 1949 supplement.

         Annotated bibliographies prepared as surveys of research
     and investigation in the Caribbean and adjoining areas.
                                                         Ref.no.15

87   Caribbean Organization
         A catalogue of Caribbean Commission and Caribbean
     Organization publications / Caribbean Organization. - Hato Rey,
     Puerto Rico : Central Secretariat, 1962. - 11p.

         A price catalogue arranged under subject headings such as
     agriculture, education, housing and trade with reports and
     periodicals listed separately. Out of print items included.
                                                              UWI-T

88   Caribbean Regional Library
         [List of books on the Caribbean] / Caribbean Regional
     Library. - [Puerto Rico : Caribbean Regional Library], [196-?].
     - [i], 37p.

                                                              NLG

                                24

89   Casa de las Américas. Biblioteca José A. Echeverria
        Bibliografía sobre las Antillas / Biblioteca José A.
     Echeverria. - Havana, Cuba : [Biblioteca José Antonio
     Echeverria], 1976. - [4], 97 leaves
        Mimeographed

        First section (p.1-25) lists items on the Caribbean in
     general while the second is devoted to Jamaica (p.26-99). Entries
     are arranged by subject. Bibliography was prepared on the
     occasion of Carifesta 1976.

                                                                   NLG

90   CLEGERN, WAYNE M.
        British Honduras ; colonial dead end, 1859-1900 / Wayne M.
     Clegern. - Baton Rouge : Louisiana State University Press,
     1967. - vii, 214p. - (Louisiana State University studies :
     Social science series ; no.12)
        Bibliography: p.193-200

        Annotated listings arranged alphabetically by author under
     bibliographic aids, official materials, periodical literature,
     printed documents.
                                                                 UWI-T

91   COMITAS, LAMBROS
        Caribbeana 1900-1965 : a topical bibliography / Lambros
     Comitas. - Seattle : University of Washington Press for
     Research Institute for the Study of Man, 1968. - xliv, 909p.

        Includes references to periodical articles as well as books
     and pamphlets on the non-Hispanic Caribbean divided thematically
     into ten sections each subdivided into topically related
     chapters. Library and geographical codes are given for each
     entry with several cross-listings. Indexed by author and
     geographical area.
                                                                 UWI-T

92   COMITAS, LAMBROS
        The complete Caribbeana, 1900-1975 : a bibliographic guide
     to the scholarly literature / Lambros Comitas ; under the
     auspices of the Research Institute for the Study of Man. -
     Millwood, N.Y. : KTO Press, 1977. - 4v. (2,193p.)

        An updating and expansion of his previous work (Ref.no.91)
     this is a substantial guide with over 17,000 references to the
     "published knowledge of the Caribbean in the twentieth century."
     One volume each devoted to People, Institutions, Resources and
     Indexes. Arrangement is by topics and author and geographic
     indexes are provided. Library locations are given in most cases
     and cross-listings are frequent. Coverage of the wider Caribbean
     excludes Haiti, Cuba, Puerto Rico and the Dominican Republic.
                                                                 UWI-T

93 Commonwealth Institute
        Commonwealth in the Caribbean : an annotated list /
    compiled by the Commonwealth Institute and the National Book
    League. - London : The Commonwealth Institute and the National
    Book League, 1969. - 16p.

        Prepared for the Commonwealth in Books exhibition in 1969,
    the reading list includes sections on description and travel,
    history, politics and government, economics and language and
    literature.
                                                            UWI-T

94 Commonwealth Institute
        The Commonwealth in the Caribbean : selected reading list
    for advanced study prepared in consultation with the librarian
    of the Royal Commonwealth Society / Commonwealth Institute. -
    [London] : Commonwealth Institute, 1966. - 5p.
        Mimeographed
                                                            UWI-T

95 Commonwealth Institute
        Readers guide to the Commonwealth / [compiled by the
    National Book League and Commonwealth Institute]. 2nd ed. -
    London : National Book League, 1971. - 213p.

        Entries which are annotated are arranged under country or
    region by genre and then alphabetically by author. Section on
    the Caribbean is divided into non-fiction, imaginative literature
    and children's books.
                                                            UWI-T

96 Commonwealth Institute
        A teacher's guide to study resources : Eastern Caribbean /
    Commonwealth Institute. - London : Commonwealth Institute,
    1973. - 19p.

        Selective listings arranged alphabetically by author under
    each country. Includes slides.
                                                            UWI-T

97 Commonwealth Institute
        A teacher's guide to study resources : Jamaica, Bahamas,
    North Caribbean and Bermuda / Commonwealth Institute. -
    London : Commonwealth Institute, 1974. - 21p.

        Select list of books, pamphlets and teaching material
    (wall charts, slide sets, recordings, filmstrips, specimens etc.)
    covering the Turks and Caicos Islands as well as those quoted in
    the title.
                                                            UWI-T

98 Commonwealth Institute. Library
        The Caribbean : selected reading lists for advanced study.
    - London : Commonwealth Institute, [1969?]-
        Annual

        Compiled and revised annually in consultation with the
    Librarian of the Royal Commonwealth Society. The lists are
    arranged alphabetically by author under broad subject headings,
    such as geography, flora and fauna, government and politics etc.
    All entries are annotated.
                                                            UWI-T

99 Commonwealth Institute. Library and Resource Centre
        Caribbean : arts, literature and music / Library and
    Resource Centre. - [London] : Commonwealth Institute Library
    and Resource Centre, 1973. - 3 leaves.

        43 items listed under books and periodical articles.
    Includes creative writings and criticism.
                                                            UWI-T

100 CUNDALL, FRANK
        Bibliography of the West Indies (excluding Jamaica) /
    by Frank Cundall. - Kingston, Jamaica: Institute of Jamaica,
    1909. - New York : Johnson Reprint, 1971. - 179p.

        Chronologically arranged under countries it includes
    entries for Barbados, Dominica, Montserrat, Antigua, St. Kitts-
    Nevis, Virgin Islands, Bahamas, Honduras, British.
                                                            UWI-T

101 DAY, ALLISON
        Library in the multi-racial secondary school : a
    Caribbean book list / Allison Day
        In School librarian. - Vol.19 (Sept.1971)
        Also published by: Commonwealth Relations Commission
                                                        Ref.no.5
                                                        Apr.1972

102 EASTON, DAVID K.
        Sources for the study of Caribbean culture / David K.
    Easton
        In Caribbean : its culture / edited by A. Curtis Wilgus. -
    Gainesville, [Fla.] : University of Florida Press, 1955.
    (Caribbean Conference series 1 ; v.5)

        A bibliographic essay treating British territories in a
    separate section.
                                                            UWI-T

103   EDWARDS, FRANCIS
        West Indies : a catalogue of books, maps, etc. including
      sections on Guiana slave trade and buccaneers and pirates /
      Francis Edwards. - London : [Francis Edwards Ltd.], 1929. -
      60p.
        Catalogue no.519, 1929

                                                                      ICS

103a GATES, BRIAN
        Afro-Caribbean religions / edited by Brian Gates. - London :
      Ward Lock Educational, 1980. - iv, 204p.
        Bibliography: p.187-198

        Arranged in two groups: (1) Africa and (2) Caribbean which
      includes books and reference material for teachers; books for the
      classroom; myths, legends and folklore; fiction, kits and audio-
      visual material (films, records and tapes). Some items deal with
      aspects of religion.

                                                                     UWI-T

104   Great Britain. Parliament. House of Commons
        General indexes ... / House of Commons. - Shannon : Irish
      University Press, 1968. - 8v. - (British parliamentary
      papers : Index 1-8)
        Facsimile reprint of the original.

        Covering the period 1696-1899 the indexes are an essential
      guide to the Bills, Reports, Accounts and Papers printed by order
      of the House of Commons and by command, during the nineteenth
      century. Reports of select committees, commissions of enquiry,
      etc. and other topics of West Indian interest are covered.

                                                                     UWI-T

105   Guyana. National Library
        Caricom book exhibition, July 12-17, 1976 : a catalogue /
      prepared by Joy Duncan and Gwyneth Browman. - Georgetown,
      Guyana : National Library, 1976. - 30p.
        Mimeographed

        Entries covering industry, tourism, The Common Market,
      education, health, agriculture and home economics are arranged by
      Dewey classification. Material consists mainly of items readily
      available in the Reference and Lending Departments of the
      National Library.

                                                                     UWI-T

106   Guyana. National Library
        Guyana and Caribbean integration : a bibliography ; based
      on the Book Exhibition to mark the 3rd Anniversary of the
      Republic of Guyana / prepared by the National Library. -
      Georgetown, Guyana : National Library, 1973. - vi, 26p.

A general bibliography (165 items) of books and articles
on the region under the headings - General, Religion, Culture,
Politics and Government, Economics, Education, Health. Includes
references to a few Guyanese newspaper articles and typescript
papers.

UWI-T

107 HALLEWELL, L.
Latin American bibliography : a guide to sources of infor-
mation and research / edited by L. Hallewell. - London :
Institute of Latin American Studies for the SCONUL Latin
American Group, 1978. - 227p.

A basic introduction to sources of information including
categories such as library catalogues and inter-lending services
as well as forms of material - manuscripts and archives, maps,
atlases, theses - rather than specific subjects, all in one
alphabetical order. Aimed at students, teachers and researchers
in the field (especially in the U.K.), the work covers "all the
Americas south of the Rio Grande including the adjacent
islands ..." in practical summaries listing major bibliographies
and other reference sources.

UWI-T

108 Hamburg. Welt-Wirtschafts-Archiv. Bibliothek
Karibishe Inseln / HWWA. - Hamburg / HWWA, 1957-60. - 2v. -
(Auslandskunde : Literaturnachweis über die Gebiete Wirtschaft
und Politik, Recht und Technik : Länder-Abteilung ; no.12)

Vol.1 covers British Caribbean territories arranged by
territory and within this by subject. Includes articles in
periodicals.

TCL

109 Hamburg. Welt-Wirtschafts-Archiv. Bibliothek
Mittlelamerika und karibischer Raum / HWWA. - Hamburg :
HWWA, 1956. - 114p. - (Auslandskunde : Literaturnachweis über
die Gebiete Wirtschaft und Politik, Recht und Technik :
Länder-Abteilung ; no.10)

800 references.

Ref.no.5
1958, p.35

110 HANKE, LEWIS
Caribbean bibliography / Lewis Hanke. - p.202-209
In The Caribbean at mid-century / edited by A. Curtis
Wilgus. - Gainesville, Fla. : University of Florida Press,
1951. - (Caribbean Conference series 1 ; vol.1)

29

A brief and general essay on the state of the art in the region underlining needs.

UWI-T

111 HANKE, LEWIS
      Caribbean bibliography : an appraisal of present needs /
      Lewis Hanke. - p.713-715
      In Caribbean Commission monthly information bulletin. -
      Vol.4, no.8 (1954)

      An essay on the need for national (retrospective, current
and selective) bibliography in the region citing beginning efforts
in the field, including plans then in train for the Current
Caribbean Bibliography. Delivered as a lecture at the University
of Florida sponsored conference on "The Caribbean at mid-century"
in Dec.1950.

UWI-J

112 HART, RICHARD
      Slaves who abolished slavery / Richard Hart. - [Mona],
      Jamaica: Institute of Social and Economic Research, U.W.I.,
      1980. - vii, 248p.
      Vol.1 of: Blacks in bondage

      157 items arranged in sections - Books, Articles,
Periodicals - followed by a list of official documentary series and
unpublished manuscripts, letters and papers.

UWI-T

113 HURWITZ, E.F.
      Caribbean studies, Part I / E.F. Hurwitz. - p.487-492,
      494-502
      In Choice. - Vol.12, no.4 (June-July 1975)

      A bibliographic essay sections of which cover (1) The
Caribbean, (2) The Commonwealth Caribbean and (3) Commonwealth
Caribbean on a Nation to Nation Basis. Items on the Caribbean
are discussed under Bibliographies and General Histories of the
Region, Social Sciences and the Challenge of Caribbean Diversity,
and Periodicals, while those on the Commonwealth Caribbean appear
under Bibliographies, Economics, Anthropology, Political Science
and East and West Indies. The third section deals with individual
countries - Jamaica , Trinidad and Tobago, Barbados, Leeward and
Windward Islands, Bahamas. Each section is followed by a list of
the works cited.

UWI-T

114 KRAAL, J.F.
      Bibliografie van auteurs vithet Caribische gebied Engels,
      Frans, Nederlands / J.F. Kraal. - p. 211-217

<u>In</u> West-Indische Gids. – Vol.35 (Mar.1955)

Ref.no.5
1956, p.36

115 LE CLERC, CHARLES
      Bibliotheca Americana : histoire, geógraphie, voyages,
archéologie et linguistique des deux Amériques et des îles
Philippines / rédigée par Ch. Le Clerc. – Paris : Maison-
neuve, 1878. – 737p.
      Supplement no.1. – 1881. – 102p.
      Supplement no.2. – 1887. – 128p.
      1961 reprint

      Includes a section with over 100 references to works on the
Greater and Lesser Antilles. Jamaica, Dominica, Trinidad, St.
Lucia, Barbados, Grenada are featured in two brief sections.
                                                        UWI-T

116 LEVY, CLAUDE
      Emancipation, sugar and federalism : Barbados and the West
Indies, 1833-1876 / Claude Levy. – Gainesville, Fla. : University Presses of Florida, 1980. – viii, 206p. – (University of
Florida Center for Latin American Studies. Latin American
monograph series ; 25).
      Bibliography: p.187-194

      Introduced by a short bibliographic essay the bibliography
includes manuscripts, newspapers, government publications and
other general sources of information on the British West Indies.
                                                        UWI-T

117 LOWENTHAL, DAVID
      A selected West Indian reading list / David Lowenthal. –
p.101-135
      <u>In</u> West Indies Federation : perspectives on a new nation /
edited by David Lowenthal. – New York : Columbia University
Press with the American Geographical Society and Carleton
University, 1961

      Includes "the most important and comprehensive writings on
the West Indies" as well as [a selection] of works of more
limited scope or significance. Arranged under 6 heads: (1)
Government Reports and Official Documents relating to West Indies
Federation arranged chronologically, (2) Physical Geography, (3)
History, (4) Contemporary Affairs, (5) Belles-lettres, (6)
Periodicals and Newspapers.
                                                        UWI-T

118 McGill University. McLennan Library
    Caribbeana : a student's guide to reference resources /
   compiled by Suzy Slavin. - [Montreal] : McGill University,
   1974. - [i], 6p.

    The guide comprises eight sections : - Handbooks, Current
Bibliography, Retrospective Bibliography, Periodical Indexes,
Biography, Literary Bibliography, Directories and Theses. Entries
are annotated and classification numbers given.

                    UWI-T

119 MINTZ, SIDNEY W.
    Caribbean transformations / Sidney W. Mintz. - Chicago :
   Aldine Publishing Company, 1974. - xii, 355p.
   Bibliography: p.329-342

    Wide-ranging references including sociology and economics
of peasant societies in the wider Caribbean area; some specific
references for Jamaica among many of general West Indian
interest.

                    UWI-T

120 MITCHELL, SIR HAROLD
    Caribbean patterns : a political and economic study of the
   contemporary Caribbean / Sir Harold Mitchell. - Edinburgh :
   W. and R. Chambers, 1967. - xix, 520p.
   Bibliography: p.408-451

    About 1,000 items arranged regionally for the wider
Caribbean area. P.423-434 relate to the Commonwealth territories
and arrangement is by type of source-documents, newspapers,
periodicals, year-books and studies subdivided into books and
pamphlets and articles.

                    UWI-T

121 National Book League
    The Commonwealth in books, 1964 / National Book League. -
   London : The National Book League, 1964. - 126p.

    "An annotated listing of monographic works, dealing with
Commonwealth countries, topically arranged. Useful in bringing to
light West Indies titles. The great majority are current
imprints."

                  Ref.no.15
                  Vol.27

122 New York (State). Foreign Area Materials Center
    Guide to reference sources on Africa, Asia, Latin America,
   and the Caribbean, Middle East and North Africa and Russia and
   East Europe : selected and annotated / edited by James R.

Kennedy. - Williamsport, Pa. : Bro-Dart Pub. Co., 1972. - xiv, 73p. - (Occasional publication ; no.17)
    Latin America and the Caribbean: p.35-44

"Provides well annotated entries to 47 of major reference sources covering social sciences and humanities."
                                                                    Ref.no.19
                                                                    p.931

123 NEYMEYER, ROBERT
        Commonwealth Caribbean bibliography : books, articles and reviews in the humanities and social sciences from non-Caribbean sources / [compiled by] Robert Neymeyer. - Iowa City, Iowa : Neymeyer, 1978. - 26p.
        Mimeographed

    288 references mainly to journal articles on the region appearing outside of it in 1978. Arranged alphabetically by author within subject sections such as anthropology, archaeology, economics, education, government and politics, and literature. Includes a country index.
                                                                    UWI-T

124 PROUDFOOT, MARY
        Britain and the United States in the Caribbean : a comparative study in methods of development / Mary Proudfoot. - London : Faber, 1954. - xxi, 434p. - (Colonial and comparative studies / edited by Margery Perham)
        Bibliography: p.363-369

    Abbreviated references arranged alphabetically by author. Includes commission and other special reports with descriptive notes in some cases.
                                                                    UWI-T

125 RAGATZ, LOWELL J.
        A bibliography of articles, descriptive, historical and scientific, on colonies and other dependent territories, appearing in American geographical and kindred journals [through 1934] / Lowell J. Ragatz. - London : A. Thomas, 1935. - 2v.
        Vol.1. - 122p.

    Includes the Bahama islands (p.53-54), the Bermudas (p.54-55), British Guiana (p.56-58), British Honduras (p.58), British West Indies (p.59-62).
                                                                    UWI-T

126 RAGATZ, LOWELL J.
        A bibliography of articles descriptive, historical and scientific, on colonies and other dependent territories,

appearing in American geographical and kindred journals /
compiled by Lowell J. Ragatz and Janet Evans Ragatz. - 2nd
ed. - Ann Arbor, Mich. : University Microfilms, 1971. - 2v.
  Xerographic reprint of: 2nd ed. published 1951
  Vol.1. - 214p. - Vol.2. - 149p.

  Vol.1: Section on British Empire includes British Guiana
and British Honduras (p.56-58) and British West Indies (p.59-62).
Vol.2: Section on British Empire includes British Guiana and
British Honduras (p.27-28) and British West Indies (p.28-30).

UWI-T

127 RAGATZ, LOWELL J.
     The fall of the planter class in the British Caribbean,
     1763-1833 : a study in social and economic history / Lowell J.
     Ragatz. - New York : Octagon Books, 1971. - xiv, 520p.
       Reprint of: 1st ed. - [S.l.] : The American Historical
     Association, 1928
       Bibliographical notes: p.461-490

     Wide-ranging essay-type notes are provided under several
headings including (1) guides, indexes and bibliographies, (2)
manuscripts, sub-divided into the several groups of papers, (3)
general and (4) local histories, (5) economic literature, (6) the
slave trade, slavery, abolition and emancipation. Comments are
evaluative and critical.

UWI-T

128 Recent books
     In Caribbean review. - Vol.1, no.1 (1969)- . - San Juan,
     Puerto Rico : Caribbean Review, Inc., 1969 --
       Quarterly

     Originally published in Puerto Rico as a book review paper
this title moved to Florida International University and broadened
its scope. Compiled by Marian Goslinga in recent years the
listings of new books are arranged alphabetically by author
within such broad subject groups as biography, description and
travel, economics, language and literature and politics and
government. Coverage is of the wider Caribbean area.

UWI-T

129 REID, DORCAS WORSLEY
     An annotated bibliography of books on Spanish and South
     America and the West Indies / Dorcas Worsley Reid. - p.313-
     326
       In Hispania. - Vol.20 (1937)

     "Lists books of general character published in the United
States after 1920."

Ref.no.20
p.42

34

130   Royal Empire Society
        Best books on the British Empire : a bibliographical guide
    for students / by Evans Lewin. - 2nd.ed. - London : Royal
    Empire Society, 1945. - 100p. -- (Royal Empire Society biblio-
    graphies ; no.12)
        West Indian colonies: p.74-77
        Later edition of 1948 subsequently revised by Flint
    (Ref.no.131)

        Sub-divided into sections on administration, history and
    native races following more general works.
                                                                    TCL

131   Royal Commonwealth Society
        Books on the British Empire and Commonwealth : a guide for
    students / [edited] by John E. Flint. - London : Oxford
    University Press [for] Royal Commonwealth Society, 1968. - vi,
    66p.
        The Caribbean: p.61-64

        Updating of earlier works edited by Evans Lewin.
    Selective listings of descriptive, geographic, economic, literary,
    historical and political works mainly published after 1940.
    Includes a general section on the Caribbean and one on particular
    islands and territories in alphabetical author order.
                                                                    UWI-T

132   SABIN, JOSEPH
        Bibliotheca Americana : a dictionary of books relating to
    America, from its discovery to the present time / by Joseph
    Sabin. - Amsterdam : N. Israel, 1961/1962. - 29v. in 15
        "Unchanged reprint of the edition published: New York,
    1868."

        The West Indies are included in the scope of this famous
    work. Alphabetical author arrangement using subject entries for
    anonymous works. One such section under West Indies covers 16
    pages and another under Jamaica, 14 pages. Library locations are
    given for rare items. Brief notes mainly bibliograpical in
    nature are given.
                                                                    UWI-T

133   SMITH, JOHN RUSSELL
        Biblioteca americana : a catalogue of a valuable collection
    of books, pamphlets, manuscripts, maps, engraved portraits
    illustrating the history and geography of North and South
    America and the West Indies / John Russell Smith. - London :
    [s.n.], 1865. - 308p.
                                                                Ref.no.3

134   STANCIL, CAROL F.
      The Bermuda triangle : an annotated bibliography / by Carol
F. Stancil. -[Los Angeles] : Reference Section, College
Library, UCLA, 1973. - 10p.

      The bibliography consists of forty-four entries which
include books, periodical articles, newspaper articles, correspondence and government publications.
                                                            UWI-T

135   STARKEY, OTIS P.
      The economic geography of Barbados : a study of the
relationship between environmental variations and economic
development / by Otis P. Starkey. - Westport, Conn. : Negro
Universities Press, [1939]. - 228p.
      Bibliography: p.213-219

      Alphabetical author list of books (including many early
works), government reports and a few articles on Barbados and the
West Indies as a whole.
                                                            UWI-T

136   STEVENS, H.
      Rare Americana : a catalogue of historical and geographical
books, pamphlets and manuscripts relating to America / H.
Stevens. - [S.l. : s.n.], 1927. - vii, 578p.
                                                              RCS

137   THOMPSON, LAWRENCE S.
      The new Sabin : books described by Joseph Sabin and his
successors, now described again on the basis of examination of
originals, and fully indexed by title, subject, joint author
and institutions and agencies / Lawrence S. Thompson. - Troy,
N.Y. : The Whitson Publishing Company, 1974- . - v.
      Index to entries / Lawrence Thompson. - 1974- . - v.

      Ongoing publication. Two vols. of the main work and two
index volumes published so far. Aims to improve on the accuracy
of entries in Sabin (Ref.no.132) since most of the works listed
have been seen by the compiler in the original or on film. The
subject index provided together with the other added entries
facilitate the tracing of material in the main body of the work
and entries for the West Indies generally and individual
countries appear in it.
                                                            UWI-T

138   Trinidad and Tobago. Central Library
      A selective list of material illustrating Caribbean
development / prepared in the Central Library of Trinidad and
Tobago on the occasion of the first Library Seminar held in

Port of Spain, Trinidad, 8th-9th June, 1963. - Trinidad,
Trinidad and Tobago : Government Printing Office, 1963. - 24p.

Alphabetical author arrangement within sections on bibliographies, histories, early and recent, government and politics,
literature and government publications.

TCL

139 Trinidad and Tobago. Central Library. Tobago Regional
     Library
         A select list of West Indian books for young people - My
     own West Indian literature : an extract from Books for all /
     compiled by the Central Library [for] Tobago Regional Library
     25th Anniversary. - [Port of Spain, Trinidad] : Government
     Printery, 1973. - 1v. - (Various pagings)
         Cover title

     Over 250 references, some annotated, to fiction and non-
fiction West Indian works for children including picture books
and folk tales. Pages are extracted from another pamphlet and
retain the original page numbering. Includes books in English
about several parts of the Caribbean including the English-
speaking areas.

TCL

140 Trinidad and Tobago. Central Library. West Indian Reference
     Section

         West Indian books for school libraries : a preliminary
     list / Central Library, West Indian Reference Section - Port of
     Spain : Central Library of Trinidad and Tobago, 1970. - 9
     leaves
         Mimeographed

     A general listing without subject divisions or annotations.
TCL

141 United States. Department of the Army
         Latin America and the Caribbean : analytical survey of
     literature / Department of the Army. - Washington, D.C. :
     Government Printing Office, 1975. - 153p. : maps. - (DA
     pamphlet ; no.550-7-1)

     Includes country-by-country surveys for the Bahamas,
Barbados, Belize, Guyana, Jamaica, Trinidad and Tobago. References
to both journal articles and monographs include descriptive
extracts and are compiled by research analysts of the U.S. Army
library. Background notes, maps, and general reading lists are
provided on each country in extensive appendices.

UWI-T

142   United States. Department of State
     Latin America and European dependencies in the Western
Hemisphere : a selected bibliography / Department of State. -
Washington, D.C. : [s.n.], 1950. - 110p.

Ref.no.145
p.5

143   United States. Library of Congress
     List of references on the West Indies / Library of Congress.
- Washington : Library of Congress, 1923. - 6p.

     58 references.

Ref.no.4
vol.4,p.6527

144   United States. Library of Congress. Division of Bibliography
     ... British possessions in the Caribbean area : a selected
list of references / compiled ... by Ann Duncan Brown under the
direction of Florence S. Hellman ... . - Washington, D.C. :
Library of Congress, 1943. - 2, 192p.
     Mimeographed

     Covers British Caribbean including Bermuda. List compiled
at the request of the Anglo-American Caribbean Commission.
Subject arrangement.

UWI-J

145   University of Miami. School of Law
     Latin America and the Caribbean : a bibliographical guide
to works in English / by S.A. Bayitch. - Coral Gables, Fla. :
University of Miami Press ; New York : Oceana Publications,
1967. - xxviii, 943p. - (Interamerican legal studies ; vol.10)

     Expanded version of an earlier (1961) work including the
non-Hispanic Caribbean among new areas of coverage. Slanted
towards economic, legal and political topics, the work is
divided into six parts with separate subject and country listings
predominating. The Caribbean is covered in two sections, p.265-
289 by subjects and p.803-926 by countries with several entries
on individual territories.

UWI-T

146   University of Southern Illinois. Lovejoy Library
     The Caribbean area : a search guide / [prepared by] Social
Science / Business Library, Lovejoy Library. - Carbondale,
Ill. : Lovejoy Library, 1972. - 13p. - (Lovejoy Library utiliza-
tion guides)

     Arranged in sections by form such as directories and hand-
books, news summaries and indexes, reference guides, bibliographies, abstract journals etc. This guide contains general
reference works which include Caribbean coverage as well as a few

specifically Caribbean items. Search strategies are outlined in
some cases and all entries carry a Library of Congress class
number and an annotation.

UWI-T

146a University of Texas. The General Libraries
        The Caribbean / by Ann H. Jordan. - Austin, Tex. : The
General Libraries, The University of Texas at Austin, 1979. -
22p. - (Selected reference sources ; 45)

TU

147 University of the West Indies
        Departmental reports to Council for the year ending ... /
University of the West Indies. - 1968-1969 - . - [Mona, Jamaica] :
University of the West Indies, 1969-
        Annual

        One composite list of staff publications was formerly
included as an appendix to the Principal's report which then
incorporated departmental reports. Latterly these are arranged
by Faculty alphabetically in a separate publication and each
departmental report includes a list of publications by members of
the faculty during the report year, as well as an account of
research work in progress. Monographs, serial articles and, in
some cases, theses and publications in press are included. Many
items relate to research in and on the West Indies.

UWI-T

148 University of the West Indies. Institute of Social and
        Economic Research (Eastern Caribbean)
        A bibliography of the Caribbean / Audine Wilkinson. - Cave
Hill, Barbados : Institute of Social and Economic Research,
University of the West Indies, 1974. - iii, 167 leaves. -
(Occasional bibliography series ; no.1)

        First of a series marking their tenth anniversary celebra-
tions and reflecting the ISER (EC) library holdings of Caribbean
material. Arranged alphabetically by territory and subdivided
within each into books, articles and documents, papers and
pamphlets.

UWI-T

148a University of the West Indies (Cave Hill). Main Library
        Caribbeana selections : glimpses of our cultural
heritage / by Jean A. Callender; contributed to the CARIFESTA
Book Exhibition at the Festival Village Complex, West Terrace,
St. James, Barbados 20th-31st July 1981. - Cave Hill, Barbados :
Main Library, University of the West Indies, 1981. - 11p.

        127 items arranged under the following headings:- General
Interest; Music and Dance; Poetry and Drama; Prose; Prose and

Poetry – Collections.   Includes some entries on the non-English-speaking Caribbean.

UWI-T

149   University of the West Indies (Mona)
         Jamaica Book Fair ... Catalogue of publications exhibited
by the University of the West Indies, Mona Campus, Jamaica
incorporating the various publications, reports and research
and independent activities and writings of staff and students. –
Kingston, [Jamaica] : U.W.I., 1972. – 9p.
         Mimeographed

         The Book Fair was sponsored by the Jamaica Library Associa-
tion. Listings are under title within separate headings for
university departments and publication series. Only titles
selected for display are included.

UWI-T

150   University of the West Indies (Mona).   Faculty of Arts and
      General Studies
         A bibliography of the University of the West Indies
Caribbean Studies 1966–1974 / by A. Theresa Elcock; submitted
in partial fulfillment of the requirements for the B.A. degree.
– Mona, Jamaica : University of the West Indies Faculty of
Arts and General Studies, 1974. – 118p.

         The author was a student in the Department of Library
Studies. Chronological listing in author order with author,
geographical and subject indexes for all the research papers
submitted as "Caribbean Studies" by final year students of the
U.W.I. in Jamaica as part of the degree requirements. This
bibliography is itself one such Caribbean study.

UWI-T

151   University of the West Indies (Mona).   Faculty of Arts and
      General Studies
         Caribbean studies – 1975 [a list] / Faculty of Arts and
General Studies. – [Mona, Jamaica : University of the West
Indies], [1975?]. – 9 leaves
         Typescript xerox copy
         Also 1976 ed. – 10 leaves

UWI-T

152   University of the West Indies (St. Augustine).   Faculty of
      Arts and General Studies
         List of Caribbean Studies theses, 1965–1970 / Faculty of
Arts and General Studies. – St. Augustine, [Trinidad] : The
University of the West Indies, Faculty of Arts and General
Studies, [1971?]. – 34p.
         Mimeographed

40

Listing by author with titles of Caribbean-topic research
projects completed by undergraduates on the St. Augustine campus
in Trinidad.

UWI-T

153 University of the West Indies (Mona). Library
       A select list of works on the British Caribbean / prepared
     by the University of the West Indies Library. - [Mona,
     Jamaica : the Library], 1964. - 13p.
       Typescript

     A listing of "the most important and basic publications for
the study of British Caribbean history." 215 items are arranged
in broad groupings under such headings as bibliographies,
historical writings pre-1900 and post-1900, slavery, sugar and the
plantation system, description and travel, social and economic
studies. Includes mainly studies of the area as a whole but a few
specialized studies of individual territories as well.

UWI-J

154 University of the West Indies (St. Augustine). Library
       Basic Caribbean reference material for foreign embassy
     collections, prepared on the occasion of SALALM XXIV June 17-
     22, 1979, Los Angeles, California / by Sandra Barnes, Maureen
     Henry [and] Annette Knight. - St. Augustine, Trinidad : Library,
     The University of the West Indies, 1979. - 43p.

     Covers the 10 members of the former West Indies Federation
as well as Guyana, the Bahamas, Virgin Islands, Bermuda and
Belize in separate sections by territory or group of territories
such as Windward Islands. A general West Indies section precedes
the country listings and each is subdivided into topics likely to
be useful in Embassy libraries, e.g., culture, cookery, history
and politics, trade and industry. Some entries briefly annotated.

UWI-T

155 University of the West Indies (St. Augustine). Library
       Serving the needs of the West Indies : the work of the
     University of the West Indies : display at the International
     Book Year Exhibition, held at the Trinidad Manufacturers'
     Association, Port of Spain, November 16-26, 1972 / Library,
     University of the West Indies. - St. Augustine, Trinidad : The
     University of the West Indies Library, 1972. - 13 leaves
       Mimeographed

     Lists publications of members of staff of the University
under broad headings - human resources and material resources.

UWI-T

156   VAUGHAN, ROBERT V.
      St. Croix, the Virgin Islands and the West Indies : a
      bibliography of a private collection / Robert V. Vaughan. -
      Christansted, Virgin Islands : [s.n.], 1971. - 36 leaves.
                                                        Ref.no.3

157   WAGENAAR HUMMELINCK, P.
      Bibliografie : articles [Bibliography] / compiled by P.
      Wagenaar Hummelinck. - p.175-234
      In Nieuwe West-Indische gids. - Vol.45, nos.2-3 (Dec.
      1966)
                                                             RIS

158   WAGENAAR HUMMELINCK, P.
      Bibliografie : articles [Bibliography] / compiled by P.
      Wagenaar Hummelinck. - p.197-247
      In Nieuwe West-Indische gids. - Vol.47, no.2 (Apr. 1970)
                                                             RIS

159   WAGENAAR HUMMELINCK, P.
      Bibliografie : separate publications [Bibliography] /
      compiled by P. Wagenaar Hummelinck. - p.262-287
      In Nieuwe West-Indische gids. - Vol.44, no.3 (Nov. 1965)
                                                             RIS

160   WAGENAAR HUMMELINCK, P.
      Bibliografie : separate publications [Bibliography] /
      compiled by P. Wagenaar Hummelinck. - p.298-335
      In Nieuwe West-Indische gids. - Vol.46, no.3 (Dec. 1968)
                                                             RIS

161   WAGENAAR HUMMELINCK, P.
      Bibliografie : separate publications [Bibliography] /
      compiled by P. Wagenaar Hummelinck. - p.84-126
      In Nieuwe West-Indische gids. - Vol.49, nos.1-2 (Nov.
      1972)
                                                             RIS

162   WAGENAAR HUMMELINCK, P.
      Bibliografie : separate publications [Bibliography] /
      compiled by P. Wagenaar Hummelinck. - p. 177-197
      In Nieuwe West-Indische gids. - Vol.49, no.3 (Dec. 1973)
                                                             RIS

163   WAGENAAR HUMMELINCK, P.
      Bibliografie : separate publications [Bibliography] /
      compiled by P. Wagenaar Hummelinck. - p.62-76
      In Nieuwe West-Indische gids. - Vol.50, no.1 (Jan.1975
                                                             RIS

164   WALROND, CHERYL
          An annotated bibliography of the available books in the
      Caribbean Regional Library / compiled by Cheryl Walrond. -
      [Georgetown : Caribbean Regional Centre for Advanced Studies
      in Youth Work], [1976]. - 58 leaves.
          April additions. - 11 leaves

                                                            Ref.no.73
                                                            1976,p.4

165   WARDEN, DAVID BAILLIE
          Bibliotheca americana ; being a choice collection of books
      relating to north and south America and the West Indies /
      David Baillie Warden. - Paris : [s.n.], 1831. - 140p.
          Another edition. - 1840. - [v], 124p.

          1,100 references.

                                                            Ref.no.4
                                                            Vol.1,p.308

166   The West Indies : a list of books and maps in the Redpath
      Library collections, published before 1910, and concerned with
      the West Indies. - [S.1 : s.n.], [n.d.]. - 6 leaves

          Alphabetical author list of books held wholly on the West
      Indies, particular islands or groups of islands as well as maps.
      Holdings are those of the Redpath Library at McGill University.
                                                            UWI-T

167   West Indies : books, maps, prints with a selection of atlases
      and general works, Central and South America, slavery and
      negroes, indians, indian languages, cultures. - Amsterdam,
      Holland : Antiquariaat "Pampiere Wereld." [19-?]. - 74p. -
      (Catalogue ; no.7)
          Mimeographed

                                                            NLG

168   Westminster City Libraries
          The sun is a shapely fire : a West Indian booklist /
      Westminster City Libraries. - London : Westminster City
      Libraries, [1972?]. - [12p.]

          Based on titles held by two branches of the Westminster
      City Libraries special West Indian collections. Outstanding
      selections only from the "remarkable outpouring of imaginative
      literature" grouped under a few broad headings.
                                                            ILAS

169   WHITTEN, NORMAN E.
        Afro-American anthropology : contemporary perspectives /
      edited by Norman E. Whitten and John F. Zwed. - New York :
      Free Press ; London : Collier-Macmillan, 1970. - x, 468p.
      References cited: p.419-449

        Alphabetical author list of items includes many on folklore,
   dialectology, religious cults, carnival, folk tales, calypso,
   social and cultural pluralism.
                                                              UWI-T

170   WILLIAMS, ERIC
        A West Indian book collection / Eric Williams. - p.59-72
        In Caribbean Commission monthly information bulletin. -
      Vol.6, no.3 (Oct. 1952)

        Bibliographic essay seeking to suggest a list of books for
   purchase by libraries in the Caribbean area. General material,
   history and literature and art are covered.
                                                              UWI-T

170a WILSON, CHARLES MORROW
        Books about Middle America / Charles Morrow Wilson. - New
      York : Middle America Information Bureau conducted by United
      Fruit Company, 1945. - 27p.
                                                                 LC

171   WULFF, ERIKA H.
        Bibliography of the Whim Greathouse Collection of books
      and pamphlets on the West Indies / compiled by Erika H. Wulff.
      - St. Croix, U.S. Virgin Islands : St. Croix Landmarks
      Society Inc., 1972. - 12, [11] leaves

        An alphabetical author listing of West Indian interest
   material held with a bias towards the Danish West Indies. No
   annotations or index.
                                                              UWI-T

172   ZIMMERMAN, IRENE
        Some notes on Caribbean bibliography and bibliographers /
      Irene Zimmerman. - p.346-353
        In The Caribbean in transition ; papers on social,
      political and economic development / edited by F.M. Andic
      [and] T.G. Mathews. - Rio Piedras, Puerto Rico : University of
      Puerto Rico, Institute of Caribbean Studies, 1965. - [Comments
      at final session] Caribbean Scholars' Conference, 2nd, Mona,
      Jamaica, April 14-19, 1964

        A bibliographic essay reviewing activities in the region
   noting leading contributions, proposals and needs for future
   development.
                                                              UWI-T

Accessions Lists

173   Barbados. Central Bank
        List of additions to the catalogue of the library. - No.1
      (1975)- . - Bridgetown, Barbados : Central Bank, 1975-
        Quarterly

        West Indian additions not separately identified. Material
arranged by Universal Decimal Classification using broad subject
headings.
UWI-T

174   Barbados. Department of Archives
        List of printed accessions, 1964-1967 / compiled by the
      Department of Archives. - [Bridgetown], Barbados : Department
      of Archives, 1968. - 74p.
        Mimeographed

        1,522 references to "government publications and selected
unofficial publications for Barbados and ... comparative material
for the West Indies and the Caribbean " collected from the
inception of the Archives Department.
UWI-T

175   Barbados Public Library. West Indian Collection
        Additions list / Barbados Public Library, West Indian
      Collection. - No.1 (1967)- . - Bridgetown, [Barbados] :
      Public Library, 1967-
        Quarterly
        Mimeographed

        Includes unpublished material such as addresses, speeches,
reports and individual issues of West Indian serial publications
in an alphabetical subject arrangement. Full bibliographic
references, but no annotations, class numbers or index are
provided.
UWI-T

176   Bibliographic guide to black studies / The Research
      Libraries of the New York Public Library. - 1975- . - Boston :
      G.K. Hall, 1976-

        Includes publications catalogued during the year by the
Schomburg Center for Research in Black Culture and serves as an
annual supplement to the Dictionary Catalog (Ref.no.48). From
1977 items are classified by the Dewey Decimal system. An
invaluable acquisitions guide, cataloguing and research tool.
NYPL

176a Bibliographic guide to Latin American studies. - Vol.1 (1978)- .
      - Boston : G.K. Hall, 1979-

Serves as an annual supplement to the Catalog of the
Latin American Collection of the University of Texas at Austin
(Ref.no.62).

TU

177 Caribbean Community Secretariat. Information and Documentation
     Section
        New additions / Information and Documentation Section,
     Caribbean Community Secretariat. - Nos.1 and 2 (Jan./Feb.
     1980)- . - [Georgetown, Guyana] : Caribbean Community
     Secretariat, Information and Documentation Section, 1980-
        Monthly

        Continues: Ref.no.178.

UWI-T

178 Caribbean Community Secretariat. Library
        List of additions and publications catalogued / Caribbean
     Community Secretariat Library. - Nos.1 (1971)-No.9 and 10 (Nov/
     Dec. 1979). - ⌊Georgetown, Guyana⌋ : Caribbean Community
     Secretariat Library, 1971-1979
        Frequency varies
        Continued by: Ref.no.177.

        An index to the Universal Decimal Classification numbers
     used and a subject index precede the listing of documents,
     articles, new journal titles, and monographs in classified order
     with some brief annotations.

UWI-T

179 Caribbean Development Bank. Library
        List of acquisitions / Caribbean Development Bank Library.
     - [Wildey, Barbados] : Caribbean Development Bank, 1975-
        Irregular
        Description based on Apr./May 1979 issue

        Includes a West Indian section at the beginning of each
     issue. Entries are arranged under country by UDC numbers and
     subdivided by subject within each section using classification
     numbers. Sections listing documents of international organiza-
     tions such as the UN also include some West Indian material.

UWI-T

180 Caribbean Organization. Library
        Selective list of recent additions to the library - Vol.1
     (Sept. 1962)-Vol.3, no.3 (Oct. 1964). - [Hato Rey, Puerto
     Rico] : Caribbean Organization Library, 1962-1964
        Title in English and French

        Continued by: Ref.nos.181-182.

UF

181 Caribbean Regional Library
         List of new acquisitions / Caribbean Regional Library. –
     January/February (1974)– . – [Hato Rey, Puerto Rico] :
     Caribbean Regional Library, 1974–
         Bimonthly
         Continues: Ref.no.180.

     Alpabetical author arrangement with Dewey classification
numbers provided and full catalogue card information. Acquisitions cover material on the wider Caribbean area served by the
Caribbean Organization and CODECA, its successor.
                                                         UWI-T

182 Caribbean Regional Library
         Selective list of recent additions to the library. – Vol.1,
     no.1 (Mar. 1966)–Vol.1, no.6 (Jan. 1967). – Hato Rey, Puerto
     Rico : Caribbean Economic Development Corporation, 1966–1967
         Bimonthly

         Continues: Ref.no.180; continued by: Ref.no.71.
                                                         UWI-T

183 Christian Action for Development in the Caribbean (CADEC).
     Documentation Service
         List of recent acquisitions / CADEC. – Bridgetown,
     [Barbados] : CADEC Documentation Service, 1973. – 5p.

     Includes a list of newsletters and journals received
regularly, with Caribbean items predominating, and a list of CADEC
publications.
                                                         UWI-T

184 Commonwealth Institute Library and Resource Centre
         Caribbean : General, no.1 / Commonwealth Institute Library
     and Resource Centre. – [London] : Commonwealth Institute
     Library and Resource Centre, 1977. – 2 leaves

     Items cover topics such as bibliography and libraries,
economy, education, geography and maps, history and biography,
fiction, poetry, music, politics and sociology.
                                                         UWI-T

185 Commonwealth Institute Library and Resource Centre
         New materials : Guyana and Belize, no.1 / Commonwealth
     Institute Library and Resource Centre. – [London] : Common-
     wealth Institute Library and Resource Centre, 1977. – 2 leaves

     Items on Guyana are listed under headings: – Reference
Books, General, Economy, Education, History, People, Politics,
Literature. Those on Belize appear under General, Forestry,
History, Music and Politics.
                                                         UWI-T

186   Commonwealth Institute Library and Resource Centre
          New materials : Jamaica, no.1 / Commonwealth Institute
      Library and Resource Centre. - [London] : Commonwealth
      Institute Library and Resource Centre, 1977. - 10p.

          Items are arranged in sections relating to topics such as
      art and architecture, cookery, economy, flora, geography and maps,
      language and literature, fiction, poetry and music.

                                                          UWI-T

187   Commonwealth Institute Library and Resource Centre
          New materials : Trinidad and Tobago / Commonwealth
      Institute Library and Resource Centre. - No.1. - [S.l.] :
      Commonwealth Institute Library and Resource Centre, 1977. - 7p.

          In addition to materials of a general nature lists items
      on birds, carnival, music and dance (including discs), cricket,
      economy, education, history, language and literature, drama,
      fiction, poetry, politics and sociology.

                                                          UWI-T

188   Curaçao Public Library
          Caribbean Collection ; quarterly acquisition list /
      Curaçao Public Library. - [Willemstad], Curaçao : Public
      Library, 1975-
          Mimeographed

          Arranged by subject in Dewey classification order with
      material on all parts of the Caribbean, including English,
      Spanish and Dutch-speaking territories, with the latter
      predominating.

                                                          UWI-T

189   Great Britain. Ministry of Overseas Development. [Library]
          Technical co-operation : a monthly bibliography /
      Ministry of Overseas Development. - Vol.1 (1963)- . - London:
      Ministry of Overseas Development, 1963-
          Monthly

          Mainly devoted to official publications of the Common-
      wealth received in the joint library services of the Ministry of
      Overseas Development and the Foreign and Commonwealth Office in
      London. Arranged regionally with sections for each country.
      Thus the West Indian territories are listed under America.
      Includes separate listings of unpublished reports and official
      U.K. government publications relating to developing countries.
                                                          UWI-T

190   Guyana.   Public Free Library
         Additions to the Guyana collection in the Reference
      Library / Public Free Library. - Georgetown, Guyana : Public
      Free Library, 1966
         Vol.2,no.1 :   Books. - 5 leaves
         -    no.2 :   Periodical articles. - 2 leaves
         -    no.3 :   Periodical articles. - 5 leaves

                                                                    NLG

191   Guyana.   Public Free Library
         Reference Department bulletin / Public Free Library -
      Vol.1 (1971)- . - Georgetown, Guyana : Public Free Library,
      1971-

         Lists all additions to the reference collection in Dewey
      classification order, with Guyanese and West Indian writings
      identified by symbols.   Includes lists of periodicals received
      regularly with those from the Commonwealth Caribbean separately
      identified.
                                                                  UWI-T

192   Hispanic and Luso-Brazilian Council.   Canning House Library
         British bulletin of publications on Latin America, the
      West Indies, Portugal and Spain / Canning House Library. -
      No.1 (1949)- . - London : Canning House Library, 1949-
         Semi-annual

         Includes books, essays and articles in newspapers and
      journals published in Britain on the West Indies, in one alpha-
      betical sequence by author.
                                                                  UWI-T

193   Institute of Jamaica.   West India Reference Library
         Jamaica accessions / West India Reference Library. -
      1964-1967. - Kingston : Institute of Jamaica, 1965-1967
         Annual

         Lists material published in Jamaica about Jamaica and
      written by Jamaicans.   Alphabetical arrangement by author within
      sections for books and pamphlets, manuscripts, maps and
      periodicals.   Superseded by Jamaican National Bibliography after
      1967 (Ref.nos.74, 75, 76).
                                                                  UWI-T

194   Institute of Jamaica.   West India Reference Library
         West India accessions / catalogued by WIRL. - November
      1972-February 1973 and March-August 1973. - Kingston, Jamaica :
      Institute of Jamaica, 1972-1973

Listing of material received and catalogued in one alpha-
betical author sequence with Dewey classification numbers.
Published as an experiment to test the feasibility of a West
Indian bibliography.

UWI-T

195   Norman Manley Law School. Library
         Recent additions / Law School Library. - [No.1] (Jan-Apr.
      1980)- . - Mona, Jamaica : Norman Manley Law School Library,
      1980-
         Three issues per year

         First issue includes a section on Judgments - Jamaica and
      Cayman Islands.

UWI-T

196   Research Institute for the Study of Man. Library
         Classified list of recent additions to the library. - No.1
      (1970)- . - New York : The Institute, 1970-
         Irregular

         Entries arranged in Dewey classification order include
      many Caribbean interest items.

UWI-T

197   Royal Commonwealth Society. Library
         Library notes / Royal Commonwealth Society. - London :
      Royal Commonwealth Society Library, 1972-
         Frequency varies

         Features a list of accessions in which a section on
      Caribbean territories and South America is regularly included in
      one alphabetical author sequence. This society was formerly the
      Royal Empire Society and these lists supplement its published
      catalogues although no classification numbers or subject headings
      are provided.

UWI-T

198   Trinidad and Tobago. Central Library
         West Indian reference collection : classified list of
      accessions / Central Library. - No.1 (1965)-No.38 (1968). -
      [Port of Spain, Trinidad] : Central Library, 1965-1968
         Irregular
         Mimeographed

         Half-yearly cumulative issues also published. Arranged in
      Dewey classification order.

UWI-T

199   Trinidad and Tobago.   Central Library.   West Indian Reference
      Section
            Trinidad and Tobago and West Indian bibliography : annual
      accessions / Central Library, West Indian Reference Section. –
      No.1 (1966)-No.6 (1968). – Port of Spain, Trinidad : Central
      Library, 1966–1968

            Trinidad and Tobago accessions, including periodicals and
      newspapers separately listed from West Indian material.   Alpha-
      betical author arrangement with Dewey class numbers given.
      Superseded by the National Bibliography of Trinidad and Tobago
      (Ref.no.77).

                                                                         TCL

200   Trinidad and Tobago.   Central Library.   West Indian Reference
      Section
            Trinidad and Tobago and West Indian bibliography : monthly
      accessions / Central Library, West Indian Reference Section. –
      1969–August 1974. – Port of Spain, Trinidad : West Indian
      Reference Section, Central Library of Trinidad and Tobago,
      1969–1974
            Frequency and title vary
            Mimeographed

            Annual cumulations also published (Ref.no.199)
            Continues: Ref.no.198
            Continued by: Ref.no.77

                                                                       UWI–T

201   Trinidad and Tobago.   Industrial Development Corporation
            Library bulletin : list of publications catalogued /
      Industrial Development Corporation. – Port of Spain, Trinidad :
      IDC, 1960–
            Frequency varies

            Arranged by UDC order.   West Indian items are not
      separately identified.   Includes material on the economy,
      industrial development, technology and business in Trinidad and
      Tobago.

                                                                       UWI–T

202   Trinidad and Tobago.   Ministry of Energy and Energy-based
      Industries.   Library
            List of books catalogued and periodical articles indexed /
      Ministry of Energy and Energy-based Industries Library. –
      Vol.1, no.1 (Jan.-Apr.1978)- . – [Port of Spain] : Ministry of
      Energy and Energy-based Industries Library, 1978–
            Frequency varies
            Ministry of Energy and Energy-based Industries was formerly
      Ministry of Petroleum and Mines.

This accessions list includes conference papers, official
and special reports and unpublished memoranda relevant to the
Ministry's scope of interest in the West Indies and Trinidad and
Tobago in particular in an alphabetical subject arrangement. UDC
class numbers are provided.

                                                            UWI-T

203 United States. Virgin Islands. Bureau of Libraries, Museums
     and Archaeological Services. VILINET (Virgin Islands Library
     and Information Network)
          Caribbean : recent acquisitions of Caribbean materials in
     Virgin Islands libraries / VILINET. - No.1 (June 1981)- . -
     [S.1.] : VILINET, [1981?] -
          Irregular

          Comprises material processed for special collections in
the U.S. Virgin Islands public library system and for the two
campus libraries of the College of the Virgin Islands. Classified
section arranged by Dewey classification with geographic index.
Periodicals and local documents which are covered in other network or Bureau of Libraries publications are excluded. Locations
provided.

                                                            UWI-T

204 United States. Virgin Islands. Department of Conservation and
     Cultural Affairs. Bureau of Libraries, Museums and Archaeo-
     logical Services
          Special collections accessions : recent acquisitions of
     Caribbean materials in Virgin Islands Public Libraries. -
     No.1 (1978)- . - St. Thomas, U.S. Virgin Islands : Bureau of
     Libraries, Museums and Archaeological Services, 1978-
          Irregular

          Arranged by Dewey classification numbers with appropriate
headings and a geographic index, the list includes material on
the West Indies, the wider Caribbean area and further afield
added to the library's special collections located at one or
more of four main public library outlets on the three U.S. Virgin
Islands, but Caribbean area material predominates.

                                                            UWI-T

205 University of Florida. Research Library
          Caribbean acquisitions : materials acquired by the
     University of Florida / compiled by the Technical Processes
     Department. - 1957/58- . - Gainesville, Fla. : University of
     Florida, 1959-
          Annual

          Later issues compiled by the Catalog Department. Coverage
includes all countries bordering on the Caribbean Sea.
Geographical subdivisions used within broad subject groups such

as economics, education etc. and an alphabetical index to main
entries is provided.

UWI-T

206 University of Guyana. Library
          Additions to stock / University of Guyana Library. – 1974–
     1975. – [Georgetown], Guyana : University of Guyana Library,
     1974–1975
          Monthly

UWI-T

207 University of Guyana. Library
          List of additions / University of Guyana Library. – 1976– .
     – Georgetown, Guyana : University of Guyana Library, 1976–
          Irregular
          Continues : Ref.no.206.

          Arranged in Library of Congress classification order, with
     a separate section for Caribbean Studies at the end. Arranged by
     country and alphabetically by author.

UWI-T

208 University of London. Institute of Commonwealth Studies.
     Library
          Select list of accessions / Institute of Commonwealth
     Studies. – No.1 (1965)– . – London : Institute of Commonwealth
     Studies Library, 1965–
          Mimeographed

          Regularly includes a section on the West Indies in general
     followed by the individual Commonwealth territories of the area.

UWI-T

209 University of Texas. Library. Latin American Collection
          Recent acquisitions for the Caribbean islands (excluding
     Cuba) and Guyana, French Guiana and Surinam of the Latin
     American Collection of the University of Texas Library. –
     No.1, 1962–Mar. 1967 (1968)– . – Austin, Tex. : University of
     Texas Library, Latin American Collection, 1968–

          Reproduced and reduced catalogue entries with Dewey class
     numbers in alphabetical sequence by countries including Bahamas,
     Barbados, Guyana, Jamaica, Trinidad and Tobago as well as French,
     Spanish and Dutch-speaking territories of the wider Caribbean.

UWI-T

210 University of the West Indies (Cave Hill). Faculty of Law.
     Library
          A list of materials added to the library / Faculty of Law
     Library. – 1975– . – [Bridgetown, Barbados] : Faculty of Law
     Library, University of the West Indies, 1975–

Irregular

Arranged by the Moys Classification Scheme. West Indian
items are interspersed throughout. Section on Primary Legal
Materials includes West Indian laws and other West Indian government documents.

UWI-T

211 University of the West Indies (Cave Hill). Faculty of Law.
     Library
         Quarterly accessions list of documents relating to the
     West Indies (excluding court decisions) / Faculty of Law
     Library. - 1974- . - [Bridgetown, Barbados] : Faculty of Law
     Library, U.W.I., 1974-
         Quarterly
         Title varies

         Lists all official publications - acts, gazettes, Hansards,
government notices (by number and name), etc. - acquired covering
the British Commonwealth territories of the West Indies.

UWI-T

212 University of the West Indies (Cave Hill). Institute of Social
     and Economic Research (Eastern Caribbean)
         Women in the Caribbean : accessions bulletin / Institute
     of Social and Economic Research (Eastern Caribbean). - No.1
     (Oct., Nov. 1979)- . - Cave Hill, Barbados : I.S.E.R., U.W.I.,
     1979-
         Bi-monthly?

Ref.no.72
Jan.-Mar. 1980, p.1

213 University of the West Indies (Cave Hill). Main Library
         Recent additions : West Indies Collection / Main Library.
     - Jan. 1972- . - [Cave Hill, Barbados : U.W.I. Main Library],
     1972-
         Irregular

         A listing following the broad divisions of the Library of
Congress classification.

UWI-T

214 University of the West Indies (Mona). Institute of Social
     and Economic Research. Library
         ISER : Recent additions. - Vol.1, no.1 (1968)- [19-?] ;
     vol.1, no.1 (1976)- . - Mona, Jamaica : I.S.E.R. Library, U.W.I.,
     1968-
         Quarterly

         Includes several items on and from the Caribbean region,
latterly subdivided into books, pamphlets, theses and student

project reports for the diploma in public administration.
Library of Congress class numbers, some modified, are given.

UWI-T

215 University of the West Indies (Mona). Library. Government
     Serials Section
          Quarterly accessions list of materials relating to the
     West Indies / U.W.I. Library, Government Serials Section. –
     1971– . – Mona, Jamaica : Government Serials Section, U.W.I.
     Library, 1971–
          Irregular

          Itemized listings of receipts of official serial publica-
     tions arranged by territory and serial title. Includes publica-
     tions of such regional organizations as the Caribbean Development
     Bank and Caribbean Community Secretariat.

UWI-T

216 University of the West Indies (St. Augustine). Library
          Recent acquisitions of Trinidad and Tobago imprints :
     cumulative issue of lists / University Library. – Nos.1–4
     (1973–1974). – St. Augustine, Trinidad : University of the
     West Indies Library, 1975. – (List no.5)
          Part 1: Books and pamphlets. – 143p. – Part 2: Index to
     books and pamphlets. – 100p.

          Full bibliographic entries arranged by the Library of
     Congress classification. Superseded by Trinidad and Tobago
     National Bibliography (Ref.no.77).

UWI-T

217 University of the West Indies (St. Augustine). Library.
     Social Sciences and West Indiana Division
          Caribbean studies : select list of accessions / U.W.I.
     Library, Social Sciences and West Indiana Division. – No.1
     (1976)– . – St. Augustine, Trinidad : U.W.I. Library, 1976–
          Irregular

          Previously incorporated with the Division's general list
     of accessions (Ref.no.218) this is a separate listing of newly
     acquired Caribbean material in all forms, including references to
     articles in journals. Arranged by territory with a section on
     the Caribbean in general, it includes material on and from non-
     English-speaking Caribbean territories.

UWI-T

218 University of the West Indies (St. Augustine). Library.
     Social Sciences and West Indiana Division
          Select list of accessions / U.W.I. Library, Social
     Sciences and West Indiana Division. – No.1 (1974)– . – St.

Augustine, Trinidad, Social Sciences and West Indiana
Division, U.W.I. Library, 1974-
     Irregular

     From No.2 there is a final section entitled: Caribbean
Studies which later appears separately (Ref.no.217).

                                                          UWI-T

219   University of the West Indies/University of Sussex. Centre
      for Multi-racial Studies, Barbados
           Select list of additions to the library / Centre for Multi-
      racial Studies. - No.1 (June 1968)-no.6 (Feb. 1971). - Cave
      Hill, Barbados : [Centre for Multi-racial Studies], 1968-1971
                                                          UWI-B

Government Publications
220   Great Britain. Colonial Office. Library
           Monthly list of official colonial publications / [compiled
      by the Colonial Office Library]. - No.1 (1948)-(196?) - London :
      Colonial Office Library, 1948-[196?] -

           Numbered listings in several parts including typescripts
      and papers not prepared for sale, government publications
      arranged by colonies alphabetically, colonial gazettes and
      legislation, U.K. government publications and maps. Each list
      reflects items received in the library.

                                                          TCL

221   HALLEWELL, LAWRENCE
           West Indian official publishing and U.K. official
      publishing on the West Indies, before independence and after /
      Lawrence Hallewell. - p.201-221
           In Twenty years of Latin American librarianship : Final
      report and working papers of the twenty-first Seminar on the
      acquisition of Latin American library materials, Indiana
      University, Bloomington, Indiana, May 2-6, 1976. - Austin,
      Tex. : SALALM Secretariat, 1978

           A bibliographic essay guide to the types and sources of
      official publishing on and of the West Indian territories.
      Includes such headings as laws, statutes, etc., demographic
      censuses and administrative reports for West Indian government
      publishing and early parliamentary reports, command papers and
      colonial reports for U.K. government publications on the region.
                                                          UWI-T

221a   Jamaica. National Investment Company
           A bibliography of reports and studies 1965-1981 : a
      subject index of reports and studies prepared in government

ministries, departments and other bodies / L. C. Pottinger. -
Kingston: Jamaica National Investment Company, 1981. - 3v.
                                              Ref.no.79
                                    Vol.4, no.2, Item no.329

222 Kraus-Thomson Organization Ltd.
       Official gazettes in microfilm / Kraus-Thomson Organization
     Ltd. - Nendeln, Liechtenstein : KTO Microform, [n.d.]

       Catalogue listing with prices includes the English-
     speaking Caribbean.
                                                          UWI-T

223 List of the serial publications of foreign governments, 1815-
     1931 / edited by Winifred Gregory for the American Council of
     Learned Societies, American Library Association, National
     Research Council ... . - New York : H.W. Wilson Co., 1932. -
     5p., 1, 720p.

       Entries under the name of each of the British possessions
     in the Caribbean area.
                                                          UWI-J

224 Royal Empire Society
       Overseas official publications : quarterly bulletin of
     official publications received by the Royal Empire Society,
     formerly Royal Colonial Institute, and issued in the Overseas
     British Empire or relating thereto. - Vol.1, no.1 (1927)-
     Vol.5, no.4 (1932). - London : The Society, 1927-1932. - Bound
     into 5v.

       West Indies entries in each volume under West Indies and
     the name of the territory.
                                                            RCS

225 University of the West Indies (Mona). Library
       Government serials in the University of the West Indies
     Library for the territories of Antigua, Barbados, British
     Guiana, Jamaica, Saint Lucia, Trinidad and Tobago / by
     William Gocking ; Appendix V of Working paper no. 25 ;
     submitted for the Seminar on the Acquisition of Latin American
     Library Materials (SALALM), 12th, Los Angeles, 1967. - p.198-
     222
       In Final report and working papers. - Vol.2. - Washington,
     D.C. : Pan American Union, 1968

       Separate sections for each territory with details of
     library holdings where necessary.
                                                          UWI-T

226 University of the West Indies (Mona). Library. Government
Serials Section
     West Indian government serial publications in the Univer-
sity of the West Indies Library, Mona, Jamaica / compiled by
the Government Serials Section. - [Mona, Jamaica : The
University of the West Indies Library], 1970. - 71p.
     Mimeographed
     Previously issued as an Appendix to a paper entitled:
"Bibliographical Control of Commonwealth Caribbean Government
Publications" / K.E. Ingram ; presented to ACURIL II, Barbados,
24 Nov. 1970.

     It updates a similar paper presented to SALALM XII (Ref.
no.225).

                                                          UWI-T

227 West Indies (Federation). Government
     List of publications of the government of the West Indies.
- [Port of Spain, Trinidad] : Government of the West Indies,
[1961]. - 2p. on 1 leaf
     Mimeographed

     The bibliography is subdivided by the different divisions,
ministries and sections of the (now defunct) West Indies federal
government and includes prices and frequency of publication.
                                                          TCL

Newspapers
228 British Library
     Catalogue of the Newspaper Library, Colindale. - London :
British Museum, Publications for the British Library Board,
1975. - 8v.
     Vols.3-4 : Overseas Countries, Aden-Zanzibar. Includes
the West Indies.
                                                      Ref.no.80

229 Institute of Jamaica. West India Reference Library
     A list of Jamaican and other West Indian newspapers in the
West India Reference Library / Philip Wright. - Kingston,
Jamaica : Institute of Jamaica, 1960

     Cited in 1973 list (Ref.no.230).

                                                          NLJ

230 Institute of Jamaica. West India Reference Library
     A list of West Indian newspapers / prepared by Anita
Johnson. - Kingston : Institute of Jamaica, West India
Reference Library, 1973. - 18p.

Holdings list in two sections, one arranged by title and the other by country of origin. Excludes Jamaican newspapers.

UWI-T

231 LENT, JOHN A.
Oldest existing newspapers in the Commonwealth Caribbean / John A. Lent. - p.90, 106
In Caribbean quarterly. - Vol.22, no.4 (Dec. 1976)

Lists by country with foundation date, frequency and last known year of issue all the newspapers, discontinued and continuing titles, known for the following territories: - Bahamas, Barbados, Bermuda, British Virgin Islands, Cayman Islands, Turks Islands, Jamaica, Leeward Islands, Trinidad and Tobago and the Windward Islands.

UWI-T

232 LINCOLN, WALDO
List of newspapers of the West Indies and Bermuda in the library of the American Antiquarian Society / Waldo Lincoln. - p.130-156
In American Antiquarian Society proceedings, new series. - Vol.36 (Apr. 1926)

UWI-J

233 University of London. Institute of Commonwealth Studies
Union list of Commonwealth newspapers in London, Oxford and Cambridge / compiled by A.R. Hewitt. - London : The Athlone Press for the Institute of Commonwealth Studies, 1960. - 101p.

West Indian entries arranged alphabetically by country under West Indian Federation with an index of newspaper titles. Locations included.

UWI-T

Non-Book Materials
234 American Geographical Society
A catalogue of maps of Hispanic America : including maps in scientific periodicals and books and sheet and atlas maps with articles on the cartography of the several countries and maps showing the extent and character of existing surveys / American Geographical Society. - New York : American Geographical Society, 1930. - 4v. - (Maps of Hispanic America ; publication no.3)
Vol.1 : Maps of Mexico, Central America and the West Indies. - Section III : Maps of the West Indies (p.196-280)
Vol.3 : Venezuela, Guianas, Brazil, Paraguay. - Section II : Maps of the Guianas (p.46-82)

UWI-T

235 BLOOMFIELD, VALERIE
        Caribbean films / Valerie Bloomfield. - p.278-314
        In Journal of librarianship. - Vol.9, no.4 (Oct. 1977)
        Select filmography: p.293-314

        Article tracing the development of documentary and feature
film production in the Commonwealth Caribbean with listings of
documentary, sponsored, independent and educational films, each
subdivided by country, and separate lists of film strips and
slides. Audience and content notes are provided and reviews
where available.

                                                            UWI-T

236 British Museum. Department of Manuscripts
        Catalogue of the manuscript maps, charts and plans and the
topographical drawings in the British Museum. - London :
Printed by order of the Trustees, 1844-61. - 3v.
        Reproduced photographically in 1962 by Gregg Associates,
Brussels, from the original annotated ed.
        Vol.3 : The remaining portions of Europe, Asia, Africa,
America containing maps of the West Indies.

                                                               BL

237 British Museum. Department of Printed Books
        Catalogue of printed maps, charts and plans / Department
of Printed Books. - London : [British Museum], 1967. - 15v.

        "Photolithographic edition complete to 1964" - BNB

                                                               BL

238 CAMPBELL, ELIZABETH
        A bibliography of non-book materials on the West Indies
held by the University of the West Indies, Barbados /
compiled by Elizabeth Campbell. - p.27-43
        In Bulletin of the Library Association of Barbados. -
No.8 (1978).

        173 items listed under headings : Art Prints, Filmstrips,
Maps subdivided by country, Microfiche with development plans
subdivided by country, Microfilm including newspapers and theses,
Multimedia Pack, Portfolio, Posters / Wall Charts, Sound Discs,
Sound Tapes / Cassettes. Location symbols are given.

                                                            UWI-T

239 Community Relations Commission
        Audio visual aids, aspects of community relations :
cultural and religious backgrounds, social development and
welfare, prejudice and specialized items for selected age
and interest group / Community Relations Commission. - London :
Community Relations Commission, 1970. - 31p.

                                                       Ref.no.664
                                                       Item no.16

240   Community Relations Commission
         Film catalogue, produced jointly / by Community Relations
      Commission and Race Relations Board. - London : The Commission,
      The Board, 1975. - 30p.

                                                      Ref.no.664
                                                      Item no.17

241   Food and Agriculture Organization and United Nations
      Educational, Scientific and Cultural Organization
         Soil map of the world, FAO/UNESCO Project : catalogue of
      maps. - Rome: FAO/UNESCO, 1965. - 165p.
         Title in English, French and Spanish

         Lists maps available in the World Soil Resources office
      and in the Library at FAO Headquarters in two parts; the first
      covers the world and major regions, the second individual
      countries including Barbados, British Guiana, British Antilles,
      Jamaica and Trinidad and Tobago. Maps are arranged under
      headings such as soils, climate, land use, topography, geology
      in each section.

                                                            UWI-T

242   Great Britain. Colonial Office. Library
         Catalogue of the maps, plans and charts in the library of
      the Colonial Office. - [S.l. : s.n.], 1910. - 6p.

                                                            FCO

243   Great Britain. Public Record Office
         Maps and plans in the Public Record Office / P.A. Penfold.
      - London : H.M. Stationery Office, 1975
         No.2 : America and West Indies. - 856p.

         "Covers the period 1584 to the first years of the present
      century with material of the eighteenth and nineteenth centuries
      predominating."

                                                            HLBC

244   Great Britain. War Office. Intelligence Division
         Catalogue of maps in the Intelligence Division, War
      Office ... Vol.IV. : America, West Indies and Oceana /
      compiled by J. L. Power. - [S.l. : s.n.], 1891. - [ii], [iii],
      301p.

                                                      Ref.no.4
                                                      Vol.1,p.13

245   RAGATZ, LOWELL JOSEPH
         A list of West Indian maps and plans and illustrations
      relative to the West Indies contained in the Gentleman's
      Magazine, 1731-1833 / compiled by Lowell Joseph Ragatz. -
      London : Arthur Thomas, 1934. - 2 leaves

                                                            FCO

246   TOOLEY, R.V.
          Printed maps of St. Kitts, St. Lucia and St. Vincent /
      R.V. Tooley. - London : Map Collectors' Circle, 1972. - 19,
      [25]p. - (Map collectors' series ; no.81)
          St. Christopher and Nevis : 74 maps (1650-1875)
          St. Lucia : 56 maps (1683-1889)
          St. Vincent and Bequia : 38 maps (1763-1878)
                                                                Ref.no.80

246a United States. Library of Congress
          Maps and charts of North America and the West Indies 1750-
      1789: a guide to the collection in the Library of Congress /
      compiled by John R. Sellers and Patricia Van Ee. - Washington,
      D.C.: Library of Congress, 1981. - 45p.
                                                                Ref.no.79
                                                      Vol.4, no.2, Item no.330

247   University of Texas. Institute of Latin American Studies
          A catalogue of Latin American flat maps, 1926-1964 /
      compiled by Palmyra V.M. Monteiro. - [Austin, Tex.] : Institute
      of Latin American Studies, The University of Texas at Austin,
      1967-1969. - 2v. (xvi, 395; ix, 430p.) - (Guides and biblio-
      graphies ; series 2)
          Vol.1 : Mexico, Central America, West Indies. Includes
      sections on British Honduras (Belize), Bahama Islands, Turks
      and Caicos, Jamaica and the Lesser Antilles. - Vol.2 : South
      America, Falkland (Malvinas) Islands and the Guianas.

          Maps are listed by subject type (military, political,
      topographic, population etc.) under each country or group of
      countries with the English-speaking territories fully represented.
                                                                     UWI-T

248   University of the West Indies. Department of Extra Mural
          Studies. Radio Education Unit
          Catalogue 1977 : recorded programmes / [compiled by Alma
      Mock Yen, summer 1971] ... . - Kingston, Jamaica : Radio
      Education Unit, Department of Extra Mural Studies, University
      of the West Indies, 1976. - 175p.
          Cover title
          Also published as part of "Sources for sound broadcasting
      in Jamaica"

          The catalogue lists radio programmes recorded mainly by
      staff members of the university from 1953 to 1976 as part of the
      Radio Unit's adult education programme and including much
      Caribbean interest material. All material listed is available
      on open reels or cassette recordings as well as in script form
      transcribed from the tapes. Material donated by some external
      agencies is also included. The listing is arranged by item
      numbers within such broad subject groups (in alphabetical

sequence) as African, Asian and Afro-American studies, Caribbean
studies, dance, drama, Federation, history, language and
linguistic studies, music, University of the West Indies and West
Indian writers and their works. Interviews with several prominent
West Indians are also included.

UWI-T

Periodicals and Serials
249   Caribbean Organization. Library
         Periodicals received in the library of the Central
      Secretariat / Caribbean Organization Library. - Hato Rey,
      Puerto Rico : Central Secretariat, 1963. - 34p.

UF

250   Commonwealth Secretariat
         Commonwealth directory of periodicals : a guide to
      scientific, technical and professional journals published in
      the developing countries of the Commonwealth / Commonwealth
      Secretariat. - London : Commonwealth Secretariat, 1973. - ix,
      157p.

      Listing is based on the holdings of major libraries in the
U.K. but gives no locations; it is arranged by subject headings
based on Ulrich's periodicals directory. A title but not
geographic index is provided. Each entry is briefly annotated
and includes address, sponsoring organization, number of issues
annually and price. Includes a few appropriate titles from the
larger West Indian territories. Mostly excludes annual reports
and irregular transactions.

UWI-T

251   Commonwealth Secretariat
         Commonwealth specialist periodicals : an annotated
      directory of scientific, technical and professional journals
      published in Commonwealth developing countries / Commonwealth
      Secretariat. - London : Commonwealth Secretariat, 1977. -
      [1], 140p.

      First published as Ref.no.250 ; arranged under broad
subject headings, entries include addresses, frequency, annual
subscription and short description of the periodical's aims.
There are title and country indexes. Titles from the Bahamas,
Barbados, Bermuda, Guyana, Jamaica and Trinidad and Tobago are
listed.

UWI-T

252   Conference on inter-library cooperation and exchange, San Juan,
      Puerto Rico, April 30-May 2, 1969 : official records / U.S.
      Virgin Islands, Department of Conservation and Cultural
      Affairs, Division of Libraries and Museums and Caribbean
      Regional Library - CODECA. - San Juan, Puerto Rico : Caribbean
      Economic Development Corporation (CODECA), [1970]. - 248p.

Includes a series of country reports for all the British
Caribbean territories as well as for the French, Spanish and
Dutch Caribbean. Each country report lists locally published
periodicals and newspapers at the time as follows : Barbados
(p.70-73), British Honduras (p.83), British Virgin Islands (p.87),
Dominica (p.92), Guyana (p.105-110), Jamaica (p.125-150), St.
Kitts (p.197), St. Lucia (p.200), St. Vincent (p.204).

UWI-T

253 Trinidad and Tobago. Central Library. West Indian Reference
     Section
          Annual reports, newspapers, periodicals : a list of
     holdings ; vol.1 / compiled by Joan Roberts [and] Wayne
     Lincoln. - Port of Spain, Trinidad and Tobago : Central Library
     of Trinidad and Tobago, 1981. - [2], 40p.

          Arranged in 3 sections : Annual Reports (60 items), News-
     papers (31 items), Periodicals (24 items). Annual reports of
     government departments and other official publications are
     included. Items listed are held in the West Indian Reference
     Collection.

UWI-T

254 Trinidad and Tobago. Central Library. West Indian Reference
     Section
          List of periodicals received in the West Indian Reference
     Section of the Central Library of Trinidad and Tobago :
     Trinidad and Tobago periodicals. - [Port of Spain, Trinidad :
     Central Library], [19-]. - 16 leaves
          Mimeographed

          Alphabetical title listing with publisher frequency and
     year of first issue. Closing dates are also given for defunct
     titles.

TCL

255 A Union list of serials : a project of the special libraries
     of Trinidad and Tobago. - [Port of Spain, Trinidad : s.n.],
     1979. - (various pagings)

          A working document in circulation in the country. Alpha-
     betical title listings with one or more of 24 special library
     locations given for each serial held by all the libraries
     cooperating in the project. Includes West Indian periodicals,
     newspapers, journals and government publications in series
     listed alphabetically but not separately identified as such.

UWI-T

256 University of Florida. Libraries
          Caribbean serial titles microfilmed at source / University
     of Florida Libraries. - Gainesville, Fla. : [University of
     Florida Libraries], 1963. - 1v.

Xerox copy

Filming done with a Rockefeller Foundation grant to the
University of Florida Libraries. The listing was a paper
presented at the Caribbean Archives Conference, University of the
West Indies, 1965 as an appendix to "Reproduction and exchange of
archival material relating to the Caribbean countries" by Stanley
L. West (Document 5). Includes Barbados, British Guiana,
Dominica, Nassau, Bahamas, St. Lucia and Trinidad and Tobago as
well as some non-English speaking territories.

UWI-T

257 West Indies (Federation). Federal Information Service
     Reference Library
          List of periodicals published in the West Indies and
     British Guiana / [compiled by the Federal Information Service
     Reference Library]. - [Port of Spain, Trinidad : Federal
     Information Service Reference Library] : [1961]. - 3p.
          Mimeographed

     Alphabetical title listings within separate sections on
each territory with source, frequency and price.

TCL

258 ZIMMERMAN, IRENE
          A guide to current Latin American periodicals : humanities
     and social sciences / by Irene Zimmerman. - Gainesville, Fla. :
     Kallman, 1961. - 357p.

     Four types of approach are provided to a selective list of
journals published in the region - (1) national approach
including a section on the West Indies Federation (p.222-227)
with 19 titles, (2) Subject approach with a brief essay and
listing for each subject, (3) chronological approach, with an
essay and listings by decade from 1930-1960, (4) title list with
commencing date and country of origin. All entries in the first
section are annotated.

UWI-T

Periodicals and Serials--Indexes
   259 Guyana. National Library
             Index of Caribbean periodicals : subject index / National
        Library. - [Georgetown, Guyana : National Library of Guyana],
        [1975?]. - 319p.
             Mimeographed

        The index covers Caribbean Quarterly, vol.1, no.1 (1949)-
vol.15, no.14 (1969); Caribbean Studies, vol.1, no.1 (1962)-
vol.9,no.4 (1970); and Social and Economic Studies, vol.1, no.1
(1953)-vol.18, no.4 (1969), using conventional subject headings.

UWI-T

260   Hispanic American periodicals index (HAPI) / edited by Barbara
      C. Cox. - 1975- . - Los Angeles : University of California. -
      1977-
           Annual

      First issue published by the Center for Latin American
Studies, Arizona State University. Publication suspended in
1974 and resumed in 1977 under new auspices. Includes a few West
Indian periodical titles with separate author and subject
indexing.

                                                         UWI-T

Theses
  261 BAA, ENID M.
           Doctoral dissertations and selected theses on Caribbean
      topics accepted by universities of Canada, United States and
      Europe from 1778-1968 / compiled by Enid Baa. - St. Thomas,
      Virgin Islands of the U.S. : Bureau of Public Libraries and
      Cultural Affairs, 1969. - 91p.

      This interim automated and experimental edition was later
published by the Institute of Caribbean Studies in conventional
form (Ref.no.262). 1,111 doctoral dissertations and 237 masters
theses are listed. The arrangement is alphabetical; indexes are
provided by author, date and university as well as subject in
KWIC form.

                                                         UWI-T

  262 BAA, ENID M.
           Theses on Caribbean topics, 1778-1968 / compiled by Enid
      Baa. - San Juan, Puerto Rico : Institute of Caribbean Studies
      and University of Puerto Rico Press, 1970. - v, 146p. -
      (Caribbean bibliographic series ; no.1)

      1,242 references to masters and other theses and doctoral
dissertations mainly from French, British and American universities with an index of universities by country, a geographical
index of countries studied, followed by subject and chronological
indexes.

                                                         UWI-T

  263 BLOOMFIELD, VALERIE
           West Indian and Latin American theses / compiled by
      Valerie Bloomfield. - [London : Institue of Commonwealth
      Studies], [1969?]. - 22p.
           Mimeographed

      The list is subdivided regionally including sections on
Latin America as a whole, individual countries of South America,
Central America and Mexico and the Caribbean. A final section
covers theses on West Indians in Great Britain.

                                                         UWI-T

264   BUSHONG, ALLEN D.
        Doctoral dissertations on Pan-American topics accepted by
    United States and Canadian colleges and universities, 1961-
    1965 : bibliography and analysis / compiled by Allen D.
    Bushong. - Austin, Tex. : [s.n.], 1967. - 57, [13]p.
        Issued as a: supplement to vol.2, no.2, Latin American
    research review

        A cumulation of supplements to Ref.no.272 up-dating the
    1962 work, including about 80 theses on the English-speaking
    Caribbean. Geographical, institutional and biographical indexes
    are supplied.
                                                            UWI-T

265   Commonwealth Caribbean Resource Centre (Barbados)
        Theses on the Commonwealth Caribbean, 1891-1973 / compiled
    by the Commonwealth Caribbean Resource Centre. - London,
    Ontario : Office of International Education, University of
    Western Ontario, [1974?]. - 139p.
        Mimeographed

        An alphabetical author listing of 837 entries with a
    geographical index of countries studied and an index of countries
    where theses were submitted.
                                                               UM
266   DEAL, CARL W.
        Latin America and the Caribbean : a dissertation biblio-
    graphy / edited by Carl W. Deal. - Ann Arbor, Mich. : Univer-
    sity Microfilms International, 1978. - 164p.

        A subject listing with geographical or country subdivisions
    of 7,200 theses published by University Microfilms International
    and extracted from their dissertation data base.
                                                            UWI-T

267   DEAL, CARL
        Latin America and the Caribbean II : a dissertation
    bibliography / Carl Deal. - Ann Arbor, Mich. : University
    Microfilms International, 1980 - 78p.

        Up-date of earlier work (Ref.no.266) published in 1978.
    Contains 9,168 titles. Arranged by subject and country or
    geographical division.
                                                            UWI-T

268   DOSSICK, JESSE J.
        Current dissertations on the Caribbean : doctoral research
    on the Caribbean and circum-Caribbean accepted by American,
    British and Canadian universities, 1966-1967 / Jesse J.
    Dossick. - p.89-96
        In Caribbean studies. - Vol.8, no.2 (July 1968)

Continuation of Ref.no.272, geographical listing includes items on the Caribbean and West Indies generally, the Bahamas, Jamaica and Trinidad and Tobago.

UWI-T

269   DOSSICK, JESSE J.
Current dissertations on the Caribbean : doctoral research on the Caribbean and circum-Caribbean accepted by American, British and Caribbean universities, 1968-1970 / Jesse J. Dossick. - p.127-155
In Caribbean studies. - Vol.11, no.2 (July 1971)

Further continuation and updating of Ref.no.272.

UWI-T

270   GRIFFIN, ERNEST C.
A bibliography of theses and dissertations on Latin America by U.S. geographers 1960-70 / by Ernest C. Griffin and Clarence W. Minkel. - [Washington, D.C.] : U.S. National Section, Pan American Institute of Geography and History, 1970. - 16p. - (Special publication ; no.2)

LC

271   KIDDER, FREDERICK E.
Doctoral dissertations in Latin American area studies 1960-1961 / Frederick E. Kidder. - p.191-200
In The Americas, Academy of American Franciscan history. - Vol.19, no.2 (Oct. 1962)

Classified by authors, each entry cites general field, title of the dissertation and university granting the degree.
Ref.no.15

272   KIDDER, FREDERICK E.
Theses on Pan American topics ; prepared by candidates for doctoral degrees in universities and colleges in the United States and Canada / compiled by Frederick E. Kidder and Allen David Bushong. - Washington, D.C. : Pan American Union, 1962. - 24p. - (Columbus Memorial Library bibliographic series ; no.5)

Includes topics on the British West Indies. Annual supplements appeared later and were cumulated in Ref.no.264.
Ref.no.17

273   McGill University. Centre for Developing-Area Studies
Caribbean topics : an annotated bibliography of McGill theses on Caribbean topics from 1972-1975 / compiled by Robyn Bryant [and] Amin Merani. - [Montreal: Centre for Developing-Area Studies, McGill University] [1976]. - v, 35 leaves

Full abstracts arranged alphabetically by author with a
contents listing including titles and subjects for easy scanning.
Previous listings (Ref.no.274) excluded abstracts.

UWI-T

274 McGill University. Centre for Developing-Area Studies
        Caribbean topics : theses in Canadian university libraries
/ compiled by Theo. L. Hills. - 3rd ed. - Montreal : Centre
for Developing-Area Studies, McGill University, 1971. - 21p.
        Previous editions published 1967 and 1969

        The listing is alphabetical by universities and within
these groups by subject and author. Both masters' and doctoral
theses are listed.

UWI-T

275 SIMS, MICHAEL
        United States doctoral dissertations in Third World Studies,
1869-1978 / compiled by Michael Sims. - Waltham, Mass. :
African Studies Association, 1980. - 436p.

        A listing of 19,000 doctoral dissertations in Third World
Studies. Arranged by geographic area and indexed by subject,
place name, personal name, language and ethnic group. Includes
author's name, year of completion and degree granting institution.
Areas covered : North Africa, Sub-Saharan Africa, Asia, Latin
America and the Caribbean and the Middle East." - Publisher's
leaflet

UWI-T

275a Tulane University
        A bibliography of Latin American theses and dissertations,
Tulane University 1912-1978 / compiled by Ruth R. Olivera. -
New Orleans, La.: Center for Latin American Studies, Tulane
University, 1979. - 67p.
        Alphabetical author listing of 462 items with title,
degree, date, department or school, and where possible the
supervisor of the thesis. Includes senior honors and architecture
theses, as well as master's theses and doctoral dissertations.
Subject index and index arranged by departments, schools and
areas of study.

UWI-T

276 University of London. Institute of Latin American Studies
        Theses in Latin American studies at British universities
in progress and completed / Institute of Latin American Studies. -
No. [1] (1966-1967)- . - London : Institute of Latin American
Studies, University of London, 1967-
        Annual

ILAS

277 University of London. Institute of Commonwealth Studies
        Theses in progress in Commonwealth studies ; a cumulative
     list / Institute of Commonwealth Studies. –London : Institute
     of Commonwealth Studies, University of London, 1978. - 46p.
        West Indies: p.41-43

        "Subject coverage not exhaustive" and British theses only
     listed. Cumulation covering January 1970 to October 1978 super-
     seding previous compilations. A general section on the West
     Indies is followed by individual country listings in alphabetical
     author order within each.

                                                              UWI-T

278 University of London. Institute of Latin American Studies
        Doctoral dissertations in history and the social sciences
     on Latin America and the Caribbean accepted by universities in
     the United Kingdom, 1920-1972 / compiled by David S. Zubatsky.
     - London : Institute of Latin American Studies, University of
     London, 1973. - 16p.

        Attempts to be a comprehensive guide in the humanities and
     social sciences (language and literature excluded). Theses are
     arranged alphabetically by author under country or geographical
     region. Entries include author's name, complete title and sub-
     title of the dissertation, the name of the degree, the name of
     the university to which the dissertation was submitted and the
     academic year in which the degree was conferred.

                                                        Ref.no.18
                                                             1974

279 University of the West Indies (Mona). Library
        Theses accepted for higher degrees, August 1963-July
     1974 / prepared by the University of the West Indies Library.
     - [Mona, Jamaica] : University of the West Indies Library,
     [1976]. - vii, 120p.

        Includes several theses on West Indian topics. Lists
     alphabetically by authors under each faculty the masters' theses
     and doctoral dissertations accepted from the inception of the
     university as a degree-granting body. Authors' abstracts are
     given for dissertations. Subject, author and chronological
     indexes are provided.

                                                              UWI-T

280 University of the West Indies (Mona). Library
        Theses accepted for higher degrees, August 1974-July
     1975 / prepared by the University of the West Indies Library.
     - [Mona, Jamaica : University of the West Indies Library],
     [1976]. - vii, 21p.
        Aug. 1975-July 1976. - 37p.
        Aug. 1976-July 1977. - 31p.
        Aug. 1977-July 1978 - 36p.

Supplements to the library's original list covering 1963 to 1974 (Ref.no.279) arranged in alphabetical author order by faculty and department with subject and author indexes. Includes author abstracts for all Ph.D. titles.

UWI-T

Leeward Islands

281 BROWN, J.
       Writings past and present, about the Leeward Islands / J. Brown. - St. John's, Antigua : [s.n.]. - 1961. - 74p.
Ref.no.941
Item no.397

282 MERRILL, GORDON C.
       The historical geography of St. Kitts and Nevis, the West Indies / by Gordon C. Merrill. - Mexico : [Instituto Pan Americano de Geografía e Historia], 1958. - 145p.
       Bibliography: p.134-137

       Includes references on the Leeward Islands as a whole and unpublished material listed separately from books, articles and published documents.

UWI-T

283 University of the West Indies (St. Augustine). Library
       Bibliography on Saba, Montserrat, St. Kitts-Nevis-Anguilla / Library, U.W.I. - St. Augustine, [Trinidad] : The University of the West Indies Library, [1967]. - 3 leaves
       Typescript

       Covers the history, geography, literature, natural resources and social and economic conditions of the islands.

UWI-T

Antigua

284 Great Britain. Colonial Office
       Antigua / Colonial Office. - [S.l. : s.n.], 1860. - 1 sheet. - (No.32 of a series of lists of works in the library)

       16 references.

Ref.no.4
Vol.1,p.433

285 United States. Library of Congress
       Antigua, Leeward Islands : a list of books / Library of Congress. - Washington, D.C. : Library of Congress, 1953. - 7 leaves

43 references.

Ref.no.4
Vol.1,p.433

285a Antigua. Public Library
          Bibliography: Antigua and Barbuda / Phyllis Mayers. -
     [St. John's, Antigua : Antigua Public Library], [1981]

UWI-T

285b University of the West Indies (Cave Hill). Main Library
          The road to independence: Antigua and Barbuda: a select
     bibliography / Jean A. Callender and Audine C. Wilkinson. -
     Cave Hill, Barbados: Main Library, University of the West
     Indies, 1981. - i, 16p.

          196 entries arranged under headings : Bibliographies,
     History and Politics, Economic Aspects, Social Aspects, The Arts.
     Includes articles in periodicals and government publications.

UWI-B

Non-Book Materials
  286 TOOLEY, RONALD VERE
          The printed maps of Antigua 1689-1899 / by Ronald Vere
     Tooley. - London : Map Collectors' Circle, 1969. - 11, [16]p. -
     (Map collectors' series ; 55)

          Lists 102 maps.

Ref.no.18
1977

Bahamas

  287 BARRATT, P.J.H.
          Grand Bahama / P.J.H. Barratt. - Newton Abbott, Devon :
     David and Charles, 1972. - 206p. - (The island series)
          Bibliography: p.191-197

          Items listed under separate chapters cover all aspects of
     the Bahamas. Some particularly noteworthy works are annotated.
     Also included is an extract of official reports, regulations and
     legislation relating to Freeport.

UWI-T

  288 College of the Bahamas. Library
          Bahamian Reference Collection : a bibliography / compiled
     by Paul G. Boultbee. - Nassau, Bahamas : College of the
     Bahamas Library, 1980. - 40p.

Lists material housed in the Bahamian Reference Collection
of the College of the Bahamas (Oakes Field). Consists of 234
entries arranged in seven sections - Monographs, Journal Articles,
Journals, Government Documents, Ephemera, Maps and Official
Gazettes: Includes a subject index.

UWI-T

289 College of the Bahamas. Library
     Bahamian Reference Collection : bibliography / compiled by
     Paul Boultbee. - 2nd ed. - Nassau, Bahamas : College of the
     Bahamas Library, 1981. - 57p.

Incorporates all items in first edition (Ref.no.288) as
well as items added to the collection since its publication.
Consists of 494 entries arranged in similar sections. Includes
author and subject indexes.

UWI-T

290 Great Britain. Colonial Office
     Bahamas and Turks islands / Colonial Office. - [S.l. :
     s.n.], 1860. - 2p. - (No.35 of a series of lists of works in
     the library)

20 references.

Ref.no.4
Vol.1,p.656

291 Great Britain. Foreign and Commonwealth Office. Overseas
     Development Administration. Land Resources Division
     Land resource bibliography : Bahamas / compiled by N.W.
     Posnett and P.M. Reilly. - Surrey, England : Land Resources
     Division, Overseas Development Administration, 1971. - 74p. -
     (Land resource bibliography ; no.1)

Including material on environmental sciences, agriculture
and forestry, etc., this bibliography was prepared in conjunction
with a project undertaken by the Division in assisting a
developing country.

UWI-T

Barbados

292 Barbados Public Library
     Our common heritage : authors among us / Barbados Public
     Library. - [Bridgetown, Barbados] : Barbados Public Library,
     1971. - [14]p.

Catalogue of an exhibition of Barbadiana in the Barbados
Public Library. Divided into three sections : (1) Works by
Barbadians, (2) Works by non-Barbadians and (3) Pamphlet

Literature by Barbadians and non-Barbadians. Selective listings only.

UWI-J

293 CRUICKSHANK, J. GRAHAM
    A bibliography of Barbados, I-III / J. Graham Cruickshank.
    - p.155-165, 220-225, 20-25
    In Barbados Museum and Historical Society journal. -
    Vol.2, nos.3-4, vol.3, no.1 (May, Aug., Nov. 1935)

    A series of three articles with chronological listings by
title of early works (1650 onwards) on Barbados. Excludes newspapers, manuscripts and parliamentary papers.

UWI-T

293a University of the West Indies (Cave Hill). Main Library
    Barbadian society, past and present : a select biblio-
    graphy / compiled in celebration of the fourteenth anniversary
    of the Independence of Barbados by Jean A. Callender with
    assistance from Loraine Jackson and Carlyle Best. - Cave Hill,
    Barbados : Main Library, University of the West Indies, 1980.
    - 63p.

    Entries are arranged under broad subject groups : Cultural
Aspects, Social Aspects, Economic Aspects, subdivided by topics
which include customs and folklore, drama, dance, music and art,
education, language, religion, ethnic groups, health, political
life, slavery, social structure, sport, agriculture, industry and
commerce, tourism and transportation. 540 entries.

UWI-T

Government Publications
294 Barbados. Archives Department
    Barbados government publications / Archives Department. -
    [Bridgetown, Barbados : Archives Department], [1965]. - 5p.
    Typescript

ICS

Non-Book Materials
295 CAMPBELL, TONY
    The printed maps of Barbados from the earliest times to
    1873 / Tony Campbell. - London : The Map Collectors' Circle,
    1965. - 24, [25]p. - (Map collectors' series ; 21)

    64 entries in chronological order with an index to the
map-makers, printers and engravers and several illustrations of
maps listed.

UWI-T

296 SHILSTONE, E.M.
     A descriptive list of maps of Barbados / E.M. Shilstone. -
p.57-84
     In Journal of the Barbados Museum and Historical Society.
- Vol.5, no.2 (Feb. 1938)

     A chronological and annotated list with locations in the
U.K. as well as in the author's personal collection.
                                                    UWI-T

Belize

297 BATH, SÉRGIO
     Notas para una bibliografia sobre Belize, Honduras
Británicas / Sérgio Bath. - México : Embaixada do Brasil,
1966. - [21] leaves

                                                    LC

298 Belize. National Library Service
     A bibliography of books on Belize in the National
Collection / National Library Service. - 4th ed. - Belize City,
Belize : The Central Library, Bliss Institute, 1977. - 102p.

     Unlike previous editions this listing excludes material on
the rest of the West Indies, covering only works on or by
Belizeans. Full Dewey class numbers are used in the subject
arrangement with author and title indexes provided at the end.
                                                    UWI-T

299 Belize. National Library Service
     A bibliography of published material on Belize as found in
the National Collection, The Central Library, Bliss Institute,
Belize City / edited by Leo H. Bradley. - 3rd ed. - Belize
City : National Library Service, 1975. - 54p.
     Mimeographed

     1,036 entries arranged alphabetically by author within
broad Dewey classes with an expansion in the History class to
include separate sections on topics such as the Mayas in early
history and territorial claims by Guatemala.
                                                    UWI-T

300 British Honduras. Library Service (Belize)
     A bibliography of published material on British Honduras
as found in the National Collection / compiled by L.H. Bradley,
L.G. Vernon and A.A. Dillet. - Belize, [British Honduras] :
British Honduras Library Service, 1960. - 52p.

     First of a series of similar lists with 510 entries.
                                                    Ref.no.515
                                                    p.272

301 British Honduras. Library Service (Belize City)
     A bibliography of published material on the country as
found in the National Collection, the Central Library, Bliss
Institute, Belize City / edited by Leo H. Bradley. - 2nd ed. -
Belize City : British Honduras Library Service, 1964. - 58p.

     Second of the series with 691 entries arranged in broad
subject classes by Dewey. An appendix lists items located in the
country but not available in the National Collection.

                                                            UWI-T

302 British Honduras. National Library Service
     A bibliography of published material on the country (new
supplement to the second edition) as found in the National
Collection / edited by Leo H. Bradley. - Belize City : The
British Honduras National Library Service, 1970. - 17p.

     The fourth publication in the series with 286 entries
incorporating all additions since 1964 and replacing the 1966
supplement.

                                                            UWI-T

303 GONZÁLEZ-BLANCO, PEDRO
     El problema de Belice y sus alivios / Pedro González-
Blanco. - [Mexico : s.n.], 1960. - 187p.
       Bibliography : p.123-127

                                                        Ref.no.5
                                               1951-1955, p.85

304 GRANT, C.H.
     The making of modern Belize : politics, society and British
colonialism in Central America / C.H. Grant. - Cambridge :
Cambridge University Press, 1976. - xvi, 400p.
       Bibliography : p.385-389

     Arranged alphabetically by author in major groupings for
books, articles, theses with a separate section on official
reports.

                                                            UWI-T

305 Great Britain. Foreign and Commonwealth Office. Overseas
     Development Administration. Land Resources Division
       Belize (British Honduras) / compiled by N.W. Posnett and
P.M. Reilly. - Surrey, England : Land Resources Division,
Overseas Development Administration, Foreign and Commonwealth
Office, 1973. - vi, 92p. - (Land resource bibliography ;
no.3)

Entries are arranged alphabetically by author under such subjects as agriculture, botany, economics, cultural studies, forestry, geoscience and natural resources.

UWI-T

306 MINKEL, CLARENCE W.
A bibliography of British Honduras, 1900–1970 / by Clarence W. Minkel and Ralph H. Alderman. - East Lansing, Michigan : Latin American Studies Center, Michigan State University, 1970. - 93p. - (Latin American Studies Center research report ; no.7)

Over 1,000 references on a wide variety of topics under 5 broad headings : Physical, Cultural, Economic, Political and General with 23 subdivisions.

UWI-T

307 NOYCE, JOHN LEONARD
Belize : a bibliography / John Leonard Noyce. - Brighton : Noyce, 1978. - 11p.

Ref.no.123

308 United States. Library of Congress. Division of Bibliography
British Honduras : a bibliographic list / compiled by Florence S. Hellman ... . - Washington, D.C. : [Library of Congress], 1940. - 21p.
Typescript

LC

309 WADDELL, DAVID ALAN GILMOUR
British Honduras : a historical and contemporary survey / David Alan Gilmour Waddell. - London : O.U.P., 1961. - vii, 151p.
Select bibliography : p.143–146

Issued under the auspices of the Royal Institute of International Affairs ; a bibliographic essay arranged under headings such as historical, social, economic and political with critical assessments of works cited.

UWI-T

309a WOODWARD, RALPH LEE
Belize / compiled by Ralph Lee Woodward ; edited by Sheila R. Herstein. - Oxford, England; Santa Barbara, Calif.: Clio Press, 1980. - xxii, 229p. - (World bibliographical series ; vol.21)

681 bibliographic entries include books, periodical articles, government publications, theses and dissertations. Divided into 39 subject areas such as geography, flora and fauna, prehistory and archaeology, language and dialects, human rights,

economics, environment, sports and recreation, and mass media.
Bibliography preceded by a brief history of Belize combined with
a bibliographic essay. Annotations and detailed author, title
and subject indexes.

UWI-T

310 WOOLRICH, B.M.A.
       Bibliografía sobre Belice / B.M.A. Woolrich. - Mexico :
[s.n], 1957. - 45p. - (Biblioteca Aportación histórica)

       125 references.

Ref.no.4
Vol.1,p.724

311 ZETZEKORN, WILLIAM DAVID
       Formerly British Honduras : a profile of the new nation of
Belize / William David Zetzkorn. - Newark, Calif. : Dumbarton
Press, 1975. - ix, 291p.
       Annotated bibliography: p.281-287

       Basic and comprehensive sources are listed by author and
title under subjects such as economics and the Maya and by form
for newspapers and periodicals. 79 items.

UWI-T

Bermuda

312 Bermuda. The Bermuda Library
       Bermudiana : a bibliography / The Bermuda Library. -
Hamilton, Bermuda : The Bermuda Library, 1971. - 27p.

       Compiled during International Book Year as an introduction
and guide to the special collection of Bermudiana housed in the
Reference Department of the Bermuda Library. The entries which
are arranged by subject, include newspaper and magazine articles.
Of special interest is a section listing more often used records
of the Bermuda Archives.

UWI-T

313 Bermuda Book Store
       Guide to books about Bermuda / Bermuda Book Store. -
Hamilton : The Book Store, 1972. - 14p.

Ref.no.80

314 COLE, GEORGE WATSON
       Bermuda in periodical literature : a bibliography / George
Watson Cole. - Boston : The Book Company, 1898. - 25p.
       Bulletin of bibliography pamphlet no.2

Reprinted from: the Boston Book Company's Bulletin of
bibliography nos.4-5 (1898)

UWI-J

315   COLE, GEORGE WATSON
        Bermuda in periodical literature, with occasional references
   to other works : a bibliography / by George Watson Cole. -
   Boston : The Boston Book Company, 1907. - 275p.

        This work is a reprint "with considerable additions" of two
   series from the Bulletin of Bibliography issues between vol.2,
   no.5 (October 1900) and vol.4, no.10 (January 1907). It provides
   an alphabetical title arrangement for journals with chronological
   author listings under each of these and extensive descriptive
   notes in many cases. Includes historical, descriptive and
   scientific literature with an emphasis on geology, flora and
   fauna. Subdivisions under headings such as Challenger expedition
   include botany, zoology, physics and chemistry, narrative,
   geology and petrology. A full name and subject index is provided
   (from which for example, the dates and references for hurricanes
   can be traced) and library locations in the United States are
   given.

UWI-J

316   Great Britain. Colonial Office
        Bermuda / Colonial Office. - [S.l. : s.n.], 1860. -
   1 leaf. - (No.9 of a series of lists of works in the library)

        18 references.

Ref.no.4
Vol.1,p.745

317   TUCKER, TERRY
        Bermuda : today and yesterday, 1503-1973 / Terry Tucker. -
   London : St. Martins, 1975. - 208p.
        Bibliography: p.194-199

        Alphabetical list of 95 items covering all aspects of
   Bermuda followed by various reports and recommendations made by
   experts brought in during the 1960s and a selection of manuscript
   material preserved in the Bermuda Archives. All items are
   available in the Bermuda Library.

UWI-T

318   WILKINSON, HENRY C.
        Bermuda from sail to steam : the history of the island
   from 1784-1901 / Henry C. Wilkinson. - London : Oxford
   University Press, 1973. - 2v. (951p.)
        Bibliography: Vol.2, p.929-934

Listing is arranged in sections - MSS. and Documents
Printed and Unprinted, Diaries and Publications, Newspapers,
Empire, Literary and Miscellaneous. The last two sections
include general works on the West Indies.

UWI-T

Non-Book Materials
319 PALMER, MARGARET
Printed maps of Bermuda / by Margaret Palmer. - 2nd ed.
revised. - London : Map Collectors' Circle, [1974]. - 26p. :
[31 map plates]
Originally published in 1964 as: Map Collectors' Circle
series ; no.19

This edition arranged alphabetically by cartographer with
a separate chronological list of maps.

UWI-T

British Virgin Islands

320 [British] Virgin Islands. Public Library
Tortolana : a bibliography / by V.E. Penn and E.R. Penn. -
Vol.1, no.1 (1968)- . - Road Town, Tortola, [British] Virgin
Islands : Public Library, 1968
Mimeographed

Arranged under broad subject headings by Dewey general
classes and alphabetically by author within each, the listing
indicates the library's holdings of local material. Brief list
of maps and pictures included.

TCL

321 HARRIGAN, NORWELL
The Virgin Islands story / by Norwell Harrigan and Pearl
Varlack. - [S.l.] : Caribbean Universities Press in Association
with Bowker, 1975. - xiv, 214p.
Bibliography: p.200-205

Arranged alphabetically by author under four general
headings - Books, Articles and Periodicals, Reports, and Public
Documents. Books section includes works on the West Indies as
a whole.

UWI-T

Government Publications
322 British Virgin Islands. Public Library
Government reports : a union catalogue of government
reports held in the Public Library and government departments
/ compiled by V.E. Penn ... . - [Tortola], British Virgin
Islands : Chief Minister's Office, 1975. - 19p.

Mimeographed

Compiled by the Librarian of the Public Library, the
catalogue gives code locations for 18 government units holding
the reports, studies and similar publications listed alphabetically by author. Title and subject indexes are provided and the
publications covered include studies done on behalf of the British
Virgin Islands government by outside agencies.

UWI-T

323 British Virgin Islands. Public Library
        Government reports : supplement to union catalogue ... of
     government reports ... provided with full author, title and
     subject index and a list of British Virgin Islands government
     agencies, local and overseas / compiled and edited by Verna E.
     Penn. - [Tortola], British Virgin Islands : Public Library,
     1978. - 66p.
        Mimeographed

UWI-T

Dominica

324 CRACKNELL, BASIL E.
        Dominica / Basil E. Cracknell. - Newton Abbot, Devon :
     David and Charles, 1973. - 198p. - (Islands series)
        Bibliography: p.183-190

     Arranged by the titles of chapters of the text and by
author within each section. Includes reports, conference
proceedings as well as books and journal articles. Chapter
headings include natural history, the Carib people, agriculture
and Dominican society today.

UWI-T

325 Great Britain. Colonial Office
        Dominica / Colonial Office. - [S.l. : s.n.], 1860. -
     1 leaf. - (No.33 of a series of lists of works in the
     library)

     7 references.

Ref.no.4
Vol.1,p.1652

326 Great Britain. Ministry of Overseas Development. Land
     Resources Division
        Dominica / compiled by Norman W. Posnett and Philip M.
     Reilly. - Surbiton, England : Land Resources Division,
     Ministry of Overseas Development, 1978. - v, 69p. - (Land
     resource bibliography ; no.12)

Alphabetical author listing under sections : Agriculture, Animal Science, Botany, Climatology, Crop Science, Cultural Studies, Economics, Forestry, Geo-Science, Land Tenure and Reform, Maps, Miscellaneous, Soil Science, Water Resources. Based on a searching of U.K. sources. Includes books, government documents (published in Great Britain and the W.I.) and periodical articles plus some unpublished documents not necessarily available to the public.

UWI-T

327 SHILLINGFORD, J.D.
A bibliography of the literature on Dominica, W.I. / by J.D. Shillingford, Jennifer Shillingford [and] Leona Shillingford. - Ithaca, N.Y. : Cornell University, 1972. - [iv], 98 leaves

565 entries for journal articles, conference papers and monographs arranged by author within such subject groups as geography and the environment, people and culture, government and politics, each further subdivided into topics. A list of newspapers and author index are given.

UWI-T

Non-Book Materials
328 TOOLEY, RONALD VERE
Printed maps of Dominica and Grenada / Ronald Vere Tooley. - London: Map Collectors' Circle, 1970. - 15, [18]p. - (Map Collectors' series ; 62)
Dominica: 36 maps, 1745-1898
Grenada: 64 maps, 1717-1872/3

Ref.no.18
1977

Grenada

329 Great Britain. Colonial Office
Grenada / Colonial Office. - [S.l. : s.n.], 1860. - 1 sheet. - (No. 36 of a series of lists of works in the library)

9 references.

Ref.no.4
Vol.2,p.2754

330 STEELE, BEVERLEY
[Bibliography on Grenada] / by Beverley Steele. - St. George's, Grenada : Public Library, [197-?]. - 5 leaves
Mimeographed

List of items arranged alphabetically by author covering all aspects of Grenada.

UWI-T

Guyana

331   Bibliographie de la Guyane Française ... ouvrages et articles de langue française concernant la Guyane et les territoires avoisinants / par E. Abonnenc, J. Hurault, R. Sabin ... . - Tome 1. - Paris : Editions Larose, 1957

Arranged alphabetically by author. Subject index includes section "Territoires Avoisinants" with entries on British Guiana and the Antilles.

UWI-T

332   Books on British Guiana. - p.474-485
In British Guiana directory and almanac for 1896. - Georgetown : [s.n.], [1896]

"Many other issues contain similar lists." - Benjamin

Benjamin

333   British Guiana. Bibliography Committee
Bibliography of British Guiana / compiled under the aegis of the British Guiana Bibliography Committee by its chairman, Hon. Vincent Roth, M.L.C., by direction of His Excellency, the governor. - [S.l. : s.n.], [1948]
Microfilm of typescript copy

Comprehensive bibliography covering period up to 1946. Arranged under topics according to the Dewey Decimal Classification scheme within broad subject headings such as philosophy, psychology, religion, social sciences, literature, history, etc. Includes author and subject indexes.

UWI-T

334   British Guiana. Public Free Library
Cultural and historical aspects of the people of British Guiana : select bibliography of books in the Reference Department / Public Free Library. - Georgetown (British Guiana) : Public Free Library, [1958]. - 31p.
Typescript

Prepared in response to an enquiry, the list is arranged under the following headings : British Guiana - Missions; Peoples of British Guiana; Guianese Language and Literature; Heroes of Guiana; British Guiana - History ; British Guiana - Progress.

NLG

335   British Guiana. Public Free Library
          List of books on British Guiana and by Guianese / Public
      Free Library. - Georgetown (British Guiana) : Public Free
      Library, [196-?]. - 31p.
          Typescript

      Lists books published between 1905 and 1960.

                                                                    NLG

336   CAMERON, NORMAN E.
          Guyanese library and its impact / Norman E. Cameron. -
      Georgetown, Guyana : [The author], 1971. - 40p.

          First published in the Sunday Chronicle from 2 February to
      25 May 1969 as a partial observance of the writer's 66th birthday
      and his 40th as an author. Several chapters of this publication
      are bibliographical essays dealing with Guyanese works in a
      variety of subject fields - social sciences, poetry, biography
      and history, geography, mathematics, science and drama. Included
      also is a listing of works by the author in order of date of
      publication and a chronological list of books published in Guyana
      from 1965 to 1971.

                                                                    UWI-B

337   Commonwealth Institute
          A teacher's guide to study resources : Guyana / Common-
      wealth Institute. - London : Commonwealth Institute, 1972. -
      16p.

          A select reading list for books and journal articles
      arranged by author under two main headings - Environment and
      People. The more advanced titles cited are so identified.
      Audiovisual aids and other sources of information on Guyana in
      London are also listed.

                                                                    UWI-T

338   Diary 1976. - [Georgetown, Guyana] : Designs and Graphics,
      [1975]. - [398]p.

          "Special issue to commemorate the 10th Anniversary of the
      Independence of Guyana. 365 books written by Guyanese or about
      Guyana are identified, one for each day" - Caricom Bibliography.
                                                               Ref.no.68
                                                          Vol.1 (1977), p.2

339   DUCHESNE-FOURNET, JEAN
          La main-d'oeuvre dans les Guyanes / Jean Duchesne-Fournet.
      - Paris : Librairie Plon, 1905. - xii, 199p.
          Bibliography: p.183-199

          Includes important entries on British Guiana.

                                                                    UG

340 FAUQUENOY, MARGUERITE
     Bibliographie sur les Guyanes et les territoires
avoisinants / Marguerite Fauquenoy. - Paris : O.R.S.T.O.M.,
1966. - iv, 127p.
     Mimeographed
                                                          Ref.no.43

341 FOURNIER, A.
     Bibliography of the Mazaruni area, Guyana / compiled by A.
Fournier ; edited by J. Benjamin. - Georgetown, (Guyana) :
Upper Mazaruni Development Authority, 1978. - xiv, 188p.

     Consists of approximately 1300 items arranged alphabeti-
cally by author under subject headings such as travel, archaeology,
history, Amerindians, pork-knockers and miners, health, education,
economic development, communications, hydro-power, geology,
agriculture and soils, ecology, forests. Works written in Dutch,
French, German, Portuguese, Spanish, Italian and Catalan in
addition to those in English are listed. A variety of mimeographed, typescript and manuscript material is included. Listed
in an appendix are survey maps in the Lands and Surveys Department,
Guyana (50 items). A chronological index is provided.
                                                          UWI-T

342 GARNER, OLIVIA
     List of books on Guyana / selected by Olivia Garner ; with
bibliographic details by the Public Free Library for inclusion
in the publication "Guyana - Best of All the World". -
[Georgetown : Public Free Library], [1972]. - 11 leaves
                                                          NLG

343 Great Britain. Colonial Office
     British Guiana / Colonial Office. - [S.l. : s.n.], 1860. -
(No.22 of a series of lists of works in the library)

     80 references.
                                                          Ref.no.4
                                                      Vol.2,p.2770

344 Great Britain. Parliament. House of Commons. Library
     British Guiana : a short bibliography / House of Commons
Library. - London : House of Commons, 1953. - 6 leaves. -
(Bibliography ; no.78)
     Mimeographed

     32 references.
                                                          Benjamin

345   GROOT, SILVIA W. DE
        Principaux ouvrages de langue néerlandaise, anglaise et
      allemande sur les Guyanes : géographie, historie, ethnologie,
      linguistique / Silvia W. de Groot. - Paris : Leyde, 1958. - v,
      79p.
        Mimeographed

        "Somewhat outdated now but still useful for retrospective
      materials." - Benjamin

                                                            Ref.no.3

346   Guyana. Public Free Library
        Reports on Guyana, 1946-1970 / Public Free Library. -
      Georgetown, (Guyana) : Public Free Library, 1970. - 1v.
      (various pagings)
        Typescript

        An unpublished list of material on display during the
      Republic celebrations exhibition 15-28 February 1970; it is
      arranged under the following headings - Constitution, Adminis-
      tration, Central Government and Local Government, Education,
      Miscellaneous and Annual Reports.

                                                                NLG

347   Guyana. Public Free Library
        Select bibliography of the works of Guyanese / Public Free
      Library. - Georgetown, (Guyana) : Public Free Library, 1969. -
      13 leaves
        Mimeographed

                                                                NLG

348   Guyana. Public Free Library
        A select bibliography of the works of Guyanese and on
      Guyana / prepared in the Reference Department of the Public
      Library on the occasion of Guyana Week, February 19-25, 1967.
      - 51p.

        Arranged by the Dewey classification followed by a list of
      authors and titles of their works. The selection is based on
      books available for lending in the public departments of the
      Public Library, Georgetown, and its branches. Includes works by
      non-Guyanese on Guyana and its people.

                                                              UWI-T

349   Guyana. Public Free Library
        Select list of Guyanese publications suitable for a univer-
      sity library / prepared by J. Merriman. - Georgetown, Guyana :
      Public Free Library, 1972. - 22 leaves
        Typescript

                                                                NLG

86

350   Guyana. Public Free Library
          Select list on the flora, fauna, history, superstitions,
      creole sayings and Amerindians of Guyana / Public Free Library.
      - Georgetown (British Guiana) : Public Free Library, [1964]. -
      21p.
          Typescript

          Compiled in response to an enquiry.

                                                                    NLG

351   Guyana. Public Free Library
          Works by Guyanese women authors / Public Free Library. -
      [Georgetown, Guyana : Public Free Library], [1972]. - 7 leaves
          Typescript

                                                                    NLG

352   Guyana. Public Free Library (Mackenzie)
          Select bibliography of books on Guyana and written by
      Guyanese on the occasion of the Republic celebrations February
      21-March 4, 1972 / Public Free Library (Mackenzie). -
      Mackenzie, Guyana : Mackenzie Branch, Public Free Library,
      1972. - 34p.
          Typescript

                                                                    NLG

353   HISS, PHILIP HANSON
          A selective guide to the English literature on the
      Netherlands West Indies ; with a supplement on British Guiana
      / by Philip Hanson Hiss. - New York : Netherlands Information
      Bureau, 1943. - xiii, 129p. - (Booklets of the Netherlands
      Information Bureau ; no.9)
          British Guiana: p.114-124

          Listing of books, journal articles, maps in alphabetical
      author order under such headings as economy, anthropology,
      missions, geography, science and general works.

                                                                    UWI-T

354   HURWITZ, EDITH F.
          Caribbean studies : Part II / Edith F. Hurwitz. - p.639-
      640, 642-647
          In Choice. - Vol.12, nos.5/6 (July-Aug. 1975)

          Continuation of bibliographic essay begun in the June
      issue (Ref.no.113). In addition to material on Haiti, the
      Dominican Republic, Surinam and the Virgin Islands, the issue
      covers the three Guianas. Items on Guyana include ethnic,
      historical and political studies.

                                                                    UWI-T

355 NIJHOFF, M.
      Livres anciens et modernes ... les Guyanes néerlandaises,
      anglaises et françaises, et les Antilles néerlandaises / M.
      Nijhoff. - La Haye : [Nijhoff], 1907. - 48p.
                                                          Ref.no.767
                                                          p.984

356 NOUVION, V. DE
      Extraits des auteurs et voyageurs qui ont écrit sur la
      Guyane, suivis du catalogue bibliographique de la Guyane /
      V. de Nouvion. - Paris : Imprimèrie de Béhune et Plon, 1844. -
      xxii, 616p. - (Publications de la Societé d'Etudes pour la
      colonisation de la Guyane française ; no.4)

      "Includes a significant number of items on Guyana.
      Extensive extracts of many of the works cited are given" -
      SALALM XXI.
                                                          Ref.no.767
                                                          p.984

357 Rio de Janeiro.   Instituto Braseileiro de Bibliografia e
      Documentaçao
      Amazonia : bibliografia / Instituto Braseileiro de
      Bibliografia e Documentaçao. - Rio de Janeiro : [Instituto
      Braseileiro de Bibliografia e Documentaçao], 1963-1972. - 2v.
        Vol.1 : 1614-1962. - Vol.2 : 1601-1970

      Vol.2 contains retrospective material not included in
   vol.1.
                                                          Benjamin

358 RODWAY, J.
      Chronology and bibliography of Guiana / J. Rodway. -
      [Georgetown : s.n.], [c.1885]. - 30 leaves. - (Long Collection;
      43/3)

      "Damaged and incomplete printed copy in the Long Collection
   in the University of Guyana Library. Carries annotations for
   works on the Guianas as a whole until 1835 but it has not been
   established whether it was a proof draft for something that was
   published, or even whether it was ever completed." - SALALM
   XXII.
                                                               UG

359 ROOPCHAND, T.
      [Bartica and Linden / Sosdyke settlements] : a working
      bibliography : a draft / T. Roopchand. - [S.l. : s.n.], 1979.
      - 22p.
         Mimeographed
                                                               UG

360   ROTH, V.
            Books on the bush 4/V. Roth. - p.129-133
            In Roth's pepperpot : comprised of bits and pieces, odds
      and ends of Guianese zoological, historical and general interest
      / by V. Roth. - Georgetown : Daily Chronicle Ltd., 1958
                                                                         UG

361   Royal Agricultural and Commercial Society of British Guiana
            Catalogue of a display of Guyanese books, prints, maps and
      photographs to mark the celebration of independence on 26th
      May, 1966 [during the] Independence Week celebrations / Royal
      Agricultural and Commercial Society of British Guiana. -
      [Georgetown, British Guiana : The Society], [1966]. - 11 leaves
            Mimeographed
                                                                        NLG

362   Royal Agricultural and Commercial Society of British Guiana
            Exhibition of books by Guianese authors during National
      Library Week, 12th-19th March, 1966 / Royal Agricultural and
      Commercial Society of British Guiana. - [Georgetown, British
      Guiana : The Society], [1966]. - 6 leaves
            Mimeographed

            A listing under the following headings: Philosophy and
      Religion, Sociology, Education, Textbooks, Law, Literature,
      Essays, Poetry and Drama, Fine Arts, Pure and Applied Science,
      History, Travel and Information, Guiana Editions (a series
      published by the Daily Chronicle Ltd., nos.1-12), Novels and
      Short Stories, Miscellaneous Publications.
                                                                        NLG

363   Royal Agricultural and Commercial Society of British Guiana
            Exhibition of books by Guyanese authors at the Royal
      Agricultural and Commercial Society [during] National Library
      Week, 11th-18th March, 1967. - [Georgetown, British Guiana :
      The Society], 1967. - 11 leaves
                                                                        NLG

364   Royal Agricultural and Commercial Society of British Guiana
            Exhibition of books on the history of British Guiana,
      24th-31st October, 1965 / Royal Agricultural and Commercial
      Society of British Guiana. - Georgetown : Royal Agricultural
      and Commercial Society, 1965. - 5 leaves
            Mimeographed
                                                                        NLG

365   Royal Agricultural and Commercial Society of British Guiana
            Exhibition of 17th to 20th century books of British
      Guiana at the Royal Agricultural and Commercial Society for
      "History and Culture" Week, 25th-31st October, 1964. -

[Georgetown, British Guiana : Royal Agricultural and
Commercial Society], 1964. - 6 leaves
　　Mimeographed

NLG

366　Royal Agricultural and Commercial Society of British Guiana
　　　List of the works of contemporary Guianese authors and of
works on British Guiana by contemporary authors / Royal
Agricultural and Commercial Society. - [Georgetown, British
Guiana : Royal Agricultural and Commercial Society], 1962. -
5p.
　　　Mimeographed

　　　An alphabetical listing of a book exhibition held 28 May-
9 June 1962.

NLG

367　SCHULZE, ADOLF
　　　Abriss einer Geschichte der Brüdermission : mit einem
Anhang enthaltend eine ausführliche Bibliographie zur
Geschichte der Brüdermission / Adolf Schulze. - Herrnhut :
Missionsbuchandlung der Missionsanstalt der evangelischen
Brüderunitat, 1901. - 4, 1, 336p.
　　　Bibliographie zur Geschichte der Brüdermission: p.[284]-
336

Benjamin

368　SEYMOUR, A.J.
　　　From Raleigh to Carew : the books of Guiana / A.J. Seymour
p.74-82
　　　In Kyk-over-al. - Dec. 1960

Benjamin

369　SMITH, RAYMOND T.
　　　British Guiana / Raymond Smith. - London : Oxford Univer-
sity Press, 1962. - 218p.
　　　Issued under the auspices of: Royal Institute of Inter-
national Affairs
　　　Bibliography:　p.209-213

　　　92 items including official reports (British Government
and British Guiana Government) which are listed separately.
Includes material on the history, government, ethnic groups,
social structure, and social and economic conditions of British
Guiana.

UWI-T

370　TIELE, P.A.
　　　Nederlandsche bibliographie van landen volkenkunde / P.A.
Tiele. - Amsterdam : F. Muller, 1884. - vii, 288p.

Benjamin

371   Union of Cultural Clubs (British Guiana)
         Catalogue of collection / Union of Cultural Clubs. -
      [S.l. : s.n.], [19-]
         Typescript

         Collection on permanent loan to the University of Guyana
                                                            UG

372   United States. Agency for International Development. Mission
      to Guyana
         Index to U.S.A.I.D. Guyana Memory Bank and documents
      collection. - Georgetown, Guyana : U.S.A.I.D. Mission to
      Guyana, 1972. - 82 leaves

         A listing of reports and private as well as official docu-
      ments on several aspects of development in Guyana. Arranged in
      12 broad subject sections including agriculture, economics and
      financial affairs, education, health, industrial development and
      transportation. Each section is further subdivided by relevant
      topics and the Mission's report holdings are itemized by title
      with issuing organization or author, date of publication and
      pagination.
                                                            UWI-T

373   United States. Library of Congress
         Select list of references on British Guiana / Library of
      Congress. - Washington, D.C. : Library of Congress, 1911. -
      7 leaves
         Additional references. - 1918. - 3 leaves

         89 references.
                                                            LC

374   United States. Library of Congress. Division of Bibliography
         British Guiana : a bibliographical list / compiled by
      Florence S. Hellman. - Washington, D.C. : [Library of
      Congress], 1937. - 39p.
         Typescript

         450 references.
                                                            LC

375   United States. Library of Congress. Division of Bibliography
         British Guiana : a bibliographical list / Library of
      Congress Division of Bibliography. - [Washington, D.C. :
      Library of Congress], [1940]. - 211p.
         Typescript
                                                            LC

376   United States. Library of Congress. Division of Bibliography
        A select list of references on the Guianas / compiled by
      Florence S. Hellman. - Washington, D.C. : [s.n.], 1940. -
      17p.

          158 references.

                                                                    LC

377   University of Guyana. Library
        Bibliography of current research publications by academic
      staff / University of Guyana Library. - [Turkeyen, Guyana] :
      University of Guyana, 1972. - 14p.
        Mimeographed

                                                                    UG

378   University of Guyana. Library
        A catalogue of the A.W.B. Long Collection / compiled by
      Carol Collins, Alleyne Riley [and] John Shinebourne. -
      Georgetown : [University of Guyana], 1970. - 12 leaves. -
      (University of Guyana Library series ; no.2)

        The collection donated to the library covers Guyanese
      material (books and manuscripts) collected by Mr. Long during a
      career in the Guyanese Police Force; some are very rare. Thirteen
      notebooks with memoranda, maps and including information on
      Amerindian tribes are described in the catalogue.

                                                                    UWI-T

379   University of Guyana. Library
        A catalogue of the Roth collection in the [University of
      Guyana] Library / compiled by Claire Collins and Yvonne
      Stephenson. - Georgetown, Guyana : University of Guyana
      Library, 1969. - 24, [4]p.
        Mimeographed

                                                                    UG

380   University of Guyana. Library
        Publications of members of University of Guyana staff :
      University of Guyana, 1963-1973 / University of Guyana
      Library. - Turkeyen, [Guyana] : University of Guyana Library,
      1973. - 62, 7p.
        Mimeographed

                                                                    UG

381   University of Guyana. Library
        The Roth collection : a catalogue / compiled by Carol
      Collins. - Georgetown : University of Guyana Library, 1971. -
      32p. - (University of Guyana Library series ; no.4)
        Mimeographed

A list of some of the manuscripts, books, pamphlets and
photoprints of Walter Edmund Roth donated to the university
library. Roth was an ethnologist and anthropologist and much of
the material is translated from Dutch and German.

UG

382   University of Guyana. Library
A selection of documents on Guyana / compiled by Claire
Collins and Yvonne Stephenson. - 2nd ed. - [Georgetown],
Guyana : University of Guyana Library, 1969. - 24, [2] leaves

A revised and enlarged list based on a shorter bibliography
(Ref.no.383). Includes reports of the national and international
governmental organizations, associations, political parties, etc.
grouped by broad subjects such as agriculture, economics, constitutional history, etc.

UWI-T

383   University of Guyana. Library
A selection of documents on Guyana in the library / by
Yvonne Stephenson. - Georgetown, [Guyana] : University of
Guyana, 1969 . - 17 leaves
Mimeographed

"This hastily prepared list was compiled as a token
contribution to the Conference on Sharing Caribbean Resources for
Study and Research, held in St. Thomas, Virgin Islands, in March
1969 ..." and later revised (Ref.no.382).

UWI-T

Government Publications
384   Guyana. Ministry of Information
List of publications available at Ministry of Information,
1969. - [Georgetown, Guyana : The Ministry], 1969. - 30p.

"Guyana official publications plus some titles printed by
the Government Printer."

Bloomfield

Newspapers
385   GROPP, A.E.
[List of 30 titles of early newspapers from British
Guiana] / A.E. Gropp. - p.13-14
In Field letters of the West Indies. - No.14 (19-?)

Benjamin

386   LONG, A.W.B.
[List of newspapers printed in Guyana] / A.W.B. Long
In Long Collection, 43/9. - [S.1. : s.n.], [196?]. - 16
leaves
Typescript

UG

Non-Book Materials
  387 AARONS, J.
          [List of early maps in the Caribbean Research Library /
       J. Aarons. - [S.l. : s.n.], [1976]. - 17 leaves
          Typescript

          Majority of maps are Guyanese although some other West
       Indian maps are listed.

                                                                     UG

  388 ADONIAS, I.
          A cartografia de regiao Amazônia : cataloge descriptiva
       1500-1961 / I. Adonias. - Rio de Janeiro : Conselho Nacional
       de Pesquisas, Instituto Nacional de Pesquisas de
       Amazônia, 1963. - 2v.

          Vol.2 (p.147-192) deals with the Roraima (ex-Rio Branco
       region). Includes detailed annotations.
                                                              Benjamin

  389 BAKER, M.
          Partial list of maps of the Orinoco-Essequibo region /
       M. Baker. - p.383-517
          In Report and accompanying papers of the Commission
       appointed by the President of the United States "to investi-
       gate and report upon the true divisional line between the
       Republic of Venezuela and British Guiana". - Vol.3, geographical.
       - Washington, Government Printing Office, 1897

          "The list is extensive and has important annotations.
       Includes an alphabetic index."
                                                              Benjamin

  390 Great Britain. Foreign Office
          Chronological list of the principal maps of Guiana /
       annotated by C.H. Coote ... and J. Bolton ... . - p.339-379
          In British Guiana boundary : arbitration with the United
       States of Venezuela ; appendix to the case on behalf of the
       government of Her Britannic Majesty. - London : Printed at
       the Foreign Office, 1898. - Vol.7
                                                              Benjamin

  391 Great Britain. Foreign Office
          List of maps / Foreign Office. - p.217-224
          In British Guiana boundary ; arbitration with the United
       States of Venezuela : index to cases, counter-cases and
       printed arguments of the governments of Great Britain and
       Venezuela. - London : Printed at the Foreign Office, 1898
                                                              Benjamin

392   KOEMAN, C.
          Bibliography of printed maps of Suriname, 1671-1971 / C.
      Koeman. - Amsterdam : Theatrum Orbis Terrarum, 1973. - 156p.

          Maps of Berbice, Demerara and Essequibo up to 1816:   p.101-
      117.

                                                                    Benjamin

393   LALL, KISSOON O.M.
          Mapping in Guyana since 1940 : a review and its relevance
      to national development / by Kissoon O.M. Lall. - Georgetown,
      [Guyana] : Department of Geography, University of Guyana,
      1975
          Appendix II : p.79-81

          Lists maps and plans by the Cartographic Division of the
      Lands Department.
                                                                Ref.no.107
                                                                     p.125

394   PHILLIPS, P.L.
          Guiana and Venezuelan cartography / P.L. Phillips. -
      p.681-776
          In Annual report of the American Historical Association. -
      Vol.23 (1897)

          800 references.
                                                                  Ref.no.4
                                                              Vol.2,p.2770

Periodicals and Serials
  395   LONDON, HETTY
          A selected list of non-government serials published in
      Guyana / Hetty London. - p.10-17
          In Guyana Library Association bulletin. - Vol.7, no.2
      (1978)
          65 items with information on publishers, frequency and
      subscription. Includes some entries in Ref.no.396 and excludes
      others.
                                                                      UWI-T

396   STEPHENSON, WENDA
          A selected list of current non-government serials published
      in Guyana / Wenda Stephenson. - p.13-19
          In Guyana Library Association bulletin. - Vol.5, no.3
      (1976)

          63 items with information on publisher, frequency and
      subscription.
                                                                      UWI-T

397   University of Guyana. Library
        List of current Guyanese periodicals and newspapers April/
      May 1969 / University of Guyana Library. - [Turkeyen, Guyana :
      University of Guyana Library], 1969. - 6 leaves
        Mimeographed

                                                                    UG

Jamaica

398   BAXTER, IVY
        The arts of an island : the development of culture and of
      the folk and creative arts in Jamaica, 1494-1962 (Independ-
      ence) / Ivy Baxter. - Metuchen, N.J. : Scarecrow Press, 1970.
      - 407p.
        Bibliography: p.368-386

        Arranged alphabetically by author in two sequences for
      books, pamphlets, manuscripts and newspaper and magazine articles
      with a list of radio scripts at the end.

                                                                    UWI-T

399   BRATHWAITE, EDWARD
        The development of creole society in Jamaica, 1770-1820 /
      Edward Brathwaite. - Oxford : Clarendon Press, 1971. - xi,
      374p.
        Bibliography: p.343-362

        Lists manuscript sources by location, official documents,
      newspapers, magazines and periodicals used as primary source
      material, followed by contemporary and modern printed works in
      alphabetical author order. Separate listings of journal articles
      and theses and unpublished papers. Short titles are used where
      full references appear in the footnotes. Listings cover
      several aspects of inter-cultural relationships between whites
      and blacks, masters and slaves as well as more general works on
      Jamaica.

                                                                    UWI-T

400   Commonwealth Institute. Library
        [Jamaica] : select reading list for advanced study /
      Commonwealth Institute. - London : Commonwealth Institute,
      1970. - 4p.

                                                                    Ref.no.3

401   CUNDALL, FRANK
        The press and printers of Jamaica prior to 1820 / by Frank
      Cundall. - Worcester, Mass. : The Society, 1916. - 126p.
        Reprinted from: The Proceedings of the American Antiquarian
      Society (Oct. 1916)

Includes sections on history, bibliography and a list of
the printers of Jamaica. The bibliography is arranged as follows:
(1) Newspapers, (2) Sheet Almanacs, (3) Book Almanacs, (4)
Magazines, (5) Books Printed in Jamaica.

UWI-J

402 FLOYD, BARRY
Jamaica : an island microcosm / Barry Floyd. - London :
Macmillan, 1979. - xii, 164p.
Bibliography: p.156-160

96 items arranged in eight sections: General Studies of
the West Indies; General Studies of Jamaica; Physical Features,
Flora, Fauna; History; Social and Cultural Aspects, The Arts;
Economics; Politics and Administration; Periodicals and Newspapers. The sections correspond approximately to the themes
treated in the book.

UWI-T

403 Great Britain. Colonial Office
Jamaica / Colonial Office. - [S.l. : s.n.], 1860. - 10p. -
(No.21 of a series of lists of works in the library)

175 references.

Ref.no.4
Vol.2,p.3240

404 Institute of Jamaica
Guide to Jamaican reference material in the West India
Reference Library / by Rae de Lattre. - Kingston, Jamaica :
Institute of Jamaica, 1965. - 76p.

Many entries are annotated and there is an extensive
bibliography section including library catalogues. Arranged by
broad subject groups such as education, history, law, science,
music, language and literature, sociology and economics and by
form such as periodicals and newspapers, maps, prints, films etc.
Each heading includes general Caribbean and Jamaican sections.
Includes author and title indexes.

UWI-T

405 Institute of Jamaica
Jamaica today : a handbook of information for visitors and
intending residents, with some account of the colony's
history, being a new and revised edition of the late Mr. Frank
Cundall's "Jamaica in 1928" / [edited by Philip M. Sherlock
and others]. - London : Printed by Hazell, Watson and Viney,
1940
Bibliography: p.199-204

Ref.no.5
1937-1942,p.863

406   Jamaica Library Service
        Jamaica : a select bibliography, 1900-1963 / compiled by
      the Jamaica Library Service ... in commemoration of the first
      anniversary of the independence of Jamaica, August 5th, 1963.
      - [Kingston, Jamaica] : Jamaica Independence Festival
      Committee, 1963. - 115p.

        Lists books and periodical articles in classified arrange-
      ment. Information collected from the holdings of the library of
      the University of the West Indies, the West India Reference
      Library of the Institute of Jamaica and the Jamaica Library
      Service. Unannotated. Author, subject index.
                                                              UWI-T

407   Jamaica Library Service
        Our literary heritage : a select list of books and
      periodical articles on Jamaica / Jamaica Library Service. -
      Kingston : Jamaica Library Service, 1962. - 25p. - (Its
      pamphlet ; no.23)
                                                              NLJ

408   United States. Library of Congress
        Selected references on Jamaica / Library of Congress. -
      Washington, D.C. : [s.n.], 1941. - 6 leaves

        77 references.
                                                        Ref.no.4
                                                      Vol.2,p.3240

409   University of the West Indies (Mona). Library
        [Card file of some titles published in or about Jamaica]
      ... / University of the West Indies Library. - Mona,
      [Jamaica] : University of the West Indies, 1962
        Microcard
                                                              UF

410   University of the West Indies (Mona). Institute of Education
        Index to the individual studies written by the students of
      the Moneague Teachers' College, Jamaica, 1957-1968 / University
      of the West Indies Institute of Education. - [Mona, Jamaica] :
      Institute of Education, University of the West Indies, [1968].
      - 87p.
        Mimeographed

        Lists final year student studies by subjects with author,
      title and date and provides a summary of a few studies. Topics
      in education and on divers aspects of Jamaican life predominate.
                                                              UWI-T

Government Publications
411   Institute of Jamaica
          Jamaican government publications : a bibliography compiled
      from the Periodicals Collection in the West India Reference
      Library / [by Suzette Hinds]. - Kingston : Institute of
      Jamaica, 1971. - 13p.
          Mimeographed

          Alphabetical listing under administrative authorities of
      the government with beginning and closing dates held where
      applicable but without frequency of publication.
                                                              UWI-T

412   Jamaica. Government Printing Office
          Government publications on sale at the Government Printing
      Office revised to 30th September, 1964. - [Kingston], Jamaica :
      Government Printer, 1977. - 16p.
          Earlier editions appeared in 1964 and 1967.
                                                              UWI-T

Non-Book Materials
413   Institute of Jamaica. Library
          Jamaica cartography : chronological list of maps of
      Jamaica in the library of the Institute of Jamaica, both on
      separate sheets and in books ; with some notes on the history
      of the parishes of the island / by Frank Cundall. - Kingston :
      [Institute of Jamaica], 1897. - 15p.
          Reprinted from: The Handbook of Jamaica for 1897.
                                                          Ref.no.144

414   KAPP, KIT S.
          The printed maps of Jamaica up to 1825 / by Kit S. Kapp.
      - [Kingston], Jamaica : Bolivar Press, 1968. - 36, [28]p. -
      (Map collectors' series; no.42)

          Chronological listing of 153 maps with source notes for
      many listings.
                                                              UWI-T

Periodicals and Serials
415   CHAMBERS, AUDREY
          Selected list of serials published in Jamaica / Audrey
      Chambers. - p.35-39
          In Jamaica Library Association bulletin. - 1975

          Alphabetical listing by title with addresses and
      frequency.
                                                              UWI-T

416   CHAMBERS, AUDREY
          Selected list of serials published in Jamaica / compiled
      by Audrey Chambers and Alvona Alleyne. - p.59-62
          In Jamaica Library Association bulletin. - 1977

          The list is alphabetically arranged by title giving
      address, frequency and date of first publication. It supplements
      Ref.no.415 with new titles appearing in 1975-1976. Government
      serials and house journals are excluded.
                                                              UWI-T

Theses
417   KULHAWIK, LEONARD R.
          Jamaica : a bibliography of doctoral dissertations
      relating to Jamaica accepted by U.S. colleges and universities
      to 1959 / Leonard R. Kulhawik. - p.2-3
          In Southeastern Latin Americanist. - Vol.4 (June 1960)

          Alphabetical author list covering the period 1928-1959.
                                                              NYPL

Montserrat

418   Montserrat. Public Library
          Montserrat : a bibliography / Public Library. - [Plymouth,
      Montserrat : Public Library], 1977. - 16p.

          Works about Montserrat and/or by nationals held by the
      Public Library, University Centre and the Museum. Arranged by
      broad subject headings using Dewey main classes and alphabeti-
      cally by author within each group. Includes maps, newspapers
      and phonograph records.
                                                              UWI-T

St. Lucia

419   Great Britain. Colonial Office
          St. Lucia / Colonial Office. - [S.l. : s.n.], 1860. - 1
      sheet. - (No.38 of a series of lists of works in the library)

          5 references.
                                                          Ref.no.4
                                                      Vol.4,p.5546

420   JESSE, CHARLES
          Bibliography for St. Lucia : some sources of information
      on St. Lucia's past / Charles Jesse. - p.80-83

In Iouanaloa : recent writing from St. Lucia / edited by
Edward Brathwaite. - Castries, St. Lucia : Department of Extra
Mural Studies, [The University of the West Indies], 1963

Items are arranged under headings : Archives, Authors'
Reviews, etc., Newspapers, Lives, and Books of Travel.

UWI-T

421 St. Lucia. Central Library
A list of books, pamphlets and articles on St. Lucia and
by St. Lucians covering the period 1844 to date / Central
Library. - Castries, St. Lucia : [Central Library of St.
Lucia], 1971. - 12 leaves
Mimeographed

The bibliography is arranged in two sections : (1) Books by
St. Lucians alphabetically arranged by author; (2) Books about
St. Lucians arranged by title. Both lists are selective only.
Several titles with sections only on St. Luica are included and
several articles from the Voice Statehood Souvenir. Authors
include Garnet Gordon, Arthur Lewis, Garth St. Omer, Derek
Walcott, and Roderick Walcott.

UWI-T

Newspapers
422 St. Lucia. Central Library
A chronological resumé of St. Lucian newspapers / by
Robert J. Devaux. - p.7-11
In Books, libraries and St. Lucia : three essays in
honour of International Book Year 1972 / by J.H. Pilgrim,
Robert Devaux and Colin Brock. - Castries, St. Lucia :
Government Printing Office, 1972

Covers the period 1780-1952.

UWI-T

Trinidad and Tobago

423 ANIKINA, E.B.
Trinidad i Tobago, Iamaika : Kolonial nye territorii =
Trinidad and Tobago, Jamaica : Colonial territories / E.B.
Anikina. - p.92-104, 107-112
In Latinskaia Amerika V Sovetskoi Pechati : Bibliografia
... 1946-1962 GG. - [Redkollegia : E.B. Ananova ... et al]. -
[Latin America in the Soviet Press]. - Moscow : Akademiia,
Nauk, SSSR, Institut Latinskoi Amerik, 1964

RIS

424   BURNHAM, ALAN
        A bibliography of Trinidad / prepared by Alan Burnham at
      Port of Spain. - Port of Spain : [s.n.], 1944-5-6 [sic]. - 8p.
        Typescript

        No organized arrangement. Items are numbered in sequence
      and publishers and dates quoted. The list includes several 19th
      century publications, some rare, and maps. There are personal
      handwritten notes. Some references are incomplete.
                                                                    TCL

425   Carnegie Free Library
        San Fernando : an index to some sources of information ...
      in the West Indian Section of the Carnegie Free Library /
      compiled by Zarina Yusuf ... on the occasion of the 50th
      anniversary of the Carnegie Free Library, San Fernando,
      Trinidad, West Indies, 31st March, 1969. - [San Fernando,
      Trinidad : Carnegie Free Library], [1969]. - 22p.
        Mimeographed
        Cover title

        Includes location symbols. Broad subject arrangement.
      References to photographs and material in books, journals and
      press clippings held by the library with holdings of two
      additional libraries in the country.
                                                                  UWI-T

426   DOW, HENRY
        A bibliography of Trinidad and Tobago / Henry Dow. - [Port
      of Spain : s.n.], [195-]. - [39] leaves
        Typescript

        First appeared in: Trinidad and Tobago Yearbook 1956,
      p.533-549.

        A working list in alphabetical author order with
      unauthored works under title.
                                                                  UWI-T

427   FRANKLIN, CONRADE BISMARK
        Bibliography of Trinidad and Tobago (chronologically
      arranged) / by Conrade Bismark Franklin. - [Port of Spain,
      Trinidad : s.n.], [1923]
        Photocopy
        Issued as: an appendix to the Trinidad and Tobago Year-
      book, 1923. - p.411-438

        Separate listings for books, papers, lectures, reports,
      poetical works, pamphlets, almanacs, guides and Tobago as a
      continuation of the work of the Scientific Association of
      Trinidad sixty years earlier.
                                                                  UWI-T

428   Great Britain. Colonial Office
         Tobago / Colonial Office. - [S.l. : s.n.], 1860. - 1
      sheet. - (No.37 of a series of lists of works in the library)

         5 references.
                                                          Ref.no.4
                                                          Vol.4,p.6142

429   Great Britain. Colonial Office
         Trinidad / Colonial Office. - [S.l. : s.n.], 1860. - 2p. -
      (No.31 of a series of lists of works in the library)

         30 references.
                                                          Ref.no.4
                                                          Vol.4,p.6208

430   JORDAN, ALMA
         Trinidad and Tobago [bibliography] / Alma Jordan. - p.63-
      67
         In Bibliography, documentation, terminology. - Vol.11,
      no.3 (May 1967)

         A review of bibliographical services and related activities
      in 1965 including a statement of desiderata and existing biblio-
      graphies.
                                                          UWI-T

431   SEWLAL, ENOS
         Bibliography of Trinidad and Tobago with a section on the
      West Indies (for the use of visiting students) / Enos Sewlal. -
      Port of Spain, Trinidad : Department of Agriculture, 1958. -
      xix, 77p.
         Mimeographed

         Designed as an appendix to the inventory of archives
      (Ref.no.866). The work is divided into twenty-two sections each
      introduced by a brief background essay and critical discussion of
      the major sources, followed by the listings in chronological
      order. Sections include history, geography and general infor-
      mation, Tobago, East Indian studies, skirmishes, riots, labour
      disturbances, inquiry commissions, life in Trinidad, local
      writers and their works, newspapers and magazines.
                                                          UWI-T

432   SIMMONDS, JESSICA
         Trinidad and Tobago 1900-1962 : an annotated bibliography
      / compiled by Jessica Simmonds. - [London] : The Library
      Association, 1966. - xv, 216p.

Presented as a thesis for the Fellowship of the Library Association; 1,399 entries are arranged by topics in broad class order using the UDC as a guide. Author and subject indexes are included.

UWI-T

433   Trinidad and Tobago. Central Library
      List of material on display at the Trinidad Hilton for the Seminar on the Acquisition of Latin American Library Materials, 29th April, 1973–3rd May, 1973 / Central Library. – [Port of Spain, Trinidad : Central Library], 1973. – 8p.
      Mimeographed

      Listing in author order with title, dates, publishers and addresses given of mainly Trinidad and Tobago imprints on a variety of subjects including literature, music and library science; includes separate section for serials, bibliographies and unpublished material in the field of librarianship.

TCL

434   Trinidad and Tobago. Central Library
      Select bibliography of books, pamphlets etc. on Trinidad and Tobago / prepared by the Central Library Services. – [Port of Spain, Trinidad] : Central Library Services, 1962. – 5, 6 leaves
      Mimeographed
      Supplement (Aug. 1964) in: Inter-American library relations (Jan.–Mar. 1968)

      Titles arranged alphabetically by author within sections for non-fiction, fiction and government publications.

TCL

435   Trinidad and Tobago. Central Library
      A select list of books, pamphlets and other material of Tobagonian authorship and on Trinidad and Tobago / prepared by the Central Library of Trinidad and Tobago and the Carnegie Free Library, San Fernando, on the occasion of the 25th anniversary of the Central Library of Trinidad and Tobago in Tobago. – [S.l.] : Central Library of Trinidad and Tobago and Carnegie Free Library, [n.d.]

      Includes works by C.R. Ottley, Eric Roach, J.D. Elder, Harold Telemaque and A.N.R. Robinson among Tobagonian authors.

UWI-T

436   Trinidad and Tobago. Central Library
      A selective list of books by Trinidadians and of Trinidad ... Independence Celebrations, Trinidad and Tobago, 31st August, 1962, [prepared for the International Pavilion] /

Central Library. - Port of Spain, Trinidad and Tobago: [s.n.],
1962. - 6 leaves
    Mimeographed

    This list includes sections for government publications
and local periodicals, fiction and non-fiction.

                                                              TCL

437   Trinidad and Tobago. Central Library
        Suggested list of books [for] Expo '67 / Central Library.
      - [Port of Spain, Trinidad : Central Library], 1967. - 13,
      5, 3 leaves
        Typescript

        Includes sections on anthropology, folk songs, tales and
dances, literature, plant and animal life, social sciences,
sport, archaeology, travel and guide books, history, biographies
and bibliography. Arrangement is alphabetical by author within
each section.

                                                              TCL

438   Trinidad and Tobago. Central Library
        A supplement to the "Select bibliography of books pamphlets
      etc. by Trinidadians and on Trinidad and Tobago" / prepared by
      the Central Library Services ... . - [Port of Spain, Trinidad] :
      Central Library, 1964. - 3 leaves

        Addenda for independence booklist (Ref.no.434).

                                                              TCL

439   Trinidad and Tobago. Central Library
        A West Indian reference collection : a select list of
      books, pamphlets etc. of Trinidadian authorship on Trinidad
      and Tobago and other material published in Trinidad and
      Tobago / prepared by the Central Library. - Port of Spain :
      Government Printer, 1966. - 21p.
        Mimeographed

        A cumulation of the library's previous bibliographies
concentrating on Trinidad and Tobago for which annual supplements
were projected. Arranged by Dewey classification with a separate
listing of government publications.

                                                              UWI-T

440   Trinidad and Tobago. Independence Celebrations [Committee]
        Trinidad and Tobago independence celebrations : catalogue
      of historical exhibition held in Port of Spain, Trinidad, 31st
      August-14th September, 1962 / Historical Exhibition Working
      Party. - [Port of Spain], Trinidad : Jet Printing Service,
      1962. - 22p.

308 items listed including sections on the history of
Trinidad, history of Tobago, drama, poetry and novelists of the
islands, archival documents, maps, postage stamps and original
paintings.

UWI-T

441   University of the West Indies (St. Augustine). Library
        [List of material on Trinidad and Tobago - human and
        social development, use and management of natural resources] /
        University of the West Indies Library. - [St. Augustine,
        Trinidad : University of the West Indies Library], 1977. - 2
        leaves
        Typescript

34 references to statistical data series, annual reports
and other official sources of relevant information.

UWI-T

Government Publications
442   MCDOWELL, WILHELMINA A.
        Official publications on Trinidad and Tobago, 1797-1962 /
        by Wilhelmina A. McDowell. - [Port of Spain, Trinidad : s.n.],
        [1971]. - viii, 233 leaves

Thesis submitted for the Fellowship of the Library
Association. The work is divided into 12 chapters the last of
which is a subject listing (Sears headings) chronologically under
each topic and is the major part of the bibliography. An author
index is provided. All material listed has been seen but no
annotations are given. Separate chapters are devoted to lists
of local laws, serials and Central Statistical Office publications
as well as British parliamentary papers, U.S. government and
U.N./specialized agency documents and publications on Trinidad
and Tobago.

UWI-T

443   Trinidad and Tobago. Central Statistical Office
        Current list of publications / Central Statistical Unit. -
        [Port of Spain, Trinidad] : Central Statistical Office
        Printing Unit, [1973]. - 14p.

Annotated price list periodically up-dated. Arranged by
frequency of publication - monthly, quarterly, annual, periodical
series, etc.

UWI-T

444   Trinidad and Tobago. Gazette
        List of publications obtainable from the Government
        Printer, Trinidad and Tobago / [compiled by the Government
        Printery]. - [Port of Spain], Trinidad and Tobago : Government
        Printery, 1974. - 7p.

Published as a supplement to the Trinidad and Tobago
Gazette

Sales list of annual departmental, statistical and other
special reports with serial titles available on subscription.
Until 1963 published quarterly and thereafter annually and
irregularly. Last published in 1974.

UWI-T

Government Publications--Indexes
  445 COMISSIONG, BARBARA
        Indexing Commonwealth Caribbean government publications :
        a preliminary index to Chairmen of Trinidad and Tobago
        Commissions of Enquiry / by Barbara Comissiong and Shirley
        Espinet ; Appendix to Working paper V [submitted to] the
        annual meeting of the Association of Caribbean University
        and Research Libraries (ACURIL) 2nd., Holiday Inn, Bridgetown,
        Barbados, 22-27 November, 1970. - St. Augustine, Trinidad :
        The University of the West Indies Library, 1970 . - 12p.
        Mimeographed

The index lists under chairmen the reports of commissions
and committees of enquiry set up by the government of Trinidad
and Tobago, and in a few cases by the government of the United
Kingdom. Compiled as an aid to easy identification, it includes
reports to the government by individuals and is based on holdings
of the St. Augustine library as well as the Foreign and Commonwealth Office and the Institute of Commonwealth Studies, London
University.

UWI-T

Newspapers
  446 Trinidad and Tobago. Central Library
        List of newspapers published in Trinidad and Tobago /
        Central Library. - [Port of Spain, Trinidad : Central Library],
        1967. - 2 leaves
        Typescript

Sixteen titles in alphabetical order with addresses only.

TCL

Non-Book Materials
  447 Map Collectors' Circle
        Some early printed maps of Trinidad and Tobago ; with a
        facsimile of Faden's descriptive account of the Island of
        Trinidad, 1802 / Map Collectors' Circle. - London : Map
        Collectors' Circle, 1964. - 12 [9, 17]p. - (Map collectors'
        series ; 10)

Chronological listing of 28 maps of Trinidad (1675-1899)
and 25 maps of Tobago (1677-1867).

UWI-T

448   Trinidad and Tobago. Lands and Surveys Department
          Maps produced by the Lands and Surveys Department,
      Trinidad and Tobago, Appendix I
          In Annual report of the Lands and Surveys Department 1955.
      - [Port of Spain], Trinidad : Government Printing Office,
      1957. - 37p.

          Sales list of approximately 30 sheet maps (topographical
      and cadastral) a few of which were printed in England with
      scale, a description and price for each item.
                                                          UWI-T

449   Trinidad and Tobago. Office of the Prime Minister. Public
      Relations Division. Film Unit.
          Film Catalogue / Film Unit. - Port of Spain : Film Unit,
      1972. - 1v. (loose-leaf)

          Chronological listing of films produced by the Film Unit
      the majority of which relate to Trinidad and Tobago. Mainly
      16mm and 35mm with some 60mm which were produced for television.
      Includes documentaries and news features. Alphabetical title
      index.
                                                          UWI-T

450   Trinidad and Tobago. Central Library
          List of periodicals published in Trinidad & Tobago /
      Central Library. - [Port of Spain, Trinidad : Central Library],
      1967. - 4 leaves
          Typescript

          Forty-four titles listed in alphabetical order with
      sources for each and newspapers identified by an asterisk.
                                                          TCL

                            AGRICULTURE

General

  451   Commonwealth Bureau of Agricultural Economics
            The Caribbean agricultural situation and prospects /
        Commonwealth Bureau of Agricultural Economics. - Oxford :
        Commonwealth Agricultural Bureaux, 1974. - 5v. - (Common-
        wealth Bureau of Agricultural Economics, annotated biblio-
        graphy series D ; nos.1-5)
            Cover title differs from title page

No.1 : West Indies-General - No.2 : Jamaica / compiled by
Ann Thirkell Smith - No.3 : Greater Antilles - No.4 : Lesser
Antilles - No.5 : Central America

Lists publications on the Caribbean as a whole which were
abstracted in World Agricultural Economics and Rural Sociology
Abstracts (WAERSA) from 1965 to 1973. Geographical arrangement.
West Indies General (62 items) ; Jamaica (64 items) ; Lesser
Antilles (general) (4 items) ; Barbados (11 items) ; Leeward
Islands (2 items) ; Antigua (3 items) ; Montserrat (2 items) ;
Trinidad and Tobago (30 items) ; general section on the Windward
Islands (3 items) ; St. Lucia (3 items) ; St. Vincent (2 items) ;
Dominica (6 items) ; Grenada (4 items).

UWI-T

452   Imperial College of Tropical Agriculture
        General publications issued by the Imperial College of
Tropical Agriculture. - St. Augustine, Trinidad : Imperial
College of Tropical Agriculture, [1960?]. - 3p.
        Mimeographed

A sales list of available publications of the former ICTA,
later the Faculty of Agriculture, UWI.

UWI-T

453   University of the West Indies. Department of Agricultural
        Extension
        Abstracts of graduate students' research in agriculture
1971-1973 / edited by T. Henderson. - St. Augustine, Trinidad
: Department of Agricultural Extension, University of the West
Indies, 1973. - 24p. (Research summaries ; no.1)

Includes postgraduate diploma, masters' and doctoral
research studies, copies of which are lodged in the university
library. Covers aspects of crop and livestock production,
economics, extension, soils and related biological sciences.
Only projects from Faculty of Agriculture students are included
and a subject index is provided.

UWI-T

454   University of the West Indies. Department of Agricultural
        Extension
        Abstracts of graduate students' research in agriculture,
1974-1976 / edited by T.H. Henderson. - St. Augustine,
Trinidad : Department of Agricultural Extension, University
of the West Indies, 1977. - 50p. - (Research summaries ; no.2)

Since the general concern is food in a total sense,
summaries include postgraduate student projects in food
technology conducted in the Department of Chemical Engineering

and one project in the Department of Mechanical Engineering as
well as Faculty of Agriculture projects. A subject index is
provided.

UWI-T

455 University of the West Indies. Department of Agricultural
     Economics
          Fifty years of research in tropical agriculture, 1922-1972
     : a bibliography / Thomas H. Henderson and Sandra Mahabir. -
     St. Augustine, Trinidad : Department of Agricultural Extension,
     University of the West Indies, 1976. - v, 180p.

          Includes books, monographs, bulletins, journal articles,
     unpublished research reports, graduate students' theses as well
     as student project reports considered to be of sufficient merit
     to be placed in the university library. The 2,573 entries are
     arranged in alphabetical author order and numbered consecutively
     with a subject index arranged by topics.

UWI-T

456 University of the West Indies. Faculty of Agriculture
          [List of publications of the former] Imperial College of
     Tropical Agriculture / Faculty of Agriculture. - St. Augustine,
     Trinidad : Faculty of Agriculture, University of the West
     Indies, [197?]. - 3 leaves

          An up-dated list without sale prices including all numbers
     in the Chemical, Economic, Mycological and Sugar Technology series
     and other miscellaneous publications available as of 1971.

UWI-T

457 University of the West Indies. Faculty of Agriculture
          M.Sc. and A.I.C.T.A. theses and D.T.A. and C.A.S Reports
     1960-1965 : Part I - Animal and grassland production ; Part
     II - Crop production, soils and agricultural economics /
     Faculty of Agriculture. - [St. Augustine, Trinidad] : Faculty
     of Agriculture, University of the West Indies, [1965?]. - 8p.
          Mimeographed

          A typescript supplement covers 1966-67. Arranged
     alphabetically by author within such sections as dairy husbandry,
     grassland agronomy and grassland husbandry in Part I and cocoa,
     banana, pigeon pea, sugar cane in Part II.

UWI-T

458 University of the West Indies (St. Augustine). Library
          List of postgraduate student research reports and research
     theses / U.W.I. Library. - p.380-381
          In Tropical agriculture. - Vol.42, no.4 (Oct. 1965)

Research reports accepted in 1963 and 1964 are covered in
this first listing. Prepared by the library from copies of
theses deposited. Lists appeared annually from 1965 to 1969 in
the April (no.2) issue of the journal covering reports up to the
1967/68 academic year. Each list includes Diploma in Tropical
Agriculture (DTA) reports, M.Sc. Theses and Certificate of
Advanced Studies in Tropical Agriculture essays. Arranged by
author with the name of the academic supervisor given in
parentheses. The No.3 (July 1977) issue lists research reports
and theses for the period 1971-1975.

UWI-T

459   ZUVEKAS, CLARENCE
        A partially annotated bibliography of agricultural
development in the Caribbean Region : Antigua, Barbados,
Belize, British Virgin Islands, Cayman Islands, Dominica,
Grenada, Montserrat, St. Kitts-Nevis-(Anguilla), St. Lucia,
St. Vincent, Turks and Caicos Islands / Clarence Zuvekas. –
Washington : Rural Development Division, Bureau for Latin
America and the Caribbean, Agency for International Develop-
ment, 1978. – 202p.

Mainly comprises items published since 1960. Most IBRD,
IDB and OAS reports, many of which have a restricted distribution
are not included. 1,908 entries arranged geographically.
Includes journal articles, University of the West Indies
publications, conference proceedings, theses. Crop and general
(topical) indexes provided. Library locations, with call numbers
if available, are given.

CARDI-T

Crop Science
459a   ASENJO, CONRADO F.
        Acerola / Conrado F. Asenjo. – p.371-374
        In Tropical and subtropical fruits : composition,
properties and uses / Steven Nagy and Philip E. Shaw. –
Westport, Conn. : AVI Pub. Co., 1980
        Bibliography: p.371-374

Alphabetical author listing of items mainly on the
ascorbic acid content of the West Indian cherry.

UWI-T

460   BRATHWAITE, CHELSTON W.D.
        A bibliography of plant disease investigations in the
Commonwealth Caribbean, 1880-1980 / prepared by Chelston W.D.
Brathwaite, Miranda Alcock and Rawwida Soodeen. – St.
Augustine, Trinidad : Inter-American Institute for Cooperation
in Agriculture and the University of the West Indies, 1981. –
vi, 280p. – (Miscellaneous publication ; no.328)

3,024 entries arranged alphabetically by author for all
the territories of the Commonwealth Caribbean. A general index,
a geographic index and an index of diseases arranged by crop are
provided.

UWI-T

461   Caribbean Agricultural Research and Development Institute
      (CARDI)
          Root crop investigations in the Caribbean : a bibliography
      / Glenys Barker. - [St. Augustine, Trinidad] : Caribbean
      Agricultural Research and Development Institute, 1981. - 33p.
      - (CARDI/USAID Project 538-0015)

          Arranged under headings : General (52 items) ; Aroids (41
      items) ; Cassava (28 items) ; Irish potato (24 items) ; Sweet
      potato (62 items) ; Yam (109 items). Includes D.T.A. reports
      and A.I.C.T.A. theses, M.Sc. and Ph.D. theses lodged in the
      U.W.I. library, St. Augustine.

CARDI-T

462   Caribbean Industrial Research Institute (CARIRI). Technical
      Information Services
          Storage and handling of fruits and vegetables in the
      Caribbean basin : a bibliography / compiled by Sharon Laurent.
      - St. Augustine, Trinidad : Information Service for Industry,
      Technical Information Services, CARIRI, 1977. - 20p.

          References are arranged in two sections, first by the
      fruits and vegetables individually followed by a general section,
      and secondly by authors alphabetically. Includes sections on
      avocado, banana, yam, plantain and mangoes.

UWI-T

463   CHAPMAN, T.
          List of completed research work carried out at the Imperial
      College of Tropical Agriculture on crop husbandry : Part I -
      Short term crops / T. Chapman and E. Herrera. - p.489-503
          In Journal of the Agricultural Society of Trinidad and
      Tobago. - Vol.61, no.4 (1961)
          Also reprinted in: Society paper no.890

          First part of a bibliography in thirteen sections.
      Comprises published papers and unpublished theses on brassicas,
      castor oil, cotton, fibre crops, egg-plant, ground nuts,
      legumes - general, maize, sorghum and millets. Within each
      section published papers and unpublished theses are listed
      separately in alphabetical author order.

UWI-T

464   CHAPMAN, T.
        List of completed research work carried out at Imperial
      College of Tropical Agriculture on crop husbandry : Part I -
      Short term crops / T. Chapman and E. Herrera. - p.72-91
      In Journal of the Agricultural Society of Trinidad and
      Tobago. - Vol.62, no.1 (1962)
        Also reprinted in: Society paper no.890

        Continuation of the bibliography begun in Ref.no.463.
      Published papers and unpublished theses on rice, sweet potato,
      tobacco, tomatoes and lettuce and yams, tannias and dasheen are
      listed.

                                                                  UWI-T

465   Commonwealth Agricultural Bureaux
        Plant pathology in the Caribbean / Commonwealth Agri-
      cultural Bureaux - Farnham Royal, Slough : Commonwealth
      Agricultural Bureaux, 1980. - 1291-1321p. - (Annotated
      bibliography CAB/157)

        Comprises items located in a retrospective search of
      Dialog data base. Covers diseases of citrus, sugar-cane, banana,
      coconut, beans, cacao, yam, pangola grass, rice, maize, papaya,
      ground-nut, tannia.

                                                                  UWI-T

465a FISHER, HERBERT H.
        Bibliografía parcial de investigación sobre malezas y su
      control para América del Sur, América Central, el Caribe y
      México 1942-1972 = A partial bibliography of weed research and
      control publications for South and Central America, the
      Caribbean and Mexico 1942-1972 = Bibliografia parcial sobre
      a pesquisa e o controle de ervas daninhas para America do Sul,
      America Central, Caraibas e Mexico 1942-1972 / co-ordinated
      and edited by Herbert H. Fisher and Eduardo Locatelli. -
      Corvallis, Ore. : International Plant Protection Center,
      Oregon State University, 1974. - x, 179p. - (Report 74-3)

        Arranged by country including Guyana (9 entries),
      Jamaica (55 entries), Trinidad & Tobago (85 entries), Caribbean -
      general (40 entries) and Central America including Belize. Under
      each country entries are subdivided into four categories : (1)
      Taxonomy, (2) Biology, (3) Weed Control & Physiology, (4)
      Poisonous Plants. No indexes.

                                                                  UWI-T

466   Imperial College of Tropical Agriculture
        Publications on cacao / Imperial College of Tropical
      Agriculture. - St. Augustine, Trinidad : Imperial College of
      Tropical Agriculture, 1960. - 10p.
        Mimeographed

A sales list of available publications of ICTA which
subsequently became the Faculty of Agriculture, U.W.I.

UWI-T

467 LEDIN, R. BRUCE
The Barbados or West Indian cherry / R. Bruce Ledin. -
p.1-28
In University of Florida Agricultural Experiment Station
bulletin. - 594 (1958)
Bibliography: p.25-28

40 items listed alphabetically by author mainly concerned
with the propagation, vitamin and ascorbic content and the
processing of the West Indian cherry.

UWI-T

468 United States. Department of Agriculture. Library
The banana industry in tropical America, with special
reference to the Caribbean area, 1930-1940 : a selected list
of references / compiled by Annie M. Hannay. - Washington,
D.C. : United States Department of Agriculture Library,
Bureau of Agricultural Economics, 1941. - 30p. - (Economic
Library lists ; 19)

Ninety-three references in alphabetical author order with
a subject index.

UWI-T

469 University of the West Indies (Cave Hill). Institute of
Social and Economic Research (Eastern Caribbean)
The Caribbean sugar industry : a select bibliography /
compiled by Audine Wilkinson. - Cave Hill, Barbados :
Institute of Social and Economic Research (Eastern Caribbean),
University of the West Indies, 1976. - xv, 87p. - (Occasional
bibliography series ; no.4)

Includes sections on the Caribbean in general, Cuba, the
Dominican Republic and the French Caribbean as well as the
Commonwealth territories individually. Under each country
entries are subdivided by such subjects as sugar production,
trade, technology, by-products and commissions, conferences,
symposia. Journal articles are included and location at one of
six libraries/repositories in Barbados indicated for each entry.

UWI-T

470 University of the West Indies (St. Augustine). Department of
Biological Sciences
A preliminary list of literature on pigeon pea (Cajanus
cajan L. Millsp.) plant pathology / R.F. Barnes. - St.
Augustine, Trinidad : Department of Biological Sciences, 1973.
- 23p. - (Bulletin ; no.1)

114

Prepared in the context of the Grain Legume Research
Programme of the Faculty of Agriculture the list includes brief
abstracts. Entries arranged alphabetically by author.

UWI-T

471 University of the West Indies (St. Augustine). Library
Bibliography on the banana / University of the West Indies
Library. - [St. Augustine, Trinidad : Library, University of
the West Indies], [197-?]. - 3 leaves
Typescript

40 references to books and articles mainly on the West
Indies banana industry.

UWI-T

472 University of the West Indies (St. Augustine). Library
A select bibliography on vegetables and food crops, fruits
and ornamentals ; prepared on the occasion of the American
Society for Horticultural Science, Tropical Region, sixteenth
annual meeting and Caribbean Food Crops Society sixth annual
meeting, July 7-13, 1968 / by Shirley Espinet ... Maritza
Pantin ... and Barbara Comissiong. - St. Augustine, Trinidad :
University of the West Indies Library, 1968. - 26 leaves

A selection of works published and unpublished done at the
Imperial College of Tropical Agriculture and its successor, the
UWI Faculty of Agriculture. Includes unpublished theses and
articles published by members of the faculty. The 174 items
listed cover legumes, lettuce, okra, peppers and egg plant,
tomatoes, bananas, citrus, mangoes, pawpaws, pineapples and
ornamentals.

UWI-T

473 University of the West Indies (St. Augustine). Library
Tropical root crops : a select bibliography ; prepared on
the occasion of the International Symposium on Tropical Root
Crops, 2nd-8th April, 1967 / by Shirley Evelyn ... Barbara
Comissiong ... and Alma Jordan ... . - St. Augustine, Trinidad
University of the West Indies Library, 1967. - 15 leaves

A compilation of works, published and unpublished, done on
tropical root crops at the Imperial College of Tropical Agriculture and its successor, the Faculty of Agriculture of the
University of the West Indies. Includes theses and articles
published by members of the faculty. Arranged under sections :
Aroids, Arrowroot, Potatoes - Irish, Potatoes - Sweet, Yams.

UWI-T

474   Windward Islands Banana Research Scheme
        Chronological list of published and unpublished reports
      and notes / WINBAN. - [Castries, St. Lucia] : Windward Islands
      Banana Research Scheme, 1969. - 9p.

        135 references to reports (some in a series of Research
      Notes), journal articles and many unpublished items produced by
      the Scheme listed in 3 periods : (1) 1959-1963 when the Scheme
      operated from ICTA/UWI in Trinidad, (2) 1963-1966 under WINBAN
      administration, (3) 1966-1969 with a professional staff of more
      than two persons.

                                                                UWI-T

475   Windward Islands Banana Research Scheme (WINBAN)
        Subject list of published and unpublished reports and
      notes / WINBAN. - [Castries, St. Lucia] : Windward Islands
      Banana Research Scheme, [1969?]. - 17p.
        Mimeographed

        Listing of staff publications from the scheme. Issued
      complementary to a chronological list (Ref.no.474) using the same
      item numbers re-arranged under 22 subject areas such as diseases
      of bananas, experimental techniques, fruit quality, nematodes
      and their control and nutrition and fertilizers.

                                                                UWI-T

Economics
476   Food and Agriculture Organization of the United Nations
        Bibliography of food and agricultural marketing (second
      series) : publications in West European languages relating to
      other countries other than the U.S.A. and Canada with summary
      contents / Food and Agriculture Organization of the United
      Nations. - No.1 (1972) - . - Rome : F.A.O., 1972-
        Biannual

        First series covering the period 1950-1969 appeared as
      sets of looseleaf sheets. Entries appear under subject headings :
      (1) Marketing Theory, Research Methodology, Teaching Material;
      (2) Marketing Organization and Costs by areas or commodities;
      (3) Transport, Packing and Initial Processing; (4) Storage and
      Management of Stocks; (5) Grading, Standardization and Quality
      Control; (6) Information, Advisory and other Facilitating
      Services; (7) Market Facilities (assembly, wholesale, retail);
      (8) Marketing Enterprises and Management; (9) Co-operative and
      other voluntary group marketing; (10) Government Participation
      in and Regulation of Marketing. Commodity, geographical and
      author indexes provided. Entries for Caribbean and individual
      countries appear in the geographical index.

                                                                UWI-T

477 McGill University. Department of Geography
        Tropical research : fieldwork and theses / Department of
     Geography. - [Montreal]: Department of Geography, McGill
     University, [196-?]. - 4 leaves
        Mimeographed

        Lists theses and continuing research projects by author
within three geographic groups : (1) Barbados, (2) The Caribbean
Region (other than Barbados) and (3) Guyana. Includes several
land use studies and the wider Caribbean region in its scope.
                                                            UWI-T

478 University of the West Indies (Cave Hill). Institute of Social
     and Economic Research (Eastern Caribbean)
        Agricultural diversification in a small economy : the case
     for Dominica / J.M. Marie. - Cave Hill, Barbados : Institute
     of Social and Economic Research, University of the West Indies,
     1979. - 119p. - (Occasional paper ; no.10)
        Bibliography: p.114-119

        55 references in alphabetical author order to government
reports and serial publications as well as monographs chiefly on
the banana industry and other crops in Dominica and the West
Indies as a whole.
                                                            UWI-T

479 University of the West Indies (St. Augustine). Library
        The economics of the sugar industry in the West Indies /
     Library, University of the West Indies. - [St. Augustine,
     Trinidad : The University of the West Indies Library], 1970. -
     8 leaves
        Typescript

        Items which are arranged geographically include articles
from West Indian newspapers and periodicals.
                                                            UWI-T

480 University of the West Indies (St. Augustine). Library
        List of references on small scale farmers in Trinidad and
     Barbados / Library, University of the West Indies. - [St.
     Augustine, Trinidad : Library, University of the West Indies],
     1978. - 2 leaves

        14 references to items held in stock arranged in alpha-
betical author order.
                                                            UWI-T

481   University of Wisconsin (Madison). Land Tenure Center.
      Library
          Agricultural economy of Cuba and the Caribbean : a
      bibliography / Land Tenure Center Library. - Madison, Wisc. :
      Land Tenure Center Library, University of Wisconsin, 1973
                                                              LTCL

482   University of Wisconsin (Madison). Land Tenure Center.
      Library
          Agriculture in the economy of the Caribbean : a biblio-
      graphy of materials dealing with the Caribbean area in the
      Land Tenure Center Library ... / compiled by Teresa Anderson.
      - Madison, Wisc. : Land Tenure Center Library, University of
      Wisconsin, 1974. - 84p. - (Training and methods series ; no.
      24)

          Includes analytical entries for relevant parts of books
      and conference proceedings, journal articles, unpublished reports,
      preprints as well as books arranged under country headings
      alphabetically. Covers all the British, French and Dutch
      territories.
                                                              UWI-T

Indexes
483   AGRINTER (Sistema Interamericano de Información para las
      Ciencias Agrícolas)
          Indice agrícola de América Latina y el Caribe / AGRINTER.
      - Vol.10, no.1 (1975)- . - Turrialba, Costa Rica : Centro
      Interamericano de Documentación e Información Agrícola IICA-
      CIDIA. - 1975-
          Quarterly

          Continuation of Ref.no.484. Literature indexed comprises
      articles in serials, books, technical reports, pamphlets, theses,
      maps, standards, conference papers, meetings etc. published in
      South America, Central America, Mexico and the Caribbean. Data
      contributed by national participating centres (including
      Jamaica and Trinidad and Tobago) and by IICA-CIDIA, the
      co-ordinating centre of AGRINTER. Information is organized
      according to the procedures of the International Information
      System for the Agricultural Sciences and Technology - AGRIS.
      Non-Spanish language material is translated into Spanish and
      adapted where necessary. Index is arranged in three sections :
      (1) Literature Indexed, which is categorized according to the
      table of contents, (2) Analytical Index (KWIC) and (3) Author
      Index.
                                                              UWI-T

484   AIBDA (Asociación Interamericana de Bibliotecarios y
      Documentalistas Agrícolas)

Bibliografía agrícola Latinoamericana y del Caribe /
AIBDA. - Vol.1, no.1-vol.9, no.4. - Turrialba, Costa Rica :
AIBDA, 1966-1974
        Formerly: Bibliografía agrícola Latinoamericana

        Index to the literature of agriculture and the allied
sciences published in Latin America and Caribbean countries and
in other parts of the world relevant to agriculture in this area.
From 1972 it was based on contributions received from institutions
participating in AGRINTER and received at the library of IICA-
CIDIA, Turrialba. Entries arranged under broad subject headings
include articles in journals, monographs, technical reports,
theses, proceedings of conferences and meetings. Covers the
English-speaking Caribbean. Author and subject indexes.
                                                        UWI-T

485 University of the West Indies (St. Augustine). Library
        CAGRINDEX : abstracts of the agricultural literature of the
     English-speaking Caribbean. - 1979-80 experimental issue /
     compiled by Miranda Alcock. - St. Augustine, Trinidad :
     Library, University of the West Indies. - 1980
        To be published annually

        Arrangement and bibliographic format based on that used in
AGRINDEX Classified section with broad subject categories and
a commodity index. Includes articles from Tropical Agriculture,
the journal of the Faculty of Agriculture, U.W.I. and items
published in the region and received by the library.
                                                        UWI-T

Livestock Science
  486 University of the West Indies. Department of Livestock Science
        Published papers relating to animal and grassland
     husbandry, 1933 to present date, in chronological order /
     prepared by S.J. Cowlishaw. - [St. Augustine, Trinidad:
     Department of Livestock Science, University of the West Indies],
     [1970]. - 5 leaves
        Mimeographed

        List of 90 items from leading agricultural journals
including Tropical Agriculture and the Journal of the Agricultural
Society of Trinidad and Tobago.
                                                        UWI-T

487 University of the West Indies. Faculty of Agriculture
        Index to articles on animal husbandry in Tropical
     agriculture : journal of the Faculty of Agriculture, 1924-
     1970. - St. Augustine, Trinidad : Faculty of Agriculture,
     U.W.I., 1971. - 11p.
        Mimeographed

Alphabetical author arrangement within broad subject
sections for general items followed by diseases and pests,
nutrition, pastures and management and physiology. Only some
items are of specific West Indian interest.

UWI-T

488   University of the West Indies. Faculty of Agriculture.
      Department of Livestock Science
         A.I.C.T.A. theses and D.T.A. reports of research work
      carried out in Trinidad at I.C.T.A. and U.W.I. on grassland
      and livestock / [prepared by S.J. Cowlishaw]. - [St. Augustine,
      Trinidad : Department of Livestock Science, University of the
      West Indies], [196-?]. - 16 leaves
         Mimeographed

         Listing by title with author and date only under descrip-
      tive subject headings such as dairy farm surveys in Trinidad,
      grass root studies and grazing behaviour studies.

UWI-T

489   WILSON, P.N.
         List of completed research work carried out at the Imperial
      College of Tropical Agriculture on animal and grassland
      husbandry / by P.N. Wilson and E. Herrera. - p.63-86
         In Journal of the Agricultural Society of Trinidad and
      Tobago. - Vol.61, no.1 (1961)
         Also reprinted in: Society paper no.886

         The bibliography lists published papers and unpublished
      theses in sections : Animal Husbandry in general; Dairy Husbandry;
      Poultry Husbandry, Poultry Progeny Testing, Pig Husbandry;
      Grassland; Agronomy and Grassland Husbandry; Grazing Behaviour
      Studies; Feeding of Farm Livestock; Animal Nutrition; Animal
      Physiology and Animal Health. Within each section published
      papers and unpublished theses are listed separately in alpha-
      betical author order.

UWI-T

Soil Science
490   Commonwealth Bureau of Soils
         Soils and agronomy in the Commonwealth Caribbean Islands
      1946-1967 / Commonwealth Bureau of Soils. - Harpenden,
      England : Commonwealth Bureau of Soils, 1968. - 19p. -
      (Annotated bibliography ; 1278)

         106 references.

Ref.no.492,vol.3
p.110

491   Commonwealth Bureau of Soils
        Soils of the Caribbean islands / Commonwealth Bureau of
      Soils (1967-1977). - Harpenden, England : Commonwealth Bureau
      of Soils, 1978. - (Annotated bibliography ; 1932)

        101 references.

                                                                      CBS

492   United States.   Agency for International Development.   Office
      of Agriculture
        Bibliography of soils of the tropics / by Arnold C.
      Orvedal. - Washington, D.C. : Development Support Bureau,
      Office of Agriculture, U.S. Agency for International Develop-
      ment, 1975. - 3v. - (Agricultural technology for developing
      countries technical series bulletin ; no.17)
        Vol.2 : Tropics in general and South America. - 1977. -
      242p. - Vol.3 : Tropics in general, Middle America and West
      Indies. - 1978. - 178p.

        Emphasis on soil geography including some references on
      geology, geomorphology, climate and land use in this context, but
      excluding soil chemistry, soil physics and soil microbiology
      except as relevant to soil geography.   Arranged alphabetically by
      author within geographic headings with texts and maps separately
      listed in each case.   Items on Guyana appear in Vol.2 (p.142-143).
      West Indian Islands are given extensive coverage in Vol.3 in
      groups such as Antigua and Barbuda, Bahamas, the Colony of Turks
      and Caicos Islands, St. Vincent, Carriacou and the Grenadines,
      Dominica and St. Lucia or individually (Barbados, Cayman Islands,
      Jamaica, Trinidad and Tobago).   Items on Belize also appear in
      Vol.2 (p.43-45).

                                                                    UWI-T

493   University of the West Indies.   Department of Soil Science
        Bibliography of soil science and fertilizer agronomy for
      the Commonwealth Caribbean / I.S. Cornforth. - St. Augustine,
      Trinidad : Department of Soil Science, University of the West
      Indies, 1969. - 97p.

        Over 1,100 references to work done in the region,
      collected from various sources and classified by a numerical
      system with a keyword index.

                                                                    UWI-T

Grenada

494 BRIERLEY, JOHN S.
     Small farming in Grenada, West Indies / by John S.
Brierley. - Winnipeg, Canada : Department of Geography,
University of Manitoba, 1974. - xxviii, 308p.
     Bibliography: p.300-308

     Arranged alphabetically. Includes references to agri-
culture in the economy and land use in the West Indies as a whole
with a few unpublished theses and reports as well as journal
articles and books.

                                                      UWI-T

Guyana

495 Guyana. National Science Research Council
     Agricultural research in Guyana, 1920-1977 : a bibliog-
raphy / compiled by C.D. Knee ... and edited / by V.L.
Kallicharan. - Georgetown, Guyana : National Science Research
Council, 1978. - vi, 155p.

     Based on an extensive documentation project with over
1,000 entries. Arranged by AGRIS subject categories with
commodity divisions, the bibliography omits routine extension
literature, progress reports and descriptive material as well as
forestry references. Author, commodity and geographical indexes
included. Categories include agriculture, geography and history,
education, extension and advisory work, plant production,
economics, development and rural sociology, animal production
and aquatic sciences and fisheries.

                                                      UWI-T

496 United States. Agency for International Development
     An annotated bibliography of agricultural development in
Guyana / K.P. Jameson. - Washington, D.C. : Development
Studies Program, U.S.A.I.D., 1977. - 41p. - (General working
document ; no.1)
     Mimeographed

                                                    Benjamin

497 University of the West Indies (St. Augustine). Library
     References to the literature of Guyanese agricultural
research / University of the West Indies Library. - [St.
Augustine, Trinidad : Library, University of the West Indies],
1976. - 2 leaves
     Typescript

     List of 12 items includes periodicals and library
catalogues.

                                                      UWI-T

Crop Science
498 BISESSAR, S.
          Bibliography of rice in Guyana / S.Bisessar. - p.64-68
          In The Farm journal of Guyana. - Vol.27, no.3 (Sept. 1966)

          Arranged alphabetically by author. 81 items covering
     cultivation, pests and diseases, storage problems of rice and
     the industry as a whole. Includes journal articles from Caribbean
     and non-Caribbean sources and theses.
                                                            UWI-T

499 KENNARD, C.P.
          A bibliography of rice in Guyana : 1921-1975 / C.P.
     Kennard. - [S.l. : s.n.], 1975. - 25 leaves
          Typescript

          "Prepared under the auspices of the Guyana Rice Board,
     Research and Extension Division" - Benjamin
                                                            UG

Soil Science
500 Commonwealth Bureau of Soils
          Bibliography on the soils of British Guiana and Suriname
     (1946-1964) / Commonwealth Bureau of Soils. - Harpenden,
     England : Commonwealth Bureau of Soils, [196-?]. - 7p.
          Mimeographed

          38 references to journal articles and monographs in
     inverse chronological order.
                                                            UWI-T

501 Commonwealth Bureau of Soils
          Soils of Guyana, Surinam and French Guyana, 1946-1974 /
     Commonwealth Bureau of Soils. - Harpenden, England :
     Commonwealth Bureau of Soils, 1975. - (Annotated bibliography;
     1776)

          98 references.
                                                            CBS

502 Guyana. Department of Agriculture
          Records of soil survey investigations / by E.J.A. Khan. -
     Georgetown : Department of Agriculture, 1959. - 17p.
                                                       Ref.no.495
                                                       Item no.1029

503 Guyana. Ministry of National Development and Agriculture
      A bibliography of soil science research in Guyana /
     compiled by K. Gordon and H.A.D. Chesney. - [Georgetown,
     Guyana] : Ministry of National Development and Agriculture,
     1973. - 40p.

                                                Ref.no.495
                                                Item no.1028

Jamaica

504 BARKER, G.H.
      Bibliography of literature relating to research and
     development in the agricultural sector of Jamaica, 1959-
     1970 / G.H. Barker. - Kingston : Inter-American Institute of
     Agricultural Science, 1980. - 20 leaves.

                                                    CARDI-T

505 EDWARDS, DAVID
      Report on an economic study of small farming in Jamaica /
     David Edwards. - [Mona, Jamaica] : Institute of Social and
     Economic Research, U.W.I., 1961. - 370p.
      Bibliography : p.350-355

      Arranged alphabetically by author with a separate section
   on government reports.

                                                    UWI-T

506 Jamaica. Ministry of Agriculture and Fisheries. Agricultural
     Planning Unit
      A select bibliography of reference material providing an
     introduction to the study of Jamaican agriculture / by Edgar
     S. Steer. - Kingston, Jamaica : Agricultural Planning Unit,
     Ministry of Agriculture and Fisheries, 1970. - 40p.

      Update of Ref.no.507. Items arranged alphabetically by
   author within six sections : General Studies; Special Studies
   and Reports; Crop Production; Livestock Production; Fishing;
   Annual Reports. Each section further subdivided by topics.

                                                    UWI-T

507 Jamaica. Ministry of Agriculture and Lands. Division of
     Economics and Statistics
      A select bibliography of reference material providing an
     introduction to the study of Jamaican agriculture / by
     Edgar S. Steer. - [Kingston], Jamaica : Division of Economics
     and Statistics, Ministry of Agriculture and Lands, 1963. -
     35 leaves
      Mimeographed

                                                    UWI-T

508   United States Agency for International Development. Bureau
      for Latin America and the Caribbean. Rural Development
      Division
          An annotated bibliography of agricultural development in
      Jamaica / compiled by Frank A. Erickson with assistance from
      Elizabeth B. Erickson. - [Washington, D.C.] : Organisation
      for International Cooperation and Development, U.S. Department
      of Agriculture, Development Planning Group, 1979. - 197p. -
      (Working document series ; Jamaica)

          Covers selected aspects of agriculture only and mostly
      post-1962 material with one of eight library locations in Jamaica
      provided. Some Library of Congress class numbers and U.S. library
      locations also provided. Entries are arranged alphabetically by
      author within 12 broad subject groups including agriculture :
      policy and planning, commodities, extension, education, etc.
      Special classification symbols are assigned to each of these
      groups and each entry is assigned symbols to indicate its subject
      matter. Annotations are critical.
                                                                ECLA-T

Trinidad and Tobago

509   Trinidad and Tobago. Ministry of Agriculture, Lands and
      Fisheries. Central Experiment Station. Library
          A bibliography of publications available for distribution
      compiled on the occasion of the National Agricultural
      Exhibition, 15th-24th September, 1977 / Central Experiment
      Station Library. - [Centeno, Trinidad : Central Experiment
      Station Library], 1977. - 5 leaves

          Alphabetical listing with free publications separated
      from sale items.
                                                                UWI-T

ANTHROPOLOGY

510   CLERMONT, NORMAN
          Bibliographie annotée de l'anthropologie physique des
      Antilles / Norman Clermont. - Fonds St. Jacques, Martinique :
      Centre de Recherches Caraïbes, Université de Montréal, 1972
      [i.e., 1973]. - 51p.

          212 numbered references (annotated in French) to journal
      articles, theses and a few papers on biological aspects of the
      peoples of the wider Caribbean area. Includes such topics as
      anthropometry, genetics, blood groups, dental and growth studies

for different ethnic groups with geographic and theme indexes
and an indication of the country or countries to which each item
refers in the text.

UWI-T

511 GOODWIN, R. CHRISTOPHER
       A selected bibliography in physical anthropology in the
     Caribbean area / by R. Christopher Goodwin and A. Gus Pantel.
     - p.531-540
       In Revista/Review interamericana. - Vol.8, no.3 (Fall
     1978)

       Alphabetical author arrangement in two sections : (1)
     Osteology (79 items), (2) Living Populations (118 items). Covers
     English, Spanish, French and Dutch-speaking Caribbean. Several
     items on Jamaica.

UWI-T

512 MINTZ, SIDNEY W.
       An anthropological approach to the Afro-American past : a
     Caribbean perspective / Sidney W. Mintz [and] Richard Price. -
     Philadelphia : Institute for the Study of Human Issues, 1976.
     - iii, 64p. - (ISHI occasional papers in social change ; 2)
       Bibliography : p.51-64

       Arranged alphabetically by author and chronologically
     under each author. Includes references to the music and other
     cultural aspects of the African diaspora and slave societies in
     the West Indies.

UWI-T

513 PANTEL, A. GUS
       A bibliography of physical anthropology in the Caribbean /
     A. Gus. Pantel. - p.163-177
       In Anuario científico. - Vol.2, no.2 (1977)

       Arranged in two sections : A. Prehistoric Populations;
     B. Living Populations. Entries covering the English, French and
     Spanish Caribbean, are arranged alphabetically by author. The
     items listed are mainly articles from journals.

Ref.no.18
1979

514 ROUSE, IRVING
       The entry of man into the West Indies / edited by Irving
     Rouse. - New Haven, Conn. : Dept. of Anthropology, Yale
     University, 1960. - 26p. - (Yale University publications in
     anthropology ; no.61)
       Bibliography : p.24-26

Bibliography arranged alphabetically by author. Mainly monographs.

UWI-T

Belize

515 LINES, JORGE A.
Anthropological bibliography of aboriginal Guatemala-British Honduras / Jorge A. Lines. - Provisional ed. - San José, Costa Rica : Tropical Science Center, 1967. - xiv, 309p. - (Tropical Science Center occasional paper ; no.6)
British Honduras (Belice) : p.271-285

Title and text in English and Spanish. Includes journal articles and a few entries on natural sciences. Prepared during Associated Colleges of the Midwest Central American Field Program.

UWI-T

515a MCGLYNN, EILEEN A.
Middle American anthropology : directory, bibliography and guide to UCLA library collections / Eileen A. McGlynn. - Los Angeles : UCLA Latin American Center and University Library, 1975. - 131p.

"A reference guide to the library of the University of California, Los Angeles, but also useful as a guide to Mesoamerican anthropology in general."

Ref.no.309a
Item no.679

Trinidad and Tobago

516 NEWSON, LINDA A.
Aboriginal and Spanish colonial Trinidad : a study in culture contact / by Linda Newson. - London : Academic Press, 1976. - 344p.
Bibliography : p.314-332

Lists primary sources (archives, printed documents and contemporary works) separately from secondary sources in alphabetical author order. Extensive references on a wide range of relevant subjects for the study of man in early Trinidad and the West Indies.

UWI-T

ARCHAEOLOGY

517   BULLEN, RIPLEY P.
          Archaeology of Grenada, West Indies / Ripley P. Bullen. -
      Gainesville, Fla. : University of Florida, 1964. - 67, [15]p. -
      (Contributions of the Florida State Museum. Social Sciences ;
      no.11)
          Bibliography : p. 15-67

          A list of 29 items arranged chronologically by author.
      Entries on the English-speaking Caribbean include journal articles
      and theses.

                                                                UWI-T

Bahamas

518   GRANBERRY, T.
          Cultural position of the Bahamas in Caribbean archaeology /
      T. Granberry. - p.133-134
          In American antiquity. - Vol.22 (Oct. 1956).

                                                                Ref.no.5
                                                                1957, p.21

Belize

519   THOMPSON, JOHN ERIC
          Excavations at San José, British Honduras / by John Eric
      Thompson ; with appendix by Anna O. Shepherd. - Washington,
      D.C. : Carnegie Institution, 1939. - xi, 1,202p. - (Carnegie
      Institution. Publication ; no.506)
          References: p.287-290

                                                                Ref.no.5
                                                                p.205

Trinidad and Tobago

520   BULLBROOK, J.A.
          On the excavation of a shell mound at Palo Seco, Trinidad,
      B.W.I. / J.A. Bullbrook. - New Haven, [Conn.] : Yale
      University Press, 1953. - 114p. - (Yale University publica-
      tions in anthropology ; no.50)
          Bibliography: p.112-114

          Consists of 63 items dealing mainly with archaeology in
      Trinidad but including a few items on British Guiana, the Lesser
      Antilles, Puerto Rico and Martinique. General histories of
      Trinidad and the West Indies are also listed.

                                                                UWI-T

ARCHITECTURE

Guyana

521   Guyana. Public Free Library
          Architecture in Guyana / Public Free Library. -
      Georgetown, (Guyana) : Public Free Library, 1971. - 1 leaf
          Typescript

                                                          NLG

ART

522   CHEVRETTE, VALERIE
          Annotated bibliography of the precolumbian art and
      archeology of the West Indies / Valerie Chevrette. - New
      York : Library, Museum of Primitive Art, 1971. - 18p. -
      (Primitive art bibliographies ; no.9)

                                                        UWI-J

Belize

522a KENDALL, AUBYN
          The art and archaeology of pre-Columbian Middle America :
      annotated bibliography of works in English / Aubyn Kendall. -
      Boston : G.K. Hall, 1977. - 324p.

          "Containing 2,147 annotated entries, this compilation
      represents one of the most important bibliographical tools on
      the Maya and other pre-Columbian peoples of Middle America. The
      bibliography is organized alphabetically by authors, including
      both books and periodical articles. An ample subject index,
      p.315-24, many works dealing with the Belize region."

                                                    Ref.no.309a
                                                    Item no.680

BIOGRAPHY

Collective

523   Carnegie Free Library
          West Indian authors : a select bio-bibliography / Carnegie
      Free Library. - San Fernando, Trinidad : Carnegie Free
      Library, 1980. - 28p.

Mimeographed

Listing of the works of 25 writers based on the library's
collection. Items arranged chronologically under author.
Biography of each author is provided.

UWI-T

524 Guyana. Public Library
        Commonwealth Caribbean writers : a bibliography / compiled
     by Stella E. Merriman and Joan Christiani. - Georgetown,
     Guyana : Public Library, 1970. - iv, 98p.

        A listing of works by and on L. Edward Brathwaite, Jan
     Carew, Wilson Harris, John Hearne, George Lamming, Vic Reid,
     Philip Sherlock, Sylvia Wynter. Includes addresses and forewords
     to publications, reviews of works, biographical sketches and
     information on portraits of the writers.

UWI-T

525 HERDECK, DONALD
        Caribbean writers : a bio-bibliographical-critical
     encyclopedia / edited by Donald E. Herdeck. - Washington,
     D.C. : Three Continents Press, 1979. - xiv, 943p.
        Associate editors: Maurice A. Lubin, John Figueroa,
     Dorothy Alexander Figueroa, José Alcantara Almánzar. General
     editor: Margaret Laniak-Herdeck.

        Bibliography is divided into four sections : v.1 :
     Anglophone Literature from the Caribbean (p.17-259) - v.2 :
     Francophone Literature from the Caribbean (p.261-547) - v.3 :
     Literature from the Netherlands Antilles and Surinam (p.549-595)
     - v.4 : Spanish Language Literature from the Caribbean (p.597-
     943). The main work is preceded by an essay on West Indian
     writing, followed by a list of writers from the West Indies (by
     country) and a list of writers born outside of the West Indies
     (by country). Each volume consists of entries for each author
     arranged alphabetically and containing biographical information,
     lists of writings arranged by genre and biographical/critical
     sources. There are also sections on West Indian Literature and
     Culture : Bibliographies ; The West Indies : Critical Studies ;
     and West Indian Literature : General Anthologies and Collections.

UWI-T

526 KIDDER, FREDERICK E.
        Hemispheric role of the Caribbean political leaders : a
     bibliography of current biography / Frederick E. Kidder. -
     p.193-202
        In The Caribbean: its hemispheric role / edited by A.
     Curtis Wilgus. - Gainesville, [Fla.] : University of Florida
     Press, 1967. - (Caribbean conference series 1 ; v.17)

A bibliographic essay emphasizing the relevance and importance of biography in the history of the twentieth-century Caribbean with a list of prominent leaders in the region.

UWI-T

527   Royal Commonwealth Society
Biography catalogue of the Library of the Royal Commonwealth Society / by Donald H. Simpson. - London : The Royal Commonwealth Society, 1961. - 511p.

Lists all the library's biographical holdings including analytics for periodical articles, accounts of the work of artists and writers and studies of individual portraiture. Arranged in two sections : (1) Individual Biographies and (2) Collective Biography and country indexes. The former includes entries for such prominent West Indians as Marcus Garvey, Arthur Andrew Cipriani and Learie Constantine, with dates of birth and death, full references to biographies in the collection and a brief description of their spheres of activity and contributions made. The second section includes the Caribbean (p.420-422) with chronological references to collective bibliographies followed by a listing of the distinguished personalities on whom information is included.

UWI-T

528   University of the West Indies (St. Augustine). Library
Creative writers in Trinidad and Tobago : a bibliography prepared on the occasion of the formal opening of the John F. Kennedy Library, 30 January, 1970 / by Maritza Pantin ... and Diane Hunte ... . - St. Augustine, Trinidad : University of the West Indies Library, 1970. - 34p.

The list covers critical works on each author as well as the author's individual works; both monographs and periodical literature are included.

UWI-T

529   VINSON, JAMES
Contemporary dramatists / edited by James Vinson. - 2nd ed. - London : St. James Press ; New York : St. Martin's Press, 1977. - xiv, 1088p.

Listings include Douglas Archibald, Mustapha Matura, Errol Hill (Trinidad); Barry Reckord (Jamaica); and Derek Walcott (St. Lucia). Entry for each dramatist consists of a biography, a bibliography, a comment by the dramatist on his plays if he chose to make one, and a signed critical essay on his work.

UWI-T

530   VINSON, JAMES
        Contemporary novelists / James Vinson. - 2nd ed. -
      London : St. James Press ; New York : St. Martin's Press,
      1976. - xvii, 1636p.

        Listings include Michael Anthony, C.L.R. James, Earl
      Lovelace, Shiva Naipaul, V.S. Naipaul, Samuel Selvon (Trinidad),
      Austin C. Clarke, George Lamming (Barbados), John Hearne, Vic
      Reid, Andrew Salkey (Jamaica), O.R. Dathorne, Wilson Harris,
      Christopher Nicole, Edgar Mittelholzer (Guyana), Jean Rhys
      (Dominica). Location of manuscript collections given.
                                                              UWI-T

531   VINSON, JAMES
        Contemporary poets / edited by James Vinson. - 2nd ed. -
      London : St. James Press ; New York : St. Martin's Press,
      1975. - xv, 1849p.

        Included in the listings for about 1,000 poets are entries
      for 9 West Indian poets : Edward Brathwaite, Martin Carter,
      Frank Collymore, John Figueroa, Wilson Harris, A.L. Hendriks,
      Edward Lucie-Smith, A.J. Seymour and Derek Walcott. Each entry
      consists of a biography, a full bibliography (including works
      other than poetry), a comment by the poet on his work if he
      chose to make one, and a signed critical essay on his work.
      Gives locations of authors' manuscript collections.
                                                              UWI-T

Individual

532   Author bibliography of works by Douglas Taylor. - [S.l. :
      s.n.], [1960?]
        Mimeographed

        Using the Handbook of Latin American Studies 1936-1959 as
      its source, the bibliography lists works mainly of anthropological/
      linguistic interest and centred around the Dominica Caribs.
                                                                TCL

533   Bibliography of Daniel J. Crowley. - [S.l. : s.n.], [196-?]. -
      4 leaves
        Typescript

        51 references to published and unpublished articles
      include West Indian and African interest material (especially
      Bahamian, St. Lucian and Trinidadian) - carnival, folklore,
      ethnomusicology, anthropology.
                                                              UWI-T

534 CAMERON, NORMAN E.
     Guide to the published works of a Guyanese author and
     playwright / by Norman E. Cameron. - Georgetown, [Guyana] :
     Labour Advocate Printery, 1966. - 47p.

     Covers a period of almost 40 years.

                                                                              UG

535 CAMPBELL, H.
     A selective bibliography of works by Walter Rodney / H.
     Campbell. - Brighton : The Author, [1981]. - 3p.

                                                                             ICS

536 Carnegie Free Library. West Indian Reference Section
     Dr. Eric Eustace Williams 1911-1981 : a listing of the
     library's holdings of works by and about Dr. Williams /
     Carnegie Free Library. - San Fernando, Trinidad : Carnegie
     Free Library, 1981. - 12p.
     Mimeographed
     Cover title

     85 items under headings : Books, Addresses, Articles,
     Related Material, Periodicals, Review Articles, Information
     Files.

                                                                           UWI-T

537 CRONON, E. DAVID
     Black Moses : the story of Marcus Garvey / E. David
     Cronon ; with a foreword by John Hope Franklin. - Madison,
     Wisc. : University of Wisconsin Press, 1969. - 278p.
     Bibliography: p.227-236

     A description of the primary and secondary sources
     followed by a list of items arranged alphabetically. Included
     are unpublished theses and articles in various journals.

                                                                           UWI-T

538 DAVIS, LENWOOD G.
     Marcus Garvey : an annotated bibliography / compiled by
     Lenwood G. Davis and Janet L. Sims. - Westport, Conn. :
     Greenwood Press, 1980. - 192p.

     Contains references to books and articles by and about
     Marcus Garvey.

                                                                             ICS

539 An exhibition of publications by Dr. Eric Williams at the
     Trinidad Hilton (Ballroom) on Thursday, 27th August, 1970 and
     continuing at Stephens Bookroom from Saturday, 29th August
     to Saturday, 12th September. - [S.l. : s.n.], 1970. - 4
     leaves
     Mimeographed

Listing similar to Ref.no.560 with 104 items listed in
title order with date of publication and a format description for
leaflets, pamphlets, etc. Cooperative input by the National
Archives, Central Library of Trinidad and Tobago, Trinidad Public
Library, P.N.M. Publishing Company and Stephens Book Department.

UWI-T

540   FAIRBANKS, CAROL
        Black American fiction : a bibliography / by Carol
      Fairbanks and Eugene A. Engeldinger. - Metuchen, N.J. ;
      London : The Scarecrow Press, 1978. - 351p.
        Bibliography on Claude McKay: p.198-202

        155 items arranged under headings : Novels, Short
Fiction, Biography and Criticism, Reviews.

UWI-T

541   FARRIER, FRANCIS QUAMINA
        List of plays written by Francis Quamina Farrier. -
      [Georgetown, Guyana : F.Q. Farrier], 1971. - 1 , 5p.
        Mimeographed

        Chronological listing. Includes synopsis and cast for
each play and a biographical sketch of the author.

NLG

542   FAX, ELTON C.
        Garvey ; the story of a pioneer black nationalist /
      Elton C. Fax. - New York : Dodd, Mead, 1972. - xxii, 305p.
        Bibliography: p.291-296

        Consists of four sections : Books, Unpublished
Manuscripts, Magazines and Pamphlets, and Newspapers. Apart
from general works on black nationalism in Africa and America it
contains several items on Garvey and Garveyism.

UWI-T

543   GOLDSTRAW, IRMA E.
        Derek Walcott : a bibliography of published poems with
      dates of publication and variant versions, 1944-1979 / Irma
      E. Goldstraw. - St. Augustine, Trinidad : Research and
      Publications Committee, University of the West Indies, 1979. -
      43p.

        Listings indicate both the source of first publication and
variant versions for all poems up to March 1979. Arranged in
sections devoted to individual anthologies followed by listings
of those poems published only in journals and unpublished poems
broadcast on the BBC. A list of periodicals and newspapers
cited is provided with addresses and an index to titles of books
and poems with some first lines also included.

UWI-T

134

544   GREEN, CAROL
        Claude McKay 1890-1948 : a bibliography / Carol Green. -
Huntington, W.V. : James E. Morrow Library, Marshall University,
1973. - 4p.

                                                            Wasserman
                                                            p.171

545   Guyana. National Library
        A.J. Seymour : a bibliography / compiled by Joan
Christiani. - Georgetown, Guyana : National Library, 1974. -
vii, 110p.
        Mimeographed

        Arranged in two main sections : Works by A.J. Seymour,
and Works on A.J. Seymour. The first section includes addresses,
articles, book reviews and creative writing. The second is
devoted to criticisms of the author's works, reviews and
biographical sketches.

                                                            UWI-T

546   Guyana. Public Free Library
        Edgar Austin Mittelholzer, 1909-1965 / Public Free
Library. - [Georgetown], Cuyana : Public Free Library, 1968. -
[23], 13p.
        Mimeographed
        Cover title

        This bibliography preceded by copies of manuscript
tributes, was published for an exhibition at the Public Free
Library during Guyana Week, 1968. Includes book reviews,
biographical sketches and articles on the author as well as a
listing of his works.

                                                            UWI-T

547   HAMNER, ROBERT D.
        Critical perspectives on V.S. Naipaul / edited by Robert
D. Hamner. - Washington, D.C. : Three Continents Press, 1977. -
300p.
        Annotated bibliography: p.263-298

        Annotated and expanded version of Ref.no.548.

                                                            UWI-T

547a HAMNER, ROBERT
        Mythological aspects of Derek Walcott's drama / Robert
Hamner. - p.35-58.
        In Ariel. - Vol.8, no.3 (July 1977)

Note 11 at the end of the article (p.57) lists 21 plays
arranged in chronological order. Some of the dates are aproximate
while others are the dates of the latest versions of plays which
were written earlier.

UWI-T

548 HAMNER, ROBERT D.
V.S. Naipaul : a selected bibliography / Robert D. Hamner.
- p.36-44
In Journal of commonwealth literature. - Vol.10, no.1
(August 1975)

The listing is arranged in two main sections: Primary
Sources and Secondary Sources. The first is subdivided into (a)
books in order of publication and (b) articles and stories by
Naipaul appearing in collections or serial publications. Secondary
sources list (a) book reviews in order of publication of the
books and (b) books and articles with exact page references.

UWI-T

549 HELMREICH, WILLIAM B.
Afro-Americans and Africa : black nationalism at the
crossroads / compiled by William B. Helmreich. - Westport,
Conn. : Greenwood Press, 1977. - xxxiii, 74p. - (African
Bibliographic Center. Special bibliographic series, new
series ; no.3)

Items arranged in two parts : (1) General Bibliography
of Works on Afro-Americans and Africans and (2) Afro-Americans
and Africa : a Selected Bibliography. The first part is
divided into several sections one of which is devoted to Marcus
Garvey and comprises 17 items. A few items on Marcus Garvey
appear in the second part.

UWI-T

550 Institute of Jamaica. West India Reference Library
Marcus Mosiah Garvey, 1887-1940 : a bibliography /
[compiled by] A. Silvera. - [Kingston, Jamaica] : West India
Reference Library, Institute of Jamaica, 1975. - 27, [1]p.

A list of holdings of material at the Institute of Jamaica
West India Reference Library. Entries are arranged under broad
subject headings and include newspaper articles. Updates
Ref.no.551.

UWI-T

551 Institute of Jamaica. West India Reference Library
Marcus Mosiah Garvey, 1887-1940 : a reading list of
printed material in the West India Reference Library / compiled
by Audrey Leigh. - [Kingston, Jamaica] : West India Reference
Library, Institute of Jamaica, 1973. - [1], 13p.

136

Mimeographed

Items which include books, pamphlets, microfilms and
manuscripts are arranged under subject headings : Bibliography,
Biography, Garvey's Writings and Publications, Garveyism and
Black Consciousness. Selected articles from Jamaican newspapers
are also listed.

UWI-T

552   JACOBS, FRED RUE
        Jean Rhys : a bibliography / Fred Rue Jacobs. - Keene,
     Calif. : Loop Press, 1979. - 32p.

        Entries arranged under headings : Works by Jean Rhys (33
     items), Translations by Jean Rhys (4 items), Works about Jean
     Rhys (63 items), Selected Reviews (48 items). Description of
     manuscript material reprinted from : Stratford's "The Arts
     Council Collection of Modern Literary Manuscripts" is included.

UWI-T

553   LA GUERRE, JOHN GAFFAR
        Cyril Lionel Robert James, 1901- : an annotated biblio-
     graphy / by John Gaffar La Guerre. - [St. Augustine, Trinidad :
     University of the West Indies], 1971. - 11 leaves
        Mimeographed

        A bio-bibliography. Eight pages of text interwoven with
     bibliographic references in a brief unfolding of James' activities
     from the age of 20. Includes 3½ page list of works at the end
     which are not repeated in the text while others in text are
     omitted here. Not all references are full.

UWI-T

554   List of books by Dr. Eric Williams on display at Stephens,
     Todd and Fogarty's Ltd. - [Port of Spain, Trinidad : Stephens
     Bookstore], 1969. - 5p.
        Typescript

        A list prepared on the occasion of the formal launching of
     the author's "From Columbus to Castro." Alphabetical title
     listing of 77 items - lectures, speeches and books - with one of
     the following three locations : the National Archives, the
     Central Library or the Bookstore at which the display took
     place.

TCL

554a LÓPEZ, MANUEL D.
        Claude McKay / compiled by Manuel D. López. - p.128-134
        In Bulletin of bibliography and magazine notes. - Vol.29,
     no.4 (Oct.-Dec. 1972)

Arranged in two parts : Works by McKay and Works about
McKay. The first part covers Autobiography (5 items), Poems in
Periodicals and Books (44 items), Novels (3 items), Poems-Books
(4 items), Short Stories (1 item), Other Works (2 items),
Reviews (10 items), Additional Sources comprising phonograph
records (2 items) and Manuscript Collections in the Schomburg
Collection of Negro Literature and History. Arrangement in
chronological order within each section. Part II lists items
under Bibliography (14 items), Obituaries (9 items), Reviews
with sub-sections - Autobiography (13 items), Novels (52 items),
Poetry (25 items), Short Stories (Collected) (11 items), Other
Works (10 items), Critical Studies and Comments (16 items);
Unpublished Works (2 items).

UWI-T

555 MARTIN, TONY
       Race first : the ideological and organizational struggles
    of Marcus Garvey and the Universal Negro Improvement
    Association / Tony Martin. - London : Greenwood Press, 1976. -
    421p. - (Contributions in Afro-American and African studies ;
    no.19)
       Bibliography : p.375-395

       An introductory essay on sources is followed by (1)
articles, books and pamphlets, (2) phonograph records and extant
newspapers and magazines published by the Garveys (Marcus and
Amy), followed by a list of manuscript and archival collections
and newspaper clipping collections. Secondary sources of all
kinds are then listed in a single alphabetical sequence with a
final listing of eight newspapers and journals not previously
mentioned.

UWI-T

556 MELLOWN, ELGIN W.
       A bibliography of the writings of Jean Rhys with a
    selected list of reviews and other critical writings / Elgin
    W. Mellown. - p.179-202
       In World literature written in English. - Vol.16, no.1
    (Apr. 1977)

       Arranged in sections : (2) Books by Jean Rhys, (b) Books
with Contributions by Jean Rhys, (c) Periodicals with Contributions by Jean Rhys, (d) Translations by Jean Rhys, followed by
a section on Selected Critical Studies of Jean Rhys consisting
of periodical and newspaper articles. Listings of works by the
author describe the British and American first editions and give
an account of subsequent editions and impressions. Reviews of
each edition are included.

UWI-T

557 QUESTEL, VICTOR
      Trinidad Theatre Workshop : a bibliography / Victor
      Questel. - p.53-59
      In Kairi (1976)

      Comprises a chronological listing of Walcott's plays with
publication and performance dates, historical data relating to
dates and places of performance of stage productions of the
Trinidad Theatre Workshop since 1959, reviews by Derek Walcott
appearing in the Trinidad Guardian and Sunday Guardian, interviews with Derek Walcott and articles and references by and about
Derek Walcott in relation to the evolution of the Trinidad
Theatre Workshop.

                                                                UWI-T

558 QUESTEL, VICTOR
      Walcott's hack's hired prose : a bibliography of Derek
      Walcott's articles on architecture, sculpture and painting
      while a critic for the Trinidad Guardian / Victor Questel. -
      p.64-67
      In Kairi (1978)

      Items which are listed chronologically are annotated.
                                                                UWI-T

559 STANTON, ROBERT J.
      A bibliography of modern British novelists / Robert J.
      Stanton. - Troy, N.Y. : Whitson, 1978. - 2v.
      Bibliography of Jean Rhys : p.753-769
                                                            Ref.no.552
                                                                p.15

560 Trinidad and Tobago. Central Library. West Indian Reference
      Section
      A list of books written by Dr. Eric Williams, Prime
      Minister of Trinidad and Tobago ; compiled from the stock of
      the West Indian Reference Section ... . - Port of Spain :
      Central Library, 1968. - 4 leaves
      Typescript

      Includes journal articles, official addresses and other
locally published items as well as his standard works with
foreign imprints.

                                                                  TCL

561 [Trinidad and Tobago. Ministry of Health. Medical Library]
      J. Lennox Pawan 1887-1957 : a chronological bibliography,
      preliminary list / compiled and prepared by the Medical
      Librarian and Staff, General Hospital, Port of Spain [for]
      8th Annual Lennox Pawan Memorial Lecture, Thursday, 20th
      November, 1969... . - Port of Spain : Government Printery,
      1969. - 2p.

22 items in chronological order including items of
interest to medical research in Trinidad especially on the
vampire bat and rabies.

UWI-T

562 Trinidad and Tobago. Ministry of Health. Medical Library
         List of publications : Michael H. Beaubrun / Medical
     Library. - [Port of Spain, Trinidad : Medical Library]
     [196-?]. - 4p.

     48 items which are arranged chronologically include
articles, conference papers and addresses.

UWI-T

563 Trinidad and Tobago. Ministry of Health. Medical Library
         Selected writings of Mr. Rodney Maingot, F.R.C.S., F.R.S.
     during the period 1957-1973 / prepared by Medical Library
     staff for "the Inaugural Schering Corporation Lecture,"
     Tuesday, 13th January 1976. - Port of Spain : Medical Library,
     General Hospital, 1976. - 3 leaves.

     Lists 17 items not specifically of Caribbean interest
appearing in medical journals.

UWI-T

564 University of Guyana. Library
         Theodore Wilson Harris : a select list of works and
     criticism / Library, University of Guyana - [Turkeyen,
     Guyana] : University of Guyana Library, 1978. - 9p.
         Mimeographed

     Comprising items held in the University Library, the
bibliography includes novels, short stories, articles and reviews
by the author as well as works about him.

UWI-T

565 University of the West Indies (St. Augustine). Library
         List of titles by (or edited by) Eric Williams in the
     U.W.I. (St. Augustine Collection). - [St. Augustine, Trinidad :
     Library, The University of the West Indies], 1969. - 3 leaves.
         Typescript

     Includes monographs, speeches and newspaper articles.

UWI-T

566 WILLIAMS, D.
         Giglioli in Guyana, 1922-1972 / D. Williams. - Georgetown :
     National History and Arts Council, 1973. - 68, 16p. - (Library
     of biography ; no.1)

Biographical notes, and published work of Giglioli (p.69-84).

Benjamin

567 WILLIAMS, DANIEL T.
The perilous road of Marcus Garvey : a bibliography and some correspondence / compiled by Daniel T. Williams
In Eight negro bibliographies / compiled by Daniel T. Williams. - New York : Kraus Reprint, 1970.

Ref.no.550
p.1

568 WREN, M.
List of articles and publications written by Dr. George Giglioli / M. Wren. - p.1-7
In Guyana medical science library bulletin. - Vol.3, no.2 (1 Sept. 1972)

Benjamin

BIOLOGY

569 WESTERMAN, J.H.
Nature preservation in the Caribbean : a review of literature on the destruction and preservation of flora and fauna in the Caribbean area / by J.H. Westerman. - Utrecht : Foundation for Scientific Research in Surinam and the Netherlands Antilles, 1953. - 106p.

Literature of a predominantly local nature appears in the text while that of a more general nature is listed in the Selected Bibliography (p.104-106). Includes material on the English-speaking Caribbean as a whole and on Trinidad and Tobago, the Bahama Islands, Jamaica and Dependencies, British Guiana, British Honduras, Barbados and the Leeward and Windward Islands specifically.

UWI-T

Bahamas

570 Bibliography of the natural history of the Bahama Islands / Gillis, R. Byrne and W. Harrison. - [Washington, D.C.] : Smithsonian Institution, 1975. - (Atoll research bulletin ; no.191)

Ref.no.751
p.16

Bermuda

571 COLE, GEORGE WATSON
     Bermuda and the Challenger expedition : a bibliography
     giving a summary of the scientific results obtained by that
     expedition at and near Bermuda in 1873 / George Watson Cole. –
     Boston : [s.n.], 1901. – 15, [1] p.

     Printed for private distribution. 50 references.
                                                          Ref.no.4
                                                          Vol.1, p.745

Guyana

572 EIGENMANN, C.H.
     The freshwater fishes of British Guiana, including a study
     of the ecological groupings of species, and the relation of
     the fauna of the plateau to that of the lowlands / C.H.
     Eigenmann. – Pittsburgh : Carnegie Institute, 1912. – xx,
     578p. – (Memoirs of the Carnegie Museum ; vol.8)
     Bibliography : p.530–554

                                                                 LC

573 GOODLAND, J.R.
     The ecology of Guyana : a bibliography of environmental
     resources / J.R. Goodland and P. Strum. – Monticello, [Ill.] :
     Vance Bibliographies, 1978. – 44p. – (Public administration
     series : bibliography ; P.61)

                                                           Benjamin

574 RODWAY, JAMES
     The "Schomburghs" in Guiana / James Rodway. – p.1–29
     In Timehri. – Vol.3 (New series) (1889)
     Bibliography : p.25–29

     List of the principal books and articles written by Sir
     Robert Schomburgh comprising 42 items arranged chronologically.
     Mainly devoted to the flora and fauna of British Guiana.
                                                              UWI-T

575 University of Guyana
     Bibliography of phytogeography, plant ecology and related
     subjects in Guyana / Alan Cooper. – Turkeyen, [Guyana] :
     Department of Biology, University of Guyana, 1974 . – 17p.

     References to journal articles and monographs in alpha-
     betical author order on a wide variety of topics in agriculture
     and related biological sciences in two sections : (1) Guyana,
     (2) Other Countries.
                                                              UWI-T

Trinidad and Tobago

576 Trinidad and Tobago. Central Library. West Indian
     Reference Section
          List of books on the flora and fauna of Trinidad and
     Tobago / West Indian Reference Section, Central Library. -
     [Port of Spain, Trinidad] : Central Library, 1963. - 2 leaves
          Typescript

          10 titles in alphabetical author order.

                                                          TCL

                              BOTANY

577 Lloyd Library
          ... Bibliography relating to the floras of North America
     and the West Indies : embracing botanical section R of the
     Lloyd Library. - Cincinnati, Ohio : The Lloyd Library, 1913. -
     ii, 355-417p. - (Bibliographical contributions from the Lloyd
     Library, Cincinnati, Ohio ; no.9, Jan. 1912)

          1,000 references.

                                                     Ref.no.4
                                                   Vol.1, p.950

577a MORTON, JULIA F.
          Atlas of medicinal plants of Middle America : Bahamas to
     Yucatan / Julia F. Morton. - Springfield, Ill. : Charles C.
     Thomas, 1981. - xxiii, 1420p.
          Bibliography: p.1297-1319

          Of the 563 items arranged alphabetically by author, twenty
     items relate specifically to the English-speaking Caribbean.
                                                          UWI-T

578 New York. Botanical Garden. Library
          Plants of the Caribbean area / Library, New York Botanical
     Garden. - [New York : The New York Botanical Garden Library],
     [197-?]. - 3 leaves
          Mimeographed

          Alphabetical list of 26 items.

                                                          UWI-T

579 United States. Virgin Islands. Bureau of Libraries and
     Museums
          An annotated bibliography of West Indian plant ecology /
     by Philip W. Rundel. - St. Thomas, Virgin Islands of the

                              143

United States : Bureau of Libraries and Museums, Department of
Conservation and Cultural Affairs, Government of the Virgin
Islands, 1974. - 70p. - (Bibliography series ; 1)

571 annotated references mainly to journal articles,
arranged alphabetically by author and covering the Greater and
Lesser Antilles as well as the Bahamas and the Cayman Islands.
Coverage of pre-1900 publications is selective. "Under an
alphabetical index of islands or island groups, papers dealing
with each area have been categorized" into the following seven
subject areas : Vegetation, Flora/Floristics, Economic Plants/
Forestry, Climate, Soils, Impact of Man on Vegetation, Paleobotany, Other Ecological Studies.

UWI-T

Barbados

580 WATTS, DAVID
Man's influence on the vegetation of Barbados, 1627-1800 /
David Watts. - Hull : University of Hull, 1966. - vii, 96p. -
(Hull University occasional papers in geography ; no.4)
Bibliography: p.93-96

Includes relevant manuscript lists of plants preserved in
the Sloane manuscripts of the British Museum, other manuscripts
and theses as well as early printed works.

UWI-T

Guyana

581 BOERBOOM, J.H.A.
Bibliography of the vegetation of Guiana, Surinam and
French Guiana (S.A.) / J.H.A. Boerboom. - p.269-272
In Excerpta botanica. - Sectio B-M, no.4 (1970).

Benjamin

582 GRAHAM, EDWARD H.
Flora of the Kartabo region : British Guiana / Edward H.
Graham. - p.17-292
In Annals of the Carnegie Museum. - Vol.22 (1933-34)
Bibliography: p.277-292

UWI-J

COMMERCE AND TRADE

583   Caribbean Commission. Central Secretariat. Statistical Unit
        Select bibliography of trade publications with special
      reference to Caribbean trade statistics : a manual for the
      guidance of research workers in identifying useful sources of
      trade statistics and of published ground rules in the
      preparation of trade accounts/compiled in the Statistical
      Unit ... [by Allan Morais]. - Port of Spain, Trinidad :
      Statistical Unit, Research Branch, Caribbean Commission, 1954.
      - 54p.
        Mimeographed

        Entries are annotated and arranged by agency issuing the
      publication. Two international sections with publications of
      world organisations - U.N. agencies - and regional organisations
      such as the Caribbean Commission itself, are followed by national
      references outside and within the Caribbean, territory by
      territory.

                                                                  UWI-T

584   United States. Bureau of Foreign and Domestic Commerce
        Publications on Latin America and the West Indies : brief
      review of information available to manufacturers and
      exporters in bulletins issued / by the Bureau of Foreign and
      Domestic Commerce. - Washington, D.C. : Government Printing
      Office, 1914. - 15p. - (Miscellaneous series ; no.17)

                                                                    LC

585   United States. Tariff Commission
        Commercial policies and trade relations of the European
      possessions in the Caribbean area : a report on recent
      developments in the trade of the European possessions in the
      Caribbean area with special reference to trade with the
      United States / Tariff Commission. - Washington, D.C. : U.S.
      Government Printing Office, 1943. - xiii, 324p.
        Bibliography : p.323-324

        76 items listed include material on the British
      possessions.

                                                                  UWI-T

COMMUNICATION

586 Black list : the concise and comprehensive reference guide to
      black journalism, radio and television, educational and
      cultural organizations in the USA, Africa and the Caribbean. -
      2nd ed. - New York : Black List, 1975. - 2v.

Vol.1 :   Afro-America U.S.A.
Vol.2 :   International

The international section covers Africa and the Caribbean.
Includes lists of West Indian newspapers and periodicals and
items on Barbados, Guyana, Jamaica and Trinidad.

UWI-J

587 LENT, JOHN A.
British Caribbean mass communications bibliography / by
John A. Lent. - [S.l. : s.n.], 1971. - 34 leaves
Mimeographed

Items are arranged under headings : Caribbean; Common-
wealth Caribbean; Antigua; Bahamas; Barbados; Bermuda; Dominica;
Grenada; Jamaica; Montserrat, St. Christopher (St. Kitts), Nevis,
Anguilla, St. Lucia, St. Vincent as one group and Trinidad and
Tobago. They include numerous journal and newspaper articles.

UWI-T

588 LENT, JOHN A.
Caribbean mass communication : a comprehensive bibliography
/ compiled by John A. Lent. - Waltham, Mass. : Crossroads
Press, 1981. - 152p. - (Crossroad's archival and bibliographic
series)

2,653 entries. Material is indexed by author and arranged
within topical geographical units.

LC

589 LENT, JOHN A.
Caribbean mass communications : selected information
sources / John A. Lent. - p.111-125
In Journal of broadcasting. - Vol.20, no.1 (Winter 1976)

Most of the 81 items are annotated. Includes bibliographies, directories, periodical and newspaper articles, theses
and general sources which include such information. Sections on
the Caribbean in general, British Caribbean with items on
Bahamas, Bermuda, Jamaica, Leewards, Trinidad and Tobago and the
Windwards, as well as French, Netherlands and Spanish Caribbean
sections.

UWI-T

590 LENT, JOHN A.
Mass communications bibliography of the English-speaking
Caribbean / John A. Lent. - p.159-202
In Caribbean studies. - Vol.14, no.2 (July 1974)
(published 1980)

Listing is arranged by country with a general Caribbean section and each is subdivided into books and pamphlets, and periodical articles, essays and other material. There are entries for Antigua, Barbados, Bermuda, Dominica, Grenada, Jamaica, Montserrat, St. Kitts-Nevis-Anguilla, St. Lucia, St. Vincent and Trinidad and Tobago.

UWI-T

591 LENT, JOHN A.
        Third World mass media and their search for modernity : the case of Commonwealth Caribbean, 1717-1976 / by John A. Lent. - Lewisburg, Pa. : Bucknell University Press ; London : Associated University Press, c1977. - 405p.
        Bibliography : p.361-391

        Items arranged alphabetically by author under sections : General, The West Indies, Bahamas, Barbados, Bermuda, Jamaica, Leeward Islands, Trinidad and Tobago, Correspondence, Interviews.
UWI-T

592 Temple University. School of Communications. Department of Journalism
        Mass media in the Commonwealth Caribbean : recent bibliographic sources / by John A. Lent. - Philadelphia : Department of Journalism, School of Communications, Temple University, 1976. - 18p. - (Communications research report ; no.7)

        Supplement up-dating previous work (Ref.nos.587 and 589). Consists of 284 entries, three-fifths of which are newspaper articles or reports published primarily in late 1975 and early 1976. Arranged by country with sub-divisions for broadcasting, film, print media, freedom of the press, etc.
UWI-T

Guyana

593 SANDERS, RON
        Broadcasting in Guyana / Ron Sanders. - London : Routledge and Kegan Paul, 1978. - xiv, 77p. - (Case studies on broadcasting systems)
        Bibliography : p.76-77

        18 references to papers, addresses and official reports arranged alphabetically by author.
UWI-T

CRIMINOLOGY

594   PRYCE, KEN
        Caribbean criminology : a bibliography / by Ken Pryce and
      Kaye Larbi. - [S.l. : s.n.], [1979?]. - 22p.
        Mimeographed

        319 items arranged under headings : (2) Crime - General
      Aspect, (b) Family, Adolescence, Illegitimacy, Marriage, (c)
      Delinquency, (d) Probation, Rehabilitation, (e) Police, (f) Drug
      Abuse, Addiction etc., (g) Alcoholism, (h) Prostitution and
      Sexual Deviance, (i) Suicide, (j) Deviant Groups and Behaviour,
      (k) Legal Administration and Legal History and Procedure, (l)
      Jamaica Gun Court, (m) Specific Cases, (n) Corruption, (o) Social
      Psychology, (p) Small Communities and Social Problems, (q) Law
      and Labour Relations, (r) Penology, (s) Social Works. Entries
      which cover Guyana, Jamaica, Trinidad and Tobago, Barbados,
      Grenada, Windwards and Leewards, St. Lucia, St. Kitts, Dominica,
      St. Vincent, Antigua, Bermuda, Bahamas, St. Kitts-Nevis-Anguilla,
      British Virgin Islands, French and Dutch-speaking islands and the
      U.S. Virgin Islands, include periodical articles, conference
      proceedings, commissions and committees of enquiry, theses,
      reports of government departments.
                                                                UWI-T

Jamaica

595   University of the West Indies (Cave Hill). Faculty of Law.
      Library
        Causes, levels, patterns and remedies of crime in Jamaica
      [a bibliography] ; as held in the University of the West
      Indies Law Faculty Library / compiled by Fay Durrant. - [Cave
      Hill, Barbados : Law Faculty Library, University of the West
      Indies], 1975. - 3 leaves

        Includes a list of LLB theses (UWI) for 1973 and 1974,
      references to parts of books, journal articles and official
      reports.
                                                                UWI-T

DANCE

Trinidad and Tobago

596   University of the West Indies (St. Augustine). Library
        Dance in Trinidad and Tobago : a list of references to
      the literature held in the Library, U.W.I., St. Augustine. -
      St. Augustine, Trinidad : Library, U.W.I., 1980. - 1 leaf
      Mimeographed

        12 items including journal articles.

                                                            UWI-T

DESCRIPTION AND TRAVEL

597   COX, EDWARD GODFREY
        A reference guide to the literature of travel including
      voyages, geographical descriptions, adventures, shipwrecks
      and expeditions / by Edward Godfrey Cox. - Seattle : University
      of Washington, 1935-49. - 3v. - (University of Washington
      publications in language and literature)
        Volume 2 : The New World. - 1938. - vii, 591p.

        Chapter 6 (p.198-235) covers the West Indies from 1553-
      1799. Arrangement of entries is chronological and most items
      are extensively annotated. Contributions to the Royal Society
      Volumes and individual voyages printed in Hakluyt and Purchas
      are omitted. A personal names index is included.

                                                            UWI-T

598   FOSTER, HARRY LA TOURETTE
        The Caribbean cruise / by Harry La Tourette Foster ;
      revised by William W. Harris. - New ed. - New York : Dodd,
      Mead and Company, 1939. - ix, [1], 350p.
        Bibliography : p.339-344

                                                          Ref.no.5
                                                    1937-1942, p.237

599   National Book League
        Commonwealth travel and description / National Book
      League. - London : the National Book League, 1966. - 16p.

        Annotated list prepared for the Commonwealth in Books
      Exhibition. Arranged geographically. Contains items on Guyana,
      Jamaica and West Indies.

                                                            UWI-T

600   PARMER, CHARLES B.
        West Indian odyssey : the complete guide to the islands
      of the Caribbean / by Charles B. Parmer. - New York : Dodge
      Publishing Company, [1937]. - xvii, 285p.
        Bibliography: p.275-280

                                                    Ref.no.5
                                          1937-1942, p.1742

601   ROBERTS, WALTER ADOLPHE
        Lands of the inner sea, the West Indies and Bermuda /
      Walter Adolphe Roberts. - New York : Coward-McCann, [1948]. -
      xiii, 301p. - (Invitation to travel series)
        Bibliography : p.287-288

                                                    Ref.no.5
                                           1947-1950, p.779

602   SJÖGREN, BENGT
        Vägen till glömda öar ; Bengt Sjögren. - [Göteborg] :
      Zinderman ; [Stockholm : Seelig], 1967. - 268, [1] p., [16]
      leaves of plates
        Bibliography : p.261-263

                                                         LC

Leeward Islands

603   DE LEEUW, HENDRIK
        Crossroads of the buccaneers / Hendrik De Leeuw. -
      Philadelphia; London : J.B. Lippincott Company, [c1937]. -
      414p.
        Bibliography : p.401-409

                                                    Ref.no.5
                                           1937-1942, p.928

Bermuda

604   TWEEDY, MARY JOHNSON
        Bermuda holiday / Mary Johnson Tweedy ; introduced by Sir
      Alexander Hood. - New York : Crown Publishers, [1950]. -
      162p.
        Bibliography : p.154-156

                                                    Ref.no.5
                                            1947-1950, p.70

ECONOMICS

605 BROWN, ADLITH
     A review of the study of economics in the English-speaking
     Caribbean / by Adlith Brown and Havelock Brewster. - p.48-68
     In Social and economic studies. - Vol.23, no.1 (1974)
     Selected bibliography : p.58-68

     171 items in sections : (a) Policy, Planning (b) Social
Accounts (c) Production, Investment, Consumption (d) Finance
Taxation, Monetary Policy (e) External Trade and Payments.

                                                     UWI-T

606 Caribbean Community Secretariat publications. - p.27-31
     In Caricom bulletin. - No.1 (Aug. 1978)

     53 items published by the Caribbean Community Secretariat
arranged alphabetically by title.

                                                     UWI-T

607 HANNAYS, IRMA
     Basic reference works on economics Appendix II / Irma
     Hannays. - p.24-37
     In Library resources for research in the Caribbean -
     Economics (English-speaking areas) / by Irma Hannays ;
     [Working paper no. IID submitted for the Conference of the
     Association of Caribbean University and Research Libraries
     (ACURIL) ... 3rd, Universidad Central de Venezuela, Caracas,
     Venezuela], 1971. - San Juan, Puerto Rico : General
     Secretariat, ACURIL, 1971

     Listing of basic documents, reports and other reference
sources emanating from the area. Arranged alphabetically by the
individual countries of the region with periodicals listed
separately in each section.

                                                     UWI-T

608 Harvard University. Law School
     Bibliography on taxation in underdeveloped countries / Law
     School of Harvard University. - Cambridge : Law School,
     Harvard University, 1962. - (International program in taxa-
     tion). - 75p.

     Approximately 2,100 references divided into sections :
General, Regions, Countries. Items on Bahamas (p.20), Barbados
(p.20), Bermuda (p.20), British Guiana (p.24), Jamaica (p.48),
Trinidad (p.69) as well as West Indies (p.74) included

                                                     UWI-T

609 HAZLEWOOD, ARTHUR
     The economics of development : an annotated list of books
     and articles published 1958-1962 / Arthur Hazlewood. - London :

Oxford University Press for the Oxford University Institute
of Commonwealth Studies, 1964. - xii, 104p.

Sequel to his earlier work (Ref.no.610), this is a general
bibliography but includes references of specific interest to
individual territories and to the Caribbean area as a whole.
Arranged in broad subject sections such as historical studies,
area studies, national income and components, population, labour
and management, government, agriculture, land and commerce, and
transport. Nine references on Jamaica specifically with a few
others on Barbados, British Honduras, Montserrat, St. Kitts-
Nevis-Anguilla. Index of authors and editors and an index of
places.

UWI-T

610 HAZLEWOOD, ARTHUR
The economics of "under-developed" areas : an annotated
reading list of books, articles and official publications /
compiled by Arthur Hazlewood. - 2nd ed. - London : Oxford
University Press for the Institute of Commonwealth Studies,
1959. - xii, 150p.

Includes publications appearing up to 1958, later updated
in Ref.no.609. Over 1,000 references subdivided into 12 sections
on such topics as agriculture and land, general surveys, population and labour, national income, consumption and development and
economic development with indexes of authors and editors as well
as places. Includes some references on the West Indies as a
whole and on the more developed territories individually.

UWI-T

611 Howard University
The economic future of the Caribbean / edited by E.
Franklin Frazier and Eric Williams. - Washington, D.C. :
Howard University Press, 1944. - 94p. - (Seventh annual
conference of the Division of Social Sciences)
Bibliography : p.91-94

56 items arranged in two sections: (a) Official Reports
and (b) Unofficial Studies. The first section is subdivided
under headings : Great Britain, United States, Anglo-American
Caribbean Commission and Bibliographies, and the second is
arranged under Books and Pamphlets, and Articles.

UWI-T

612 MATHEWS, THOMAS
Los estudios de la historia económica del Caribe (1585-
1910) ; ponencia presentada al XXXIX Congreso de Americanistas
en Lima, Peru, Agosto, 1970 / Thomas Mathews. - Hato Rey :
Instituto de Estudios del Caribe, Universidad de Puerto Rico,
1970. - 46 leaves in various foliations

An essay review of works on Caribbean economic history, followed
by a bibliography with 298 references in author order, including journal articles, and a theme index broken down by territories. Topics

covered include the sugar industry, commercial policy, plantation
economy and migration.
                                                               UWI-T

613   PALMER, RANSFORD W.
        Caribbean dependence on the United States economy/ Ransford W.
Palmer. - New York : Praeger Publishers, 1979. - xiv [1], 173p. -
(Praeger special studies).
Bibliography : p.166-173

        Arranged under sections : Books, Journal Articles,
Public Documents (subdivided by countries - Barbados, Guyana,
Jamaica, Trinidad and Tobago, United States). Many of the books
and articles listed relate to the economy, industries and
politics of the region. The public documents consist mainly of
annual statistics, including trade and population.
                                                               UWI-T

614   Selected bibliography on employment and income distribution
      in the Caribbean. - [S.1. : s.n.], 1971. - 5p.

        In addition to a general section on economics and politics
includes sections on such topics as agriculture, land tenure,
wage, price, productivity and income distribution. Numerous
periodical articles are cited.
                                                               UWI-T

615   Trinidad and Tobago. Ministry of Planning and Development.
      Library
        Cooperatives : a bibliography of material available in the
      library / P. Raymond. - [Port of Spain, Trinidad] : Ministry
      of Planning and Development, 1979. - 6p.
        Mimeographed
        Comprises 18 items on the West Indies as a whole and four
      items on Trinidad and Tobago.
                                                               MF-T

616   United States. Department of State. Division of Libraries
      and Reference Services. Office of Intelligence
        Economic studies of underdeveloped countries : Latin
      America and Caribbean area / Division of Libraries and
      Reference Services. - Washington, D.C. : [s.n.], 1950. - 90p.
      - (Bibliography ; no.52)
                                                            Ref.no.5
                                                      1947-1950, p.110

617   University of the West Indies (St. Augustine). Faculty of
      Social Sciences. Department of Economics
        Caribbean economic problems : reading list / L. Best. -
      St. Augustine, [Trinidad] : Department of Economics, University
      of the West Indies, 1975. - 6p.

        Arranged in six broad sections as follows : I. Economic
Problems of the Caribbean - II. Historical Underdevelopment of
Caribbean Economy - III. Models of Caribbean Economy - IV. Sector
Studies - V. Problem Areas and Policy Issues - VI. Caribbean
Economic Thought and Methodology. Sections IV and V are in turn
subdivided by sectors and issues such as agriculture, industrial-
zation, tourism.
                                                               UWI-T

618 University of the West Indies (St. Augustine). Library
       Economics : West Indies / University of the West Indies
     Library. - [St. Augustine, Trinidad : Library, University of
     the West Indies], 1970. - 6 leaves
       Typescript

     Arranged by form of material and then alphabetically by
  author.

                                                            UWI-T

Indexes

619 Caribbean Community Secretariat. Library
       Caricom Common Market Council : index to documents of the
     9th meeting, September 1976 / Library, Caribbean Community
     Secretariat. - Georgetown : C.C.S., 1976

       Classified.

                                                              CCS

620 Caribbean Community Secretariat. Library
       Caricom Common Market Council : index to documents of the
     11th meeting, September 1977 / Library, Caribbean Community
     Secretariat. - Georgetown : C.C.S., 1978

       Classified.

                                                              CCS

621 Caribbean Community Secretariat. Library
       Subject index to the decisions and recommendations of the
     eleventh meeting of the Common Market Council of Ministers,
     Georgetown, Guyana, 14-15 September, 1977 / Library,
     Caribbean Community Secretariat. - Georgetown : C.C.S., 1978

       Classified.

                                                              CCS

Land Tenure and Reform

622 MELICZEK, HANS
       Bibliography on land tenure and related subjects in St.
     Lucia and other Caribbean territories / compiled by Hans
     Meliczek. - Castries : Ministry of Trade, Industry, Agri-
     culture and Tourism, 1973. - 12p.
       Mimeographed

     Arranged alphabetically by author under the following
  sections : (A) Monographs and Articles Referring to St. Lucia,
  (B) Monographs and Articles Referring to the West Indies

Including St. Lucia, (C) Monographs and Articles Referring to
Individual Territories in the West Indies, (D) Legislative
Provisions of St. Lucia [pertaining to land tenure]. Covers land
tenure in St. Lucia together with studies on the general
economic and social situation in that country, plus studies on
land tenure in other Caribbean countries.

ECLA-T

623 University of Wisconsin (Madison). Land Tenure Center
        Agrarian reform in Latin America : an annotated biblio-
     graphy / Land Tenure Center, University of Wisconsin. -
     Madison, Wisc. : Land Tenure Center, University of Wisconsin,
     1974. - 667p. - (Land economics monographs ; 5)

        Over 5,000 annotated entries. Includes a Caribbean
general bibliography (p.1575-1578) of 23 items listed alphabetically by author. Author (individual and corporate) and
subject indexes provided.

UWI-T

Guyana

624 Guyana. Bank of Guyana. Research Department
        A bibliography of documents relating to the economy of
     Guyana / Bank of Guyana. - Georgetown : Bank of Guyana, 1968.
     - iii, 23p.
        Mimeographed
        Cover title

UWI-LL

625 Guyana. Ministry of Economic Development
        A bibliography of recent reports relating to the economy
     of Guyana / Wilfred L. David. - [Georgetown, Guyana] :
     Development Planning Team, Ministry of Economic Development,
     1970. - 47p.
        Mimeographed

        This listing of 494 reports provides author, title and
date information. Covers mainly the last ten years but includes
important older titles. Since some authors and dates are missing
the bibliography is incomplete in this sense. Location marks are
given for one of ten sources and agencies in Guyana. Arrangement
is under seven broad headings : (1) Agriculture, (2) Mining,
(3) Manufacturing, (4) Electricity, Water and Sanitary Services,
(5) Commerce, Trade, Economic Affairs and Statistics, (6) Transport, Storage and Communication, (7) Services (including Health
and Education).

UWI-T

626   Guyana. Public Free Library
          Bibliography on co-operatives / prepared by Public Free
      Library in collaboration with Co-operatives Division, Ministry
      of Economic Development. - Georgetown, Guyana : Public Free
      Library, 1971. - ix, 64p.
          Mimeographed

          A general bibliography which includes sections on
      cooperatives in Guyana (p.49-58) and the Co-operative Republic
      of Guyana (p.63-64). Includes many unpublished items and
      locations for each title. Compiled for the first anniversary of
      the Cooperative Republic of Guyana.

                                                              UWI-T

627   University of Guyana. Library
          Material on co-operatives in the U.G. [University of
      Guyana] Library. - [Turkeyen, Guyana : Library, University of
      Guyana], [c1971]. - 2 leaves
          Typescript

                                                                 UG

Jamaica

628   [Jamaica Library Service]
          Production in action : put your shoulder to the wheel /
      [Jamaica Library Service]. - Kingston : Jamaica Library
      Service, 1977. - 35p.

          Prepared for the annual independence exhibition of the
      Jamaica Library Service.

                                                         Ref.no.76
                                                         1977, p.4

Trinidad and Tobago

629   SOLOMON, MERVYN M.
          [Bibliography] / prepared by Mervyn M. Solomon. - [S.l. :
      s.n.], 1981. - [10] leaves
          Mimeographed

          54 items comprising studies, position papers, conference
      reports, speeches and similar work completed by the officers of
      the Central Bank of Trinidad and Tobago. Arranged chronologi-
      cally.

                                                               CB-T

630   Trinidad and Tobago. Central Bank. Research Library
          Bibliography of national economic literature / compiled by
      Maria Brewster for SALALM XXIII, London, July 16-22, 1978. -
      [Port of Spain, Trinidad : Central Bank], 1978. - 45p.

          Lists published and unpublished economic literature on
      Trinidad and Tobago available in the bank library in several
      sections. Includes a chronological list of staff papers and
      addresses with a subject index to these, other bank publications,
      government fiscal publications, departmental reports and separate
      lists of periodical publications from different sources within
      and outside the country.
                                                             UWI-T

631   Trinidad and Tobago. Ministry of Planning and Development.
      Library
          Co-operatives : a bibliography of material available in
      the library, Ministry of Planning and Development. - [Port of
      Spain, Trinidad : Ministry of Planning and Development
      Library], 1979. - 6p.
          Mimeographed

          Comprises 18 items on Trinidad and Tobago and four on the
      Caribbean generally.
                                                             MF-T

632   Trinidad and Tobago. Ministry of Planning and Development.
      Library
          Material on employment, manpower and related subjects in
      the Library. - [Port of Spain, Trinidad : Library, Ministry
      of Planning and Development], 1970. - 49p.
          Mimeographed

          74 items on employment, unemployment, wages, manpower,
      vocational training, industrial relations/labour laws, migration
      in Trinidad and Tobago, and 7 entries for the West Indies
      generally.
                                                             MF-T

633   Trinidad and Tobago. Ministry of Planning and Development.
      Library
          Transportation economics / Ministry of Planning and
      Development Library. - [Port of Spain, Trinidad : Ministry
      of Planning and Development Library], 1975. - 8p.
          Mimeographed

          Comprises 18 items on the Caribbean and 7 on Trinidad and
      Tobago.
                                                             MF-T

EDUCATION

634   ALTBACH, PHILIP G.
      Higher education in developing nations : a select
      bibliography / Philip G. Altbach ; with the assistance of
      Bradley Nystrom. - Cambridge, Mass. : Center for International
      Affairs, Harvard University, 1970. - 118p. - (Occasional
      papers in international affairs ; no.24)

      Covers the period 1945-1968.

                                                                   LC

635   ALTBACH, PHILIP G.
      Higher education in developing nations : a select
      bibliography, 1969-1974 / Philip G. Altbach and David H.
      Kelly. - New York : Praeger Publishers, 1974. - ix, 229p. -
      (Praeger special studies in international economics and
      development)
      Published in cooperation with the International Council
      for Educational Development.

      Continues Ref.no.634. Includes about 2,400 listings from
   85 countries. Over half the listings are journal articles and
   there are some 300 dissertations. The section on Latin America
   includes the Caribbean (10 items), Guyana (4 items).

                                                                 UWI-T

636   BENNETT, HAZEL E.
      Basic reference works on the subject by countries / Hazel
      E. Bennett. - p.14-16
      In Library resources for research in education in the
      Caribbean / by Hazel E. Bennett ; Working paper no.III B
      submitted for the Conference of the Association of Caribbean
      University and Research Libraries (ACURIL) ... 3rd,
      Universidad Central de Venezuela, Caracas, Venezuela,
      November 7-12, 1971. - San Juan, Puerto Rico : General
      Secretariat, Association of Caribbean University and Research
      Libraries, 1971

      Arranged by the individual countries of the English-
   speaking Caribbean.

                                                                 UWI-T

637   Caribbean Commission
      A bibliography of education in the Caribbean / compiled
      by V.O. Alcala. - [Port of Spain], Trinidad : Central
      Secretariat, 1959. - ix, 144p.

638   Community Relations Commission
        Education for a multi-racial society : a bibliography for
      teachers / Community Relations Commission. - 3rd ed. - London :
      Community Relations Commission, 1974. - 39p.

        Arranged in sections such as reference books, history,
      geography, selected fiction, home economics, music, anthologies,
      bibliographies. Each section contains items of West Indian
      interest.
                                                                UWI-T

639   Education in the West Indies : a bibliography. - p.167-173
        In Revista/Review interamericana. - Vol.2, no.2 (Summer
      1972)

        A compilation done by the UWI Library, Trinidad for the
      director/editor of the journal with post-1958 material held in
      the library. Excludes all items recorded in Comitas (Ref.no.91)
      and Baa (Ref.no.262). Includes government and other special
      reports, journal articles and books.
                                                                UWI-T

640 HART, ESTELLITA
        Bibliographical sources on education in the Caribbean /
      Estellita Hart. - p.267-268
        In The Caribbean : contemporary education / edited by
      A. Curtis Wilgus. - Gainesville, Fla. : University of Florida
      Press, 1960. - (Caribbean conference series 1 ; vol.10)

        A bibliographic essay covering the wider Caribbean area.
                                                                UWI-T

641 LAUERHASS, LUDWIG
        Education in Latin America : a bibliography / Ludwig
      Lauerhass and Vera Lucía Oliveira de Araújo Haugse. -
      Boston : G.K. Hall, 1981. - 431p. - (UCLA Latin American
      Center publication. Reference series; v.9)

        Arranged by country and then classified into four main
      subject groups : Education in General, In-school Education,
      Out-of-school Education and Educational Planning and Adminis-
      tration. Country coverage includes Belize, Guianas, Jamaica,
      and Trinidad and Tobago with a general section on the smaller
      islands.
                                                                   LC

641a PARKER, FRANKLIN D.
        American dissertations on foreign education : a biblio-
      graphy with abstracts. Vol. X, Central America, West Indies,
      Caribbean and Latin America (general) / edited by Franklin D.
      Parker and Betty June Parker. - Troy, N.Y. : Whitson Publishing,
      1979. - 620p.

"Abstracts of 229 doctoral dissertations on all aspects of
education in the region by title. The bibliography is organized
alphabetically by authors, with a subject and geographical index
appended."

Ref.no.309a
Item no.681

642 POSTON, SUSAN L.
        Non formal education in Latin America : an annotated
     bibliography / by Susan L. Poston. - Los Angeles : University
     of California, 1976. - 268p. - (UCLA Latin American Center
     publications. Reference series ; vol.8)

        The listing is arranged first by country with topical
     subdivisions under headings such as basic education, literacy,
     vocational skill training, agricultural training and multi-
     faceted programs. Includes brief sections on Guyana, Jamaica,
     Trinidad and Tobago as well as a broad section on Central
     America and the Caribbean. References to books and journal
     articles provided.

LC

643 PURUSHOTHAMAN, M.
        The education of children of Caribbean origin : select
     research bibliography / M. Purushothamam. - [S.l.] : Centre
     for Information and Advice on Educational Disadvantage, 1978. -
     37p.

        Originally compiled for a conference on the linguistic
     needs of West Indian children in 1977. Entries are arranged
     under four main headings : (a) Reviews/Critiques, (b) Research
     Findings and Conclusions from Studies in the United Kingdom,
     (c) Education in the Caribbean, (d) A Sample of Five Studies from
     the United States. Each section except the third includes
     abstracts of significant publications. Section (b) covers topics
     such as ability, attainment, achievement, racial awareness,
     behaviour disturbances, school curriculum and social and cultural
     background.

UWI-T

644 Regional Committee on Family Life and Sex Education for Latin
     America and the Caribbean (CRESALC)
        Family life education publications in the Caribbean : the
     report of a study and an annotated bibliography on publica-
     tions for family life education in the Caribbean / Michael H.
     Alleyne. - [S.l. : CRESALC], 1980. - 66p.
        Annotated bibliography: p.10-41

        49 items arranged under sections: (A) Reports of Meetings,
     (B) Curriculum/Syllabus Outlines, (C) Text Books, (D) Enrichment
     Material, (E) Flyers/Pamphlets, (F) Analyses, (G) Studies,

(H) Family Life Education Teacher Guides, (I) General Reference
Manuals. Annotations are extensive.

UWI-T

645 SHINEBOURNE, JOHN
A bibliography on technical education in the Caribbean /
compiled by John Shinebourne. - Georgetown : University of
Guyana Library, 1970. - [3], 35p. - (University of Guyana
Library series ; no.1)

208 references cover 1946 to 1969, include materials in
English, Spanish and French, and embrace all the islands of the
Caribbean and the Guianas. Arranged alphabetically by author
within five broad sections : (1) Bibliographies, (2) Technical
and Industrial Education, (3) Vocational Education, (4) Agricultural Education, (5) Medical Education, followed by brief
indexes to theses included and by geographic areas of the region.

UWI-T

646 Trinidad and Tobago. Central Library. West Indian Reference
Collection
A list of books on agricultural education, home economics
education, labour economics, technical education, and trade
and industrial education compiled from the stock of the West
Indian Reference Section ... . - [Port of Spain, Trinidad :
Central Library], 1968. - 3p.
Typescript

TCL

647 Trinidad and Tobago. Central Library. West Indian Reference
Section
List of books on education in the West Indies (with
emphasis on secondary education in Trinidad) / prepared by
the Central Library Services. - [Port of Spain, Trinidad] :
Central Library Services, 1964. - 2 leaves
Mimeographed

26 references to reports, books, conference proceedings,
with a few journal articles and school annuals. Some Caribbean
library locations are provided.

TCL

648 University of Guyana. Library
Holdings on education in the West Indies / Library,
University of Guyana. - [Turkeyen, Guyana : Library,
University of Guyana], [1976]
Mimeographed

UG

A Bibliography of Bibliographies

649 University of the West Indies (Mona). Institute of Education.
Documentation Centre
Caribbean education : reading list / Institute of Education
Documentation Centre. - [Mona, Jamaica : Documentation Centre,
Institute of Education, U.W.I.], [1968]. - 41p.

UWI-J

650 University of the West Indies (Mona). Institute of Education.
Documentation Centre
Caribbean educational project July 14-August 12, 1968,
sponsored by U.W.I. and A.A.C.T.E. : reading list / Institute
of Education Documentation Centre. - [Kingston, Jamaica] :
Documentation Centre, Institute of Education, 1968. - 34p.
Mimeographed

Detailed subject arrangement. Theses on West Indian
education are listed separately on p.29-34.

TCL

651 University of the West Indies (Mona). School of Education
Select bibliography of education in the Commonwealth
Caribbean, 1940-1975 / compiled by Amy Robertson, Hazel
Bennett and Janet White. - Mona, Jamaica : Documentation
Centre, School of Education, University of the West Indies,
1976. - 196p.

Covers 15 English-speaking islands or groups of islands
(e.g., Turks and Caicos, Cayman Islands) and Guyana, including
much unpublished material such as student studies submitted for
the Bachelor's degree. Sections on the individual territories
are followed by subject groupings such as curriculum development,
levels of education, handicapped education and national development, school libraries, teaching methods, etc. A name index and
locations throughout the region are provided. Appendices include
theses accepted at universities abroad and professional journals
published in the region, both selective.

UWI-T

652 University of the West Indies (St. Augustine). Library
Universities in the third world : a select bibliography /
Library, U.W.I. ; prepared on the occasion of the U.W.I.
Joint STAPEC/Open Lecture series. - St. Augstine, [Trinidad :
University of the West Indies], 1980. - 31p.

Arranged under broad topics : (a) Role of the University,
(b) University and the State, (c) Universities in Developing
Countries, and (d) Governance of Universities. Includes sections
on the Caribbean Region (English-speaking) (p.8-10) and the
University of the West Indies (p.14). Principally a listing of
material held in the St. Augustine library, the bibliography
includes monographs, articles in journals and dissertations.

UWI-T

Guyana

653 RAGHUBEER, E.
        Bibliography on education in Guyana / E. Raghubeer. -
     [S.l. : s.n.], 1977. - 143 leaves
        Photocopy

        "This is a working photocopy of cards for a comprehensive
     bibliography undertaken by the University of Guyana Library for
     the Ministry of Education, Social Development and Culture" -
     Benjamin.
                                                                    UG

654 University of Guyana. Library
        Technical education in Guyana / Library, University of
     Guyana. - [Turkeyen, Guyana : University of Guyana Library],
     1975. - 3 leaves
        Mimeographed
                                                                    UG

Jamaica
Indexes

655 Jamaica. Ministry of Education. Library
        Author index of selected articles on education in Jamaica
     / Ministry of Education Library. - [Kingston, Jamaica] :
     Ministry of Education Library, [1964?]. - 15p.
        Mimeographed
        Cover title
                                                                  UWI-J

656 Jamaica. Ministry of Education. Library
        Subject index of selected articles on education in
     Jamaica / Ministry of Education Library. - Kingston, [Jamaica],
     Ministry of Education Library, 1966. - 2p., 1, 16p.
        Mimeographed

        Includes a list of periodicals received in the library of
     the Ministry of Education.
                                                                  UWI-J

Trinidad and Tobago

657 Trinidad and Tobago. Ministry of Planning and Development
        Education in Trinidad and Tobago / compiled by Patricia
     Raymond. - [Port of Spain, Trinidad] : Ministry of Planning
     and Development, 1971. - 7p.
        Mimeographed

62 items including reports of the government of Trinidad and Tobago, World Bank education projects, UNESCO and reports on educational television, technical education and adult education.

MF-T

658   University of the West Indies (St. Augustine). Library
Bibliography on the history of education in Trinidad and Tobago / Library, University of the West Indies. - [St. Augustine, Trinidad : Library, University of the West Indies] [196-?]. - 3 leaves

Arranged by form of source material including reports, legislation and journals.

UWI-T

Periodicals and Serials -- Indexes
659   CUTHBERT, ZINKA
The educational journal of Trinidad and Tobago : index 1965-1976 / compiled by Zinka Cuthbert. - [S.l. : s.n.], 1979. - 14p.

A two-part index providing subject and author approaches. The subject index uses subject headings in alphabetical order for articles appearing in the journal over a 10 year period.

UWI-T

ETHNIC GROUPS

660   CAMPBELL-PLATT, KIRAN
Ethnic minorities in society : a reference guide / Kiran Campbell-Platt. - London : Community and Race Relations Unit of the British Council of Churches and Runnymede Trust, 1976. - 55p.
Bibliography : p.52-54

Includes items on West Indian immigration, race relations, housing, employment, etc.

UWI-T

661   CROSS, MALCOLM
Race relations, social class and social change : a comparative study of Guyana and Trinidad, 1930-1970 ; a working bibliography / compiled by Malcolm Cross. - [S.l. : s.n.], 1970. - 43p.
Mimeographed

The bibliography was compiled for a particular study and is recognized by the author as incomplete. It is divided into three main sections : (a) Official Publications in chronological

order, (b) Unofficial Publications in alphabetical author order,
(c) Periodicals. The second section is the most extensive
including books and pamphlets, journal articles and published
papers, and unpublished theses.

UWI-T

662   Institute of Race Relations
        Coloured immigrants in Britain : a select bibliography /
compiled by A. Sivanandan. - 3rd ed. - London : Institute of
Race Relations, 1969. - v, 110p. - (Institute of Race
Relations ; special series)

        Lists works published during the period 1950-1969. Based
on the holdings of the Institute's library and compiled by its
librarian, the listings are arranged under subjects such as
health, education, housing, immigration, etc. and include mostly
post-1950 material. Separate listings of relevant parliamentary
debates, periodicals and organizations issuing publications are
provided as appendices, and there is an author index.

UWI-T

663   LAWRENCE, DANIEL
        Black migrants : white natives ; a study of race relations
in Nottingham / Daniel Lawrence. - London : Cambridge University
Press, 1974. - 251p.
        Bibliography : p.241-246

        Official publications, monographs and journal articles
(including many references on West Indians) arranged alphabetically
by author.

UWI-T

664   MADAN, RAJ
        Colored minorities in Britain : a comprehensive biblio-
graphy, 1970-1977 / Raj Madan. - Westport, Conn. : Greenwood
Press, 1979. - xi, 199p.

        Divided into 15 sections : General Works, Immigration,
History and Politics, Racism, Law and Legislation, Inter-ethnic
Relations, Employment, Social Conditions, General Culture,
Family and Community Life, Education, Housing, Health, Social
Sciences, Race Relations in the Mass Media. Subdivided into
sub-sections for books and periodical articles including pamphlets,
government publications, theses and dissertations. Appendix A
lists titles and addresses of periodicals that deal primarily
with race relations in Britain. Appendix B lists names and
addresses of organizations concerned with British colored
minorities' problems. Author, title and subject indexes.

UWI-T

665   RUTTER, M.
        Children of West Indian immigrants / M. Rutter. - p.261-
      262, 15-17, 122-123
        In Journal of child psychology and psychiatry. - Vol.15-16
      (Oct. 1974-Apr. 1975)
                                                    Ref.no.5
                                              Aug. 1975, p.155

666   SCOBIE, EDWARD
        Black Britannia : a history of blacks in Britain / by
      Edward Scobie. - Chicago : Johnson Publishing Company, 1972. -
      316p.

        Short bibliographies appear at the end of each of the 18
      chapters, including journal and newspaper articles as well as
      monographs. Includes section on entertainers and World War II
      featuring West Indian blacks.
                                              ·   UWI-T

667   University of Guelph. Library
        West Indians in Canada : a selective annotated bibliography
      / by Flora Helena Blizzard. - Guelph, Canada : The Library,
      University of Guelph, 1970. - 41p. - (Bibliography series ;
      no.1)

        This compilation aims at reflecting West Indian immigrant
      assimilation by Canadian society and recording the "noteworthy
      cultural contributions" to Canadian life during the last hundred
      years. But a negro West Indian bias results from dearth of other
      information. Includes listings of monographs, serial articles,
      non-book materials and an author/name index ; library locations,
      mainly in Ontario, are provided.
                                                    UWI-T

668   University of the West Indies (St. Augustine). Library
        East Indians in the Caribbean : a select bibliography
      prepared on the occasion of the UNESCO-UWI Conference on the
      East Indians in the Caribbean, September 16-22, 1979 /
      by Lynda Quamina and Kaye Larbi. - St. Augustine, Trinidad :
      Library, The University of the West Indies, [1979]. - [1],
      48p.

        Principally a listing of material held in the university
      library. Arranged under the main themes discussed at the
      conference, viz., History, Sociology, Politics, Economics,
      Cultural Forms and Literature; includes monographs, articles in
      journals and dissertations.
                                                    UWI-T

Barbados

669   SHEPPARD, JILL
        The "Redlegs" of Barbados : their origins and history /
      by Jill Sheppard ; foreword by Sir Philip Sherlock. - Millwood,
      N.Y. : KTO Press, 1977. - xiv, 147p. - (The Caribbean :
      historical and cultural perspectives)
        Bibliography : p.139-142

        Arranged according to sources which include lists of
      emigrants, manuscripts and official documents as well as news-
      papers and journal articles.
                                                            UWI-T

Belize

669a   DAVIDSON, WILLIAM V.
        Black Carib (Garifuna) habitats in Central America /
      William V. Davidson. - p.85-94
        In Frontier adaptations in lower Central America / edited
      by Mary W. Helms and Franklin O. Loveland. - Philadelphia:
      Institute for the Study of Human Issues, 1976.

        "A cultural geographer details the distribution of Black
      Carib settlements on the eastern coast of Central America
      including six in Belize (Stann Creek, Hopkins, Georgetown, Seine
      Bight, Punta Gorda and Barranca). This is an extension of
      Davidson's earlier article, 'The Caribs (Garifuna) of Central
      America: a map of their realm and a bibliography of research',
      Belizean Studies, vol.2, no.6 (Nov. 1974), p.15-25."
                                                      Ref.no.309a
                                                      Item no.321

Trinidad and Tobago

670   SAROOP, HAYMAN CECIL
        A bibliography of selected materials on the East Indian
      communities of the Caribbean area (1838-1975) / Hayman Cecil
      Saroop. - El Dorado, Trinidad : [s.n.], 1979. - i, 9p.
        Typescript

        Alphabetic author list of 105 items the majority of which
      deal with East Indians in Trinidad and Tobago and Guyana with a
      few others on Jamaica, Surinam, Martinique, Guadeloupe, and the
      West Indies generally. Items include many journal articles and
      some Colonial Office reports.
                                                            UWI-T

ETHNOGRAPHY

671 GOWER, CHARLOTTE D.
     The northern and southern affiliations of Antillean
culture / by Charlotte D. Gower. - New York : Kraus Reprint,
1964. - 60p. - (Memoirs of the American Anthropological
Association ; no.35, 1927)
     Bibliography : p.51-60

     Arranged alphabetically by author and chronologically
under each. Includes monographs, journal articles and reports on
the archaeology and anthropology of the wider Caribbean area.
Includes references to the West Indian territories.

                                                    UWI-T

Bahamas

672 LA FLAMME, ALAN G.
     An annotated ethnographic bibliography of the Bahama
Islands / Alan G. La Flamme. - p.57-66
     In Behaviour science research. - Vol.11, no.1 (1976)

     "Useful bibliography for anthropologists interested in the
Bahamas" - HLAS.
                                                   Ref.no.15
                                        Vol.39 (1977), no.1225

Trinidad and Tobago

673 FIGUEREDO, ALFREDO E.
     A revised aboriginal ethnohistory of Trinidad / Alfredo
E. Figueredo and Stephen D. Glazier. - p.259-262
     In Seventh International Congress for the Study of pre-
Colombian Cultures of the Lesser Antilles, Universidad Central
de Caracas, Caracas, Julio 11-16 de 1977. - [S.l.] : Centre
de Recherches Caraïbes, 1978
     Bibliography : p.261-262

     20 references in alphabetical author order.

                                                    UWI-T

674 GLAZIER, STEPHEN D.
     An annotated, ethnographic bibliography of Trinidad / by
Stephen D. Glazier. - [S.l. : s.n.], [n.d.] - iii, 40, [2]p.

     The 165 items listed comprise articles, books and
unpublished theses. A subject index is provided.
                                                    UWI-T

675   Trinidad and Tobago.   Central Library
        List of references on the Ciboney, Arawak and Carib in the
      West Indian Reference Section / Central Library. - [Port of
      Spain, Trinidad : Central Library], 1969. - 3 leaves
        Typescript

        17 references to books and journal articles citing
      specific pages relevant.

                                                                    TCL

                              ETHNOLOGY

676   LEFFALL, DOLORES C.
        The black experience in Africa, Latin America and the
      Caribbean : a selected bibliography of articles appearing in
      periodicals, 1973-1974 / Dolores C. Leffall. - p.352-395
        In Journal of negro history. - Vol.59, no.4 (Oct. 1974)
        The Caribbean : p.387-393

        Caribbean listing is subdivided by subjects such as
      cultural heritage, economic conditions, education, history,
      literature, religion, politics, travel and urban development.
                                                                    UWI-T

677   NODAL, ROBERTO
        A preliminary bibliography on African cultures and black
      peoples of the Caribbean and Latin America / Roberto Nodal. -
      Milwaukee : Department of Afro-American Studies, University
      of Wisconsin, 1972. - 48p. - (Afro-American studies report ;
      no.1)

        A general bibliography on black cultures and societies of
      Latin America and the Caribbean area, it contains separate
      sections on the English-speaking Caribbean (excluding Jamaica)
      (p.38-41) and Jamaica (p.42-43).   There is also a section on the
      general Caribbean.
                                                                    UWI-J

678   POLLAK-ELTZ, ANGELINA
        Cultos afroamericanos / Angelina Pollak-Eltz. - Caracas :
      Facultad de Humanidades y Educación, Instituto de Investiga-
      ciónes Históricas, Universidad Católica "Andrés Bello," 1972.
      - 258, [12]p.
        Bibliography : p.251-258

References arranged alphabetically by author are mainly
to monographs and include entries on shango, obeah, voodoo,
shakers, shouters and other African-based religious cults.

UWI-T

679   PRICE, R.
Caribbean fishing and fishermen : a historical sketch /
R. Price. - p.1381-1383
In American anthropology. - Vol.68 (Dec. 1966)

Ref.no.5
1967, p.39

680   TAYLOR, DOUGLAS MACRAE
The Black Carib of British Honduras / Douglas MacRae
Taylor. - New York : Wenner-Gren Foundation for Anthropological
Research, 1951. - 176p. - (Viking fund publications in
anthropology ; no.17)
Bibliography : p.172-176

UWI-J

681   WORK, MONROE N.
A bibliography of the Negro in Africa and America /
compiled by Monroe N. Work. - New York : Argosy-Antiquarian,
1965. - xxi, 698p.
Reprint ed.
First published 1928

17,000 entries covering significant publications in
different languages issued before 1928. Material listed under
two main sections : The Negro in Africa; The Negro in America.
In section 3 of the latter - Present Conditions of the Negro in
the West Indies and Latin America (p.637-660) - items on the West
Indies are listed under the following subject headings : Present
Conditions of the Negro in the West Indies and Central America;
Present Conditions of the Negro in South America; Folklore of the
Negro in the West Indies and South America; Folk Music of the
Negro in the West Indies and South America; The Negro and
Literature in the West Indies and South America : a Bibliography
of Bibliographies on the West Indies.

UWI-T

Belize

682   THOMPSON, JOHN ERIC
... Ethnology of the Mayas of southern and central
British Honduras / John Eric Thompson. - Chicago : [Field
Museum of Natural History], 1930. - 2, 1, 27-213p. - (Field
Museum of Natural History publication ; no.274. Anthropo-
logical series ; vol.17, no.2)
Bibliography : p.196-203

Includes a short historical bibliography on British
Honduras and a listing of over 100 books and articles referred to
in the book in one alphabetical arrangement by author.

UWI-J

Guyana

683 DERBYSHIRE, D.C.
     Preliminary bibliography of northern Carib / by D.C.
Derbyshire. - London : Linguistic Section, Hixkaryana Research
Project, University College, [1977?]. - 11p.
     Mimeographed

Benjamin

684 Guyana. National Library
     Select list of books on Guyana and its multi-racial
society / National Library. - Georgetown : National Library,
1975. - 4 leaves
     Typescript

NLG

685 Guyana. Public Free Library
     Bibliography of the Africans in Guyana / Public Free
Library. - Georgetown, (Guyana) : Public Free Library, 1971. -
4 leaves
     Typescript

     Lists books and periodical articles.

NLG

686 Guyana. Public Free Library
     Books on the background and origin of the people of
Guyana / Public Free Library. - Georgetown : Public Free
Library, [19-?]. - 10 leaves

NLG

687 Guyana. Public Free Library
     East Indian life in Guyana / Public Free Library. -
Georgetown, (Guyana) : Public Free Library, 1970. - 1 leaf
     Typescript

     Items comprise books only.

NLG

688 KABDEBO, THOMAS GEORGE
     Guide to the literature of the Amerindians of Guyana / by
Thomas George Kabdebo ... . - [London] : Library Association,
1975. - 289p.
     F.L.A. thesis

Aimed at all would-be students of Amerindian affairs, the text discusses the literature on the original inhabitants of Guyana, including sources and the condition of the material. The bibliography (p.99-256) covers works from 1596 to 1970 with full descriptions, notes and critical summaries. Library locations and classification numbers are provided and a general index of authors, titles and subjects cited concludes the work.

UWI-T

689 MENEZES, MARY NOEL
British policy towards the Amerindians in British Guiana, 1803-1873 / by Mary Noel Menezes. - Oxford : Clarendon Press, 1977. - xiii, 326p.
Bibliography : p.298-314

Lists bibliographies and guides, primary sources, manuscript and printed and secondary sources separating contemporary accounts from later works with articles and periodicals in a final section.

UWI-T

690 O'LEARY, TIMOTHY J.
Ethnographic bibliography of South America / Timothy J. O'Leary. - New Haven, Conn. : Human Relations Area Files, 1963. - xxiv, 387p. - (Behaviour science bibliographies)

UG

691 OSGOOD, CORNELIUS
British Guiana archaeology to 1945 / Cornelius Osgood. - New Haven, [Conn.] : Yale University Press, 1946. - 65p. - (Yale University publications in anthropology ; no.36)
Bibliography : p.64-65

Includes several items on the Indians of British Guiana and the archaeology of that country. Alphabetical author arrangement.

UWI-T

692 ROTH, WALTER EDMUND
An introductory study of the arts, crafts and customs of the Guiana Indians / by Walter Edmund Roth. - New York : Johnson Reprint Corporation, 1970. - 25-745p.
Reprint of 1916 ed.
Bibliography : p.63-68

Originally published by the U.S. Government Printing Office as a paper accompanying the 38th Annual Report of the U.S. Bureau of American Ethnology. 162 items, many of them dealing with the Indians of Guyana. Includes some works on Guyanese history and natural history.

UWI-T

693   SINGH, K.B.
          The Jung Bahadur Singh Collection / K.B. Singh. - [S.l. :
      s.n.], [1976]. - 18 leaves
          Typescript

          "Lists, with annotations, photographs and other visual
      items relating to the life of J.B. Singh and East Indian cultural
      development in Guyana. This small collection is presently
      deposited in the University of Guyana Library" - Benjamin.
                                                                    UG

694   STEWARD, JULIAN H.
          Handbook of South American Indians / edited by Julian H.
      Steward. - New York : Cooper Square Publishers, 1963. - 7v.

          All volumes have extensive bibliographies, several of them
      containing items on the ethnology, ethnography, anthropology,
      languages, linguistics of the aborigines of Guyana.
                                                                  UWI-T

695   University of Guyana. Library
          East Indians in the Caribbean and Guyana : a bibliography
      based on the resources of the University of Guyana Library. -
      Turkeyen, Guyana : University of Guyana Library, 1975. - 8
      leaves
          Mimeographed
                                                                    UG

Jamaica

696   Institute of Jamaica. West India Reference Library
          The maroons of Jamaica : a bibliography / Rosalie Williams.
      - [Kingston, Jamaica : Institute of Jamaica], [1974?]

          Prepared for an exhibition at the Institute of Jamaica,
      the bibliography was not published.
                                                              Ref.no.18
                                                                    1974
                                                            Item no.238

697   WILLIAMS, JOSEPH J.
          Whence the "black Irish" of Jamaica? / Joseph J.
      Williams. - New York : Dial Press, 1932. - vip., 3 leaves,
      97p.
          Bibliography : p.76-90

          "Surveys the literature on the origins of the Black
      Jamaicans called Black Irish including some oral historical
      sources" - Szwed and Abrahams.
                                                                  UWI-J

Trinidad and Tobago

698   University of the West Indies (St. Augustine). Library
         List of references on cultural and religious practices of
      Hindus in Trinidad and Tobago / University of the West Indies
      Library. - [St. Augustine, Trinidad : Library, University of
      the West Indies], 1977. - 2 leaves

         23 references to reports, journal articles and monographs
      (theses, pamphlets, books) on Indians in Trinidad and Tobago
      generally. Arranged in alphabetical author order.
                                                            UWI-T

                          ETHNOMUSICOLOGY

699   BLOOMFIELD, VALERIE
         Caribbean recordings : notes on sources with a select
      discography / Valerie Bloomfield. - p.47-72
         In Journal of librarianship. - Vol.8, no.1 (Jan. 1976)
         Select discography : p.62-66
         References and bibliography : p.66-72

         Select discography comprises a selection of commercial
      sound discs listed under categories : General; Folk Music; Cult
      and Religious Music; Calypso; Steelband; Reggae; Ska and Rock
      Steady and Spoken Word. Items in references and bibliography are
      listed under sections : Bibliographies, Institutions, Music in
      General, Calypso, Calypso-Collections, Folk Music, Cult and
      Religious Music, Dance, Steelband, Other Instrumental, Reggae,
      Spoken Word : Broadcasting.
                                                            UWI-T

700   MALM, KRISTER
         Writings on ethnic music and mesomusic in the Lesser
      Antilles including Aruba, Bonaire, Curaçao, Tobago, Trinidad
      and the Virgin Islands : a bibliography / by Krister Malm. -
      [Uppsala], Sweden : Institute of Musicology, University of
      Uppsala, 1969. - 10p.

         An author arrangement list which includes brief annotations
      for journal articles and monographs.
                                                            UWI-T

701   University of the West Indies (St. Augustine). Library
         Caribbean music, dance, ethnomusicology : a select
      bibliography / University of the West Indies Library. - [St.
      Augustine, Trinidad : U.W.I. Library], [197-?]. - 6 leaves
         Typescript

Includes sections on the calypso, carnival, dance, songs
and the steelband.

UWI-T

Jamaica

702   DAVIS, STEPHEN
         Reggae blood lines : in search of the music and culture of
      Jamaica / text by Stephen Davis ; photography by Peter Simon.
      - London : Heinemann Educational Books, 1979. - 216p.
         Jamaica discography / compiled by Don Williams: p.211-216

         Information given includes record label, record number and
      album title.

UWI-T

703   TROYNA, B.S.
         An annotated bibliography : reggae / B.S. Troyna. - p.18-
      19
         In CRC journal. - Vol.5, no.2 (Feb. 1977)

         21 items alphabetically arranged by author. Includes 2
      items specifically on Bob Marley.

UWI-T

Trinidad and Tobago

704   HILL, ERROL
         The Trinidad carnival : mandate for a national theatre /
      Errol Hill. - Austin : University of Texas Press, 1972. -
      139p.
         Bibliography : p.127-129

         A list of books and articles in alphabetical author order
      including some unpublished items, followed by a list of 14
      Trinidad newspapers of the 19th and 20th centuries with dates
      including closure for defunct titles.

UWI-T

705   LIVERPOOL, HOLLIS URBAN LESTER
         Carnival in Trinidad and Tobago : its implications for
      education in secondary schools / by Hollis Urban Lester
      Liverpool. - St. Augustine, [Trinidad] : School of Education,
      University of the West Indies, 1977. - 107p.
         Bibliography : p.102-107

"Dissertation submitted for Diploma in Education programme." Forty-one items, some annotated, chiefly on carnival and related cultural and educational considerations.

UWI-T

706 Trinidad and Tobago. Central Library. West Indian Reference Section
List of books on Carnival in Trinidad / prepared by the Central Library Services of Trinidad and Tobago. - [Port of Spain, Trinidad] : Central Library, 1965. - 2 leaves

Includes 24 references to books (citing relevant sections), pamphlets and journal articles, a few of which are not held by the library.

TCL

707 University of the West Indies (St. Augustine). Department of English
A selected bibliography on the calypso and oral tradition of Trinidad and Tobago / Department of English. - [St. Augustine, Trinidad] : Department of English, The University of the West Indies, 1972. - 2p.
Mimeographed

The 38 items listed include periodical and newspaper articles as well as monographs and theses.

UWI-T

708 University of the West Indies (St. Augustine). Library
Carnival, the steelband and the calypso : a list of references to the literature held in the library ... . - St. Augustine, Trinidad : University of the West Indies, 1978. - 3p.

Brief listings in author order for monographs and journal articles under the three subject areas.

UWI-T

FOLKLORE

709 Caribbean Organization. Library
Caribbean folklore : selective list of books and articles / Caribbean Organization Library. - Puerto Rico : [Caribbean Organization] Central Secretariat, 1963. - 13p.
Mimeographed

NLG

710 PARSONS, ELSIE WORTHINGTON (CLEWS)
      Folk-lore of the Antilles, French and English / Elsie
      Worthington Parsons. - New York : The American Folk-lore
      Society, 1933, 1936, 1943. - 3v.
          Volume 3 : 1943. - 487p.
          Bibliography and abbreviations : p.1-12

      Over 300 references to folk tales and collections as well
  as commentaries published in journals and as books.
                                                              UWI-J

711 SZWED, JOHN F.
      Afro-American folk culture : an annotated bibliography of
      materials from North, Central and South America and the West
      Indies / John F. Szwed and Roger D. Abrahams with Roger Baron
      ... . - Philadelphia : Institute for the Study of Human
      Issues, c1978. - 2v. - (Publications of the American Folklore
      Society. Bibliographical and special series ; v.31-32)
          Pt.1 : North America
          Pt.2 : The West Indies, Central and South America

      Includes material on folklore, music, dance, religion,
  cookery, dress, language, jokes and recreation. The six major
  sections - Bibliography, General, North America, Caribbean,
  Central America and South America - are further subdivided by
  country. Books, journals, magazines, newspapers and phonograph
  records published from the early 19th century through 1973 are
  listed. There are subject and geographic indexes and descriptive
  annotations.
                                                              UWI-T

712 Trinidad and Tobago. Central Library. West Indian Reference
      Collection
      A selective list of books, periodical literature and
      pamphlet material on folklore in the West Indies / compiled
      from the stock of the West Indian Reference Collection of the
      Central Library. - Port of Spain : Central Library, 1968. -
      7p.
                                                              TCL

713 Trinidad and Tobago. Central Library. West Indian Reference
      Section
      List of books and articles on folklore in the West Indies
      / Central Library. - [Port of Spain, Trinidad] : Central
      Library, 1969. - 4 leaves
                                                              TCL

714 TWINING, MARY ARNOLD
      Caribbean folklore / Mary Arnold Twining. - Atlanta, Ga. :
      Atlanta University, [1971]. - 13 leaves. - (Center for African
      and African-American Studies CAAS bibliography ; no.6)
                                                              UWI-J

715 TWINING, MARY
       Towards a working folklore bibliography of the Caribbean
     area / Mary Twining. - p.69-77
     In Black lines. - Vol.2, no.1 (Fall 1971)
                                                          Ref.no.92
                                                      Item no.1.0276

716 UDAL, JOHN SYMONDS
       Obeah in the West Indies / John Symonds Udal. - p.255-295
     In Folklore. - Vol.26 (1915)

       Includes a review of writings on obeah.
                                                          Ref.no.711
                                                       Item no.695

717 WILLIAMS, JOSEPH JOHN
       Voodoos and obeahs ; phases of West India witchcraft / by
     Joseph John Williams. - New York : Dial Press, 1932. - xixp.,
     1 leaf, 257p.
       Bibliography : p.237-248

       Based on works found in the Boston College library, the
     bibliography is divided into three sections: (1) ... for African
     Ophiolatry, (2) ... for Haitian Voodoo and (3) ... for Jamaica
     Obeah, Myalism and Revivalism with over 50 references to general
     reports, laws and books arranged alphabetically by author.
                                                               UWI-J

Bahamas

718 PARSONS, ELSIE WORTHINGTON (CLEWS)
       Folktales of Andros Island, Bahamas / Elsie Worthington
     Parsons. - Lancaster, Pa. ; New York : American Folklore
     Society, [1918]. - xx, 170p.
       Bibliography : p.xvii-xx.
                                                                    LC

Guyana

719 Guyana. Public Free Library
       Culture, customs, beliefs and folklore and legends /
     Public Free Library. - Georgetown, (Guyana) : Public Free
     Library, 1971. - 7 leaves
       Typescript

       Arrangement is by ethnic groups.
                                                                   NLG

720 SINGH, K.B.
     'Kali Mai Puja' : a study of Guyanese East Indian folk
     cult in its socio-cultural context / K.B. Singh. - [S.1. :
     s.n.], 1977. - 112 leaves

     "Gives a detailed set of annotations for tapes of this
     movement made by K.B. Singh for the University of Guyana
     Library" - Benjamin.

                                                              UG

721 University of Guyana. Library
     Recordings of folklore, drama and music made in Guyana
     1971-3 / [by Peter Kempadoo]. - Georgetown : University of
     Guyana Library, 1974. - 22p.
     Mimeographed

     "Items are arranged by place where the recording was made
     ... Details of each recording are given. Tapes are housed in the
     University of Guyana library" - ACURIL VI (Ref.no.2).

                                                              UG

Jamaica

722 BECKWITH, MARTHA WARREN
     Black roadways : a study of Jamaican folk life / by Martha
     Warren Beckwith. - Chapel Hill : University of North Carolina
     Press, 1929. - xvii, 243p.
     Bibliography : p.229-233

     Alphabetical list of 69 references including articles from
     journals.

                                                            UWI-T

Trinidad and Tobago

723 Trinidad and Tobago. Central Library. West Indian Reference
     Section
     Folk tales of Trinidad and Tobago : a short list of
     holdings / West Indian Reference Section, Central Library. -
     Port of Spain, Trinidad : Central Library, [197-?]. - 1 leaf
     Typescript

     Lists 10 locally published works.

                                                              TCL

724   Trinidad and Tobago.   Central Library.   West Indian
      Reference Section
         List of folk tales in information files, 1963-1975 / West
      Indian Reference Section, Central Library. - Port of Spain,
      Trinidad : Central Library, [196-?]. - 2 leaves
         Typescript

         Indexes local folk tales appearing in 4 local newspapers,
      one of which has since become defunct.

                                                                  TCL

                               FORESTRY

725   Caribbean Commission.   Caribbean Research Council.   Committee
      on Agriculture, Nutrition, Fisheries and Forestry
         Forest research within the Caribbean area / Committee on
      Agriculture, Nutrition, Fisheries and Forestry, Caribbean
      Research Council. - Washington, D.C. : [Caribbean Commission],
      1947. - 128p.
         Bibliography : p.85-107

         Arranged geographically under headings : (a) Barbados,
      Leeward Islands and Windward Islands, (b) British Guiana, (c)
      Cuba, (d) Guadeloupe, Martinique and French Guiana, (e) British
      Honduras, (f) Jamaica, (g) Puerto Rico, (h) Surinam, (i) Trinidad
      and Tobago.   Includes official publications and periodical
      articles.   195 entries on the English-speaking Caribbean.

                                                                UWI-T

725a LAMB, F. BRUCE
         A selected, annotated bibliography on mahogany / F. Bruce
      Lamb. - p.17-37
         In Caribbean forester. - Vol.20, nos. 1 & 2 (Jan.-June
      1959).

         240 items covering the English-speaking and wider
      Caribbean.   Includes many entries on British Honduras and a few
      on the Bahamas, Jamaica and Trinidad and Tobago.   Arranged by
      the Oxford Decimal System of Classification for Forestry with
      brief annotations and an author index.

                                                                UWI-T

Guyana

726 [British Guiana. Forestry Department]
     Bibliography [on] forestry, British Guiana / Forestry
     Department. - [S.l. : s.n.], 1947. - 9 leaves
     Photocopy
                                                              UG

727 Guyana. National Science Research Council
     Forests and forestry : a select bibliography with special
     reference to Guyana / compiled by Lloyd S. Harry ; edited by
     Shirley Alonzo. - Georgetown, Guyana : National Science
     Research Council, 1975. - 100p.
                                                              UG

728 WELCH, I.A.
     Selected list of reports, papers, etc. dealing with forest
     valuation and forest reconnaisance surveys, aerial photo-
     interpretation, geology, soils and forest resource development
     available from Forest Department records . I.A. Welch. - George-
     town : Forest Department, 1967. - 11 leaves
     Mimeographed
                                                          Benjamin

Trinidad and Tobago

729 BELL, T.I.W.
     Management of the Trinidad Mora forests with special
     reference to the Matura Forest Reserve / by T.I.W. Bell. -
     [Port of Spain], Trinidad and Tobago : Forestry Division,
     [1971]. - ix, 70p.
     Bibliography : p.65-67

     64 references arranged alphabetically by author including
     journal articles, government reports, conference papers and other
     monographs on forestry.
                                                            UWI-T

730 Trinidad and Tobago. Ministry of Agriculture, Lands and
     Fisheries. Forestry Division. Library
     Forestry in Trinidad and Tobago : a select bibliography ;
     compiled on the occasion of the XI Commonwealth Forestry
     Conference, Trinidad, 7-26 September, 1980 / Library, Forestry
     Division. - St. James, [Port of Spain] : Library, Forestry
     Division, Ministry of Agriculture, Lands and Fisheries, 1980.
     - ii, 24p.
     Mimeographed

Subject arrangement based on the broad divisions of the
Oxford System of Decimal Classification for Forestry. 282 items
are listed under sections : General, Environmental Factors,
Silviculture, Forest Injuries and Protection, Forest Mensuration
and Management, Utilization of Forest Products. Most of the
material listed is available in the Forest Division Library and
includes publications by the Division's staff.

UWI-T

731 Trinidad and Tobago. Ministry of Planning and Development
     Forest and forest products / Patricia Raymond. - [Port of
Spain, Trinidad : Ministry of Planning and Development],
[197-?]. - 2p.
     Mimeographed

     11 items. Prepared for a proposed bibliography of Trinidad
and Tobago.

MF-T

GEOGRAPHY

732 BLUME, HELMUT
     Beiträge zur Klimatologie Westindiens / Helmut Blume. -
p.288-289
     In Erdkunde. - Vol.6 (Dec. 1962)

Ref.no.5
1963, p.296

733 BLUME, HELMUT
     Die Britischen Inseln über dem Winde (Kleine Antillen) /
Helmut Blume. - p.286-287
     In Erdkunde. - Vol. 15 (Dec. 1961)

Ref.no.5
1963, p.296

734 BLUME, HELMUT
     The Caribbean islands / Helmut Blume ; translated by
Johannes Maczewski and Anne Norton. - London : Longman, 1974.
- 464p.
     Bibliography (up to 1966): The West Indies as a whole, and
major subregions. - p.384-436
     Supplement 1967-1970. - p.437-449

     Includes books, periodical articles, conference papers
and reports. Covers the Greater and Lesser Antilles with general
sections devoted to geographic surveys, topography, climate, the
sea, flora and fauna and the Amerindian aborigines as well as

population and economy followed by detailed lists for individual
territories and groups. The supplement is arranged in alphabetical
author order.

UWI-T

735 PAGNEY, PIERRE
Le climat des Antilles / Pierre Pagney. - Paris : Institut
des Hautes Etudes de l'Amérique Latine, 1966. - 379p. -
(Université de Paris. Travaux et mémoires de l'Institut des
Hautes Etudes de l'Amérique Latine ; 15)
Bibliography: p.351-364

Ref.no.5
Apr. 1972, p.154

736 Union Géographique Internationale
Bibliographie géographique internationale 1960 ... avec le
concours de l'Organisation des Nations Unies pour l'Education,
la Science et Culture (UNESCO) / Union Géographique Internationale. - Paris : Centre National de la Recherche Scienti-
fique, 1962. - 865p.

UWI-J

737 University of the West Indies. Faculty of Natural Sciences.
Geography Department
A bibliography of the Caribbean area for geographers /
compiled by Anne V. Norton. - Mona, [Jamaica] : Department of
Geography, University of the West Indies, 1971. - 3v. (418p.).
- (U.W.I., Mona, Jamaica : Department of Geology and Geography.
Geography Division occasional publications ; no.7)

Includes British Honduras, Guyana and all the islands of
the Caribbean Sea.

UWI-J

738 University of the West Indies (Mona). Faculty of Natural
Sciences. Geography Department
Undergraduate research papers in geography at the University
of the West Indies, 1968-1970. - [Mona], Jamaica : Department
of Geography, University of the West Indies, 1970. - xvi, 53
leaves

Whole issue of the department's Research Notes (no.4,
1970) devoted to bibliography. Listings in section A cover
Jamaica and are arranged alphabetically by author under topics :
Urban Geography, Economic Geography - Agriculture and Agricultural
Marketing, Economic Geography - Industrialisation, Economic
Geography - Tourism, Economic Geography - Trade, Physical
Geography - Climatology and Biogeography, Special Regional Studies.
Section B covers non-Jamaican topics and items are arranged
alphabetically by author under the following countries : Barbados,

Dominica, Trinidad. Section C lists the papers arranged by
authors while in Section D they are arranged by year of submission.
Abstracts of papers arranged by topics follow the listings.

UWI-T

739 WEST, ROBERT COOPER
        Middle America : its land and peoples / Robert Cooper West
     and John P. Augelli. - Englewood Cliffs, N.J. : Prentice Hall,
     1966. - 482p.

        Selected references at the end of each chapter on the
     geography, land use, agriculture and economy of the countries
     discussed. There are chapters on the Greater Antilles, including
     Jamaica, the Lesser Antilles and the Bahamas.

UWI-T

Belize

740 United States. Weather Bureau
        An annotated bibliography of the climate of British
     Honduras / J.A. Wallace and Angelo F. Spano, Foreign Area
     Section, Office of Climatology ... ; sponsored by the Air
     Weather Service Climatic Center, U.S. Air Force. - Washington,
     D.C. : [s.n.], 1962. - 17p.
        Cover title

LC

Guyana

741 CUMMINGS, LESLIE PETER
        Bibliography [on the Guianas] : [Section II] / Leslie
     Peter Cummings. - Turkeyen, Guyana : University of Guyana,
     [1968?]. - 46p.
        Mimeographed

        This is the second part of a bibliography of the Guianas
     in preparation. It is biased towards articles and reports on
     geography, and towards material located in London.

UWI-T

742 United States. Weather Bureau
        Bibliography on the climate of the Guianas : British,
     French, Surinam (Dutch or Netherlands) / by Simon J. Roman. -
     Washington, D.C. : [s.n.], 1957. - 31p.

LC

GEOLOGY

743   Bibliography and index of geology. - Vol.38 (1974)- . - Boulder,
      Col. : Geological Society of America. - 1974-
          Monthly
          From v.1 (1934)-v.37 (1973) published as : Bibliography
      and index of geology exclusive of North America

          Some issues contain entries on the West Indies.
                                                    Ref.no.745

744   BOWIN, C.O.
          Geophysical study of the Cayman Trough / C.O. Bowin. -
      p.5172-5173
          In Journal of geophysical research. - Vol.73 (Aug. 1968)

          Lists 40 items some of which deal with West Indian geology
      as a whole. There are a few on the Caymans and one on the geology
      of Jamaica.
                                                            UWI-T

745   Caribbean Industrial Research Institute (CARIRI)
          Bibliography of geological literature of possible relevance
      to work of Regional Beach Erosion Control Programme / CARIRI. -
      St. Augustine, [Trinidad] : CARIRI, 1972. - 10p.

          Comprises primary and secondary source material held in the
      Library of the University of the West Indies, St. Augustine, the
      Seismic Research Unit, U.W.I., St. Augustine, the Technical
      Information Service, CARIRI and the computer-based GEO-RFF
      (Geological Reference File) maintained by the American Geological
      Institute. 68 items arranged alphabetically by author under
      headings : Caribbean-Regional (10 items), Lesser Antilles (6
      items), Leeward Islands (5 items), Windward Islands (1 item),
      Anguilla (3 items), Antigua (2 items), Barbados (21 items),
      Dominica (3 items), Grenada (4 items), Montserrat (13 items),
      St. Kitts-Nevis (2 items), St. Lucia (4 items), St. Vincent (5
      items). Includes a listing of Geological Research in Progress
      in the Caribbean during 1970. Many journal articles and govern-
      ment reports.
                                                            UWI-T

746   MATTSON, PETER H.
          Theses in geological sciences in the Caribbean / Peter H.
      Mattson. - p.97-102
          In Caribbean journal of science. - 2 (1962)

          A list of theses submitted to U.S. and Canadian universi-
      ties and colleges through 1957. Arranged by country or area
      studied. Includes Venezuela and the Dutch West Indies as well

as the English-speaking islands. This Caribbean listing was
compiled from a larger bibliography.

UWI-T

747 MATTSON, PETER H.
     West Indies island arcs / edited by Peter H. Mattson –
Stroudsburg, Penn. : Dowden, Hutchinson and Ross, 1977. –
xiii, 382p. – (Benchmark papers in geology ; 33)
     Bibliography : p.361–368

     Lists of references are included at the end of each of the
papers some of which cover Caribbean and Middle America tectonics,
sedimentary environments in Trinidad and the geology of Jamaica.
In addition the general bibliography at the end of the work cites
articles on significant mapping projects in chronological order
by project.

UWI-T

748 PUTNAM, P.C.
     Geological literature on Central America, 1529–1924 / P.C.
Putnam. – [Cambridge] : Massachusetts Institute of Technology,
1924
     Part 2 of Thesis (M.S.). – Massachusetts Institute of
Technology, Boston, 1924

     Includes the wider Caribbean area.

Ref.no.746

749 RICHARDS, HORACE GARDINER
     Annotated bibliography of quaternary shorelines, 1945–
1965 / Horace Gardiner Richards [and] Rhodes W. Fairbridge. –
Philadelphia : Academy of Natural Sciences, 1965. – vii, 280p.
– (Academy of Natural Sciences, Philadelphia. Special publi-
cation ; 6)
     Supplement 1965–1969. – 1970. – 240p. – (Academy of
Natural Sciences, Philadelphia. Special publication ; 10)

     The supplement includes 36 references to the Caribbean.
Ref.no.745
Item no.11.10

750 RUTTEN, LOUIS M.R.
     Bibliography of West Indian geology / Louis M.R. Rutten.
– Utrecht : Bij N.V.A. Oosthoek's Uitg. Mij, 1938. – viii,
103p.
     Added title : Geographische en geologische mededelingen,
pub nit het Geographisch en vit het Mineralogisch – geodogisch
instituut der Jijksuniversiteit te Utrecht, Physiograhisch
geologische reeks no.16.

UWI-T

751   United Nations
        Caribbean small islands water resources assessment develop-
ment management : a first bibliography of geology, hydrogeology and water resources / prepared by Peter Hadwen ... in
collaboration with U.W.I. Seismic Research Unit, British
Development Division, Canadian International Development
Agency, Government Hydrologist, Barbados. - Bridgetown,
Barbados : United Nations, 1980. - 59 leaves. - (CAR/79/ROI)
        Mimeographed
        Cover title

        Arranged in two sections - Country Bibliographies and
Regional Bibliographies (selected list). References in the first
section (p.4-56), mainly English language, are arranged under
country and by date with location of copies where known. Those
in the second section are chronologically arranged. Included are
journal articles, proceedings, symposia, unpublished theses and
reports. The bibliography covers geophysics, geology, geothermics
and water resources. Trinidad and Tobago and Jamaica are
excluded.

                                                                    UWI-T

752   University of Miami (Coral Gables, Florida). Institute of
      Marine Science
        Regional bibliography of Caribbean geology : technical
report / compiled by L.K. Fink. - Miami, Fla. : [s.n.], 1964.
- 65p. - (Mimeographed report ; no.64-3)
        Mimeographed
                                                            Ref.no.70
                                              Vol. 12-14, 1962-64

Bahamas

753   CANT, R.V.
        Annotated bibliography of groundwater in the Bahamas :
U.N. ground-water project informal report no.18 for Ministry
of Works and Utilities, Nassau, Bahamas / R.V. Cant. - [S.l. :
s.n.], 1979
                                                           Ref.no.751
                                                                p.12

Guyana

754   [BARRON, C.N.]
        A further guide to mineral exploration in Guyana : forming
a supplement to Bulletin 38 and containing notes on over fifty
of the more interesting prospects brought to light in the
period 1965-1969 / C.N. Barron. - [Georgetown : Geological
Survey], [1969?]. - 1v. (various pagings)

Mimeographed

Includes a list of Geological Survey publications.

Benjamin

755   DIXON, C.G.
      Bibliography of the geology and mining of British Guiana /
      by C.G. Dixon and H.K. George. - Georgetown, British Guiana :
      Government Printery, 1964. - iv, 87p. - (Geological survey of
      British Guiana bulletin ; 32)

      Based on material in the Geological Survey library.
   Abstracts are provided for each of the papers quoted and
   additional lists of the references are provided in both chronological and geographical arrangements.

UWI-T

756   GIBBS, A.
      Bibliography for the Oko-Blue Mountains regions : geology
      / A. Gibbs. - [S.l. : s.n.], 1977. - 4 leaves
      Typescript

UG

757   GIBBS, A.
      Field report on the Mazaruni-Puruni expedition, 1977 /
      A. Gibbs. - [S.l. : s.n.], 1977. - 4 leaves
      Typescript

      "To be published shortly by the Geological Survey of
   Guyana. Includes a significant bibliography." - Benjamin

UG

758   Guyana. Ministry of Geological Survey
      List of publications and maps as at 31st December 1972 /
      Ministry of Geological Survey. - Georgetown, Guyana :
      Geological Survey Department, [1973]. - 23p.
      Mimeographed

      "Earlier lists, with variations, have been published" -
   Benjamin. Includes annual reports, bulletins, conference
   proceedings, mineral resources pamphlets, miscellaneous papers
   and reports, maps, records of the Geological Survey.

NLG

759   MCDONALD, J.R.
      A guide to mineral exploration in Guyana / J.R. McDonald.
      - [Georgetown], Guyana : Geological Survey of Guyana, Ministry
      of Natural Resources, 1968. - iii, 91p. - (Bulletin 38)
      Bibliography: p.72-88

      37 expedition reports and other miscellaneous reports are
   listed, followed by a list of Geological Survey publications and

maps, annual reports, mineral resources pamphlets, special
reports, printed geological maps, aeromagnetic maps, inter-Guiana
Geological Conferences and Caribbean Geological Conferences.

UWI-T

760   SINHA, N.K.P.
        Geomorphic evolution of the Northern Rupununi Basin,
   Guyana / by N.K.P. Sinha. - Montreal : Department of Geography,
   McGill University, 1968. - 131p. - (McGill University savanna
   research project.   Savanna research series ; no.11)
        Bibliography: p.125-312

        Lists mainly journal articles, reports and theses in
   alphabetical order by author. Includes references on geology,
   climate and vegetation in Guyana among more general works relevant
   to the study.

UWI-T

Indexes
   761   Guyana. Geological Survey Department. Library
            [Index of reports in the Geological Survey Department
        Library, Guyana.]. - [S.l. : s.n.], [196-?-197-?]. - 157p.
            Typescript

        "Cumulative index of published and unpublished reports and
   articles by the staff of the Geological Survey" - Benjamin

GSL

Jamaica

762   KHUDOLEY, K.M.
        Paleogeography and geological history of Greater Antilles
   / K.M. Khudoley and A.A. Meyerhoff. - [Boulder, Colo.] :
   Geological Society of America, 1971. - xiv, 199p. - (The
   Geological Society of America memoir ; 129)
        Bibliography : p.167-186

        References are arranged alphabetically by author and
   include only Jamaica of the former British territories.

UWI-T

763   KINGHORN, MARION
        Bibliography of Jamaican geology / edited by Marion
   Kinghorn. - [Norwich, England : Geo. Abstracts, University of
   East Anglia], [1977]. - 150p.

        Includes dissertations, other monographs and periodical
   articles in geochemistry, marine geology and pollution as well
   as in traditional geology but excludes government agency reports.

An appendix covers the Cayman Islands, a former dependency of
Jamaica. Index of second authors and a key word-out-of-context
subject index.

UWI-J

764   MATLEY, C.A.
        Some recent contributions to the geology of Jamaica with a
      bibliography / C.A. Matley. - p.676-688
        In Handbook of Jamaica 1923 / by Frank Cundall. - Kingston,
      Jamaica : Government Printing Office, 1923

        Chronological listing covering 1707 to 1922 appears as an
      appendix.

UWI-J

Trinidad and Tobago

765   SUTER, H.H.
        The general and economic geology of Trinidad, B.W.I. /
      by H.H. Suter. - London : H.M.S.O., 1954. - 134p.
        "Reprinted, with amendments, from: Colonial Geology and
      Mineral Resources, vol.2, nos.3 and 4 and vol.3, no.1"
        Bibliography : p.123-127

        Over 150 references to journal articles and monographs
      mainly on Trinidad, arranged alphabetically by author.

UWI-T

HISTORY

766   The Cambridge history of the British Empire / edited by E.A.
      Benians, Sir James Butler, C.E. Carrington. - Cambridge :
      University Press
        Vol.3 : The Empire-Commonwealth, 1870-1919. - 948p.
        Reprinted: 1967
        Bibliography / compiled by A. Taylor Milne. - 1959. -
      p.769-908

        Lists manuscript collections in public and private archives
      with official papers and publications in Part I and other works
      subdivided by form and period of publication in Part II. Includes
      some references to the West Indian colonies.

767   The Cambridge history of the British Empire / general editors
      J. Holland Rose, A.P. Newton, E.A. Benians. - Cambridge :
      University Press
          Vol.2 :   The growth of the new empire, 1783-1870. - 1940.
      - 1066p.
          Reprinted: 1961
          Bibliography / A.P. Newton and A. Taylor Milne. - 1940. -
      p.882-1004

          Extensive lists of manuscript collections in public and
      private archives, official papers and publications including
      parliamentary papers dealing with the British West Indies in
      chronological order.   Includes separate listings of contemporary
      and later works on the West Indies, Bermuda, British Honduras
      and British Guiana (p.976-985).

                                                                    UWI-T

768   CHAFFEE, WILBER A.
          Dissertations on Latin America / by Wilber A. Chaffee and
      Honor M. Griffin. - Austin, [Tex.] : Institute of Latin
      American Studies, the University of Texas at Austin, 1973. -
      xi, 62p. - (Guides and bibliographies series; 7)

          This listing which attempts to collect all of the doctoral
      dissertations done on topics on Latin American history during the
      period 1960-1970 includes sections on the Caribbean generally,
      Belize, Jamaica and B.W.I., and the Guianas.   The entries are
      grouped by country and arranged alphabetically within each group
      by author.

                                                                    UWI-T

768a CROUSE, NELLIS M.
          French pioneers in the West Indies, 1624-1664 / Nellis M.
      Crouse. - New York : Octagon Books, 1977 [c1940]. - 294p.
          Reprint
          Bibliography: p.273-281

          33 references with full and evaluative annotations to
      works of travel, description and especially history, embracing
      many islands, British and French, with which Frenchmen were
      involved.   Grenada, St. Christopher, St. Lucia, St. Vincent and
      Antigua are all included.

                                                                    UWI-T

769   GOVEIA, ELSA V.
          A study on the historiography of the British West Indies
      to the end of the nineteenth century / Elsa V. Goveia. -
      Mexico : Instituto Panamericano de Geografía e Historia, 1956.
      - 183p. - (Instituto Panamericano de Geografía e Historia.
      Comisión de Historia [Publicaciones] 78 Historiografías ; 2)

A comprehensive bibliographic analysis of histories of the British West Indies taken in chronological order. Based on printed histories available in the libraries of the University College of the West Indies and the Institute of Jamaica, it excludes manuscript material and twentieth century imprints. Extensive footnotes and a chronological list of chief works cited are provided.

UWI-T

770 GRIFFIN, CHARLES C.
Latin America : a guide to the historical literature / [edited by] Charles C. Griffin. - Austin, [Tex.] : University of Texas Press for the Conference on Latin American History, [1971]. - xxx, 700p. - (Conference on Latin American history publications ; no.4)

Coverage includes the British West Indian territories as part of the non-Hispanic Caribbean in each of the sections devoted to reference, general and background works as well as those of the independence and post-independence periods. Entries annotated and indexed by author.

UWI-T

771 GRIFFIN, GRACE GARDNER
Writings on American history, 1906-1937/38 : a bibliography of books and articles on United States and Canadian history published during the year[s] 1906-1937/38 ; with some memoranda on other portions of America / by Grace Gardner Griffin. - Washington, D.C. : Government Printing Office, 1908-1942. - 31v.

"There are entries in each volume under British West Indies and/or under West Indies which are specially valuable for finding detailed bits of historical information" - Brown.

Ref.no.144

772 HANHAM, H.J.
Bibliography of British history 1851-1914 ; issued under the direction of the American Historical Association and the Royal Historical Society of Great Britain / compiled and edited by H.J. Hanham. - Oxford : Clarendon Press, 1976. - xxvii, 1606p.
Ch.3 : External relations

Section on the British West Indies (p.185-188) comprises 31 annotated entries.

UWI-T

773 HARING, CLARENCE HENRY
The buccaneers in the West Indies in the xvii century / by Clarence Henry Haring. - New York : E.P. Dutton, 1910. - viii, 298p.

192

Sources and bibliography :   p.275–287

Lists manuscript sources in England located in the Public
Record Office, the British Museum and the Bodleian Library,
manuscript sources in France and printed sources. Several
important secondary works are also described in detail and others
are listed.

UWI–T

774   JACOBS, P.M.
History theses 1901–70 : historical research for higher
degrees in the universities of the United Kingdom / compiled
by P.M. Jacobs. – [London] : Institute of Historical Research,
University of London, 1976. – viii, 456p.

List contains theses completed and approved for the degree
of B.Litt. and doctor's and master's degrees in universities of
the United Kingdom, also a few B.D., B.Phil. and B.Sc. theses.
Titles of theses are arranged chronologically under main headings
further subdivided by topics. Author and subject indexes are
provided. Section on America covers West Indies, British Guiana
and British Honduras (94 entries). Items include material on
Bahamas, Bermuda, Jamaica, Barbados, Leeward Islands, Windward
Islands, St. Kitts, Nevis, Trinidad, Tobago. Apart from history
there are theses on politics and government, sociology, education,
economics, law.

UWI–T

775   LEWIN, P.E.
West Indies, Bermuda and the Falkland Islands / by P.E.
Lewin and W.C. Hill. – p.497–503
In Bibliographie d'histoire coloniale, 1900–1930 / Congrès
international d'histoire coloniale. Paris, 1932

Includes sections on bibliography and archives, general
history, biographical history, constitutional history, and
economic history. The Congress was organized by the Societé
de l'Histoire des Colonies Françaises.

UWI–T

776   MARSHALL, WOODVILLE K.
Historical writing on the English Caribbean since c.1940 ;
a status report / Woodville K. Marshall. – [Cave Hill,
Barbados : University of the West Indies], [1972]. – 10p.
Mimeographed

Bibliographic essay.

UWI–B

777   MARSHALL, WOODVILLE K.
      A review of historical writing on the Commonwealth
      Caribbean since c.1940 / Woodville K. Marshall. - p.271-307
      In Social and economic studies. - Vol.24, no.3 (1975)
      Revised version of a paper which was prepared for a
      conference on "Caribbean Man and his Environment" sponsored by
      the Association of Caribbean Universities and Research
      Institutes and held at U.W.I., Cave Hill on 2-7 Jan. 1973.

      Bibliographic essay covering the specialist literature,
      political and constitutional history, economic history, social
      history, bibliography and the general literature. Includes many
      "modifications or reproductions of doctoral dissertations." The
      bibliography comprises 305 items arranged in alphabetical author
      order.

                                                                UWI-T

778   MATHEWS, THOMAS
      Historical writing in the Caribbean / Thomas Mathews. -
      p.4-6
      In Caribbean review. - Vol.21, no.3 (Fall 1970)

      Bibliographic essay which critically reviews the most
      important historical writings on the Caribbean.

                                                                UWI-T

779   MORALES CARRIÓN, ARTURO
      Puerto Rico and the non-Hispanic Caribbean : a study in the
      decline of Spanish exclusivism / Arturo Morales Carrión. -
      3rd ed. - [San Juan] : University of Puerto Rico Press, 1974.
      - xii, 160p.
      Bibliography: p.144-151

      Arranged in sections : Bibliographical Aids; Primary
      Sources; Manuscripts; Primary Sources : Printed Documents and
      Contemporary Accounts; Secondary Works Including Periodical
      Articles.

                                                                UWI-T

780   MORRELL, W.P.
      British overseas expansion and the history of the Common-
      wealth : a select bibliography / by W.P. Morrell. - 2nd ed. -
      London : Historical Association, 1970. - 48p. - (Historical
      Association. Helps for students of history ; no.63)

                                                                   BL

781   NODAL, ROBERTO
      An annotated bibliography of historical materials on
      Barbados, Guyana and Trinidad-Tobago / Roberto Nodal. -
      Milwaukee, Wisc. : Department of Afro-American Studies,

University of Wisconsin, 1974. - 34 leaves. - (Afro-American
studies report ; 7)

Ref.no.18
1976

782   PARES, R.
        Manning the navy in the West Indies, 1702-63 / R. Pares. -
      p.31-60
        In Royal Historical Society of London transactions S4. -
      Vol.20 (1937)

        Bibliographical footnotes.

Ref.no.5
1937-1942, p.1743

783   RAGATZ, LOWELL JOSEPH
        A guide for the study of British Caribbean history, 1763-
      1834, including the abolition and emancipation movements /
      compiled by Lowell Joseph Ragatz. - Washington, D.C. : U.S.
      Government Printing Office, 1932. - viii, 725p.
        Also published separately as: House document no.818,
      71st Congress, 3rd Session and as: Vol.3 of the Annual report
      of the American Historical Association, 1930

        It is arranged in alphabetical author order under such
headings as manuscripts, documents, legislative journals,
historical writings, description and travel, medical works,
religion in the Caribbean colonies, and abolition and emancipation
literature, further subdivided by country. All entries are fully
annotated and an index with authors, titles, subjects and proper
names is provided. The compilation is "based on material in 69
repositories, both public and private, in seven countries"
including the library of the Institute of Jamaica but locations
are not given. Among noteworthy features are sections on the
British West Indian press (p.391-400) and foreign West Indian
newspapers (p.401-404).

UWI-T

784   RAGATZ, LOWELL JOSEPH
        A list of books and articles on colonial history and
      overseas expansion published in the United States 1900-1930 /
      compiled by Lowell Joseph Ragatz. - Ann Arbor, Mich. :
      Edwards Brothers, 1939. - 2p., 1, 45p.

        "A portion of this list was originally published as an
appendix to: Colonial studies in the United States during the
twentieth century." Supplemented by Ref.nos. 785 and 786.

LC

785   RAGATZ, LOWELL JOSEPH
        A list of books and articles on colonial history and
overseas expansion published in the United States in 1931 and
1932 / compiled by Lowell Joseph Ragatz. - London : A. Thomas,
1933. - 2p., 1, 41p.

        "Prepared for the meeting of the Commission internationale
d'histoire coloniale to be held in Warsaw, Poland in August
1933." Supplements Colonial Studies in the United States During
the Twentieth Century [published 1932].

                                                                    LC

786   RAGATZ, LOWELL JOSEPH
        A list of books and articles on colonial history and
overseas expansion published in the United States in 1933,
1934 and 1935 / compiled by Lowell Joseph Ragatz. - London :
A. Thomas, [1936]. - vi, 91p.

        "Prepared for the annual meeting of the Commission
internationale d'histoire coloniale."

                                                                    LC

787   RAGATZ, LOWELL JOSEPH
        The study of recent and contemporary Caribbean dependencies
history / Lowell Joseph Ragatz. - p.317-327
        In The Caribbean : British, Dutch, French, United States /
edited by A. Curtis Wilgus. - Gainesville, [Fla.] : University
of Florida Press, 1958. - (Caribbean conference series 1 ;
vol.8)

        Bibliographic essay underlining research gaps and needs.
A list of newspapers of the region with commencing dates is
provided as a footnote.

                                                                    UWI-T

788   RAGATZ, LOWELL JOSEPH
        Writings on the Caribbean dependencies, 1928-1959 / by
Lowell Joseph Ragatz. - [Columbus : Ohio State University],
[1958]. - 74p.
        Mimeographed
        Pre-print edition

        Alphabetical author listing of books and journal articles
grouped geographically under the following headings :   the
Dependencies Collectively, the British Caribbean, the Danish
West Indies, the Dutch Caribbean, the French Caribbean, the
Former Spanish West Indies, the Old Swedish West Indies, the
American Caribbean (including the Canal Zone) and the Caribbean
Commission. Each section is subdivided first by territories
and then into entries on general, economic, social, political,
cultural and scientific topics. No annotations.

                                                                    UWI-T

789   RODNEY, WALTER
        Supplement to Bibliography of the Caribbean / compiled by
      Walter Rodney. - [Mona, Jamaica : ISER, U.W.I.], [1965]. -
      1v. (various pagings)
        Mimeographed draft

        A supplement to Barham's similar compilation (Ref.no.78).
      Covers only works in history in alphabetical author arrangement.
                                                                  UWI-T

790   A selective list of books providing contemporary accounts for
      the teaching of West Indian history. - [S.l. : s.n.], [1960?].
      - 4p.
        Mimeographed

        Arranged in three sections :   (1) Collections of Documents
      with Relevant Material, (2) Histories and (3) Other Contemporary
      Authorities. The reading list is aimed at secondary school
      pupils and is based on material available either at the University
      of the West Indies Library or the library of the Institute of
      Jamaica which provide the only clues to its origins. Includes
      very brief annotations.
                                                                  UWI-T

791   University of the West Indies (Cave Hill). Library
        The English-speaking West Indies - post-emancipation
      1831-1865 ; holdings of main library U.W.I., Cave Hill. -
      [Cave Hill, Barbados] : U.W.I. Main Library, [1980]. - 24p.
        Mimeographed

        Alphabetical author listing of monographic works and
      journals in separate sequences.
                                                                  UWI-T

792   University of the West Indies (Mona)
        A selected reading list of books on West Indian history /
      Elsa V. Goveia. - [Mona, Jamaica] : U.C.W.I., 1960. - 12
      leaves
        Mimeographed

        A student reading list of books only, subdivided into
      several sections relating to topics such as imperial expansion
      and policy, slavery and the slave trade, the French Revolution
      in the West Indies etc., with brief notes introducing some
      sections.
                                                                  UWI-T

793   University of the West Indies (Mona). Library
        A select list of works on the British Caribbean ... /
      Library, U.W.I. . - Mona, Jamaica : University of the West
      Indies Library, 1964. - 13p.

Mimeographed
Also published as: Appendix VII of Working paper no.25,
submitted to SALALM XII at Los Angeles.

Listing of the most important and basic works for the
study of British Caribbean history.   Includes out of print and
rare items identified as such.   Excludes works on medicine,
natural sciences and creative writing.

UWI-T

794   University of the West Indies (St. Augustine).   Library
West Indian history (1750-1850) / U.W.I. Library. - [St.
Augustine, Trinidad : University of the West Indies Library],
[197-?]. - 4 leaves
Typescript

Items are arranged alphabetically by author in two
sections - Bibliographies and General.

UWI-T

795   VANDERWAL, RONALD L.
An annotated bibliography prepared for "Prehistory of the
West Indies" / by Ronald L. Vanderwal. - Kingston, Jamaica :
The Institute of Jamaica, 1967. - 6 leaves

References to journal articles arranged alphabetically by
author and subdivided by date of publication.   Includes some
references to the wider Caribbean area.   Annotations are
evaluative and locations are included for the Institute's
collections.   Some items unavailable in Jamaica are so indicated.

UWI-J

796   WADDELL, D.A.G.
The British West Indies in the historiography of the
British Empire-Commonwealth / D.A.G. Waddell. - Durham, N.C. :
[s.n.], 1966

"A shorter discussion of histories than Goveia's but comes
closer to date."

Ref.no.941
Item no.7

797   West Indies Festival of Arts, 1958.   Historical Exhibition
Working Party
Catalogue of historical exhibition held in the Rotunda of
the Red House, Port of Spain, Trinidad, 22nd April-3rd May,
1958 / Historical Exhibition Working Party. - Port of Spain :
Caribbean Commission, [1958]. - 10p.
Mimeographed

Arranged according to groupings in the exhibition such as
maps.   Includes over 50 historical documents on the West Indies.
                                                                UWI-T

798 WILLIAMS, ERIC
        A bibliography of Caribbean history : a preliminary essay ;
     Part 1 : 1492-1898 / by Eric Williams. - [S.l. : s.n.],
     [1965?]. - 46p.
        Mimeographed
        Previously appeared in: Caribbean historical review, nos.
     3-4 (Dec. 1954), p.208-250. The paper was prepared for the
     Caribbean archives conference, University of the West Indies,
     1965 but not published in the report.

        A bibliographic essay reviewing and evaluating available
     material (primary and secondary sources) in five broad periods
     of Caribbean history :   (1) The Spanish Monopoly, 1492-1655,
     (2) The Anglo-French Rivalry, 1656-1783, (3) The Abolition of
     Slavery, 1784-1898, (4) The American Mediterranean, 1899-1940,
     (5) The Movement for Caribbean Self-government, 1940-1955.
                                                                UWI-T

799 WILLIAMS, ERIC
        From Columbus to Castro : the history of the Caribbean,
     1492-1969 / Eric Williams. - London : Deutsch, 1970. - 576p.
        Bibliography: p.516-558

        Essay with listings subdivided into five broad periods :
     (1) 1492-1655 - The Spanish Monopoly, (2) 1656-1783 - The Anglo-
     French Rivalry, (3) 1784-1898 - The Abolition of Slavery, (4)
     1899-1940 - The American Mediterranean, (5) 1940-1969 - The
     Movement for Caribbean Independence. Sections subdivided as
     necessary into documentary material, first-hand accounts,
     secondary sources, catalogues of manuscripts, local histories
     etc. Includes separate sections on the British, French, Spanish,
     Danish and Netherlands territories under the abolition of
     Slavery. This is a later version of an earlier publication (Ref.
     no.798).
                                                                UWI-T

Archival and Manuscript Materials
 800 ANDREWS, CHARLES MCLEAN
        Guide to the manuscript materials for the history of the
     United States to 1783, in the British Museum, in minor London
     archives, and the libraries of Oxford and Cambridge / by
     Charles McLean Andrews and Frances G. Davenport. - Washington,
     D.C. : Carnegie Institution of Washington, 1980. - xiv, 499p.

        Arranged by the location of the materials with a full
     index. Includes references on the islands.
                                                                  LC

801   ANDREWS, CHARLES MCLEAN
        Guide to the materials for American history to 1783 in
      the Public Record Office of Great Britain / by Charles M.
      Andrews. - Washington, D.C. : Carnegie Institution of
      Washington, 1912-14. - 2v.
        Vol.1 :   The State papers. - xi, 346p.
      America and the West Indies :   p.112-266

        Includes Colonial Office papers on America and the West
      Indies listed by class and series numbers with sections devoted
      to each island or group and brief descriptions; a key to the old
      and new reference numbers in the Colonial Office is provided in
      an appendix (B) and a full index to subject and place names.

                                                                    LC

802   Baptist Missionary Society
        Papers relating to the West Indies 1813-1914 / catalogued
      by Mary M. Evans. - London : Baptist Missionary Society, 1964.
      - 26p.
        Mimeographed

        Catalogue is divided into six sections which include
      Jamaica, British Honduras, Bahamas and Trinidad.   Comprises
      letters written by or to missionaries, committee minute books,
      deeds of mission property and other miscellaneous papers relating
      to the BMS.

                                                                  UWI-T

803   Caribbean archives conference, University of the West Indies,
      Mona, Jamaica, September 20-27, 1965. - Report. - [Kingston,
      Jamaica : Government Printer], [1965?]. - 510p.

        The first conference was held under the joint sponsorship
      of the Government of Jamaica and the University of the West
      Indies.   Report includes 29 papers presented, many with lists
      and descriptions of the archival records relating to the Caribbean
      in repositories within and outside the area.   Scope includes
      British, Dutch, French and American affiliated territories of the
      Caribbean.

                                                                  UWI-T

804   Carnegie Institution of Washington
        Guide to British West Indian archive materials, in London
      and in the islands for the history of the United States / by
      Herbert C. Bell, David W. Parker and others. - Washington,
      D.C. : Carnegie Institution of Washington, 1926. - ix, 435p. -
      (Carnegie Institution of Washington publication ; no.372)

        Provides "special guidance to a body of widely scattered
      archival material, for the history of the British colonial empire
      in America and of the United States ... before 1815." It lists

Colonial Office papers by island. Brief account of the papers
of the West India Committee in London and a series of descriptions in alphabetical order of the archives of the individual
islands follow. Full subject index provided.

UWI-T

805 Great Britain. Public Record Office
        Catalogue of microfilm / Public Record Office. - [S.l. :
     s.n.], 1976. - 101p.

        Lists most of the records of which the Public Record Office
holds master negatives on microfilm. Items arranged in alphabetical order of the headings of each group of records and
numerical order of the classes within each group. Under the
heading Colonial Office there are 58 items relating to individual
West Indian territories.

UWI-T

806 Great Britain. Public Record Office
        Guide to the contents of the Public Record Office, revised
     (to 1960) ... . - London : Her Majesty's Stationery Office,
     1963. - 3v.
        Vol.1 : Legal records, etc. - 249p.
        Vol.2 : State papers and departmental records. - 410p.
        Vol.3 : Documents transferred 1960-1966, 1968. - 191p.

        Annotated lists of records held, arranged by administrative
provenance and fully indexed. Covers all the territories of the
region including non-British islands.

UWI-T

807 Great Britain. Public Record Office
        List of Colonial Office records : Vol.4 West Indies [to
     1946] / Public Record Office. - Millwood, N.Y.: Kraus-
     Thomson Organization, by arrangement with Her Majesty's
     Stationery Office, London, 1977. - iv, 339p. - (Lists and
     indexes supplementary series ; no.15)
        Public Record Office lists and indexes originally
     published: H.M. Stationery Office between 1892 and 1936
     reprinted: Kraus-Thomson Organization.

        Other compilations amplifying or continuing the printed
series available only in typescript or manuscript have been
reproduced and issued by the Kraus-Thomson Organization in the
supplementary series. This list is arranged by country :
Antigua and Montserrat, Bahamas, Barbados, Bermuda, Cayman
Islands, Dominica, Grenada, Jamaica, Leeward Islands, Montserrat,
Nevis, St. Christopher, St. Lucia, St. Vincent, Tobago, Trinidad,
Turks and Caicos Islands, Virgin Islands, West Indies, and
Windward Islands, subdivided by type of record. These include

original correspondence, acts, sessional papers, government
gazettes, correspondence, and indexes.

UWI-T

808   Great Britain.   Public Record Office
          The records of the Colonial and Dominions offices / by
       R.B. Pugh. - London : Her Majesty's Stationery Office, 1964. -
       120p. - (Public Record Office handbooks ; no.3)
          Section III :   Annotated list of record classes

          Following on section II which provides an elementary guide
       to the general types of records generated, section III provides a
       brief and simple introduction to each territory covered in
       alphabetical order and a short-list of the record types or
       classes with their numbers, dates of coverage and the number of
       volumes held as at 30 June, 1962.

UWI-T

809   Great Britain.   Scottish Record Office
          Source list of material relating to West Indies and South
       America in Scottish Record Office. - [Edinburgh] : Scottish
       Record Office, [1965]. - 20p.
          Mimeographed

          Listing of records, letters and other private papers from
       the 17th to the 19th century. Arranged by record title alpha-
       betically. Includes several references to the West Indian
       islands but there is no index.

UWI-T

810   Historical Records Survey
          Descriptive catalogue of the Du Simitière papers in the
       Library Company of Philadelphia / prepared by the Historical
       Records Survey Division of Professional and Survey Projects,
       Works Projects Administration. - Philadelphia, Pa. : The
       Historical Records Survey, 1946. - 2p. l, [iii]-iv, 196p.
          Reproduced from typewritten copy

NYPL

811   INGRAM, K.E.
          Manuscripts relating to Commonwealth Caribbean countries
       in United States and Canadian repositories / K.E. Ingram. -
       St. Lawrence, Barbados : Caribbean Universities Press in
       association with Bowker Publishing Company, 1975. - xxiv,
       422p.

          Comprises "manuscript material relating to Bermuda, the
       Bahamas, British Honduras, Jamaica ... The Cayman Islands, the
       Turks and Caicos Islands, the logwood cutting areas of the Bay
       of Honduras and the Mosquito Coast to mid-19th century, the
       British [Virgin] Islands ... Anguilla, St. Kitts, Nevis, Antigua,

Barbuda, Redonda, Montserrat, Dominica, St. Lucia, St. Vincent, Barbados, Grenada and the Grenadines, Trinidad and Tobago and Guyana." Entries for each repository are arranged chronologically and the repositories grouped by names of states and of cities within each state.

UWI-T

812   MANROSS, W.W.
      The Fulham papers in the Lambeth Palace Library : American colonial section ; calendar and indexes / compiled by W.W. Manross. - Oxford : Clarendon Press, 1965. - xxii, 524p.

      Includes sections on the West Indies. Items are arranged chronologically by country. Each of the main collections listed - Calendar, Ordination Papers, Missionary Boards - contains items relating to the West Indies chronologically arranged within country. Indexes of names and topics referred to in the summaries of documents as well as names appearing in the documents are provided. Important source for the history of the church in the colonies and for colonial history generally.

UWI-T

813   PADRÓN, FRANCISCO MORALES
      Archival material on the Lesser Antilles located in the archives of the Indies, Seville (Spain) / Francisco Morales Padrón. - p.131-152
      In Report of the Caribbean archives conference, Mona, Jamaica, September 20-27, 1965. - (Document 3(D) (II))

      Description and listings of documents and maps relating to the Lesser Antilles housed in the General Archives of the Indies (Seville), the National Library, and the Palace (Madrid), the Archives of Simancas (Valladolid) and the National Library of Paris. Includes documents relating to the Windwards, Bermudas, Dominica and Trinidad. See also Ref.no.803.

UWI-T

814   PARES, RICHARD
      Public records in British West India islands / Richard Pares. - p.149-157
      In Bulletin of the Institute of Historical Research. - Vol.7, no.21 (Feb. 1930)

      An essay enlarging on the information supplied by the Carnegie Institution of Washington guide (Ref.no.804) "for the islands of Jamaica, Barbados, Antigua and St. Kitts - the four most important collections for the history of the West Indies in the old Empire." No listings are provided.

UWI-T

815 PAULIN, CHARLES O.
     Guide to the materials in London archives for the history
     of the United States since 1783 / by Charles O. Paulin. -
     Washington, D.C. : Carnegie Institution of Washington, 1914. -
     642p.

          Includes entries for Bahamas, Barbados, Jamaica, etc.
                                                        Ref.no.681
                                                          p.657

816 RAGATZ, LOWELL JOSEPH
     A checklist of House of Commons sessional papers relating
     to the British West Indies and the West Indian slave trade and
     slavery, 1763-1834 / compiled by Lowell Joseph Ragatz. -
     London : The Bryan Edwards Press, [1923]. - 42p.

          Listing is in three parts as follows : Part I. - Bills
     Printed by Order of the House of Commons - Part II. - Parlia-
     mentary Reports - Part III. - Accounts and Papers. Each part is
     subdivided into topics including names of territories.
                                                          UWI-T

817 [RAGATZ, LOWELL JOSEPH]
     A checklist of House of Lords sessional papers relating to
     the British West Indies and to the West Indian slave trade and
     slavery, 1763-1834 / Lowell Joseph Ragatz. - London : The
     Bryan Edwards Press, [1931]. - iiip., 1 leaf, 13p.
                                                          UWI-J

818 RAGATZ, LOWELL JOSEPH
     A guide to the official correspondence of the governors of
     the British West India colonies with the Secretary of State,
     1763-1833 / compiled by Lowell Joseph Ragatz. - London : The
     Bryan Edwards Press, [1923]. - 79p.
          Also 2nd ed. 1929. - 55p.

          Listed in "groups arranged in alphabetical order; the
     communications from a given colony chronologically" giving the
     series numbers used in the Public Record Office in Britain.
     "Save for a change in format the 2nd ed. is identical with the
     earlier one" - Preface.
                                                          UWI-T

819 TYSON, GEORGE F.
     A guide to manuscript sources in United States and West
     Indian depositories relating to the British West Indies
     during the era of the American revolution / by George F.
     Tyson. - Wilmington, Del. : Scholarly Resources Inc., 1978. -
     xviii, 96p.

Identifies and describes manuscript collections in the
United States and Caribbean depositories covering the period
1763-1783 with special emphasis upon materials relating to
Antigua, the Bahamas, Barbados, Bermuda, the British Virgin
Islands, Dominica, Grenada, Jamaica, Montserrat, Nevis, St. Kitts,
St. Lucia, St. Vincent and Tobago.

UWI-T

820   United States. Library of Congress. Division of Manuscripts
        List of the Vernon-Wager manuscripts in the Library of
      Congress / compiled under the direction of Worthington
      Chauncey Ford. - Washington, D.C. : Government Printing Office,
      1904. - 148p.

        "Prepared by Mr. John C. Fitzpatrick." The papers comprise
      "the correspondences of two men, Sir Charles Wager and Edward
      Vernon. They cover a very interesting period in the history of
      the English operations in the West Indies ... when Britain was
      contesting with Spain the supremacy in the West Indies."

Ref.no.144
Item no.151

821   United States. National Archives
        Materials in the National Archives relating to the
      Caribbean region / [compiled by Ralph G. Lounsbury]. -
      [Washington, D.C. : U.S. Government Printing Office], 1942. -
      10p. - (Reference information circular ; no.7)
        Processed

        A general description of records relating to the Caribbean
      including the British Caribbean during the nineteenth and
      twentieth centuries. Detailed lists of materials are not given
      but it is indicated that these can be prepared for specific
      subjects on request to the Director of Reference Service, the
      National Archives. Some of the records described are confidential
      in character and special authorization may be necessary for their
      use.

UWI-J

822   United States. National Archives and Records Service. General
      Services Administration
        Guide to materials on Latin America in the National
      Archives of the United States / by George S. Ulibarri and
      John P. Harrison. - Washington, D.C. : National Archives and
      Records Service, General Services Administration, 1974. -
      xii, 489p.

        Supersedes the guide to Materials on Latin America in the
      National Archives (vol.1, 1961), compiled by J.P. Harrison.
      Includes descriptions of pertinent records of the executive,
      legislative and judicial branches of government not included in
      the earlier work. Contains a name and subject index and
      appendices. Materials on the English-speaking Caribbean appear

under headings : British West Indies, West Indies and individual
countries. The description of records usually provides information as to type, purpose, content, chronological span and
quantity.

UWI-T

823   United States. Virgin Islands. Island Resources Foundation
      Preliminary report on manuscript materials in British
archives relating to the American revolution in the West
Indian islands / by George F. Tyson, Jr. and Carolyn Tyson. -
St. Thomas, U.S. Virgin Islands : Island Resources
Foundation, 1974. - xvii, 56p.

      "Published under the auspices of the American Revolution
Bicentennial Commission of the Virgin Islands." Covers mainly
records at the Public Record Office with selections from four
other British archives arranged by archive subdivided by
individual islands with brief annotations.

UWI-T

824   University of Oxford. Rhodes House Library
      Manuscript collections (excluding Africana) in Rhodes
House Library, Oxford / compiled by Louis B. Frewer. -
Oxford : Bodleian Library, 1970. - 61p.

      Includes a section on the West Indies in general and
Bahamas, Bermuda, British Guiana and British Honduras. Entries
are arranged alphabetically by author.

UWI-T

825   University of the West Indies. Library
      Manuscripts in the library of the University of the West
Indies / by William Gocking ; Appendix IV of Working paper
no.25 submitted for the Seminar on the Acquisition of Latin
American Library Materials (SALALM) ... 12th, Los Angeles,
1967. - p.182-187
      In Final report and working papers [of the Seminar]. -
Washington, D.C. : Pan American Union, 1968. - Vol.2

      A preliminary listing in chronological order. Includes
letters, papers, travel journals, a typescript novel, postcards
and photographs on the West Indies.

UWI-T

826   WALNE, PETER
      Guide to manuscript sources for the history of Latin
America and the Caribbean in the British Isles / edited by
Peter Walne ; with a foreword by R.A. Humphreys. - London :
Oxford University Press in collaboration with the Institute
of Latin American Studies, University of London, 1973. - xx,
580p. - (Guide to sources for the history of Latin America;
British Isles)

Survey lists of material in public and private hands
throughout the British Isles, arranged by country and record
offices for public records and by type of business for business
archives. Fully indexed and including several references to the
British Caribbean territories.

UWI-T

827   WARDLE, D.B.
        List of records relating to Caribbean countries (or in
the British Museum or National Maritime Museum) in England and
Wales / D.B. Wardle. - p.503-510
        In Report of the Caribbean archives conference, Mona,
Jamaica, September 20-27, 1965. - (Item 4 United Kingdom)

Items are arranged by country. See also Ref.no.803.

UWI-T

828   WARDLE, D.B.
        Records relating to Caribbean countries in the Public
Record Office, London / D.B. Wardle. - p.471-498
        In Report of the Caribbean archives conference, Mona,
Jamaica, September 20-27, 1965. - (Item 3 United Kingdom)

Lists records of the Colonial Office by country. See also
Ref.no.803.

UWI-T

829   WROTH, LAWRENCE C.
        Acts of French royal administration concerning Canada,
Guiana, the West Indies and Louisiana, prior to 1791 : a list
/ compiled by Lawrence C. Wroth and Gertrude Annan. - New
York : New York Public Library, 1930. - 151p.

List contains 1,302 separately printed acts, including
variant issues and different editions, and 790 acts taken from
printed collections. Chronological arrangement is based upon
the date of the royal signature. There is a classified table of
matters bringing together under a small number of headings acts
related to the West Indies. Acts concerning the English-speaking
West Indies can be located through the index. Locations of
copies of acts are given.

UWI-T

Periodicals and Serials
   830 Committee on Latin America
          Latin American history with politics : a serials list /
          edited ... by C.J. Koster ; with a preface by R.A. Humphreys
          and a note on periodical indexes by A.J. Walford. - Farn-
          borough, England : Gregg for COLA, 1973. - 165p. - (Latin
          American serials ; vol.2)

Arranged by areas which include Caribbean area (9 entries),
Bahamas (2 entries), Barbados (6 entries), Bermuda (9 entries),
British Honduras (3 entries), Cayman Islands (1 entry), Guyana
(15 entries), Jamaica (36 entries), Leeward Islands (3 entries),
Trinidad and Tobago (12 entries), Windward Islands (5 entries).
Includes newspapers and government publications. British library
locations are given.

IIR-T

Leeward Islands

Archival and Manuscript Materials
831 BAKER, EDWARD C.
A guide to the records in the Leeward Islands / by Edward
C. Baker. - Oxford : Basil Blackwell for the University of the
West Indies, 1965. - x, 102p.

Covers the Leeward Islands Federation, Antigua, Barbuda,
Montserrat, Nevis, St. Christopher (St. Kitts), Anguilla and the
British Virgin Islands. Based on the second in a series of
surveys of records undertaken by the History Department of the
University of the West Indies with a Rockefeller Foundation
grant. Itemized listings are arranged by location of the record
groups. Includes newspaper holdings. Indexed.

UWI-T

Windward Islands

Archival and Manuscript Materials
832 BAKER, EDWARD C.
A guide to records in the Windward Islands / by Edward C.
Baker. - Oxford : Basil Blackwell for the University of the
West Indies, 1968. - xii, 95p.

Covers Grenada, the Grenadines, St. Vincent, St. Lucia
and Dominica. For each country the listing is arranged by
location of the records which are mostly scattered between
several government offices, schools, the public libraries and
churches. Indexed. Includes newspaper holdings.

UWI-T

833 University of Puerto Rico. Institute of Caribbean Studies
Windward Islands records catalogue / Institute of Caribbean
Studies. - [San Juan], Puerto Rico : Institute of Caribbean
Studies, University of Puerto Rico, 1964. - 1v. (various
pagings)
Supplement to : Caribbean studies, vol.4, no.1 (Apr.
1964)

A list of government and ecclesiastical records for
Dominica, St. Lucia, St. Vincent and Grenada. Locations are
given.

UWI-T

Bahamas

834 CRATON, MICHAEL
     A history of the Bahamas / Michael Craton. - London :
     Collins, 1962. - 320p.
     Bibliography : p.293-302

     Lists primary and secondary sources followed by material
dealing with various periods of Bahamian history. The latter
include works on natural history, archaeology and anthropology
and sources of documents relating to the General Archive of the
Indies at Seville. Included also are works on the West Indies
as a whole.

UWI-T

Archival and Manuscript Materials
835 British Museum
     List of documents relating to the Bahama islands in the
     British Museum and Record Office, London. - Nassau : The
     Nassau Guardian, 1910. - 63p.

Ref.no.144

836 SAUNDERS, D. GAIL
     Guide to the records of the Bahamas / D. Gail Saunders and
     Edward A. Carson. - Nassau, Bahamas : Government Printing
     Department, 1973. - xvi, 109, 28p.

     "Compiled as a result of the collecting, examining,
sorting and listing of the records" which were largely centralized
at the time of setting up the Public Record Office of the Bahamas.
Includes a list of important Bahamian records in foreign repositories, chiefly the Public Record Office in London. An index of
names and subjects is provided.

UWI-T

Barbados

837 Barbados. Public Library
     Barbadiana : a list of works pertaining to the history of
     the island of Barbados / prepared in the Public Library to
     mark the attainment of independence. - Bridgetown, [Barbados] :
     Barbados Public Library, 1966. - 44p.

Entries arranged alphabetically under subject groups such as historical, descriptive, government and politics, social and economic and education. Full bibliographic information is provided but no annotations or indexes.

UWI-T

Archival and Manuscript Materials
  838 CHANDLER, MICHAEL J.
       A guide to records in Barbados / by Michael J. Chandler. - Oxford : Basil Blackwell for the University of the West Indies, 1965. - xi, 204p.

       Based on a survey of records in the English-speaking territories undertaken by the History Department of the University of the West Indies with a Rockefeller Foundation grant. Arranged mainly according to the location of the records in 1961 grouped under broad classes such as central government records, local government, semi-public, private and ecclesiastical records. A section on manuscript collections describes holdings of the Barbados Public Library and the Barbados Museum and Historical Society. Indexed. Includes newspapers held.

UWI-T

  839 CHANDLER, MICHAEL J.
       List of archives in official repositories in Barbados / Michael J. Chandler. - p.282-286
       In Report of the Caribbean archives conference, Mona, Jamaica, September 20-27, 1965. - (Item 1 Barbados)

       Items are listed under central government bodies. Two small collections of manuscripts are described. See also Ref.no.803.

UWI-T

  840 CHANDLER, MICHAEL J.
       List of archives not in official repositories in Barbados / Michael J. Chandler. - p.409-419
       In Report of the Caribbean archives conference, Mona, Jamaica, September 20-27, 1965. - (Item 2 Barbados)

       Archives are grouped under Central Government and Local Government. See also Ref.no.803.

UWI-T

  841 HANDLER, JEROME P.
       A guide to source materials for the study of Barbados history, 1627-1834 / by Jerome P. Handler. - Carbondale : Southern Illinois University Press, 1971. - xiii, 205p.

Detailed guide to books, pamphlets, broadsheets, parliamentary papers, newspapers, prints and manuscripts; annotated,
indexed and including library locations in the U.S., U.K. and the
Caribbean.

UWI-T

842   Instituto Panamericano de Geografía e Historia. Comisión de
      Historia
            Lista de documentos microfotografiados en Barbados por la
      Unidad Móvil de Microfilm de la UNESCO / Comisión de Historia.
      - p.199-227
            In Guía de los documentos microfotografiados por la
      Unidad Móvil de la UNESCO. - México : [s.n.], 1963

            An introductory historical summary on the Barbados Public
      Library where the originals are housed is followed by two main
      listings of handwritten and printed materials microfilmed
      quoting reel numbers for each item. Includes Council minutes,
      Blue Books, official gazettes, newspapers with details of main
      contents in each case. Includes an alphabetical index of the
      main contents for the printed materials listed.

UWI-J

843   Unesco. Mobile Microfilm Unit
            List of microfilmed materials at the Barbados Public
      Library / Francisco Sevillano Colón. - Barbados : [s.n.],
      1960. - 23p.
            Mimeographed

            Lists main items microfilmed. These include handwritten
      microfilmed materials - Minutes of Council (transcripts made in
      the first quarter of the 19th century), printed materials -
      miscellaneous newspapers, the official gazettes and Barbados
      Blue Books.

UWI-T

844   University College of the West Indies (Mona)
            Guides to records microfilmed by U.C.W.I. in Barbados,
      July, October 1960 ; March-August 1961. - [Mona, Jamaica] :
      U.C.W.I. [1961?]. - 1v.
            Mimeographed
            Archivist: M.J. Chandler

            Microfilming was done as part of the University College
      of the West Indies' survey and preservation programme for
      archives in the West Indies. Several guides are bound together
      in this collection including Barbados General Agricultural
      Society records, Methodist Church, Moravian Church, Chamber of
      Commerce and school records, as well as House of Assembly
      minutes, other official records and a few newspapers. Over 100
      microfilm reels are identified in a convenient serial listing of
      the project.

UWI-T

Indexes
845 ALLSOPP, DOROTHY Y.B.
         The Journal of the Barbados Museum and Historical Society
     author/title index to Volume 1, no.1 (November 1933) to Volume
     35, no.2 (March 1976) / compiled by Dorothy Y.B. Allsopp for
     the Commonwealth Caribbean Resource Centre, Bridgetown,
     Barbados. - Barbados : COMCARC, 1976. - 58, [1] leaves
         Mimeographed
         Supplement to: Subject index / compiled by Michael
     Chandler.

         Extracts from newspapers and proceedings of meetings of
     the Society excluded.

                                                               UWI-T

846 CHANDLER, M.
         Subject index to the Journal of the Barbados Museum and
     Historical Society, Volumes 1-31 and Bulletins 1-8 (November
     1933-August 1966) / M. Chandler. - [Bridgetown, Barbados :
     s.n.], [1967?]

                                                         Ref.no.845

Belize

847 ASTURIAS, FRANCISCO
         Belice / Francisco Asturias. - 2nd ed. aumentada. -
     Guatemala : [Tipografía Nacional de Guatemala], 1941. - 2p.,
     1, 7-177p.
         Bibliography : p.173-175

                                                               UWI-J

848 DONOHOE, WILLIAM ARLINGTON
         A history of British Honduras / William Arlington
     Donohoe. - New York : Colrite Offset Print Company, [1947]. -
     118p.
         Bibliography : p.[105]-116
         First published: Montreal : Provincial Publishing Company,
     [1946]

                                                               UWI-J

Bermuda

849 TUCKER, TERRY
         Bermuda : today and yesterday 1503-1973 / by Terry Tucker.
     - London : Robert Hale and Company, 1975. - 208p.
         Bibliography : p.194-199

Alphabetical list of items which includes government documents and newspapers followed by lists of reports and recommendations made by experts brought in during the 1960's and manuscript material in the Bermuda archives. All items are to be found in the Bermuda Library.

UWI-T

850 WILKINSON, HENRY CAMPBELL
Bermuda in the old Empire : a history of the island from the dissolution of the Somers Island Company until the end of the American Revolutionary War, 1684-1784 / by Henry Campbell Wilkinson. - London ; New York : Oxford University Press, 1950. - xi, 457p.
Bibliography : p.442-447

LC

British Virgin Islands

Archival and Manuscript Materials
851 A list of the archives of the British Virgin Islands. - p.287-297
In Report of the Caribbean archives conference, Mona, Jamaica, September 20-27, 1965. - (Item 1 British Virgin Islands)

Documents not in fair to good condition are so described. Items are listed according to type of record. See also Ref.no. 803.

UWI-T

Grenada

Archival and Manuscript Materials
852 NARDIN, J.C.
The old records of Grenada ... (translated from an article published in the Revue of [sic] française d'histoire d'outre-mer, Vol.49 (1962) ; p.117-140) / J.C. Nardin. - p.327-345
In Report of the Caribbean archives conference, Mona, Jamaica, September 20-27, 1965

Bibliographic essay. See also Ref.no.803.

UWI-T

Guyana

852a RODNEY, WALTER
A history of the Guyanese working people, 1881-1905 / Walter Rodney. - Baltimore ; London : Johns Hopkins University

Press, 1981. - xxv, 282p. - (Johns Hopkins studies in
Atlantic history and culture)
    Bibliography :   p.265-274

    Bibliographic essay covering the Guyana National Archives
and Public Record Office, Archives in the United Kingdom, Newspapers, Printed Pirmary Sources, Secondary Sources and Oral
Sources, followed by a list of 133 items arranged alphabetically
by author.   Includes works on the history and politics of British
Guiana as well as items on its ethnic groups.

UWI-T

Archival and Manuscript Materials
 853   MENEZES, MARY NOEL
        An annotated bibliography of governors' dispatches (British
    Guiana) : selected years, 1781-1871 (C.O.111/1(1781) -
    C.O.384(1871) and C.O.884/1-19 / Mary Noel Menezes. -
    [Turkeyen, Guyana] : Department of History, University of
    Guyana, 1978. - 62p.
        Mimeographed

Ref.no.73
1979, p.3

 854   Raleigh and Guiana. - [S.l. : s.n.], [196-?]. - 7 leaves
        Mimeographed

    102 entries alphabetically arranged.   Includes material
published in the eighteenth and nineteenth centuries.   In addition
to English, French and Spanish language items are also listed with
some references on the Venezuela/Guyana border issue.

UWI-T

 855   ROESSINGH, M.P.H.
        Guide to the sources in the Netherlands for the history of
    Latin America / by M.P.H. Roessingh. - The Hague : Government
    Publishing Office, 1968. - 232p. - (Guide to the sources of
    the history of nations. A. Latin America. III. Two sources
    preserved in the Netherlands)
        Bibliography :   p.13-29

UWI-J

Jamaica

 856   CRATON, MICHAEL
        A Jamaican plantation : the history of Worthy Park, 1670-
    1970 / Michael Craton and James Walvin. - London : W.H. Allen,
    1970. - xi, 344p.
        Bibliography :   p.332-336

Subdivided into primary and secondary sources, the listing
is arranged by locations for manuscripts and alphabetically by
author for printed secondary material. Includes several manuscripts from the Worthy Park sugar estate.

UWI-T

857 LONG, ANTON V.
        Jamaica and the new order, 1827-1847 / by Anton V. Long. –
     [Mona, Jamaica] : Institute of Social and Economic Research,
     University of the West Indies, 1956. – iv, 167p. – (I.S.E.R.
     special series ; no.1)
        Bibliography : p.138-157

        Cited works arranged by form of material in six sections,
including manuscript sources, official and semi-official papers
and journals, newspapers and periodicals and contemporary
published materials as well as later published works and theses.
Most items are annotated.

UWI-T

858 MARSALA, VINCENT JOHN
        Sir John Peter Grant, governor of Jamaica, 1866-1874 : an
     administrative history / by Vincent John Marsala. – [Kingston,
     Jamaica] : Institute of Jamaica, 1972. – 125p. – (Cultural
     heritage series ; vol.3)
        Bibliography : p.120-125

        Divided into primary and secondary sources for cited works
and subdivided by form of material including government publications and newspapers. Uncited items listed separately and
subdivided into historical, geographical and sociological titles.

UWI-T

859 MARX, ROBERT F.
        Port Royal rediscovered / by Robert F. Marx. – New York :
     Doubleday, 1973. – 304p.
        Bibliography : p.290-295

        References mainly to journal articles and general works
including the Port Royal story as well as a list of relevant
archaeological reports by the author.

UWI-T

Archival and Manuscript Materials
  860 BLACK, CLINTON V.
        A list of the records in the Jamaica archives by main
     groups with an indication of extent and approximate covering
     dates, as well as a note of the contents of the neighbouring
     Island Record Office and Registrar General's Department /
     Clinton V. Black. – p.371-378

In Report of the Caribbean archives conference, Mona,
Jamaica, September 20-27, 1965. - (Item 1. Jamaica,

Items are listed under headings : Public, Semi-public,
Private, Gifts and Deposits and Ecclesiastical. See also Ref.no.
803.

UWI-T

861 INGRAM, KENNETH EVERARD
Sources of Jamaican history, 1655-1838 : a bibliographical
survey with particular reference to manuscript souces /
Kenneth Everard Ingram. - Zug, Switzerland : Inter Documentation Company, 1976. - 2v. (1,310p.)

Includes descriptions of material in British, Jamaican,
North American, Spanish and other European repositories and
sources based on surveys conducted by the author over a number of
years. Fully indexed. The author was University Librarian,
University of the West Indies.

UWI-T

862 Jamaica. Archives
An exhibition of official documents relating to the 1865
Morant Bay rebellion in the Jamaica Archives, Spanish Town,
1965. - Kingston, [Jamaica] : Jamaica Information Service,
1965. - 20p.

Consists of a brief list of 12 documents without annotations
and reproductions of the documents with a few facsimiles.

UWI-T

Trinidad and Tobago

863 ANDERSONS, EDGARS
Senie Kurzemnieki Amerikā un Tobāgo Kolonizācija = The
ancient Couronians in America and the colonization of Tobago /
Edgars Andersons. - p.351-364
In Dangava (1970)

Ref.no.5
1976, p.479

864 WILLIAMS, ERIC
History of the people of Trinidad and Tobago / Eric
Williams. - London : Andre Deutsch, 1964. - x, 292p.
Bibliography : p.283-286

A bibliographic essay including a listing of 23 important
reports of commissions of enquiry and identifying other major
works in relation to their period of coverage and contribution to
the field.

UWI-T

Archival and Manuscript Materials
   865 BENJAMIN, WILHELMINA A.
            A check-list of documents on Trinidad and Tobago (in the
        libraries and archives of England, Scotland, Spain and France)
        / Wilhelmina A. Benjamin. - [S.1. : s.n.], 1976. - 42 leaves
            Mimeographed

            Compiled during a survey in 1967 the list is arranged by
        the record sources (Public Record Office, Rhodes House Library,
        Scottish Record Office, Biblioteca Nacional, Spain, etc.) and
        grouped by type within these sections. Guides and lists precede
        the listing for each source.

                                                                  UWI-T

   866 SEWLAL, ENOS
            List of archives of Trinidad and Tobago / Enos Sewlal. -
        p.379-407
            In Report of the Caribbean archives conference, Mona,
        Jamaica, September 20-27, 1965. - (Item 1 Trinidad and
        Tobago)

            Items are listed under government departments and various
        other depositories including the Trinidad Public Library, City
        of Port of Spain Archives, Borough of San Fernando Archives, and
        the Archives of the Historical Society of Trinidad and Tobago.
        See also Ref.no.803.

                                                                  UWI-T

Indexes
   867 Historical Society of Trinidad and Tobago
            Index to publications 1-299 / compiled by Gertrude
        Carmichael and N. Montgomery Gordon. - [Port of Spain],
        Trinidad and Tobago : Government Printer, 1941. - xxxivp.

            Indexes the first group of the Society's published papers
        on the history of the islands providing "a very considerable
        fund of accurately documented information to which the student of
        West Indian history will inevitably have recourse in referring
        to any particular period or major theme."

                                                                  UWI-T

   868 Historical Society of Trinidad and Tobago
            Index to publications 300-1000 / compiled by Gertrude
        Carmichael. - [Port of Spain], Trinidad, B.W.I. : Government
        Printing Office, 1951. - lxxviiip.

            Detailed index of names and subjects occurring in the
        second set of the Society's published historical documents.
        Sequel to Ref.no.867.

                                                                  UWI-T

HOUSING AND PLANNING

869 Great Britain. Department of Scientific and Industrial
     Research. Building Research Station
         Housing and planning in the West Indies / Building
     Research. - Watford, [England] : Building Research Station,
     DSIR, 1948. - 6p. - (Library bibliography ; no.134)

         Mimeographed

         56 items include the West Indies in general, British
     Guiana, British Honduras and Bermuda.

                                                          UWI-T

870 MACKENZIE, DONALD R.
         A bibliographic overview of housing in developing
     countries : annotated / by Donald R. Mackenzie and Erna W.
     Kerst. - Monticello, Ill. : Council of Planning Librarians,
     1977. - 281p. - (Council of Planning Librarians exchange
     bibliography ; 1225-1227)

         Bibliography is divided into seventeen topical sections
     with geographical sub-sections. Includes items on the West
     Indies.

                                                          UWI-T

INDUSTRIAL RELATIONS

871 LUTCHMAN, HAROLD A.
         Select bibliography : industrial relations and trade
     unionism in Guyana and the West Indies / Harold A. Lutchman. -
     p.291-301
         In Interest representation in the Public Service : a
     history of the Guyana Public Service Association / by Harold
     A. Lutchman. - Guyana : Public Service Association, 1973

         Includes sections on Guyana, Trinidad, Barbados,
     Associated States and Jamaica as well as on the West Indies as a
     whole. Addresses, seminar papers, articles, reports and books
     are listed in alphabetical order by author.

                                                          UWI-T

872 University of the West Indies (Mona). Institute of Social and
     Economic Research
         Statutory regulation of collective bargaining with special
     reference to the Industrial Relations Act of Trinidad and

Tobago / Chuks Okpaluba. – Mona, Jamaica : Institute of Social
and Economic Research, University of the West Indies, 1975. –
ix, 183p.
Bibliography :   p.101–114

120 items, not exclusively West Indian, arranged under
headings :   Books and Periodicals, Public Documents, Lists of
Statutes Cited.   Covers labour relations, trade unionism in
Guyana, Trinidad, Jamaica.   List of statutes cited includes trade
union ordinances and trade disputes and industrial relations acts
in the various West Indian territories.   List of references is
followed by a list of table of cases, 21 of which relate to the
Commonwealth Caribbean, and unreported industrial court judgments
(Trinidad and Tobago) (29 items).

UWI–T

Jamaica

873   Jamaica Library Service
        Trade unionism in Jamaica : a select bibliography /
Jamaica Library Service. – Kingston : Jamaica Library Service,
1975. – 7p.

Prepared "specifically for the launching of Prime
Minister Manley's book "A Voice at the Workplace" – foreword.

Ref.no.76
1976, p.3

INDUSTRY AND TECHNOLOGY

874   Caribbean Commission. Caribbean Research Council. Committee
on Agriculture, Nutrition, Fisheries and Forestry
        The sugar industry of the Caribbean / Caribbean Research
Council, Caribbean Commission. – Washington, D.C. : [s.n.],
1947. – xiii, 343p. – (Crop enquiry series ; no.6)
        Bibliography :   p.269–335

Extensive listings on sugar cane arranged under headings :
Barbados, British Guiana, Imperial College of Tropical Agriculture,
Jamaica, Leeward Islands, Antigua, Puerto Rico, Trinidad and
Tobago. Topics covered include botany, chemistry, insect pest
control, milling, clarification, crystallization, soils, sugar
technology, experiments, tillage, yields.

UWI–T

875   Caribbean Commission. Library
        [List of references with some information on] rum (history
      and fabrication) : letter / by Berthe Canton. - Port of Spain,
      Trinidad : Caribbean Commission Library, 1958. - 3 leaves
            Typescript

        Letter response to an enquiry providing annotated list of
      four references plus 19 more cited in full from one of the works
      listed and including references to rum manufacture in Jamaica,
      Puerto Rico and other Caribbean territories.

                                                              TCL

876   GIRVAN, NORMAN
        Corporate imperialism : conflict and expropriation ;
      transnational corporations and economic nationalism in the
      third world / Norman Girvan. - New York : M.E. Sharpe, 1976. -
      243p.
            Bibliography :   p.229-232

        Arranged alphabetically by author. Includes references on
      the bauxite and petroleum industries of Jamaica, Guyana and
      Trinidad and Tobago, state participation and nationalization.

                                                              UWI-T

877   GIRVAN, NORMAN
        Towards technology policies for the Caribbean / by Norman
      Girvan ; with the collaboration of P.I. Gomes and Donald B.
      Sangster. - [Turkeyen, Guyana] : Institute of Development
      Studies, University of Guyana; Mona, Jamaica : Institute of
      Social and Economic Research, University of the West Indies,
      1978. - [5], iii, 365p. - (Caribbean technology policy studies
      project. General study)
            Mimeographed
            Bibliography : p.354-365

        101 references in alphabetical author order highlighting
      publication dates (mostly of the seventies).

                                                              UWI-T

878   REBEL, THOMAS P.
        Sea turtles and the turtle industry of the West Indies,
      Florida and the Gulf of Mexico / Thomas P. Rebel. - Revised
      edition. - Coral Gables, Fla. : University of Miami Press,
      1974. - 250p.
            Bibliography :   p.143-242

        Annotated entries arranged alphabetically by author,
      followed by a general subject index. Some 20 references speci-
      fically on the Caribbean with a few more on the Bahamas,
      Bermuda and Cuba.

                                                              UWI-T

879 Trinidad and Tobago. Central Library. West Indian Reference
     Section
         List of books on fisheries in the West Indian Reference
     Section of the Central Library Services. - [Port of Spain,
     Trinidad : Central Library Services], 1964. - 1 leaf
         Typescript

         Alphabetical author listing.

                                                                    TCL

880 Trinidad and Tobago. Industrial Development Corporation.
     Library
         Select bibliography on fiscal incentives / Industrial
     Development Corporation Library. - [Port of Spain, Trinidad] :
     Industrial Development Corporation Library, [1972]. - 5
     leaves

         A brief general listing including comparative studies and
     some items of Caribbean origin and/or interest on taxation, duty
     concessions and export promotion policies.

                                                                  UWI-T

881 Trinidad and Tobago. Ministry of Planning and Development
         UNDP/FAO Caribbean fishery development projects / compiled
     by Patricia Raymond. - [Port of Spain, Trinidad] : Ministry of
     Planning and Development, [1977]. - 2p.
         Mimeographed

                                                                   MF-T

882 University of the West Indies. Faculty of Engineering.
     Department of Mechanical Engineering
         List of theses, publications, reports and brief descrip-
     tions of current work on solar energy and related subjects /
     U.W.I., Department of Mechanical Engineering. - St. Augustine :
     Department of Mechanical Engineering, U.W.I., 1972. - 2 leaves

         Lists nine items including two publications by a faculty
     member and student theses or project reports as well as on-going
     research projects in the field.

                                                                  UWI-T

883 University of the West Indies (St. Augustine). Library
         [List of work done on sugar cane wax at ICTA] / UWI
     Library. - [St. Augustine, Trinidad : U.W.I. Library], 1976. -
     2 leaves
         Typescript

         Six references to papers and articles in a letter response
     to an enquiry.

                                                                  UWI-T

Barbados

Periodicals and Serials - Indexes
  884   Barbados sugar industry review : index to volume 1-4 / Sugar
        Producers' Association. - [Warren's, Barbados] : Sugar
        Producers' Association, 1979. - 12p.
            Mimeographed

Ref.no.72
Jan.-Mar. 1980, p.1

Dominica

  885   University of the West Indies. Institute of Social and
        Economic Research
            Industrial development of Dominica / by R.L. Williams. -
        [Mona], Jamaica : Institute of Social and Economic Research,
        University of the West Indies, 1971. - 100p.
            Bibliography :   p.93-100

            References arranged by chapters include survey reports on
        industries such as citrus and cocoa, journal articles and some
        unpublished items.

UWI-T

Guyana

  886   GIRVAN, NORMAN
            Making the rules of the game : company-country agreements
        in the bauxite industry / Norman Girvan. - [Mona, Jamaica] :
        Department of Economics, U.W.I., 1971. - 72, 3p. - (Department
        of Economics working paper ; no.3)
            Bibliography :   3 leaves

            19 items arranged alphabetically by author consisting
        mainly of government documents relating to the bauxite industry
        in British Guiana and Jamaica. Entries include agreements
        between the governments and bauxite companies.

UWI-T

  887   [Guyana. Ministry of Agriculture. Fisheries Department]
            [List of reports on fisheries (Guyana)] / Fisheries
        Department. - [Georgetown, Guyana : Fisheries Department,
        Ministry of Agriculture], [1976?]. - 4 leaves
            Typescript

UG

Jamaica

888 FOSTER, PHILLIPS
     The structure of plantation agriculture in Jamaica /
     Phillips Foster [and] Peter Creyke. - College Park, Md. :
     Agricultural Experiment Station, University of Maryland, 1968.
     - viii, 102p. - (Miscellaneous publication ; 623)
     Selected bibliography :   p.99-102

     Arranged by author in two sections - Books, Bulletins,
Reports and Articles and Papers. References cover mainly the
economic aspects of the sugar industry in Jamaica.
                                                              UWI-T

889 WIDDICOMBE, STACEY H.
     The performance of industrial development corporations :
     the case of Jamaica / Stacey H. Widdicombe. - New York :
     Praeger Publishers, 1972. - xxvi, [419]p.
     Bibliography :   p.409-419

     Select bibliography of 116 items lists Jamaica Industrial
Development Corporation reports and publications, other official
reports and publications and non-official publications dealing
with the economy and industrial development of Jamaica.
                                                              UWI-T

890 WILLIAMS, R.L.
     The coffee industry of Jamaica : growth, structure and
     performance / R.L. Williams. - [Mona], Jamaica : Institute of
     Social and Economic Research, U.W.I., 1975. - x, 82p.
     Bibliography :   p.75-80

     99 references arranged alphabetically by author including
economic and agricultural viewpoints and some items relevant to
other Caribbean territories.
                                                              UWI-T

Trinidad and Tobago

891 HANNAYS, IRMA
     Special collection : bibliography of all publications of
     the Trinidad and Tobago Industrial Development Corporation,
     November 1971 / by Irma Hannays. - p.13-19
     In Library resources for research in the Caribbean -
     Economics (English-speaking areas) / Irma Hannays; working
     paper no.IID submitted for the Conference of the Association
     of Caribbean University and Research Libraries (ACURIL) ...
     3rd, Universidad Central de Venezuela, Caracas, Venezuela,
     November 7-12, 1971. - San Juan, Puerto Rico : Association of
     Caribbean University and Research Libraries, 1971

Mimeographed

Alphabetically arranged by title under the units of the Corporation responsible for the publications.

UWI-T

892   Trinidad and Tobago. Industrial Development Corporation
      Bibliography of all publications of the Economic Studies
      and Planning Division of the Industrial Development Corporation
      / Trinidad and Tobago Industrial Development Corporation. -
      Port of Spain : I.D.C. Library, 1977. - 3p

Lists all publications prepared in the ESPD from its inception in 1969 to 1977.

IDC-T

893   Trinidad and Tobago. Industrial Development Corporation
      Bibliography of handouts and seminar papers prepared for
      "Industry Week 1975" / Trinidad and Tobago Industrial Develop-
      ment Corporation. - Port of Spain : I.D.C. Library, 1975. -
      3p.

Lists publications describing the work of the I.D.C. and the services it offers, as well as the papers prepared for the symposium on "The Prospects of a Metal Forming and Metal Working Industry in Trinidad and Tobago."

IDC-T

894   Trinidad and Tobago. Ministry of Planning Development
      Fishing industry : Trinidad and Tobago / Ministry of
      Planning and Development. - [Port of Spain, Trinidad] :
      Ministry of Planning and Development, [1972?]. - 2p.
      Mimeographed

18 items comprising UNDP, FAO, Caribbean Fisheries Development Project reports. Prepared for a proposed bibliography of Trinidad and Tobago.

MF-T

895   Trinidad and Tobago. Ministry of Planning and Development
      Hotel development : Trinidad and Tobago / compiled by
      Patricia Raymond. - [Port of Spain, Trinidad] : Ministry of
      Planning and Development, [197-?]. - 2p.
      Mimeographed

Consists of 12 items. Prepared for a proposed bibliography of Trinidad and Tobago.

MF-T

896   Trinidad and Tobago. Ministry of Planning and Development
        Hotel training : Trinidad and Tobago / compiled by
      Patricia Raymond. - [Port of Spain, Trinidad] : Ministry of
      Planning and Development, [197-?]. - 1p.
        Mimeographed

        Comprises eight items on Trinidad and Tobago and two on
      the Caribbean as a whole. Prepared for a proposed bibliography
      of Trinidad and Tobago.

                                                                    MF-T

897   Trinidad and Tobago. Ministry of Planning and Development.
      Library
        A list of material available in the Library, Ministry of
      Planning and Development : sugar and sugar by-products. -
      [Port of Spain, Trinidad : Library, Ministry of Planning and
      Development], 1978. - 7p.
        Mimeographed

        26 items on Trinidad and Tobago, 18 on the Caribbean
      generally.

                                                                    MF-T

898   Trinidad and Tobago. Ministry of Planning and Development.
      Library
        Trinidad and Tobago : petroleum / compiled by Patricia
      Raymond. - [Port of Spain, Trinidad] : Ministry of Planning
      and Development, 1971. - [5]p.
        Extract from: Bibliography on petroleum, petro-
      chemicals, natural gas / Patricia Raymond

                                                                    MF-T

899   University of the West Indies (St. Augustine). Library
        [List of references on the role of the petroleum
      industry in the economy of Trinidad and Tobago] / U.W.I.
      Library. - [St. Augustine, Trinidad : U.W.I. Library], 1977. -
      1 leaf
        Typescript

        Nine references to theses, reports, journal articles and
      pamphlet items compiled in response to a request.

                                                                    UWI-T

225

INTERNATIONAL RELATIONS

900 GLASSNER, MARTIN IRA
        The foreign relations of Jamaica and Trinidad and Tobago,
    1960-1965 / Martin Ira Glassner. - p.116-153
        In Caribbean studies. - Vol.10, no.3 (Oct. 1970)
        Bibliography: p.151-153

        79 items mainly about international relations and regional
    co-operation arranged under headings : Books, Articles, Docu-
    ments, Miscellaneous.

                                                            UWI-T

901 Great Britain. Ministry of Overseas Development. Library
        British aid : a select bibliography / Library, Ministry of
    Overseas Development. - 5th revised ed. - [S.l. : Library,
    Ministry of Overseas Development], 1969. - 27p.
        Mimeographed

        483 references based on the library's collection arranged
    under such topics as legislation, area studies, education,
    natural resources, public administration and including a few
    references on the Caribbean. Revised periodically.

                                                            UWI-T

902 KRESLINS, JANIS A.
        Foreign affairs bibliography : a selected and annotated
    list of books on international relations 1962-1972 / Janis A.
    Kreslins. - New York : R.R. Bowker for Council on Foreign
    Relations, 1976. - xvii, 921p.

        Fifth "Foreign Affairs Bibliography." Includes entries
    for West Indies and the Caribbean (p.300-312), Jamaica (p.310-
    312), other islands (p.312). Entries for South America include
    the Guianas (p.336). Those on British Honduras appear in the
    section on Central America (p.297). See also Ref.nos.903,
    905, 906, 908.

                                                            UWI-T

903 LANGER, WILLIAM L.
        Foreign affairs bibliography : a selected and annotated
    list of books on international relations 1919-1932 / by
    William L. Langer ... [and] Hamilton Fish Armstrong ... . -
    New York ; London : Harper for Council on Foreign Relations,
    [1933]. - xxvii, 551p.

        "An enlarged and completely revised list based on biblio-
    graphies published quarterly since 1922 in : "Foreign Affairs."
    Short general West Indies section (p.200-220). Very brief
    annotations provided to 10 titles on the English-speaking

Caribbean. Also has separate sections on Haiti, Cuba, etc. but
not Lesser Antilles. See also Ref.nos. 902, 905, 906, 908.

                                                          UWI-J

904 PHILLIPS, PETER
       The business sector and Jamaican foreign relations : a
     study of national capitalist orientations to third world
     relations / Peter Phillips. - p.146-168
       In Social and economic studies. - Vol.26, no.2 (June 1977)
       References: p.166-168

       27 references on foreign policy in the West Indies and the
     third world.

                                                          UWI-T

905 ROBERTS, HENRY L.
       Foreign affairs bibliography : a select and annotated list
     of books on international relations, 1942-52 / Henry L. Roberts
     and others. - New York : Harper, 1953. - xxii, 727p. - (Council
     on Foreign Relations. Publication)
       Also published: London : Royal Institute of Foreign
     Affairs.

       Third Foreign Affairs Bibliography. See also Ref.nos.902,
     903, 906, 908.

                                                          LC

906 ROBERTS, HENRY L.
       Foreign affairs bibliography : a selected and annotated
     list of books on international relations 1952-1962 / Henry L.
     Roberts assisted by Jean Gunther ... Janis A. Kreslins, Mary
     L. Ryan and Nancy L. Guller. - New York : R.R. Bowker Company
     for the Council on Foreign Relations, 1964. - xxi, 752p.

       Fourth Foreign Affairs bibliography. Section on the West
     Indies and the Caribbean (p.265-276) includes items listed under
     headings : General, Jamaica, Other Islands (with some items on
     Anguilla, Leeward and Windward Islands and Trinidad and Tobago).
     Entires on British Honduras (p.261) appear in the section on
     Central America and items on the Guianas (p.296-297) are listed
     in the section devoted to South America. Six items on British
     Guiana. Entries are briefly annotated. See also Ref.nos.902,
     903, 905, 908.

                                                          UWI-T

907 University of Guyana. Library
       Canada-Caribbean relations : a select bibliography based
     on resources in the University of Guyana Library. - [Turkeyen,
     Guyana : University of Guyana Library]. - 10 leaves
         Typescript

                                                          UG

908 WOOLBERT, ROBERT GALE
      Foreign affairs bibliography : a selected and annotated
     list of books on international relations 1932–1942 / Robert
     Gale Woolbert. – New York : R.R. Bowker for the Council on
     Foreign Relations, 1969. – xxi, 703p.
      Reprint of: 1945 ed.
      Sequel to: Foreign affairs bibliography, 1919–1932
     (Ref.no.903)

      Section on general West Indies (p.269–273) includes items
  on the English-speaking Caribbean. A few items on British Guiana
  are listed in the section on the Guianas (p.287).

                                                            UWI-T

                        LANGUAGE AND LINGUISTICS

909 Bibliographie créole succincte = Concise creole bibliography.
      – p.27–36
      In Les receuils du C.E.R.A.G. (Centre d'Etudes Regionales
     Antilles-Guyane). – No.1 (1973)

                                                            RIS

910 CARRINGTON, LAWRENCE D.
      Determining language education policy in Caribbean socio-
     linguistic complexes / Lawrence D. Carrington. – p.27–43
      In International journal of the sociology of language. –
     8 (1976)
      References: p.41–43

      Includes many items on language, linguistics and creole
  languages of the Caribbean. Entries for British Guiana, British
  Honduras, Jamaica, St. Lucia, Trinidad and Tobago, Dominica.
                                                            UWI-T

911 CRAIG, DENNIS R.
      Bidialectal education : creole and standard in the West
     Indies / Dennis R. Craig. – p.93–136
      In International journal of the sociology of language. –
     8 (1976)
      References: p.127–136

      Includes several items on creole languages, dialect
  language teaching and linguistics in the Caribbean.
                                                            UWI-T

912 CRAIG, D.R.
      Language-education research in the Commonwealth Caribbean
     / D.R. Craig. – p.23–26

In Caribbean journal of education. - No.1 (June 1974)
References : p.30-36

Alphabetical author list of 116 items on language,
linguistics, creole and pidgin languages, dialect, language
teaching. Several items relate to Jamaica, Guyana and Trinidad
while a few appear for Dominica, Antigua, Grenada, St. Lucia and
the Cayman Islands.

UWI-T

913 CRAIG, DENNIS R.
The sociology of language learning and teaching in a creole
situation / Dennis R. Craig. - p.101-116
In Caribbean journal of education. - Vol.5, no.3 (Sept.
1978)
References : p.112-116

50 entries including works on pidgins and creole in the
West Indies.

UWI-T

914 DILLARD, J.L.
Towards a bibliography of works dealing with the creole
languages of the Caribbean area, Louisiana and the Guianas /
J.L. Dillard. - p.84-95
In Caribbean studies. - Vol.3, no.1 (Apr. 1963)

Author describes bibliography as an addition to Rubin's
work (Ref.no.922). Alphabetical author arrangement of books,
pamphlets and periodical articles.

UWI-T

915 EDWARDS, VIV
Black British English : a bibliographical essay on the
language of children of West Indian origin / Viv Edwards. -
p.1-25
In Sage race relations abstracts. - Vol.5, no.3-4 (Sept.
1980)

Bibliographic essay covering the language of West Indians
and their descendants in Britain. Works dealing with Caribbean
creole languages, languages of West Indians in Britain,
linguistics and dialect interference, and attitudes to West
Indian speech are described. Essay also covers works on West
Indian verbal skills and educational policy towards language of
West Indian children. List of 90 items follows the essay.
Includes many periodical articles and theses.

UWI-T

916   EDWARDS, VIV
        The West Indian language issue in British schools :
      challenges and responses / Viv Edwards. - London ; Boston :
      Routledge and Kegan Paul, 1979. - vii, 168p. - (Routledge
      education books)
        Bibliography :   p.155-163

        161 items arranged alphabetically by author. Includes
      general works on West Indians in Britain, their education, social
      and economic conditions, and works of fiction of relevance.
                                                                    UWI-T

917   ERIC Clearinghouse for Linguistics. Center for Applied
      Linguistics
        A preliminary bibliography of American English dialect /
      Center for Applied Linguistics. - [Washington, D.C. : CAL,
      ERIC], [1969]. - 2, 55 leaves
        Mimeographed

        Negro dialects of the Caribbean (items 525-565).
                                                                    LC

918   Institute of Jamaica. West India Reference Library
        Caribbean languages : a bibliography ; from the collection
      in the West India Reference Library / prepared by Rosalie
      Williams. - [Kingston, Jamaica] : Institute of Jamaica, 1970. -
      21p.
        Mimeographed

        Items are arranged alphabetically by author within sections
      which include English language textbooks, Antigua, Barbados,
      British Guiana, British Honduras, Jamaica, St. Lucia, Tobago and
      Trinidad. There are also sections on the Arawak and Carib
      languages.
                                                                    UWI-T

919   Language and development : the St. Lucian context ; final
      report of a seminar on an orthography for St. Lucian creole
      held at Caribbean Research Centre, Barnard's Hill, Castries,
      St. Lucia, January 29-31, 1981 and arranged by Caribbean
      Research Centre, St. Lucia and Folk Research Centre. -
      Castries, St. Lucia : Caribbean Research Centre and Folk
      Research Centre, 1981. - 9, [2], 2, 4 leaves
        Mimeographed

        Appendix D : Materials on creole languages available in
      the Morne Educational Complex Library. - 4 leaves

36 items listed under headings : Bibliographies,
Directories, Grammars, Phonetics, Dictionaries, Educational
Implications, Development, Social Implications, Study and
Teaching, Literature, Periodicals. Several items relate to St.
Lucian creole or patois while others are concerned with Caribbean
creole languages generally.

UWI-T

919a NODAL, ROBERTO
A bibliography, with some annotations, on the creole
language of the Caribbean, including a special supplement on
Gullah / compiled by Roberto Nodal. - Milwaukee, Wis. :
Department of Afro-American Studies, University of Wisconsin,
1972. - 53p. - (Afro-American studies. Report ; no.2)

"An excellent, partly annotated bibliography on the entire
Caribbean region, with references to many journal articles"

Ref.no.309a
Item no.355

920 PRIMUS, WILMA JUDITH
Creole and pidgin languages in the Caribbean : an annotated
bibliography / compiled by Wilma Judith Primus ; submitted to
the Library Association in fulfillment of the requirements for
the Fellowship of the Library Association. - [S.l. : s.n.],
1974. - vi, 156 leaves
Mimeographed

An expansion of an earlier work (Ref.no.927) providing
annotations and based on the collections of three Caribbean
libraries and the University of Texas at Austin. 790 entries
arranged by language of origin - English-based, French-based and
Spanish/Portuguese-based creoles - with sections under the
relevant territories in each case embracing some parts of the
wider Caribbean area. Includes an author index and a list of
the journals cited.

UWI-T

921 REINECKE, JOHN E.
A bibliography of pidgin and creole languages / compiled
by John E. Reinecke [and others]. - Honolulu : University of
Hawaii Press, 1975. - 804p. - (Oceanic linguistics special
publication ; no.14)

Includes a section (p.373-431) on the West Indies
comprising 65 entries on West Indian (or Caribbean) English
followed by 177 entries on Jamaica, 72 on Trinidad and Tobago,
84 on Guyana and briefer sections on Barbados, Antigua and Belize
among others. 103 references on West Indian dialect in literature
are provided with an indication of the author's country of origin
in each case. Separate treatment is given to French-based

creoles with a few entries on Dominica, St. Lucia, Grenada and Trinidad. Most entries are annotated. Indexes to (a) authors, (b) Christian scriptures, (c) anonymous titles and (d) periodicals in creole/pidgin languages are provided.

UWI-T

922 RUBIN, JOAN
      A bibliography of Caribbean creole language / Joan Rubin.
    - p.51-61
     In Caribbean studies. - Vol.2, no.4 (1963)

     Comprises works dealing with all the creole languages of the Antilles, Caribbean area, Louisiana and the Guianas. Items which include references covering the linguistic, socio-linguistic or historical aspects of the languages are listed alphabetically by author.

UWI-T

923 TAYLOR, DOUGLAS
      Languages of the West Indies / Douglas Taylor. - Baltimore : Johns Hopkins University Press, 1977. - xix, 278p. - (Johns Hopkins studies in Atlantic history and culture)
     Bibliography: p.270-278

     Arranged chronologically within alphabetical author listings. Includes references on Amerindian languages especially Island-Carib in St. Vincent and Dominica as well as creole languages.

UWI-T

924 University of Guyana. Library
      List of materials of interest to linguists working in the Caribbean area / Library, University of Guyana. - [Georgetown, Guyana : University of Guyana Library], [1970?]. - 13 leaves

     Originally prepared for the Senate Sub-Committee for Linguistics, University of the West Indies, it comprises 350 entries alphabetically arranged within 10 subject groups.

UG

925 University of the West Indies. Senate Sub-Committee for Linguistics
      Materials relevant to Caribbean Linguistics held in libraries of that region : preliminary list / [compiled by L.D. Carrington] for Senate Sub-Committee for Linguistics. - [St. Augustine, Trinidad : Senate Sub-Committee for Linguistics, University of the West Indies], 1970. - 61p.

     Entries arranged alphabetically under specific libraries of the wider Caribbean region (including Haiti and the Dominican Republic) with subdivisions by language groupings. Holdings of

the Institute of Jamaica predominate and include sections on
slavery and emancipation, migrants, etc.

                                                        UWI-T

926 University of the West Indies (Mona). Library
        Towards a bibliography of materials of interest to
     linguists working in the Caribbean area : materials at the
     Library, University of the West Indies, Mona / A. Jefferson.
     - Mona, [Jamaica] : Library, University of the West Indies,
     [1971]. - [20]p.
        Mimeographed

        Alphabetical author arrangement with Library of Congress
     classification numbers and a list of periodicals cited. Not
     indexed.

                                                        UWI-T

927 University of the West Indies (St. Augustine). Library
        Creole and pidgin languages in the Caribbean : a select
     bibliography prepared on the occasion of the UNESCO/UWI
     Conference on Creole Languages and Educational Development,
     July 24-28, 1972 ... / by Wilma J. Primus ... . - St. Augustine,
     Trinidad : Library, The University of the West Indies, 1972. -
     iii, 80p. - (Bibliographic series ; no.5)

        594 numbered entries divided into five main sections :
     Bibliographies, General Works, English, French and Spanish/
     Portuguese-based Creoles and Pidgins with each section further
     subdivided by countries and in alphabetical author order within
     these. Includes listings of reviews of works listed and an
     author index. Later up-dated by Ref.no.920.

                                                        UWI-T

Guyana

928 GIBSON, K.
        A handbook of the Edwards collection of tapes, University
     of Guyana / K. Gibson. - [S.l. : s.n.], 1977. - 16 leaves
        Photocopy

        "This collection, based largely on the linguistic research
     of Walter Edwards is presently deposited in the University of
     Guyana Library" - Benjamin.

                                                          UG

929 GOEJE, C.H. DE
        The Arawak language of Guiana / by C.H. de Goeje. -
     Amsterdam : Koninklijke Akademie van Wetenschappen, 1928. -
     309p.
        Bibliography : p.9-13

                                                     Benjamin

930   Guyana. National Library
        Creolese relating to Guyana / National Library. -
      Georgetown : National Library, 1975. - 4 leaves
        Typescript

                                                                NLG

931   WILLIAMS, JAMES
        ... Grammar notes and vocabulary of the language of the
      Makucki Indians of Guiana / James Williams. - St. Gabriel-
      Mödlung near Vienna, Austria : "Anthropos,", 1932. - 2, 1,
      [3]-113p.
        Bibliography: p.21-46.

                                                                LC

                                LAW

932   British Institute of International and Comparative Law.
      Commonwealth Legal Advisory Service
        A bibliography of publications on West Indian law
      (including Guyana, British Honduras and the Bahamas) and on
      legal topics concerning the West Indies / Commonwealth Legal
      Advisory Service. - [London : British Institute of International
      and Comparative Law], 1970. - 19p.
        Mimeographed

        Arranged in three parts, the first with general works on
      law of the West Indies, parliamentary papers and articles in the
      International and Comparative Law Quarterly, the second with
      material on each territory/island of the Commonwealth Caribbean
      grouped separately, and a third part with textbooks relevant to
      the law of the West Indies.

                                                              UWI-T

933   DWYER, F.X.
        A bibliography of current statute law for British colonies
      in the Western hemisphere / F.X. Dwyer. - p.338
        In Proceedings of the first conference of the American Bar
      Association. - 1941

                                                          Ref.no.941
                                                          Item no.9

934   DYRUD, JOHN
        Collection of West Indian legal materials in the Common-
      wealth Caribbean : report on field trip sponsored by the Ford
      Foundation and undertaken by the University of the West Indies
      Faculty of Law Library / submitted by John Dyrud. - [Cave Hill,
      Barbados] : Faculty of Law Library, 1973. - [49], [55] leaves

Includes a country-by-country essay review of basic legal
materials and how to acquire them followed by listings of material
acquired in each of 12 Commonwealth territories including the
Bahamas, British Virgin Islands and the ten members of the former
federation. Lists include unpublished theses, official reports,
gazettes, Hansards, laws and statutes etc. arranged under the
name of the territory or by author.

UWI-T

935   Great Britain. Colonial Office
List of the laws dealing with the emigration from the
British West Indian colonies to foreign countries / Colonial
Office. - [S.l. : s.n.], 1908. - 1p. - (Cd. ; 3827)

Ref.no.53
Vol.3, p.532

936   MAXWELL, LESLIE F.
The British Commonwealth, excluding the United Kingdom,
Australia, New Zealand, Canada, India and Pakistan / compiled
by Leslie F. Maxwell. - 2nd ed. - London : Sweet and Maxwell,
1964. - vii, 459p. - (A legal bibliography of the British
Commonwealth of Nations ; v.7)
Part 4 : Central and South America and the Southern
Atlantic (p.278-369)

Coverage includes the Bahamas, British West Indies
(Barbados, Jamaica, Cayman Islands, Turks and Caicos Islands),
Leeward Islands, Tobago, Trinidad, Windward Islands, British
Guiana and British Honduras.

UWI-T

937   MAXWELL, W. HAROLD
A complete list of British and colonial law reports and
legal periodicals arranged in alphabetical and in chronological
order with bibliographical notes / compiled by W. Harold
Maxwell and C.R. Brown. - 3rd ed. - Toronto : The Carswell
Company, 1937. - viii, 141, [1]p., 2 leaves, 59p.
On cover : Check list of British and colonial reports,
periodicals and Canadian statute law

Includes entries under Bahamas, Barbados, Bermuda, British
Guiana, Jamaica, St. Lucia, Trinidad and Tobago, West Indies,
Windward Islands.

UT

938   MEEK, C.K.
Colonial law : a bibliography with special reference to
native African systems of law and land tenure / by C.K. Meek.
- London : Oxford University Press for Nuffield College, 1948.
- xiii, 58p.

RCS

939   NEWTON, VELMA
      Historical perspective of law reporting in the English-
      speaking Caribbean : a case for regional law reporting / Velma
      Newton. - p.37-44
      <u>In</u> West Indian law journal (Oct. 1978)
      Appendix I : West Indian law reports and digests (p.41-
      44)

      Items are listed by country.

                                                              UWI-B

940   NEWTON, VELMA
      Law in Caribbean society : an annotated guide to the
      University of the West Indies Law in Society dissertations
      1973-77 / Velma Newton and Sylvia Moss. - [Mona ; Cave Hill ;
      St Augustine] : Research and Publications Fund Committee,
      U.W.I., 1980. - vi, 151p.

      177 items arranged under subjects such as Amerindians,
      constitutional and administrative law, constitutional law,
      consumer protection, courts and legal profession, criminal law
      and criminology, crimes aboard aircraft, criminology, customary
      law, family law, affiliation, family courts, inheritance and
      succession, insurance, automobile, international law, labour law,
      land law, land use and tenure, press law and torts. Includes
      appendices of Table of Cases and Table of Statutes arranged in
      the same subject groupings as the main works and a list of
      secondary sources. Author index provided. Dissertations deal
      with the Commonwealth Caribbean as a whole and individual
      countries.

                                                              UWI-T

941   PATCHETT, KEITH W.
      British colonization (Caribbean, Central and South
      America) / Keith W. Patchett. - [Brussels] : Editions de
      l'Institut de Sociologie, Université Libre de Bruxelles,
      1970. - 52p. - (Bibliographical introduction to legal history
      and ethnology / edited by John Glissen ; F7)
      On cover : Etudes d'histoire et d'ethnologie juridiques

      Survey listing of the legal materials of some 17
      territories under the British Crown up to the 1960's. Arranged
      alphabetically by territories and subdivided into General Works,
      Legislation and Law Reports, Public Law and Private Law with an
      extensive section on the West Indies in general with similar
      subdivisions. The author was then Dean of the Faculty of Law,
      U.W.I.

                                                              UWI-T

942   University of London.   Institute of Advanced Legal Studies
         Union list of commonwealth law in libraries in Oxford,
      Cambridge and London / Institute of Advanced Legal Studies. –
      London : Institute of Advanced Legal Studies, University of
      London, 1952. – [v], 120p. – (Publication ; no.2)

         1,000 references.

                                                                    BL

942a University of the West Indies (Cave Hill)
         Lawyers! Should thou advertise? : a bibliography of
      materials on legal ethics and lawyer advertising / Velma
      Newton. – [Cave Hill, Barbados] : University of the West Indies,
      1982. – vii, 28p.

         The 366 items divided into primary and secondary sources
      include a few items on the Commonwealth Caribbean – legislation
      on the legal profession and legal ethics and articles concerning
      lawyer advertising which appeared in the Trinidad Guardian and
      the Trinidad Express.

                                                                  UWI-T

943   University of the West Indies (Cave Hill). Faculty of Law.
      Library
         A bibliography of a representative selection of material
      by Law Faculty personnel / Faculty of Law Library. – Cave Hill,
      Barbados : Faculty of Law Library, University of the West Indies
      Indies, 1981

         Compiled to accompany a display mounted in the library to
      commemorate the Decennial Celebrations of the Faculty of Law
      1970/71–1980/81.

                                                                 UWI-LL

943a University of the West Indies (Cave Hill). Faculty of Law.
      Library
         Legal literature and publishing in the Commonwealth
      Caribbean : a working paper / Velma Newton. – Cave Hill,
      [Barbados] : Faculty of Law Library, 1979. – [ii], 137p.
         Mimeographed

         Section 2 (p.11–69) covering Commonwealth Caribbean Legal
      Literature includes several chapters, in the style of biblio-
      graphic essays, dealing with primary legal materials – Legislation,
      Law Reports, Judgments – and secondary legal materials including
      bibliographies, official documents, monographs, periodical
      literature and unpublished material.

                                                                  UWI-T

944   University of the West Indies (Cave Hill). Faculty of Law.
      Library
          The legal literature of the Commonwealth Caribbean - 1978
      update : a bibliography / compiled by Velma Newton. - Cave
      Hill, Barbados : Faculty of Law Library, The University of the
      West Indies, 1978. - 92p.

          Consists of three sections covering primary sources,
      secondary materials and conditions affecting legal publishers.
      The bibliography which updates Ref.no.949 is the first of a two-
      part project on the legal literature of the Commonwealth. Items
      are listed under country headings and subdivided by subject. An
      author index is provided.
                                                             UWI-T

945   University of the West Indies (Cave Hill). Faculty of Law.
      Library
          West Indian law : a bibliography of writings by University
      of the West Indies Faculty of Law staff / compiled by S.G.
      Moss and V.E. Newton. - [Cave Hill], Barbados : Faculty of Law
      Library, The University of the West Indies, 1976. - 14, iiip.

          The bibliography which includes published and unpublished
      works held by the Faculty of Law Library, Cave Hill, comprises
      148 entries arranged alphabetically by author. Name index
      provided.
                                                             UWI-T

946   University of the West Indies (Cave Hill). Faculty of Law.
      Library
          West Indian primary legal materials : a checklist of West
      Indian law reports, mimeographed judgments, government depart-
      mental reports, legislation and parliamentary records held by
      the Faculty of Law Library on June 30th, 1977 / compiled by
      Velma Newton. - Cave Hill, [Barbados] : Faculty of Law Library,
      University of the West Indies, [1977]. - 58p.
          Mimeographed

          Listing separates law reports and judgments from govern-
      ment reports and both sections are divided by territory.
                                                             UWI-T

947   University of the West Indies (Cave Hill). Faculty of Law.
      Library. Public Services Section
          A list of newspaper clippings added to the library. -
      March-May 1979- . - [Cave Hill, Barbados] : Faculty of Law
      Library, University of the West Indies, 1979-
          Irregular

          Items arranged by subject comprise articles of legal
      interest, mainly from West Indian newspapers.
                                                             UWI-T

947a   University of the West Indies (Cave Hill). Institute of Social
        and Economic Research (Eastern Caribbean)
             Civil rights with special reference to the Commonwealth
        Caribbean : a select bibliography / Velma Newton. - Cave Hill,
        Barbados : Institute of Social and Economic Research (Eastern
        Caribbean), University of the West Indies, 1981. - vii, 110p.

             890 entries covering primary and secondary sources and
        including references to the fundamental rights provisions of
        Commonwealth Caribbean constitutions, judgments of Commonwealth
        Caribbean superior courts. Sections include civil rights,
        discrimination, freedom of association, race relations, liberty
        of the press, minorities, ombudsman and race discrimination, with
        items on the Commonwealth Caribbean. Author and country indexes.
                                                               UWI-T

948   University of the West Indies (Cave Hill). Institute of
        Social and Economic Research (Eastern Caribbean)
             Legal literature and conditions affecting the legal
        literature and publishing in the Commonwealth Caribbean : a
        bibliography / Velma Newton. - Cave Hill, Barbados : Institute
        of Social and Economic Research, University of the West Indies,
        1979. - 108p. - (Occasional bibliography series ; no.6)

             711 items arranged under headings : (a) Primary Sources,
        subdivided into Legislation ; Law Reports and Digests and (b)
        Secondary Sources, subdivided into Published Bibliographies ;
        Post-1973 Published Secondary Sources ; Post-1973 Unpublished
        Secondary Sources ; and Legal and Other Periodicals. Topics are
        further subdivided by country. Collections of legislation, West
        Indian legislation and West Indian Law reports and digests, West
        Indian Supreme Court and other judgments held by the Faculty of
        Law Library, Cave Hill and indices to judgments, LL.B. Law in
        Society II dissertations are listed. Author index provided.
                                                               UWI-T

949   University of the West Indies (Mona). Institute of Social and
        Economic Research and Faculty of Law
             A bibliographical guide to law in the Commonwealth
        Caribbean / compiled by Keith Patchett and Valerie Jenkins. -
        [Mona], Jamaica : Institute of Social and Economic Research
        and Faculty of Law, 1973. - xvi, 80p. - (Law and society in
        the Caribbean ; no.2)

             Prepared as a tool for research workers in the field, the
        847 references listed include numerous works which are either
        unpublished or have been produced for limited publication.
        Arranged under geographical and subject headings. Author and
        subject indexes are provided.
                                                               UWI-T

950 WILLIAMS, W.E.
     Bibliography of published and unpublished legal materials
     of members of the Faculty of Law, University of the West
     Indies / W.E. Williams. - Cave Hill, Barbados : [s.n.], 1975. -
     11p.

                                                        UWI-LL

Indexes
  951 EARNSHAW, W.
       A digest of laws relating to shipping, navigation,
       commerce and revenue in the British colonies, in America and
       the West Indies / W. Earnshaw. - London : [s.n.], 1818.
                                                   Ref.no.941
                                                   Item no.131

  952 FURTADO, W.A.
       Index to the laws of England specially relating to the
       colonies and British possessions abroad / W.A. Furtado. -
       [Kingston], Jamaica : [s.n.], 1890. - iii, 52p.

           750 references.

                                                   Ref.no.4
                                                   Vol.2, p.2641

  953 Trinidad and Tobago. High Court. Law Library
       Subject index to the West Indian reports of volumes 9-16,
       (1965-1971) / prepared by the Law Library, High Court. - Port
       of Spain. - [Port of Spain], Trinidad : Government Printer,
       1974. - 120p.

           Alphabetical subject arrangement with details of juris-
       diction and page, volume and year of the relevant report.
                                                        UWI-T

  954 The West Indian reports. - Vol.18, (1974) ; including consoli-
       dated tables and index to volumes 9-18 (1965-1972). - London :
       Butterworths, 1975. - 598p.
       Consolidated tables and index : p.425-598

           Alphabetical list of cases reported from Barbados, Guyana,
       Jamaica, Trinidad and Tobago, West Indies Associated States,
       Windward and Leeward Islands as well as cases judicially considered,
       statutes, etc. judicially considered followed by an alphabetically
       arranged subject index.
                                                        UWI-T

  955 The West Indian reports. - Vol.8 (1965) ; including consoli-
       dated tables and index to volumes 1-8 (1958-1965). - London :
       Butterworths, 1966. - 571p.
       Consolidated tables and index : p.438-571

Alphabetical lists of cases reported from the former
Federal Supreme Court of the West Indies, the British Caribbean
Court of Appeal, the Courts of Appeal and Supreme Courts of the
main Commonwealth Caribbean territories as well as Privy Council
cases on appeal from them. A subject index to these cases
follows, arranged under legal topics such as bankruptcy, arrest,
criminal law, sale of land, etc. with detailed subdivisions
under each heading.

UWI-T

956   University of the West Indies (Cave Hill). Faculty of Law.
      Library
           British West Indian cases index : subject index to the
      judgments of the courts of the former British West Indies and
      Commonwealth Caribbean territories as held in the University
      of the West Indies Law Faculty Library, Cave Hill, Barbados up
      to May 31, 1975 / compiled by Fay Durrant. - Cave Hill,
      Barbados : U.W.I., Faculty of Law Library, 1975. - 260p.
           First supplement, June 1975-Jan. 1976 / compiled by Velma
      Newton. - 1976. - 89p.
           Second supplement, Jan.-Dec. 1976 / compiled by Velma
      Newton. - 1976. - 59p.
           Third supplement, Jan. 1977-Dec. 1978 / compiled by Velma
      Newton. - iv, 138p. - [1979?].

UWI-LL

Leeward Islands
Indexes

957   BAYNES, E.W.
           Alphabetical index of the short titles to the acts of the
      Leeward Islands ..., 1925 / E.W. Baynes. - Antigua : [s.n.],
      1926. - 9p.

Ref.no.948
Item no.168

958   CAMACHO, M.V.
           Tables of the federal statutes of the Leeward Islands /
      M.V. Camacho. - [Antigua:s.n.], 1925. - 81p.

Ref.no.948
Item no.169

959   An index to the federal acts of the general legislature of the
      colony of the Leeward Islands from 1872 to 1889. - [Antigua:s.n.],
      [1890]. - 32p.

           350 references.

Ref.no.4
Vol.3, p.3478

960   Leeward Islands. Laws, statutes, etc.
           Index to the laws of ... the Leeward Islands and presi-
       dencies / D.H. Semper and A.C. Burns. - [London : s.n.],
       [1911]. - 160p.

           750 references.

Ref.no.948
Item no.170

961   University of the West Indies (Mona). Library
           Index to judgments of the Leeward Islands, 1928-1956 as
       found in the Leeward Islands gazettes, 1890-1956 / Library,
       University of the West Indies. - Mona, [Jamaica] : Government
       Serials Section, U.W.I. Library, 1971. - 112p.

           Judgments are arranged by date. Page numbers and circuit
       are indicated.

UWI-LL

Anguilla

Indexes
962   Anguilla. Laws, statutes, etc.
           Consolidated index of statutes and subsidiary legislation
       to 1st January 1980 / compiled at the Faculty of Law and Law
       Library, University of the West Indies, Barbados. - [Cave
       Hill, Barbados] : Faculty of Law and Law Library, University
       of the West Indies, 1980. - iv, 64p.

           One of a series in the West Indian Legislation Indexing
       Project (WILIP) compiled in co-operation with the British
       Development Division. Indexes (1) The statutes and subsidiary
       legislation contained in the 1961 revised edition of the Laws
       of Saint Christopher, Nevis and Anguilla (Vols.1-8) ... in force
       on 24 October, 1961; (2) The laws made in Anguilla from 1971 to
       1979.

UWI-T

Antigua

Indexes
963   Antigua. Laws, statutes, etc.
           Index cumulative and consolidated to 1st January 1976 /
       [compiled by Sir Clifford Hammett]. - [Cave Hill, Barbados :
       Faculty of Law Library, University of the West Indies],
       [197-?]. - ii, 43p.

One of a series in the West Indian Legislation Indexing
Project (WILIP). Covers laws in force on 2 January, 1962 and
contained in the 1962 revised edition of the laws; the majority
of laws published from 1962-1975 and certain relevant U.K.
enactments.

CLE-T

964   Antigua. Laws, statutes, etc.
The revised laws of Antigua / prepared ... by P. Cecil
Lewis. - London : Waterlow and Sons [as] the [Antigua] Govern-
ment Printers, 1965
Vol.9 : General index. - 225p.

Alphabetical subject index using legal phrase headings
with specific subdivisions citing chapter, section and page
numbers of the laws - revised edition 1962.

TLL

965   RAE, J.S.
Revised general index to laws of Antigua to 1934 / J.S.
Rae. - [Antigua : s.n.], [1934]. - 32p.

Ref.no.948
Item no.171

Bahamas

966   JARRETT, J.R.
Law finder : a guide to legislation in force in the
Bahamas / J.R. Jarrett. - 3rd ed. - Nassau : [s.n.], 1947. -
154p.

Ref.no.941
Item no.432

Barbados

Indexes
967   Barbados. Laws, statutes, etc.
The laws of Barbados in force on the 31st day of December,
1971 ; revised edition / prepared ... by Ashley Roy Marshall
and Keith William Patchett. - Bridgetown, Barbados : Government Printer ; London : Sweet and Maxwell, 1974. - 7v.
Vol.7: General index. - 416p.

This is not a complete subject index but rather a chapter-
by-chapter index to the contents of the 385 chapters of the laws
quoting the relevant sections in a subject breakdown for each.

UWI-T

968   Barbados. Laws, statutes, etc.
        Laws of Barbados : index and appendices to the revised
      edition ; 1667-1 - 1942-8. - Bridgetown, Barbados : Advocate
      Company, 1946. - 314, ix, xip.

        Subject index using legal words and phrases and citing
   year, chapter and section for each subdivision.
                                                              TLL

969   Barbados. Laws, statutes, etc.
        Laws of Barbados index of statutes, consolidated and
      cumulative to 1st January, 1977 / Library, Faculty of Law,
      U.W.I. - Cave Hill, Barbados : Library, Faculty of Law,
      University of the West Indies, 1977. - 57p.
        Mimeographed

        One of a series in the West Indian Legislation Indexing
   Project (WILIP). Covers the Barbados Revised Laws 1971 which
   does not have a full index as well as subsequent legislation to
   1976. Excludes Appropriation and Final Appropriation Acts.
                                                              CLE-T

Belize

Indexes
   970 Belize. Laws, statutes, etc.
          Consolidated index of statutes and subsidiary legislation
        to 1st January, 1978 / compiled ... by Sir Clifford J. Hammett.
        - Cave Hill, Barbados : Faculty of Law Library, University of
        the West Indies, 1978. - 57p.

          One in the series of the West Indian Legislation Indexing
     Project (WILIP).
                                                              UWI-LL

Bermuda

Indexes
   971 DILL, THOMAS MELVILLE
          Index to the Journals of the Honourable House of Assembly
        of Bermuda, 1850-1899 / Thomas Melville Dill. - [S.l. : s.n.],
        1903. - iv, 246p.

          6,000 references.
                                                         Ref.no.4
                                                         Vol.1, p.745

972 GRAY, REGINALD
     Index to the acts of the Legislature of the island of
     Bermuda from 1690 to 1896, no.6, 1896 / Reginald Gray. -
     [S.l. : s.n.], 1896. - iv, 124p.

     3,500 references.

                                                    Ref.no.4
                                                    Vol.1, p.745

British Virgin Islands

Indexes
973 British Virgin Islands. Laws, statutes, etc.
     Consolidated index of statutes and subsidiary legislation
     to 1st January, 1978 / compiled ... by Sir Clifford J. Hammett.
     - Cave Hill, Barbados : Faculty of Law Library, University of
     the West Indies, 1978. - 56p.

     One of a series in the West Indian Legislation Indexing
     Project (WILIP).

                                                    UWI-LL

Dominica

Indexes
974 Dominica. Laws, statutes, etc.
     Laws of Dominica index of statutes and subsidiary legis-
     lation to 1st January, 1979 / [compiled by Sir Clifford
     Hammett]. - [Cave Hill, Barbados : Faculty of Law Library,
     University of the West Indies], 1979. - 72p.

     One of a series in the West Indian Legislation Indexing
     Project (WILIP).

                                                    UWI-LL

975 FORBES, A.G.
     Index to legislation in force on July 31, 1940 / A.G.
     Forbes. - Dominica : [s.n.], 1940. - 109p.

                                                    Ref.no.145
                                                    Item no.884

Grenada

Indexes
976 Grenada. Laws, statutes, etc.
     Consolidated index of statutes and subsidiary legislation
     to 1st January 1978 / compiled [by Sir Clifford Hammett] at
     the Faculty of Law and Law Library, U.W.I., Barbados. - Cave

Hill, Barbados : Faculty of Law and Law Library, University of the West Indies, 1978. - ii, 45p.

One of a series in the West Indian Legislation Indexing Project (WILIP). Covers statutes and subsidiary legislation in force on 31st December, 1958 contained in vols.1-6 of 1958 edition of the Laws of Grenada, Ordinances and Acts enacted and Statutory Rules and Orders made between 1st January, 1959 and 31st December 1977 and some of the United Kingdom legislation in force in Grenada.

CLE-T

977   Grenada. Laws, statutes, etc.
      The revised laws of Grenada in force on the 31st day of December 1958 / compiled ... by Sir Clement Malone. - St. Lucia, W.I. : Voice Publishing Company [for St. Lucia] Government Printers, 1962. - 6v.
      Index : Vol.4. - p.183-494.

TLL

978   SHERRIFF, P.M.C.
      Comparative index of the laws of the colonies of Grenada and St. Vincent up to 1905 / P.M.C. Sherriff. - Barbados : [s.n.], [1906]. - ii, 26p.

      1,000 references.

Ref.no.948
Item no.173

Guyana

979   RAMSAHOYE, F.H.W.
      The development of land law in British Guiana / F.H.W. Ramsahoye ; with a foreword by Professor O.R. Marshall. - Dobbs Ferry, N.Y. : Oceana Publications, 1966. - xli, 340p.
      Bibliography: p.323-328

      Includes 62 items directly relevant to Guyanese law.

UWI-T

980   SHAHABUDDEEN, M.
      The legal system of Guyana / M. Shahabuddeen ; with a foreword by Shridath S. Ramphal. - Georgetown, Guyana : [s.n.], 1973. - xxix, 523p.
      Bibliography: p.491-511

      Extensive listing includes a substantial number of items on Guyanese law with others on the history, government and social and economic conditions of Guyana and the history of the West Indies.

UWI-T

Indexes
  981 ABRAHAM, E.A.V.
            Digest of cases, Review Court, 1856–1891 / E.A.V. Abraham.
       - Demerara, [British Guiana] : [s.n.], 1892. - 154p.
                                                              Ref.no.941
                                                              Item no.259

  982 BELMONTE, B.E.J.C.
            An alphabetical digest and index appended of ... decisions
       of the several courts of justice in British Guiana, from 1856
       to 31st December, 1906, and of the statute laws of the colony
       ... comprising the resolutions of the States general, A.D.
       1774 and all subsequent statutes / B.E.J.C. Belmonte. - [S.l. :
       s.n.], 1907. - xiii, 419p.
            Supplementary ... digest ... 1907 to 21 August, 1908. -
       1908. - xiii, 90p.

            Main work contains 3,000 references while 40 are listed
       in the supplement.
                                                              Ref.no.4
                                                              Vol.2, p.2770

  983 British Guiana. Laws, statutes, etc.
            Index to the laws of British Guiana, alphabetically
       arranged from the year 1580 to 1880. - Georgetown, Demerara
       [British Guiana] : L. M'Dermott, 1882
            Vol.VI, Part II : General index. - 167p.

            Cites volume, number, section and page for each entry.
       Several subdivisions used under each word or phrase heading.
                                                              TLL

  984 DALTON, L.C.
            Digest of case law, 1910–1920 / L.C. Dalton. - Georgetown
       : [s.n.], 1922. - 212p.
                                                              Ref.no.941
                                                              Item no.263

  985 DALTON, L.C.
            Digest of decisions of Supreme Court of British Guiana /
       L.C. Dalton
            In West Indian Court of Appeal and Privy Council, 1931–
       1938. - Georgetown : [s.n.], 1941
                                                              Ref.no.941
                                                              Item no.264

  986 DUKE, E.M.
            Digest of decisions in the Supreme Court ..., 1931–1938 /
       E.M. Duke. - [S.l. : s.n.], 1941. - 139p.
                                                              Ref.no.941
                                                              Item no.265

987   ERSKINE, R.H.
      Digest of decisions of the Privy Council under Roman-
      Dutch law 1829-1869 / R.H. Erskine. - Demerara : [s.n.], 1882
                                                      Ref.no.941
                                                      Item no.266

988   Indexes to law reports of British Guiana, 1919-1965. -
      [Georgetown : Cameron and Shepherd], [197-?]. - 1v. (unpaged)
                                                      Ref.no.948
                                                      Item no.256

989   PASEA, G.A.
      Digest of cases affecting the Commissary's Department from
      1856-1916 / G.A. Pasea. - Georgetown : [s.n.], 1917. - 5p.
                                                      Ref.no.941
                                                      Item no.268

990   SHARPLES, O.E.
      A digest of cases decided in the Supreme Court of British
      Guiana during the years 1901, 1902, 1903, 1904, and the earlier
      half of the year 1905, including cases decided in the appellate
      jurisdiction of the court / O.E. Sharples. - [S.l. : s.n.],
      [1906]. - [11], ii, 251, xp.
      Supplement 1905-1909. - 1910. - vi, 234, xp.

      500 references are listed in the main work and 600 in the
      supplement.
                                                      Ref.no.4
                                                      Vol.2, p.2770

Jamaica

Indexes
991   Digest of the public acts of the island of Jamaica. - [Kingston
      : s.n.], 1845. - 2v.
                                                      Ref.no.948
                                                      Item no.164

992   FURTADO, W.A.
      Index to the laws of Jamaica / W.A. Furtado. - [Kingston],
      Jamaica : [s.n.], 1880. - 95p.

      2,000 references.
                                                      Ref.no.4
                                                      Vol.2, p.3241

993   FURTADO, W.A.
      Index to the laws to December 31, 1885 / W.A. Furtado. -
      [Kingston : s.n.], 1889.
                                                      Ref.no.948
                                                      Item no.167

994 FURTADO, W.A.
     Index to the laws of Jamaica / W.A. Furtado. - Jamaica :
     [s.n.], 1892. - 163p.

     3,000 references.
                                                         Ref.no.4
                                                      Vol.2, p.3241

995 GRIFFITH, W. BRANDON
     An index to the acts and laws of Jamaica, up to Law no.1
     of 1892 / W. Brandon Griffith. - [Kingston : s.n.], 1892. -
     ii, 142p.
     3rd ed. / by C.H. Yorke Slader. - 1911. - (iii), viii,
     355p.

     First ed., 10,000 entries; 3rd ed., 20,000 entries.
                                                         Ref.no.4
                                                      Vol.2, p.3241

996 Jamaica. Supreme Court
     Cumulative index including table of cases and subject
     index to judgments of the Supreme Court, Court of Appeal and
     Privy Council 1962-1971 / prepared and compiled by Mr. Justice
     C.H. Graham-Perkins, Yvonne T. Lawrence and Fay M. Williams. -
     [S.l. : s.n.], [197-?]. - 95p.

                                                          UWI-LL

997 Jamaica. Supreme Court
     Cumulative index including table of cases and subject index
     to judgments of the Supreme Court, Court of Appeal and Privy
     Council 1972-1974 / edited and compiled by Mr. Justice C.H.
     Graham-Perkins and Fay Williams. - [S.l. : s.n.], 1975.
                                                       Ref.no.948
                                                      Item no.258

998 LUNAN, J.
     Abstract of the Laws of Jamaica relating to slaves (from
     33 Chas. II-59 Geo. III) with the Slave Law at length / J.
     Lunan. - St. Jago de la Vega, [Jamaica] : [s.n.], 1819. -
     192p.
                                                       Ref.no.948
                                                      Item no.330

999 MINOT, JAMES
     A digest of the laws of Jamaica from 33 Charles II to 28
     Victoria / James Minot. - [Kingston], Jamaica : [s.n.], 1865.
     - xiii, lii, 817p.
       Supplement. - 1868. - xx, 258p.
       Continuation supplement / by William Rastrick Lee. - 1869.
     - xvi, 123p.

7,500 references; supplement, 2,000 references;
continuation, 1,000 references.

Ref.no.4
Vol.2, p.3241

Montserrat

Indexes
1000   Montserrat. Laws, statutes, etc.
         Consolidated index of statutes and subsidiary legislation
       to 1st January, 1980 / compiled at the Faculty of Law and Law
       Library, University of the West Indies, Barbados. - [Cave
       Hill, Barbados] : Faculty of Law and Law Library, University
       of the West Indies, 1980. - iv, 68p.

         One of a series in the West Indian Legislation Indexing
       Project (WILIP) compiled in co-operation with the British
       Development Division. Covers (1) The statutes and subsidiary
       legislation in force on 1 January 1962, (2) the Ordinances and
       Statutory Rules and Orders in the period 1962 to 1979 published
       as Gazette Supplements, (3) Federal laws continued in force after
       the dissolution of the West Indies, (4) Some of the Acts and
       Statutory Instruments of the United Kingdom in force or relevant
       to the laws in force in Montserrat.

UWI-T

St. Kitts-Nevis

Indexes
1001   RAE, J.S.
         Revised general index of the laws of St. Christopher and
       Nevis-Anguilla to 1937 / J.S. Rae. - [Basseterre, St. Kitts :
       s.n.], [1938]. - 92p.

Ref.no.941
Item no.434

1002   St. Christopher, Nevis and Anguilla. Laws, statutes, etc.
         Consolidated index of statutes and subsidiary legislation
       to 1st January, 1978 / compiled by Sir Clifford Hammett. -
       Cave Hill, Barbados : Faculty of Law and Law Library,
       University of the West Indies, 1978. - 56p.

         One of a series in the West Indian Legislation Indexing
       Project (WILIP).

UWI-LL

1003   St. Christopher-Nevis-Anguilla. Laws, statutes, etc.
           The revised laws of St. Christopher-Nevis and Anguilla,
       1961 / prepared by P. Cecil Lewis. - London : Waterloo and
       Sons [for] the St. Christopher-Nevis-Anguilla Government
       Printers, 1964
           Vol.9: General index. - 220p.

           Subject index citing chapter, section and page numbers.
       Arranged alphabetically under legal word and phrase headings with
       several subheadings analysing each.
                                                                    TLL

St. Lucia

1004   Guide to legislation in force 1944. - Castries, St. Lucia :
       [s.n.], 1944
                                                           Ref.no.145
                                                           Item no.887

1005   SALMON, JAMES E.M.
           Saint Lucia : law finder ; a short guide to legislation in
       force at 1st January, 1937, and to legislation no longer in
       force or modified in part at 1st January, 1937 / James E.M.
       Salmon. - [Castries, St. Lucia : Government Printer], 1937. -
       2p., 1, 62p.
                                                                   UWI-J

1006   SALMON, JAMES E.M.
           Saint Lucia : law finder ; a short guide to legislation in
       force at 1st January, 1942 / James E.M. Salmon. - Castries,
       [St. Lucia] : Government Printer, 1942. - 92p.
                                                                   UWI-J

Indexes
1007   St. Lucia. Laws, statutes, etc.
           Consolidated index of statutes and subsidiary legislation
       to 1st January 1979 / [compiled by Sir Clifford Hammett]. -
       Cave Hill, Barbados : Faculty of Law and Law Library, University
       of the West Indies, 1979. - 80p.

           One of a series in the West Indian Legislation Indexing
       Project (WILIP).
                                                                  UWI-LL

1008   St. Lucia. Laws, statutes, etc.
           Index to the laws of St. Lucia [1957-1969]. - [S.1. :
       s.n.], 1970. - 21p.

           "Commences at 1st July, 1957." Index divided into three
       parts for Acts/Ordinances, Statutory Rules and Orders, Imperial
       Legislation.
                                                                    TLL

1009   St. Lucia. Laws, statutes, etc.
       [Index to the laws of St. Lucia, 1970-1973]. - Revised
       edition. - [S.l. : s.n.], 1974. - 38p.

       A continuation of the 1957 to 1969 index (Ref.no.1008).
   Includes cross-references.

                                                          UWI-LL

1010   SHERRIFF, P.M.C.
       Index of the laws of St. Lucia (exclusive of the civil code
       and code of civil procedure) in force on the 31st December,
       1907 / P.M.C. Sherriff. - [Castries, St. Lucia : s.n.], 1908. -
       v, 34.

       1,000 references.

                                                      Ref.no.4
                                                   Vol.4, p.5546

St. Vincent

Indexes
1011   St. Vincent. Laws, statutes etc.
       Consolidated index of statutes and subsidiary legislation
       to 1st January 1978 / compiled at the Faculty of Law and Law
       Library, U.W.I., Barbados by Sir Clifford Hammett. - Cave Hill,
       Barbados : Faculty of Law and Law Library, 1978. - iii, 109p.

       One of a series in the West Indian Legislation Indexing
   Project (WILIP) compiled in co-operation with the British Development Division. Covers Ordinances and Acts in force on 4 May 1926
   contained in vols. 1 and 2 of the 1926 Revised Edition of the Laws
   of Saint Vincent, Ordinances, Acts and Statutory Rules and Orders
   published in the annual volumes from 4 May 1926 to 31 Dec., 1977
   including relevant U.K. laws referred to or republished therein.
                                                            CLE-T

1011a   Saint Vincent and the Grenadines
       Consolidated index of statutes and subsidiary legislation
       to 1st January 1980 / compiled at the Faculty of Law and Law
       Library, University of the West Indies, Barbados in co-
       operation with the Ministry of Legal Affairs, Kingstown, St.
       Vincent. - Revised edition. - [Cave Hill], Barbados : Faculty
       of Law and Law Library, University of the West Indies, 1980. -
       iii, 172p.

       One of a series in the West Indian Legislation Indexing
   Project (WILIP) compiled in co-operation with the British Development Division. Indexes Ordinances and Acts in force on 4th May
   1926 contained in volumes 1 and 2 of the 1926 revised edition of
   the statutes of St. Vincent; Ordinances and Acts from 4 May 1926
   to 31 Dec. 1979; subsidiary legislation from 1903-1979. Federal

Laws in force after the dissolution of the West Indies Federation; some of the U.K. Statutes and Statutory Instruments in force or relevant to the laws in force in St. Vincent and the Grenadines. Arranged by title with reference numbers.

UWI-T

Trinidad and Tobago

Indexes
1012 Chronological table of the royal order in council and ordinances promulgated in this colony between the 25th April, A.D. 1831 and the 30th June, A.D. 1877. - Port of Spain : [s.n.], 1877. - xvii, 142p.

   1,250 references related to Trinidad.

Ref.no.4
Vol.4, p.6209

1013 Digest of vols. 1 to 4 of Trinidad and Tobago Supreme Court judgments. - [Port of Spain], Trinidad : [s.n.], 1928. - 100p.
Ref.no.941
Item no.460

1014 Employers' Consultative Association of Trinidad and Tobago
         Index by subject to policies, principles and guidelines contained in judgments of the Industrial Court (1965 onwards) / Employers' Consultative Association of Trinidad and Tobago. - [Port of Spain] : E.C.A., 1973. - 85, 46p.
      Looseleaf
      Supplement no.1. - 1975

UWI-T

1015 Index to all the orders in council and ordinances which were either wholly or partially in force on the 31st day of December, A.D. 1871. - [S.l. : s.n.], 1872. - ii, 51p.

   500 references relating to Trinidad.

Ref.no.4
Vol.4, p.6209

1016 Index to proclamations, orders in council, regulations, etc. for the year 1945. - [Port of Spain : s.n.], 1959. - x, [250]p.

   250 references relating to Trinidad and Tobago.

Ref.no.4
Vol.4, p.6209

1017 LE GENDRE, E.
          An index to orders-in-council, proclamations, bye-laws,
      rules, regulations, etc. in force on March 31, 1943 / E. Le
      Gendre. - [Port of Spain : Government Printer], [1943]. - 75p.
                                                    Ref.no.948
                                                    Item no.178

1018 REIS, C.
          Complete subject index of ordinances / C. Reis. - [Port of
      Spain : Government Printer], [1920].
                                                    Ref.no.948
                                                    Item no.177

1019 A table of contents of all the orders in council and ordinances
      which were wholly or partially in force on the 31st December
      A.D. 1871. - [S.l. : s.n.], [1872]. - ii, 34p.

          500 references relating to Trinidad.
                                                    Ref.no.4
                                                  Vol.4, p.6208

1020 Trinidad and Tobago. Laws, statutes, etc.
          Consolidated index of statutes and subsidiary legislation
      to 1st January, 1978 / compiled at the Faculty of Law and Law
      Library, University of the West Indies, Barbados. - [Port of
      Spain], Trinidad and Tobago : Government Printer, 1978. - iii,
      138p.

          "One of a series in the West Indian Legislation Indexing
      Project (WILIP) compiled in co-operation with the British
      Development Division." The laws referred to are the Statutes
      and Subsidiary Legislation in force on 31 December 1950, Ordinances,
      and Government Notices for 1 January 1951 to 29 May 1953, Ordi-
      nances, Acts and Government Notices in the Annual Volumes of the
      Laws 1951-1976 and Acts 1-51 and Government Notices 1-219 of 1977.
      Certain of the United Kingdom Laws which are in force or are
      referred to in laws in force in Trinidad and Tobago are included.
                                                    UWI-T

1021 Trinidad and Tobago. Laws, statutes, etc.
          Laws of Trinidad and Tobago. - Port of Spain, Trinidad :
      Government Printing Office, 1902. - 3v.
          Index vol. - 798p.

          "Ordinances are arranged under suitable titles, placed in
      alphabetical order and analysed under suitable sub-headings also
      in alphabetical order." References are to sections and pages
      with numbers and volumes set out at the top of each analysis of
      an ordinance.
                                                    TLL

1022   Trinidad and Tobago. Laws, statutes, etc.
       Laws of Trinidad and Tobago. - Port of Spain, Trinidad :
Government Printing Office, 1905. - 6v.
       Vol.6 : A chronological table of ordinances from 1832 to
1904 showing those which have been repealed and the place in
the revised edition of those in force. - 38p.
                                                                    TLL

1023   Trinidad and Tobago. Laws, statutes, etc.
       Laws of Trinidad and Tobago containing the ordinances of
the colony in force on the 30th day of June 1925 ; revised
edition / prepared ... by Walter Clarence Huggard. - Port of
Spain, Trinidad : Government Printing Office, 1925
       Vol.5 : Chronological table and index. - 223p.

       Table of ordinances by number with description of subject
matter and remarks noting repeals and replacements followed by
subject index arranged alphabetically under phrase headings
further subdivided, citing chapters and page numbers for each
subheading.
                                                                    TLL

1024   Trinidad and Tobago. Laws, statutes, etc.
       The laws of Trinidad and Tobago ; revised edition ; index
/ compiled by A.R. Hewitt. - Port of Spain : Government of
Trinidad and Tobago, 1981. - 420p.
       Cover title: Laws of the Republic of Trinidad and Tobago

       Alphabetical subject arrangement further subdivided by
topics. Includes defined list of words and phrases.
                                                                  UWI-T

1025   Trinidad and Tobago. Laws, statutes, etc.
       Table of enactments, 1950-1976 / prepared by Stephanie
Daly. - Port of Spain : Pollonais and Blanc, 1977. - 38, 17p.

       Shows "the ordinances in the revised laws, 1950 and
amendments thereto and the acts and amendments thereto from 1951
to 1976." Public and private enactments listed separately by
subject with proclamation dates in one column, followed by
references and amendments/new acts in separate columns.
                                                                    TLL

1026   Trinidad and Tobago. Laws, statutes, etc.
       Table of government notices, 1950-July 1978 / prepared by
Stephanie Daly. - Port of Spain : [Pollonais and Blanc], 1978.
- 61p.
       Appendices (various pagings)

Alphabetical listing by subjects covered of all notices giving number and year followed by several detailed appendices including a chronological list of statutes by proclamation date, public health bye-laws, and sedition proclamations.

TLL

1027 Trinidad and Tobago. Law Library

Subject index to Trinidad law reports : subject index to cases reported in the Trinidad law reports, volumes 5 to 7 and 10 to 16 / Law Library, Judiciary. - [Port of Spain, Trinidad : Government Printery], 1974. - 14p.

TLL

Turks and Caicos Islands

Indexes
1028 Turks and Caicos Islands. Laws, statutes, etc.
Consolidated index of statutes and subsidiary legislation to 1st January, 1980 / Library, Faculty of Law, U.W.I. - Cave Hill, Barbados : Faculty of Law and Law Library, University of the West Indies, 1980. - 43p.

One of a series in the West Indian Legislation Indexing Project (WILIP).

UWI-LL

LIBRARIANSHIP

1028a JORDAN, ALMA THEODORA
The development of library service in the West Indies through inter-library cooperation / Alma Theodora Jordan. - Metuchen, N.J. : Scarecrow Press, 1970. - xvii, 433p.
Bibliography: p.362-394

A general bibliography which includes several references to library reports and articles on library services in the area.

UWI-T

1029 JORDAN, ALMA
Library co-operation in the West Indies, the state of the art / Alma Jordan. - p.170-194
In Libraries and the challenge of change : papers of the International Library Conference held in Kingston, Jamaica, 24-29 April, 1972 / edited by K.E. Ingram and Albertina A. Jefferson. - London : Mansell for the Jamaica Library Association and the Jamaica Library Service, 1975
References : p.189-194

145 references arranged in four sections : - Co-operative Organization; Co-operative Bibliographic and Technical Services; Co-operative Acquisitions and Sharing Resources; Other Aspects.

UWI-T

Trinidad and Tobago

1030 Library Association of Trinidad and Tobago
        Library Association of Trinidad and Tobago : bibliography
      1960-1975 / Lois Barrow and Joyce Encinas. - Port of Spain,
      Trinidad : Library Association of Trinidad and Tobago, 1975. -
      11p.

        List includes Presidents' reports to the annual general
      meetings of LATT from 1961 to 1974, addresses and lectures
      delivered to meetings of the Association, papers and reports
      presented to seminars, conferences and annual general meetings,
      reports to the Association on overseas conferences, statements
      and comments on a variety of issues in librarianship and library
      planning in Trinidad and Tobago and broadcasts given on behalf of
      the Association.

                                                              UWI-T

                              LITERATURE

1031 BAUGH, EDWARD
        Critics on Caribbean literature : readings in literary
      criticism / edited by Edward Baugh. - London : George Allen
      and Unwin, 1978. - 164p.
        Selected bibliography: p.162-164

        Arranged in sections : Prose Fiction (41 items), Poetry
      (14 items), Plays (4 items), Critical Studies (Books and
      Articles) (16 items).

                                                              UWI-T

1032 Bibliography : W.I. exiles. - p.23 and 25
        In Trinidad and Tobago review. - Vol.2, no.5 (Jan. 1978)
      and vol.2, no.6 (Feb. 1978)

        Items arranged under sections : Bibliographies Published
      Serially, Bibliographies of Individual Authors, Research Aids.
      The second section is further subdivided by genre - anthologies,
      non-fiction and critical studies of individual authors.

                                                              UWI-T

1033 Bulletin of the Association for Commonwealth Literature and
      Language Studies. - No.3 (1967). - Leeds : The Association,
      1967
        Selected bibliographies of Australian and West Indian
      literature: p.6-30

Includes a full retrospective and up-to-date list of West Indian writings compiled by John Hearne.

UWI-J

1034   CANTON, E.B.
Bibliography of West Indian literature 1900-1957 / E.B. Canton. - p.2-57
In Current Caribbean bibliography. - Vol.7 (1957)

Arrangement is by genre - novel, poetry, theatre, essay, folk literature - subdivided by countries or groups of countries. Includes items from the English-speaking Caribbean except British Honduras. Works of reference and general anthologies are also listed.

UWI-T

1035   COMISSIONG, BARBARA
Bibliography of West Indian novels and plays, 1940-1961 : submitted in part requirement for University of London Diploma in Librarianship / Barbara Comissiong. - [S.l. : s.n.], 1962. - 44p.

206 items arranged by country within each genre. Comprises novels from Barbados, British Guiana, Dominica, Jamaica, Tobago, Trinidad and plays from Barbados, British Guiana, Grenada, Jamaica and Trinidad. Author and title indexes.

UWI-T

1036   COMISSIONG, BARBARA
A select bibliography of women writers in the Eastern Caribbean (excluding Guyana) / Barbara Comissiong and Marjorie Thorpe. - p.279-304
In World literature written in English. - Vol.17, no.1 (Apr. 1978)

Comprises 380 items listed by genre within country groupings.

UWI-T

1037   DUNN, PATRICIA Y.
Selection of published bibliographic sources for the study of English Caribbean literature / Patricia Y. Dunn and Rae Wright. - p.16-23
In Library resources for research in the Caribbean : Caribbean literature in English / Patricia Dunn and Rae Wright; Working paper no. VII-B submitted for the Conference of the Association of Caribbean University and Research Libraries ... 3rd, Universidad Central de Venezuela, Caracas, November 7-12, 1971. - San Juan, Puerto Rico : Association of Caribbean University and Research Libraries, 1971

Consists of 64 items in four sections : General Reference
Works; Bibliographies, Library Accessions Lists etc.; Critical
and Other Works With Bibliographical Information; Periodicals
and Newspapers. Most entries are annotated.

UWI-T

1038 ENGBER, MARJORIE
Caribbean : fiction and poetry / compiled by Marjorie
Engber. - New York : Center for Inter American Relations,
1970. - 86p.

This is the second in a series of bibliographies being
prepared by the Center designed for students, teachers and
scholars interested in contemporary Caribbean and Latin American
literature. Lists works of fiction and poetry by Caribbean
authors published in the U.S. and U.K. from 1900 to 1970. French,
Dutch, Spanish-speaking areas included only for works translated
into English.

UWI-T

1039 FEENEY, JOAN V.
Peasant literature : a bibliography of Afro-American
nationalism and social protest from the Caribbean / by Joan
Feeney. - Monticello, Ill. : Council of Planning Librarians,
1975. - 71p. - (Council of Planning Librarians exchange
bibliography ; no.822)

"An attempt to bring together some of the more pertinent
literature written by black intellectuals" in the spirit of
"black power" in an effort "to comprehend the real meaning behind
the Black Arts Movement of American black playwrights in the
60's." Provides a tool to access "the literature of the movement
in the Caribbean which preceded the United States black awakening."
Fiction and non-fiction works are intermingled in alphabetical
author listings. Section headings include drama, dance and
personalities in theatre arts from the Caribbean, evaluations
and critiques on the works of Caribbean authors, famous political
figures of the present and recent past from the Caribbean and
books written by Caribbean authors. No annotations are given but
some sections are arranged chronologically.

UWI-T

1040 Guyana. Public Free Library
Carifesta '72 : book exhibition ; catalogue of the
Carifesta book exhibition held at the Public Free Library,
August 25-September 15, 1974. - Georgetown, Guyana : Public
Free Library, 1972. - [3], 102p.
Mimeographed

Prepared for the first Caribbean Festival of Creative Arts.
Entries grouped under Dutch, English, French, Portuguese and
Spanish-speaking countries in alphabetical author order giving
country of origin and genres followed by the list of works
exhibited (titles and dates only) for each author.

UWI-T

1041   JAHN, JANHEINZ
       Die neoafrikanische literatur : gesamtbibliographie von
den Anfängen bis zur Gegenwart / Janheinz Jahn. - Düsseldorf-
Köln : Eugen Diederichs Verlag, 1965. - xxxv, 359p.
       Also published as: A Bibliography of neo-African
literature from Africa, America and the Caribbean : London :
Deutsch ; New York : Praeger, 1965
       Includes the Antilles and Guyanas : p.132-195

       Introduction and explanatory notes are in German, English
and French. Published books, performed plays or completed
manuscripts are listed but single poems, stories or plays in
journals etc. are excluded. Authors or editors are given in
alphabetical order within each geographical division e.g.,
Antilles and Guiana. The author's country of birth is given
after his name.

UWI-T

1042   JAMES, LOUIS
       The islands in between : essays on West Indian literature
/ edited with an introduction by Louis James. - London :
Oxford University Press, 1968. - 166p.
       Select bibliography: p.160-164

       Arranged in six sections : Background, Periodicals,
Popular Culture, Fiction, Poetry, Anthologies.

UWI-T

1043   Jamaica Library Service
       Carifesta '76 : the literature of a people ; a select list
of books on the creative writings of the participating
countries in second Caribbean Festival of Arts ; book exhibition held at the Kingston and St. Andrew Parish Library,
[July 24-August 31] / Jamaica Library Service. - Kingston,
Jamaica : Jamaica Library Service, 1976. - [2], 67p.

NLG

1044   Jamaica Library Service. Kingston and St. Andrew Parish
       Library
       Contemporary West Indian literature : an annotated book-
list / prepared by the Kingston and St. Andrew Parish Library.
- [Kingston, Jamaica : The Kingston and St. Andrew Parish
Library], [1962]. - 52p.
       Cover title
       Mimeographed

Prepared for an exhibition to celebrate Jamaica's
independence in 1962. Covers the English-speaking territories
including a select list of literary magazines, fiction, poetry,
drama, music and folklore, history and travel, economic and
social and biographical references for some West Indian writers.

UWI-J

1045   JONES, JOSEPH JAY
Authors and areas of the West Indies / Joseph Jay Jones
and Johanna Jones. - Austin, Tex. : Steck-Vaughn Company,
1970. - xiv, 82p. - (People and places in World-English
literature ; no.2)
Reference bibliography of West Indian literature: p.75-77.

45 entries arranged under headings : Anthologies;
Literary History and Criticism; Background Books; Periodicals.
A supplementary list of authors and titles also appears on p.80-
82.

UWI-T

1046   National Book League
Black writing from Africa, the Caribbean and the United
States of America / National Book League. - London : National
Book League, 1975. - 36p.

"[Catalogue of an exhibition] prepared for the Second
World Black and African Festival of Arts and Culture, Lagos, 22nd
November-20th December, 1975" - Introduction.

Ref.no.18
1977

1047   Select bibliography of West Indian literature. - p.82-85
In Kyk-over-al. - Vol.3, no.11 (Oct. 1950)

Brief listings by form - poetry, fiction, history, plays,
biography and critical and social with alphabetical author
arrangement, brief title and date within each.

UWI-T

1048   University of the West Indies (Mona). Library
West Indian literature : a select bibliography / compiled
by the University of the West Indies Library. - Mona, Jamaica
: [University of the West Indies], 1964. - 32p.
Supplement 1964-1967. - 1967. - 8p.

Based on Canton (Ref.no.1034) with up-dating additions;
it is divided into six sections including historical and critical
works, folk literature/dialect, and one for each genre - prose
fiction, poetry, drama - in alphabetical order by authors. The
supplement is similarly arranged. Both include works by a few

non West Indians" when they have drawn their inspiration from
the W.I. scene."

UWI-T

1049   University of the West Indies (St. Augustine). Department of
        English
            West Indian literature : reading list / Department of
        English. - [St. Augustine, Trinidad : Department of English,
        The University of the West Indies], 1974. - 6p.
            Mimeographed

            Comprises sections on Louise Bennett, Samuel Selvon,
        Martin Carter, Edward Brathwaite, Wilson Harris, Derek Walcott,
        V.S. Naipaul, George Lamming and General Essays on West Indian
        Criticism.

UWI-T

1050   University of the West Indies (St. Augustine). Library
            Bibliography of West Indian literature / Library, U.W.I. -
        [St. Augustine, Trinidad : University of the West Indies],
        1975. - 5 leaves
            Typescript

            Listing subdivided into Bibliographies, Periodicals,
        Drama, Folktales, Novels and Short Stories, Poetry and includes
        an indication of works suitable for children in lower and upper
        age groups.

UWI-T

1051   WATSON, KARL S.
            Literature of the English and French-speaking West Indies
        in the University of Florida Libraries : a bibliography /
        compiled by Karl S. Watson. - Gainesville, Fla. : Center for
        Latin American Studies, University of Florida, 1971. - v, 26p.

            Prepared as a supplementary contribution to the papers on
        research resources presented at the third conference of the
        Association of Caribbean University and Research Libraries
        (ACURIL). Listings alphabetically by author under each of the
        countries followed by anthologies and general works on the
        Caribbean. An annotated select list of journals of literary
        interest from the English and French-speaking West Indies and an
        author index are provided.

UWI-T

1052   The West Indies. - 1964-
            In The Journal of Commonwealth literature. - No.1 (Sept.
        1965)-

This bibliography is a section in the journal's Annual
bibliography of Commonwealth literature. Compiled in 1964, 1965,
1966 by Fernando Henriques; 1967, 1968, 1969, 1970 by Kenneth
Ramchand; 1971 by Louis James; 1972, 1973 by Alvona Alleyne and
Kenneth Ramchand; 1974, 1975 by Kenneth Ramchand; 1976 by Alvona
Alleyne, Billie Goldstraw and Kenneth Ramchand; 1977 by Kenneth
Ramchand; 1978-1980 by Mark McWatt. Items arranged under
headings : Bibliographies; Poetry; Drama; Fiction; Anthologies;
Non-Fiction; Criticism; Journals.

UWI-T

Children

1053 BAHADUR, GLORIA
        Caribbean writings for children : an annotated catalogue
of an exhibition 7-19 May, 1973 / prepared by Gloria Bahadur.
- Georgetown : National Library, 1973. - [5], 29p.
        Typescript

NLG

1054 ELKIN, JUDITH
        Books for the multi-racial classroom : a select list of
children's books, showing the backgrounds of the Indian sub-
continent and the West Indies / compiled by Judith Elkin. -
2nd (revised) ed. - London : National Book League ; Birmingham
: Library Association Youth Libraries Group, 1976. - [1], 112,
[1]p. - (Library Association. Youth Libraries Group.
Pamphlets ; no.17)

        An updating of the author's 1971 list including worthwhile
children's books with geographical, cultural and religious
backgrounds of the Caribbean as well as the Indian sub-continent.

BL

1055 HILL, JANET
        Books for children : the homelands of immigrants in
Britain, Africa, Cyprus, India and Pakistan, Ireland, Italy,
Poland, Turkey, The West Indies / Janet Hill. - London :
Institute of Race Relations, distributed by Research Publi-
cations Services, 1971. - 85p. - (Institute of Race Relations ;
special series)

BL

1056 Latin America : an annotated list of materials for children /
selected by a committee of librarians, teachers and Latin
American specialists in cooperation with the Center for Inter-
American Relations. - New York: Information Center on Children's Cultures, United States Committee for UNICEF, 1969. -
96p.

The list "represents an effort to evaluate all in-print
English language materials for children." Includes material on
or from all islands of the Caribbean region. Annotations are
given as a guide.

UWI-T

1057 Trinidad and Tobago. Central Library
West Indian literature for children : booklist / [prepared
by the Central Library Children's Section for a panel
discussion at the Carnegie Free Library as part of their 50th
anniversary celebrations]. - [Port of Spain, Trinidad] :
Central Library, 1970. - 5 leaves
Mimeographed

Listing in Dewey class order with appropriate headings for
selected fiction and non-fiction works.

TCL

1058 Trinidad and Tobago. Central Library. Children's Section
Our stories : a list of 26 titles by and about West
Indians / Children's Section, Central Library. - [Port of
Spain, Trinidad] : Government Printer, 1971. - 12p.

Listings for two age groups - 9 and under and 10 and over
with synopses. Arrangement is alphabetical by author and in one
sequence. Full annotations are given.

UWI-T

Criticism
1059 ALLIS, JEANNETTE BRAUNSBERG
A survey and bibliography of critical writing on West
Indian literature 1931-1974 / by Jeannette B. Allis. - [S.l. :
s.n.], 1979. - 2v. in 1 (193; 382p.)
Vol. 2: Bibliography

A thesis submitted in partial fulfillment of the requirement for the degree of Master of Philosophy of the U.W.I. The
bibliography volume provides an index to 78 journals and newspapers in three sections : (1) a listing by critic alphabetically
and chronologically under each critic, (2) an alphabetical list
by author with author's birthplace and dates and arranged under
specific works in publication order, (3) a chronological and
annotated listing of general articles. Reviews of novels, poetry,
and collections of short stories are all included. Two major
newspapers, the Barbados Advocate and the Guyana Graphic which
were unavailable to the author are excluded.

UWI-J

1060 ALLIS, JEANNETTE B.
West Indian literature : an index to criticism, 1930-1975
/ Jeannette B. Allis. - Boston : G.K. Hall, 1981. - 353p.

Arranged in three sections :   (1) Index of Authors, (2)
Index of Critics and Reviewers, (3) Index of General Articles.
Includes reviews of novels, poetry and collections of short
stories. More than 2,000 articles dealing with over 200 authors.

                                                                    UWI-T

1061 CARNEGIE, JENIPHIER B.
      Critics on West Indian literature : a select bibliography /
      Jeniphier B. Carnegie. - Mona ; Cave Hill ; St. Augustine :
      The Research and Publications Committee, U.W.I., 1979. - 74p.

      Compiled as a research aid for students of West Indian
Literature at the Cave Hill Campus all material listed is available
at the Cave Hill Main Library. Comprises 741 items arranged in
two sections :   (a) Individual Authors, in which authors treated
in separate sections are Michael Anthony, Edward Kamau Brathwaite,
Theodore Wilson Harris, George Lamming, Roger Mais, Edgar Austin
Mittelholzer, Vidiadhar Surajprasad Naipaul, Victor Stafford
Reid, Jean Rhys, Andrew Salkey, Samuel Selvon and Derek Walcott,
(b) (i) Bibliographies and Indexes (ii) General, which includes
criticisms on West Indian literature in general. Entries are
arranged alphabetically by author within each section. Items
include articles from journals, reviews, theses and interviews.

                                                                    UWI-T

1062 GRIFFITHS, GARETH
      A double exile ; African and West Indian writings between
      two cultures / Gareth Griffiths. - London : Boyars, 1978. -
      205p. - (Critical appraisals series)
      Bibliography: p.195-202

                                                                       LC

1063 MLA International bibliography of books and articles on the
      modern languages and literature / Modern Language Association
      of America, 1922- . - New York : Modern Language Association,
      1922-

      In this annual listing the section on English language and
literature, (latterly in volume one), includes items on West
Indian literature.

                                                                    UWI-T

1064 NEW, WILLIAM H.
      Critical writings on Commonwealth literatures : a selective
      bibliography to 1970, with a list of theses and dissertations
      / compiled by William H. New. - University Park, [Pa.] : The
      Pennsylvania State University Press, 1975. - 333p.
      Bibliography on the West Indies: p.270-281

274 items arranged within sections :   Research Aids –
General and Individual Authors.   Individual authors covered are
Michael Anthony, Louise Bennett, L. Edward Braithwaite, Martin
Carter, Austin C. Clarke, Frank A. Collymore, Wilson Harris, John
Hearne, George Lamming, Edward Lucie-Smith, Claude McKay, Roger
Mais, Edgar Mittelholzer, H. Orlando Patterson, Victor Reid, Jean
Rhys, Andrew Salkey, Authur J. Seymour, Louis Simpson, Dennis
Williams.   Bibliography of theses and dissertations (p.282–312).
West Indies (p.311) divided into two sections :   West Indies,
General and West Indies, Individual Authors.

UWI-T

1065   WALKLEY, JANE
          A decade of Caribbean literary criticism : a select
       annotated bibliography / Jane Walkley. – p.187–195
          In Literary half yearly. – Vol.11, no.2 (July 1970)

          In a West Indian number of the journal guest edited by
       Arthur Drayton this article lists reviews and other critical
       works on Caribbean authors individually and general studies
       appearing in journals and monographs, with very brief summaries
       in some cases.   17 authors are covered in alphabetical order and
       all critical works listed appeared in the sixties.

UWI-J

Drama
1066   BROWN, LLOYD W.
          West Indian drama in English : a select bibliography /
       Lloyd W. Brown. – p.14–16
          In Studies in black literature. – Vol.6, no.2 (1975)
                                                    Ref.no.1052
                                          Vol.11,no.2, Dec.1976, p.125

1067   Jamaica Library Service
          Drama catalogue / Jamaica Library Service. – Kingston,
       Jamaica : Jamaica Library Service, 1963. – [i], iv, 377p.
          Mimeographed
          Bibliography of plays: p.[iii]

UWI-J

1068   Jamaica Library Service
          A select bibliography of West Indian drama / Jamaica
       Library Service. – Kingston, Jamaica : Jamaica Library
       Service, [1962]. – 4p. – (Pamphlet ; no.14)
                                                    Ref.no.205
                                          1965/66, Item no.94

1069   Trinidad and Tobago. Central Library. West Indian Reference
       Section
          West Indian plays in Central Library. – [Port of Spain,
       Trinidad] : Central Library, 1966. – 8 leaves

Typescript

56 plays listed including three published in anthologies and periodicals.

TCL

1070 University College of the West Indies. Department of Extra
      Mural Studies
          List of plays available from the Extra-Mural Department,
      UCWI. - Mona, Jamaica : [s.n.], [196-?]. - 2p.
          Mimeographed

RIS

1071 University of the West Indies (Mona). Extra Mural Department
          List of plays about the West Indies / Extra Mural Depart-
      ment, U.W.I. - [S.1. : s.n.], [196-?]. - 3 leaves
          Typescript

      The list is subdivided into one act and full length plays
and includes a two line description of each play.

TCL

1072 University of the West Indies (St. Augustine). Department of
      Extra-Mural Studies
          U.W.I. publications : Caribbean plays and other publica-
      tions published by the U.W.I. Extra-Mural Department, Trinidad
      and Tobago. - St. Augustine, [Trinidad] : Extra-Mural Depart-
      ment, U.W.I., [1967]. - 2p.

      Sales list of short, medium and full-length plays,
separately itemized by title, with author's names but not
publishing details.

UWI-T

Fiction
1073 BANDARA, S.B.
          A bibliography of Caribbean novels in English / S.B.
      Bandara. - p.141-170
          In Journal of Commonwealth literature. - Vol.15, no.1
      (Aug. 1980)

      Listing of over 500 novels from the English, Dutch, French
and Spanish-speaking Caribbean arranged alphabetically under
author with variant editions given. Based on the resources of
the collections of the Library of the U.W.I., Mona, and the West
India Reference Library, Institute of Jamaica (now the National
Library of Jamaica).

UWI-T

1074 BOXILL, ANTHONY
        A bibliography of West Indian fiction, 1900–1970 / Anthony
      Boxill. – p.20–41
        In WLWE [World literature written in English] newsletter.
      – No.19 (Apr. 1971)

        Covers works of West Indian fiction including anthologies
      and criticism contained in books, pamphlets and periodicals.
                                                            UWI-B

1075 Carnegie Free Library
        A decade of West Indian writing 1952–1963 : a chronological
      list of British West Indian novels prepared for John Hearne's
      lecture to the Library Association of Trinidad and Tobago at
      the Carnegie Free Library, San Fernando on Wednesday, 29th
      May, 1963 / Carnegie Free Library. – [San Fernando, Trinidad]
      : Carnegie Free Library, 1963. – 5 leaves
        Mimeographed

        Lists novels published in each year for the period with
      author, title and country of origin of each author.
                                                              TCL

1076 HARRIS, L.J.
        A preliminary check-list of West Indian fiction in English,
      1949–1964 / L.J. Harris and D.A. Ormerod. – p.146–149
        In Twentieth century literature. – Vol.2 (1965–66)

        Lists works published in England and the United States,
      omitting anthologies, non-fiction and fiction for children.
                                                            UWI-T

1077 Institute of Jamaica. West India Reference Library
        Caribbean fiction, 1900–1960 ; (English and American
      publishers only) / by Rosalie Williams. – Kingston, Jamaica :
      West India Reference Library, Institute of Jamaica, 1970. –
      23 leaves
        Mimeographed

                                                              NLG

1078 MURRAY, RUDY G.
        A bibliography of Caribbean novels in English / Rudy G.
      Murray. – p.3–25
        In Black images. – Vol.1, no.1 (Jan. 1972)

        Items are listed chronologically under each author.
                                                            UWI-T

1079   RAMCHAND, KENNETH
          The West Indian novel and its background / by Kenneth
       Ramchand. - London : Faber, 1970. - 295p.
          Bibliography: p.274-286

          A British Caribbean author bibliography (twentieth century)
       is followed by a chronological listing (1903-1967) and a shorter
       listing of secondary sources. Brief lists of current and defunct
       West Indian literary periodicals are also provided.
                                                                UWI-T

1080   SANDER, REINHARD W.
          Short fiction in West Indian periodicals : a check-list /
       Reinhard W. Sander. - p.438-462
          In World literature written in English. - Vol.15, no.2
       (Nov. 1976)

          The bibliography is a complete check-list of the short
       fiction published in the literary periodicals : Trinidad, The
       Beacon, Bim, Kyk-over-al, Focus and Voices. It is arranged
       alphabetically by author and entries are listed chronologically
       under author.
                                                                UWI-T

1081   SANI, RUTA MARA
          A bibliographical survey of the West Indian novel : a
       thesis submitted to the Faculty of the Graduate College in
       partial fulfillment of the Degree of Master of Science in
       Librarianship / Ruta Mara Sani. - Kalamazoo, Mich. : Western
       Michigan University, 1972. - 122p.
          Appendix A : A bibliography of West Indian novels. -
       Appendix B : An annotated bibliography of selected in print
       books

          The main body of the thesis comprises an essay and
       chronological survey of West Indian authors and their works.
       Both appendices are arranged alphabetically by author but synoptic
       annotations are provided for the latter only. Selections in
       Appendix B relate to material available in St. Thomas, where the
       study was done.
                                                                UWI-T

1082   STOELTING, WINIFRED L.
          A checklist of the West Indian fiction (excluding Cuba,
       Puerto Rico and Haiti) / Winifred L. Stoelting. - Atlanta :
       Atlanta University, [1971?]. - 5, [13] leaves. - [Center for
       African and African-American Studies. CAAS bibliography ;
       no.8]
          Cover title

Covers prose fiction of 1900–1970 and mainly novelists
who were born or grew up in the West Indies.

UWI–J

1083   Trinidad and Tobago. Central Library
           Fiction and drama by West Indian authors / [compiled by
       Central Library]. – [Port of Spain, Trinidad : Central
       Library], [1962?]. – 3p. on 2 leaves
           Mimeographed

           Arranged alphabetically by country of origin of authors.
       Latest imprints included – 1962.

TCL

1084   Trinidad and Tobago. Central Library
           Fiction by West Indian authors / Central Library. – [Port
       of Spain, Trinidad : Central Library], [19–?]. – [4]p.
           Mimeographed

           Includes imprints up to 1959. Divided into two sections :
       I.(a) By West Indian Authors (b) By Non-West Indian Authors in
       the West Indies. II. (c) Children's Books (d) Annuals and
       Guides.

TCL

1085   Trinidad and Tobago. Central Library
           Recent fiction and drama by West Indian authors /
       [compiled by the Central Library]. – [Port of Spain : Central
       Library], [1961?]. – 2p. on 1 leaf

           Arranged by country of origin of authors with separate
       fiction and drama lists.

TCL

1086   Trinidad and Tobago. Central Library. West Indian Section
           Recent fiction by West Indian authors / [compiled by the
       West Indian Section, Central Library]. – [Port of Spain] :
       Central Library, [1962?] – 2 leaves
           Mimeographed

           Similar in content to list with drama included Ref.no.
       1085.

TCL

1087   Trinidad and Tobago. Central Library. West Indian Reference
       Section
           Recent fiction by West Indian authors 1949–1963 / West
       Indian Reference Section, Central Library. – [Port of Spain,
       Trinidad] : Central Library, 1963. – 3 leaves

TCL

1088   Trinidad and Tobago.   Central Library
        A selection of West Indian novels / Central Library. –
[Port of Spain, Trinidad] : Central Library Services, 1964. –
4p.

        A listing of some of the library's holdings arranged by
country of origin of the authors.
                                                        UWI–T

Indexes
1089   SANDER, REINHARD W.
        An index to Bim, 1942–1973 / Reinhard W. Sander. – p.1–41
        In The Journal of Commonwealth literature. – Vol.11, no.1
(Aug. 1976)
        First published :   U.W.I. Extra–Mural Studies Unit,
Trinidad and Tobago (Ref.no.1091).

        Updated and revised, this listing contains all material
which was published while Frank Collymore was editor.   Arranged
in sections :   Fiction, Drama, Poetry, Articles on Literature
and Language, Art and Theatre Reviews, Book Reviews, etc.
                                                        UWI–T

1089a   SANDER, REINHARD W.
        An index to Kyk-over-al 1945–1961 / Reinhard W. Sander. –
p.421–461
        In World literature written in English. – Vol.16, no.2
(Nov. 1977)

        The index to this West Indian literary magazine, edited
and published half-yearly by A.J. Seymour in Guyana from 1945 to
1961, is divided into eight sections :   Fiction, Drama, Poetry,
Articles on Literature and Language, Articles on History and
Culture, Miscellaneous Articles, Symposia and Colloquia, and
Editorial Notes.   Each section is arranged alphabetically by
author and entries appear under each author in the order of date
of publication of the issue.
                                                        UWI–T

1090   [University of Guyana.   Library]
        Index to West Indian poetry in anthologies of poetry /
Library, University of Guyana. – [Turkeyen, Guyana : Library,
University of Guyana], [ca.1970]. – 7 leaves
        Mimeographed
                                                        UG

1091   University of the West Indies.   Extra–Mural Studies Unit
        An index to Bim, 1942–1972 / compiled and edited by
Reinhard W. Sander. – [Port of Spain], Trinidad and Tobago
Extra–Mural Studies Unit, U.W.I., 1973. – 86p. – (Art and
Civilisation series ; v.2)

"Index to the West Indian literary magazine which has been
edited and published half-yearly by Frank A. Collymore in Barbados
since 1942." Includes an introduction by Edward Baugh and
Chatting about Bim – excerpts from a conversation with Frank
Collymore in 1971. The listing is divided into sections on
fiction, poetry, book reviews, etc. and organized alphabetically
by author within each section with entries listed in the order
of their publication by issue.

UWI-T

Periodicals and Serials
1092   Committee on Latin America
          Literature with language, art and music / edited on behalf
       of the Committee by Lawrence Hallewell. – London : Committee
       on Latin America (C.O.L.A.), 1977. – 2,253p. – (Latin
       American serials ; v.3)

          One of a series of three (Ref.nos.830, 1092, 1368) union
       lists with holdings in British libraries of Latin American and
       West Indian interest periodicals, wherever published. The list
       is arranged alphabetically by country of origin and then by title
       with brief bibliographical details. Includes a note on periodical
       indexes and an index of titles, sponsors and publishers.
       Includes listings for the Bahamas, Barbados, Bermuda, Guyana,
       Jamaica, St. Lucia and Trinidad and Tobago.

UWI-T

1093   Commonwealth Institute. Working Party on Library Holdings of
       Commonwealth Literature
          Commonwealth literature periodicals : a bibliography,
       including periodicals of former Commonwealth countries, with
       locations in the United Kingdom / compiled and edited by
       Ronald Warwick. – London : Mansell, 1979. – xv, 146p.

          Includes not only "specifically literary periodicals but
       also more general magazines likely to be of interest to the
       student of Commonwealth literature." Arranged geographically
       and further subdivided under broad subject headings where
       material is extensive. Section covering the Caribbean (p.88–93)
       includes a short-title list by country followed by an alpha-
       betical list of the periodicals. A title index is provided.

UWI-T

Poetry
1094   ASEIN, SAMUEL O.
          West Indian poetry in English, 1900–1970 : a selected
       bibliography / Samuel O. Asein. – p.12–15
          In Black images. – Vol.1, no.2 (Summer 1972)

Extracted from a more comprehensive annotated bibliography in progress. Arranged alphabetically by author in four
sections : Bibliographies, Anthologies, Individual Authors and
Criticism in Monographs and Journals.

UWI-T

Barbados

Poetry
1095   BRATHWAITE, EDWARD KAMAU
Barbados poetry, ?1661-1979 : a check-list : [slavery to
the present] books, pamphlets, broadsheets / Edward Kamau
Brathwaite. - Mona, [Jamaica] : Savacou Publications, 1979. -
16p. - (Savacou bibliographical series / work in progress)

Part of a larger work in progress listing Caribbean poetry
in English. Works on some 70 poets (50 of Barbadian birth
starred) are listed alphabetically by title and author in three
main period divisions. Critical and descriptive notes about some
poets are provided and listing includes Barbados-inspired works
by non-Barbadians such as Wilfred Cartey and Derek Walcott.
Excludes publishers.

UWI-T

Guyana

1096   Guyana. Ministry of Information and Culture. National History
and Arts Council
Books published 1966-1976 / National History and Arts
Council. - p.213-222
In Independence 10 : Guyana writing / [edited by A.J.
Seymour]. - Georgetown : National History and Arts Council,
1976

Prepared in the Reference Department of the National
Library. 142 items arranged alphabetically by author in two
sections : (1) Fiction by Guyanese Authors 1966-1976, (b) Non-
fiction (class 800) by Guyanese 1966-1976.

UWI-T

1097   Guyana. National History and Arts Council. Literature Sub-
Committee
The literary tradition in Guyana / National History and
Arts Council. - [Georgetown, Guyana] : National History and
Arts Council, [c1974]. - 8p.

Bibliographic essay.

Benjamin

273

1098   Guyana. National Library
        Creative writings by Guyanese women authors / National
Library. – Georgetown, Guyana : National Library, 1975. – 3
leaves
        Typescript

                                                                    NLG

1099   Guyana. National Library
        Non-fiction (class 800) by Guyanese, 1966–1976 / National
Library. – Georgetown : National Library, 1976. – 12 leaves
        Typescript

                                                                    NLG

1100   Guyana. National Library
        Short list of material in belles-lettres (class 800) by
Guyanese published 1966–1976 / National Library. – Georgetown :
National Library, 1976. – 16 leaves
        Typescript

                                                                    NLG

1101   Guyana. Public Free Library
        Guyanese authors and their types of work / Public Free
Library. – [Georgetown, Guyana] : Public Free Library, 1969. –
3 leaves
        Typescript

                                                                    NLG

1102   Guyana. Public Free Library
        Poetry, drama, fiction written by East Indian authors from
Guyana / Public Free Library. – Georgetown : Public Free
Library, 1970. – 6 leaves
        Typescript

                                                                    NLG

1103   MCDOWELL, ROBERT EUGENE
        Bibliography of literature from Guyana / Robert Eugene
McDowell. – Arlington, Tex. : Sable Publishing Corp., 1975. –
xx, 117p.

        Listing alphabetically by author of all works Guyanese in
content or by authorship, including writers who immigrated to the
country. Includes individual references to works in anthologies
and periodicals. Genre is identified by code. The author is on
the staff of the University of Guyana.

                                                                    UWI-T

Children
1104   Guyana. National Library
        Guyanese fiction for children / National Library. –
[Georgetown, Guyana : National Library], [n.d.]. – 3 leaves
        Typescript

                                                                    NLG

Drama
1105   Guyana. Public Library
            Guyanese plays and their location : a bibliography /
       compiled by Phyllis Shepherd. - Georgetown, Guyana : Public
       Library, 1967. - [4], 17p.
            Mimeographed

            Includes unpublished plays produced on stage and radio.
       There is an index of titles and playwrights. Location marks
       indicate private as well as public library holdings.
                                                            UWI-T

1106   HILL, ERROL
            Plays of the English-speaking Caribbean, Part II : Guyana ;
       a bibliography and check-list / Errol Hill. - p.11-15
            In Bulletin of black theatre. - Vol.1, no.3 (Winter 1973)

            Alphabetical list of 175 items. Date and place of the
       first performance of the plays are given where this information
       is available as well as the present location of playscripts.
       See also Ref.nos.1111, 1116.
                                                            UWI-T

Fiction
1107   Guyana. National Library
            Fiction by Guyanese authors, 1966-1976 / National Library.
       - Georgetown : National Library, 1976. - 6 leaves
            Typescript
                                                            NLG

Poetry
1108   CAMERON, N.E.
            Guyanese poetry : covering the hundred years' period 1831-
       1931 / selected and edited by N.E. Cameron. - Georgetown :
       The Argosy Co. Ltd., 1931. - 186p.
            Kraus reprint 1970

            Bibliographic essay providing valuable criticism and
       bibliographic information about works of poetry by Guianese poets
       writing during this period.
                                                            UWI-T

Jamaica

1109   Commonwealth Institute Library and Resource Centre
            Jamaican language and literature / Commonwealth Institute
       Library and Resource Centre. - [London] : Commonwealth
       Institute Library and Resource Centre, [197-?]. - 4 leaves

60 items arranged in four sections : Language, Literature
- Collections, Fiction, Poetry.

UWI-T

1110 ALLEYNE, ALVONA
      Preliminary checklist of literary works published in
      Jamaica, 1900-1976 ; [bibliography appended to] Literary
      publishing in the English-speaking Caribbean / Alvona Alleyne.
      - p.238-248
      <u>In</u> Twenty years of Latin American librarianship : Final
      report and working papers of the Twenty-first Seminar on the
      Acquisition of Latin American Library Materials, Indiana
      University, Bloomington, Indiana, May 2-6, 1976. - Austin,
      Tex. : SALALM Secretariat, 1978

      Over 200 titles listed alphabetically by author with
      printer cited where available and date of publication. Arranged
      in four sections (following the text) by type of publisher :
      (1) Author, (2) Associations and Institutions including the
      Extra-Mural Department of the University, (3) Journals, (4)
      Publishing Firms.

UWT-T

Drama
1111 HILL, ERROL
      Plays of the English-speaking Caribbean, Part I : Jamaica ;
      a bibliography and check-list / Errol Hill. - p.9-15
      <u>In</u> Bulletin of black theatre. - Vol.1, no.2 (Winter 1972)

      281 items are listed. The date and place of the first
      production of the plays are given and for unpublished plays a
      location is provided, where known. See also Ref.nos.1106,1116.

UWI-T

Poetry
1112 BRATHWAITE, EDWARD KAMAU
      Jamaica poetry : a checklist ; [slavery to the present]
      books, pamphlets, broadsheets 1686-1978, with preface by
      Leila Thomas to mark the 30th anniversary of the Jamaica
      Library Service, 1948-1978 / Edward Kamau Brathwaite. -
      Kingston : Jamaica Library Service, 1979. - 36p.

      Part of a larger work in progress. Listing by author and
      titles of the works of 150 Jamaicans in three period divisions :
      (i) Slavery, (ii) Colonial Period and (iii) 1900 - The Present
      "establishing the voice." Notes provided on some poets ; place
      of publication and dates given but no publishers.

UWI-T

Trinidad and Tobago

1113 GONZALEZ, ANSON
       Bibliography of creative writing in Trinidad and Tobago
       1962-1977 / Anson Gonzalez. - p.26-42
       In New voices. - Vol.6, no.11 (1978)

       Items are arranged by genre - Novels, Poems, Short Stories
       and Poems, Biography, Autobiography, Plays - followed by lists of
       journals, magazines and yearbooks.
                                                                    UWI-T

1114 GONZALEZ, ANSON
       Creative writing in the Republic of Trinidad and Tobago,
       1962-1977 : a bibliography / Anson Gonzalez. - [Diego Martin,
       Trinidad] : Anson Gonzalez, 1977. - [20]p.

       Chronological list of novels by Trinidad and Tobago
       authors, alphabetical list of work by novelists resident in the
       Republic followed by lists of other creative writing by form.
       Includes a list of writing for children, a directory of national
       writers resident in 1977 and a list of local publishers interested
       in creative writing.
                                                                    UWI-T

1115 Trinidad and Tobago. Central Library. West Indian Reference
       Section
       List of literary works by Trinidadians / West Indian
       Reference Section, Central Library. - [Port of Spain, Trinidad
       : Central Library], 1963. - 2p.
       Typescript
       List of publishers [of works listed] and addresses. - [1p.]

       Works of fiction, poetry and drama are covered.
                                                                    UWI-T

Drama
1116 HILL, ERROL
       Plays of the English-speaking Caribbean, Part III :
       Trinidad and Tobago ; bibliography and check-list / by Errol
       Hill. - p.11-15
       In Bulletin of black theatre. - Vol.1, no.4 (1974)

       180 items alphabetically listed. The place and year of
       the first performance are given when known. See also Ref.nos.
       1106, 1111.
                                                                    UWI-T

Fiction
1117 GONZALEZ, ANSON JOHN
          Novels by Trinagoans (1934-1974) / Anson John Gonzalez. –
      p.[9-10]
          In Family life education : possibilities in local litera-
      ture / by Anson John Gonzalez. – Port of Spain : Publications
      Branch, Ministry of Education and Culture, 1974

          Chronological listing with brief imprint statements.

                                                              UWI-T

Indexes
1118 GONZALEZ, ANSON JOHN
          Trinidadian writers in BIM / Anson John Gonzalez. – [S.l. :
      s.n.], [1972]. – 9 leaves
          Mimeographed

          Sections cover fiction and poetry. Alphabetical author
      arrangement within each section.

                                                              UWI-T

Poetry
1119 Trinidad and Tobago. Central Library. West Indian Reference
      Section
          West Indian poetry : Trinidadian writers / West Indian
      Reference Section, Central Library. – [Port of Spain, Trinidad]
      : Central Library, 1963. – 2 leaves

          Alphabetical author listing of published poems including
      mainly works appearing in Caribbean Quarterly and Bim.

                                                                TCL

                              MEDICINE

1119a HARRISON, IRA E.
          Traditional medicine : implications for ethnomedicine,
      ethnopharmacology, maternal and child health, mental health
      and public health : an annotated bibliography of Africa,
      Latin America and the Caribbean / Ira E. Harrison and Sheila
      Cosminsky. – New York : Garland, 1976, 229p.

          "Well-organized assemblage of 1,135 references on
      numerous topics of medical anthropological interest in Latin
      American and Caribbean populations. Materials are indexed by
      author, country and subject matter."
                                              Ref.no.15, no.39, 1977
                                                      Item no.2004

1120 SCHMID, JANEIRO B.
        Bibliography and reference sources in the Caribbean /
      Janeiro B. Schmid. - p.249-268
        In The Caribbean : its health problems / edited by A.
      Curtis Wilgus. - Gainesville, [Fla.] : University of Florida
      Press, 1965. - (Caribbean conference series 1 ; v.15)

        An essay review concentrating on library resources
      available in the field of medicine in the wider Caribbean area
      (based on responses to a questionnaire) followed by a list of
      selected references including biomedical periodicals from the
      region, official reports and health legislation sources.
      Includes references for most of the English-speaking territories.
                                                            UWI-T

1121 Trinidad and Tobago. Ministry of Health. Medical Library
        Index to Caribbean medical literature / compiled by the
      Medical Library, General Hospital, Port of Spain. - Port of
      Spain, Trinidad and Tobago : Medical Library, General
      Hospital, 1976. - 69p.

        An alphabetical listing by author of over 1,000 papers,
      articles and official reports of Caribbean medical interest held
      by the library. No index is provided.
                                                            UWI-T

1122 Trinidad and Tobago. Ministry of Health. Medical Library
        Index to Caribbean medical literature : an author, title
      and subject listing of holdings at the Medical Library ;
      supplement no.1 / compiled by the Medical Library, General
      Hospital, Port of Spain. - Port of Spain, Trinidad and
      Tobago : Medical Library, General Hospital, 1978. - 36p.
                                                            UWI-T

1123 Trinidad and Tobago. Ministry of Health. Medical Library
        Index to Caribbean medical literature : an author, title
      and subject listing of holdings at the Medical Library ;
      supplement no.2 / compiled by the Medical Library, General
      Hospital, Port of Spain. - Port of Spain, Trinidad and Tobago
      : Medical Library, General Hospital, 1980. - 43p.
                                                            UWI-T

1124 Trinidad and Tobago. Ministry of Health. Medical Library
        Original research done by doctors of the Caribbean
      prepared for Commonwealth Caribbean Medical Research Council
      Twenty-first Scientific Meeting, April 21 to 24, 1976 ...
      Trinidad Hilton Hotel / compiled by Staff, Medical Library. -
      Port of Spain : Medical Library, General Hospital, 1976. - 1
      leaf folded in 6p.

Listing, arranged alphabetically by country and by author within each section, of papers, reports and journal articles on medical research of Caribbean interest.

UWI-T

1125   Trinidad and Tobago. Ministry of Health. Medical Library
        Selected list of Caribbean writings on "Heart and chest diseases" / prepared by Medical Library Staff for Caura Chest Hospital. - Port of Spain : Medical Library, General Hospital, Port of Spain, 1976. - 2 leaves
        Mimeographed

Alphabetical list of 24 items.

UWI-T

Social and Preventive

1126   University of the West Indies. Department of Social and Preventive Medicine. Documentation Unit
        Adolescence and reproductive behaviour : select bibliography / Olive Ennever and Beryl N. Fletcher. - Mona, Jamaica : Documentation Unit, Department of Social and Preventive Medicine, U.W.I., 1981. - 6 leaves. - (UNFPA Project "Family health care in the Caribbean" RLA 78/P.29
        Mimeographed

35 entries comprising pamphlets and books, about 16 of which relate to the Caribbean and particularly to Jamaica.

UWI-T

1127   University of the West Indies. Department of Social and Preventive Medicine. Documentation Unit
        Family health care : select bibliography / Olive Ennever and Beryl N. Fletcher. - Mona, Jamaica : Documentation Unit, Department of Social and Preventive Medicine, U.W.I., 1981. - 6 leaves. - (UNFPA Project "Family health care in the Caribbean" RLA 78/P.29)

30 entries comprising pamphlets and books about 12 of which relate to the West Indies and particularly to Jamaica.

UWI-T

Guyana

1128   GIGLIOLI, G.
        Malaria, filariasis and yellow fever in British Guiana : control by residual D.D.T. methods with special reference to progress made in eradicating A. Darlingi and Aedes Aegypti from the settled coast lands / G. Giglioli. - [Georgetown, Guyana] : Mosquito Control Service, Medical Department, 1948. - 228p.

Bibliography: p.217–219.

Benjamin

1129   Guyana. Public Free Library
Nutrition in Guyana / Public Free Library. – Georgetown :
Public Free Library, 1971. – 1 leaf
Typescript

NLG

1130   ROSE, F.G.
A resumé of the scientific work published by medical men
in British Guiana from 1769 to the present day / F.G. Rose and
J.E. Chow. – p.53–62
In British Guiana medical annual. – Vol.23 (1923)

A bibliographic essay covering the period 1769 to 1917.

UWI-T

1131   WREN, MAUREEN
Medical literature of Guyana : a selected bibliography
1890–1960 / Maureen Wren. – p.1–20
In Guyana medical science library bulletin (special issue).
– Vol.2, no.1 (Feb. 1971)

Consists of 185 entries arranged by subjects such as
communicable diseases, dentistry, filariasis, geriatrics,
gynaecology, etc. Includes a list of periodicals and their
abbreviations and an author index.

NLG

Jamaica

Social and Preventive
1132   RUBIN, VERA
Ganja in Jamaica : a medical anthropological study of
chronic marijuana use / Vera Rubin and Lambros Comitas. – The
Hague : Mouton, 1975. – xvii, 217p. – (New Babylon studies in
the social sciences ; 26)
Bibliography: p.197–205

References are arranged alphabetically by author and then
chronologically ; consist mainly of journal articles on cannabis
as a whole with some specifically on its medical and cultural
significance in Jamaica. Includes some references to the use of
alcohol in Jamaica.

UWI-T

MUSIC

1133 JACKSON, IRENE V.
      Afro-American religious music : a bibliography and
      catalogue of gospel music / Irene V. Jackson. - Westport,
      Conn. ; London : Greenwood Press, 1979. - 224p.

      "Author organizes the material to illuminate her conception
      of the importance of the impact of Christianity on traditional
      worship patterns of Africans in Africa and in the United States
      and the Caribbean ... The second part of the book is a catalogue
      of gospel music copyrighted between 1937 and 1965, listing
      composer or author, arranger, publishing company and the copy-
      right year."

                                              SARRA, Vol.6,no.1
                                              Feb. 1981, p.11

1134 MORSE, JIM
      Folk songs of the Caribbean / compiled by Jim Morse. - New
      York : Bantam, [n.d.]

      "Words and music of songs with brief discography."
                                              Ref.no.711
                                              p.462

1135 STEVENSON, ROBERT MURREL
      A guide to Caribbean music history : bibliographic
      supplement to a paper read at the 1975 annual meeting of the
      Music Library Association in San Juan, Puerto Rico / Robert
      Murrel Stevenson. - Lima, [Peru] : Ediciones Cultura, 1975. -
      101p.

                                                              LC

1136 THOMPSON, DONALD
      Music, theatre and dance in Central America and the
      Caribbean : an annotated bibliography of dissertations and
      theses / Donald Thompson. - p.113-140
      In Revista/Review interamericana. - Vol.9, no.1 (Spring
      1979)

      Alphabetical author arrangement. Includes items on
      music in the Bahamas, British Honduras, Jamaica, Trinidad, the
      calypso, folk songs of the Black Carib, dance in Jamaica, the
      theatre in Trinidad. Subject index is provided.
                                                              UWI-T

Guyana

1137   Guyana. Public Free Library
              Music : printed and in manuscript by Guyanese composers /
       Public Free Library. - Georgetown : Public Free Library, 1970.
       - 3 leaves
              Typescript

              Lists mainly manuscript music.

                                                                    NLG

                          NATURAL RESOURCES

1138   ASH, LEE
              Natural resources of the Caribbean : some bibliographical
       and library needs / Lee Ash. - p.301-309
              In The Caribbean : natural resources / edited by A. Curtis
       Wilgus. - Gainesville, [Fla.] : University of Florida Press,
       1959. - (Caribbean conference series 1 ; v.9)

              An essay discussing existing types of literature in the
       field and suggesting needs. No list of references is provided.
                                                                    UWI-T

1139   CUMPER, G.E.
              Bibliography of the physical resources of the region /
       G.E. Cumper. - p.266-272
              In The economy of the West Indies / edited by G.E. Cumper.
       - Kingston : Institute of Social and Economic Research,
       University College of the West Indies, 1960

              Over 100 references to reports, journal articles, books
       and papers arranged by author under each of five headings as
       follows :   (I) General and Regional, (II) Energy Sources, (III)
       Inorganic Raw Materials, (IV) Forest Resources, (V) Food and
       Water Resources.

                                                                    UWI-T

1140   WESTERMAN, J.H.
              Conservation in the Caribbean : a review of literature on
       the destruction and conservation of renewable natural
       resources in the Caribbean area, with reference to the popu-
       lation problem / by J.H. Westerman. - Utrecht : Foundation for
       Scientific Research in Surinam and the Netherlands Antilles,
       1952. - 12p. - (Foundation for Scientific Research in Surinam
       and the Netherlands Antilles publication ; no.7)

                                                                    UWI-T

Guyana

1141 BISHOPP, D.W.
         The bauxite resources of British Guiana and their develop-
      ment / compiled by D.W. Bishopp from E.E. Winter ..., Sir
      John Harrison and from other sources ; revised by E.R.
      Pollard. - Georgetown, Demerara, [British Guiana] : Daily
      Chronicle, 1955. - 123p. - (Bulletin ; no.6)
         Bibliography: p.122-123

         Lists 29 items including articles, published and
      unpublished reports.
                                                              UWI-T

1142 MILLER, BENJAMIN LEROY
         The mineral deposits of South America / Benjamin Leroy
      Miller and Joseph Singewald. - New York : McGraw-Hill Book
      Company, 1919. - ix, 598p.
         Bibliography on Guianas: p.429-433
                                                              LC

                              NUMISMATICS

1143 ALMANZAR, ALCEDO
         Latin American numismatic bibliography (including the
      Caribbean) / Alcedo Almanzar. - San Antonio, Tex. : Almanzar's
      Coins of the World, 1972. - 42p.
                                                              LC

1144 PRIDMORE, F.
         The coins of the British Commonwealth of Nations to the
      end of the reign of George VI, 1952 / by F. Pridmore. -
      London : Spink and Son, 1965
         Part 3 : Bermuda, British Guiana, British Honduras and
      the British West Indies. - 364p.
         Bibliography: p.15-16

         38 items listed in alphabetical author order, including
      several journal articles, followed by a list of "sale catalogues
      which include illustrations and descriptions of mutilated coins."
                                                              UWI-T

OCEANOGRAPHY

1145   Harvard University. Library
           Notes on the historical hydrography of the Handkerchief
       Shoal in the Bahamas / William H. Tillinghast. - Cambridge,
       Mass. : Library of Harvard University, 1881. - ii, 258-263p. -
       (Bibliographical contribution ; no.14)

           100 references.

                                                                    BL

1146   WUST, GEORG
           Stratification and circulation in the Antillean-Caribbean
       basins : Pt.1. Spreading and mixing of water types, with an
       oceanographic atlas / by Georg Wust ; with the assistance of
       Arnold Gordon. - New York : Columbia University Press, 1964. -
       201p. - (Vema research series ; no.2)
           Bibliography: p.52-54

           Includes useful references on the oceanography of the
       Caribbean. Also some items on geophysics, geology and hydrography.
                                                                    UWI-T

PHILATELY

Guyana

1147   Short philatelic bibliography
           In B.G. philatelic journal. - No.10

           "Information for this entry comes from V. Roth's Biblio-
       graphy of Guyana" - Benjamin.

                                                                Benjamin

Indexes
1148   RICKETTS, W.R.
           The British Guiana philatelic index : being a subject-
       author index of articles and notes concerning British Guiana
       philately found in philatelic literature from the beginning
       1862 to the present time / W.R. Ricketts. - p.15-22
           In B.G. philatelic journal. - No.39, pt.2 (Dec. 1925)
                                                                Benjamin

POLITICAL SOCIOLOGY

Guyana

1149 MILNE, R.S.
          Politics, ethnicity and class in Guyana and Malaysia /
      R.S. Milne. - p.19-37
          In Social and economic studies. - Vol.26, no.1 (Mar. 1977)
          References: p.33-37

          70 references including books and journal articles on
      Guyana and other West Indian territories.
                                                          UWI-T

1150 SERBIN, ANDRÉS
          Nacionalismo, ethnicidad y política en la república
      cooperativa de Guyana / Andrés Serbin. - Caracas, Venezuela :
      Editorial Bruguera Venezolana, [1980]. - 276p. - (Autores
      Latinoamericanos)
          Bibliography: p.251-276

          The bibliography is arranged in two main sections covering
      (1) Books and Articles in Journals, by author and (2) Periodical
      Publications and Pamphlets. Coverage includes race relations,
      ethnicity and politics and government.
                                                          UWI-T

1151 University of the West Indies (Mona). Institute of Social and
      Economic Research
          Race vs. politics in Guyana : political cleavages and
      political mobilisation in the 1968 general election / J.E.
      Greene. - [Mona, Jamaica] : Institute of Social and Economic
      Research, University of the West Indies, 1974. - xvii, 198p.
          Bibliography: p.177-194

          295 references to books, articles and government publica-
      tions each arranged in separate listings.
                                                          UWI-T

Jamaica

1152 University of the West Indies (Mona). Institute of Social and
      Economic Research
          Class, race and political behaviour in urban Jamaica /
      Carl Stone. - [Mona, Jamaica] : Institute of Social and
      Economic Research, University of the West Indies, 1973. - 188p.
          Bibliography: p.184-186

Arranged alphabetically by author under two headings –
Political Sociology and Jamaica; Politics and Society.

UWI-T

Trinidad and Tobago

1153   CRAIG, SUSAN E.
       Community development in Trinidad and Tobago : 1943-1973 ;
       from welfare to patronage / Susan E. Craig. – [Mona], Jamaica
       : Institute of Social and Economic Research, University of the
       West Indies, 1974. – iii, 138p. – (I.S.E.R., U.W.I. working
       paper ; no.4)
          Mimeographed
          Bibliography: p.130-138

       Arranged in four main sections for (1) Official Documents
       – Departmental and Special Reports, Council Minutes etc., (2)
       Newspapers, (3) Other Publications including unpublished theses
       listed alphabetically by author and (4) Lectures.

UWI-T

POLITICS AND GOVERNMENT

1154   BLOOMFIELD, VALERIE
       Commonwealth elections 1945-1970 : a bibliography /
       Valerie Bloomfield. – [London] : Mansell, 1976. – xvi, 306p.
          Also published: Greenwood Press, 1977

       Covers elections held in all Commonwealth countries and
       dependent territories between 1945 and 1970 with separate
       sections on each.   660 entries on the Commonwealth Caribbean
       territories each subdivided into official publications, books,
       articles and party documents.   Includes an author/name index.

UWI-T

1155   COLLINS, B.A.N.
       Select bibliography on public administration in the
       British Caribbean [since World War II] / by B.A.N. Collins. –
       p.110-112
          In Social and economic studies. – Vol.16, no.1 (1967)

       Items which are listed alphabetically by author, were
       published since World War II.

UWI-T

1156   CUNDALL, FRANK
        Political and social disturbances in the West Indies : a
brief account and bibliography / by Frank Cundall. - Kingston,
Jamaica : The Educational Supply Company for the Institute of
Jamaica, 1906. - 35p.
        Bibliography: p.29-35

        Chronological listings (1837 to 1905) indicating indi-
vidual territories by headings for pamphlets, papers, extracts
from newspapers, reports and some unpublished material mostly held
by the library of the Institute of Jamaica of which the author was
Secretary and Librarian. Includes several references to the 1865
"Morant Bay Rebellion" in Jamaica and the 1903 "Water Riots" in
Trinidad.

                                                              UWI-T

1157   DANIELS, MARIETTA
        Sources of information on contemporary Caribbean inter-
national problems / Marietta Daniels. - p.311-326
        In The Caribbean : contemporary international relations /
edited by A. Curtis Wilgus. - Gainesville, [Fla.] : University
of Florida Press, 1957. - (Caribbean conference series 1 ;
v.7)

        A bibliographic essay which treats the wider Caribbean
   area.

                                                              UWI-T

1158   DURRANT, FAY
        A bibliographical aid to the study of government and
politics in the West Indies / Fay Durrant. - p.243-270
        In Readings in government and politics of the West Indies
/ edited by Trevor Munroe and Rupert Lewis. - Mona, Jamaica :
Department of Government, U.W.I., 1971

        Augmented and edited version of previous edition (Ref.no.
1163). Includes material in published and unpublished form and
works in sociological and economic fields related to the study of
government and politics. Arranged by author under broad headings
such as politics, general elections, nationalism, race, colour
and society, trade unions and interest groups. Coverage is of
the Commonwealth Caribbean region.

                                                              UWI-T

1159   Great Britain. Colonial Office
        British dependencies in the Caribbean and North Atlantic,
1939-1952 / Colonial Office. - London : H.M.S.O. 1952. - 98p.
- (Cd.; 8575)
        Bibliography: p.78-79

Lists important U.K. publications on the West Indies under
headings : General; Political and Constitutional Development;
Economic Problems and Policy; Development and Welfare; Colonial
Government Publications and Caribbean Commission Publications.

UWI-T

1160 GREENE, J.E.
A review of political science research in the English-
speaking Caribbean : toward a methodology / J.E. Greene. -
p.1-47
In Social and economic studies. - Vol.23, no.1 (1974)

List of 174 references.

UWI-T

1161 HALSTEAD, JOHN P.
Modern European imperialism : a bibliography of books and
articles 1815-1972 / John P. Halstead and Serafino Porcari. -
Boston : G.K. Hall, 1974. - 2v.
Vol.1 : General and British Empire. - xvi, 508p.

Includes section : Britain in the Caribbean under
headings : General; Atlases; Bibliographies; Documents and
Papers; Economic and Financial. In each section periodical
articles are listed separately. 467 items.

UWI-T

1162 HEILIGER, EDWARD M.
Source materials for the study of Caribbean political
problems / Edward M. Heiliger. - p.301-317
In The Caribbean : its political problems / edited by A.
Curtis Wilgus. - Gainesville, [Fla.] : University of Florida
Press, 1956. - (Caribbean conference series 1 ; v.6)

Bibliographic essay on the wider Caribbean area without
specific references for individual territories.

UWI-T

1163 LEVY, CATHERINE
Bibliography on government and politics in the West Indies
1950-1967 / compiled by Catherine Levy and A.W. Singham. -
(S.l. : s.n.], [1968?]. - 29, 3p.
Mimeographed
Also published in: Readings in government and politics of
the West Indies / compiled by A.W. Singham and others. -
[Mona, Jamaica : U.W.I.], 1968

Covers the Commonwealth Caribbean; drawn partly from
holdings of the University library in Jamaica for whose students
the main reader was compiled. Excludes Hansards, periodical
reports of the governments and legislation. See also Ref.no.1158.

UWI-T

1164   LOWENTHAL, DAVID
        The aftermath of sovereignty : West Indian perspectives /
        edited and introduced by David Lowenthal and Lambros Comitas.
        – Garden City, N.Y. : Anchor Press, 1973. – xvii, 422p.
        Bibliography: p.[382]-410

        A selective reading list arranged alphabetically by author
    in four sections :   (1) Bibliographies, (2) General References,
    (3) Fiction and Poetry and (4) West Indian Periodicals.

                                                               UWI-T

1165   MITCHELL, SIR HAROLD
        Caribbean patterns : a political and economic study of the
        contemporary Caribbean / by Sir Harold Mitchell. – Edinburgh :
        W. and R. Chambers, 1967. – xix, 583p.
        Bibliography: p.408-452

        Includes material in all forms on politics and economics
    of the West Indies in the sixties.

                                                               UWI-T

1166   MITCHELL, SIR HAROLD
        Europe in the Caribbean : the policies of Great Britain,
        France and the Netherlands towards their West Indian terri-
        tories in the twentieth century / by Sir Harold Mitchell. –
        Edinburgh : W. and R. Chambers, 1963. – xv, 211p.
        Bibliography: p.181-199

        Section on Great Britain and British territories (p.181-
    187). This is subdivided into sections on official documents,
    unofficial documents and pamphlets, newspapers, periodicals and
    yearbooks, books and articles each in alphabetical order. There
    is a general section on the West Indies as a whole.

                                                               UWI-T

1167   MURRAY, DAVID JOHN
        The West Indies and the development of colonial government,
        1801-1834 / David John Murray. – Oxford : Clarendon Press,
        1965. – xiv, 264p.
        Bibliography: p.233-256

        Separate listings of manuscript sources in the Colonial
    Office for each territory or group followed by other manuscript
    sources and printed material. West Indies slave emancipation
    literature before and after 1835 is featured.

                                                               UWI-T

1168   Netherlands Universities Foundation for International
       Co-operation
             Developments toward self-government in the Caribbean : a
       symposium held under the auspices of the Netherlands Univer-
       sities Foundation for International Co-operation at the Hague,
       September 1955. - The Hague : W. Van Hoeve, 1955. - vii, 285p.
             Bibliography: p.271-285

             41 items arranged in sections : General, British, French,
       Netherlands, Netherlands Antilles, Surinam and the United States.
       The 74 items in the section covering the British territories
       include a number of works on the politics and government of the
       area as well as its social and economic conditions and industrial
       development.

                                                                  UWI-T

1169   National Book League
             Politics in the Commonwealth / National Book League. -
       London : National Book League, 1966. - 24p.

             Annotated list prepared for the Commonwealth in Books
       Exhibition. Includes items on Guyana, Jamaica, Trinidad and
       Tobago and the West Indies in general.

                                                                  UWI-T

1170   NIELSEN, EDWARD C.
             The proposed federation of the British West Indies /
       Edward C. Nielsen. - Washington, D.C. : [s.n.], 1951. - 133
       leaves
             Thesis (M.S.) - Georgetown University
             Bibliography: p.131-133

                                                               Ref.no.5
                                                      1951-1955, p.695

1171   A select bibliography on public administration in the
       Caribbean. - [S.l. : s.n.], [196-?]. - 7 leaves
             Mimeographed

             Items listed were published since the Second World War and
       include official documents and articles in periodicals.

                                                                  UWI-T

1172   SINGH, PAUL G.
             Bibliography of West Indian local government / Paul G.
       Singh. - p.138-146
             In Local democracy in the Commonwealth Caribbean : a study
       of adaptation and growth / Paul G. Singh. - [Port of Spain,
       Trinidad] : Longman Caribbean, 1972
             Publication part sponsored by the University of Guyana

Arranged alphabetically by author under the four main
territories covered – Barbados, Guyana, Jamaica and Trinidad and
Tobago with a general section on the West Indies.   Includes
journal articles, official reports, pamphlets and books in each
section.

UWI-T

1173 SPACKMAN, ANN
        Bibliography of documents of the West Indies, 1922-68 /
Ann Spackman. – p.592-608
        In Constitutional development of the West Indies, 1922-
1968 : a selection from the major documents / Ann Spackman. –
[Bridgetown, Barbados] : Caribbean Universities Press in
association with Bowker, 1975. – (Caribbean history bibliographical and documentation series)
        Appears as: Appendix D of the main work.

        Arranged under territorial and subject headings with
documents listed chronologically in each case.   Includes headings
such as Associated States, Federation and federal experiments,
along with the names of special commissions and of individual
territories.

UWI-T

1174 SPURDLE, FREDERICK G.
        Early West Indian government : showing the progress of
government in Barbados, Jamaica and the Leeward Islands, 1660-
1783 / Frederick G. Spurdle. – Palmerston North, New Zealand :
The Author, 1962. – 275p.
        Bibliography: p.265-271

        Lists reference works, manuscript documents by location
(Public Record Office, British Museum, Bodleian Library),
followed by printed documents and secondary sources distinguishing
contemporary and more modern works.

UWI-T

1175 Trinidad and Tobago.   Central Library
        List of material relating to foreign policy in the
Caribbean / prepared by West Indian Reference Section of the
Central Library of Trinidad and Tobago. – [Port of Spain,
Trinidad] : Central Library of Trinidad and Tobago, 1971. –
3 leaves
        Typescript

        18 references to books and pamphlets as well as a few
newspaper articles (Times only) in author order.

TCL

1176   University of Guyana. Library
          A comparative bibliography of parliament in the Common-
       wealth / Library, University of Guyana. - Georgetown :
       University of Guyana Library, [1970?]. - 10 leaves
          Typescript

          Author listing of 86 entries of which approximately half
       deal with the Caribbean.

                                                                     UG

1177   University of London. Institute of Commonwealth Studies.
       Library
          Supplement to select list of accessions January-March 1977
       : Commonwealth political parties / Library, Institute of
       Commonwealth Studies. - London : Institute of Commonwealth
       Studies, University of London, 1977. - 27p.

          Listings of publications acquired from each political
       party under country of origin followed by a similar section on
       trade unions. Entries on the West Indies (p.17-19, 26-27).

                                                                    UWI-T

1178   University of the West Indies (Cave Hill). Institute of Social
       and Economic Research (Eastern Caribbean)
          General elections in the Eastern Caribbean : a handbook /
       Patrick A. Emmanuel. - Cave Hill, Barbados : Institute of
       Social and Economic Research (Eastern Caribbean), University
       of the West Indies, 1979. - ix, 194p. - (Occasional paper ;
       no.11)
          Bibliography: p.185-194

          118 items in two main sections: - Constitutional and
       Electoral Provisions, (2) Election Reports. Each section is
       subdivided geographically with items covering Antigua, Mont-
       serrat, St. Kitts, Nevis, Anguilla, Dominica, Grenada, St. Lucia,
       St. Vincent, Barbados. A third section lists a few general items
       on politics in individual territories.

                                                                    UWI-T

1179   University of the West Indies (Mona). Institute of Social and
       Economic Research
          Controls and influences on the civil service and statutory
       bodies in the Commonwealth Caribbean : a preliminary discussion
       / by Ralph E. Gonsalves. - [Mona, Jamaica] : Institute of
       Social and Economic Research, University of the West Indies,
       1978. - 67p. - (Working paper ; no.17)
          Bibliography: p.62-67

          67 references arranged in alphabetical author order for
       books, journal articles and reports on public administration with
       special reference to the Caribbean.

                                                                    UWI-T

1180   University of the West Indies (Mona).   Institute of Social
        and Economic Research
            The politics of constitutional decolonization : Jamaica
        1944-62 / by Trevor Munroe. - [Mona], Jamaica : Institute of
        Social and Economic Research, University of the West Indies,
        1972. - xiv, 239p.
            Bibliography: p.220-234

        Lists books and theses in alphabetical order followed by
    primary sources and documents in chronological order.   Includes
    a list of newspapers, political party pamphlets and government
    publications.

                                                            UWI-T

1181   WALLACE, ELISABETH
            British Caribbean from the decline of colonialism to the
        end of Federation / Elisabeth Wallace. - Toronto ; Buffalo :
        University of Toronto Press, 1977. - vii, 27p.
            Selected bibliography: p.253-262

        182 items arranged under sections :   (1) Government
    Documents subdivided under headings - United Kingdom; Colonial
    Office; Jamaica; Trinidad and Tobago; British Honduras; the West
    Indies, (2) Monographs, (3) Articles.

                                                            UWI-T

1182   WILL, HENRY AUSTIN
            Constitutional change in the British West Indies 1880-
        1903 ; with special reference to Jamaica, British Guiana and
        Trinidad / by Henry Austin Will. - Oxford : Clarendon Press,
        1970. - xxii, 331p.
            Bibliography: p.[302]-314

        Arranged by sources which include manuscripts, official
    and private printed primary sources, contemporary pamphlets,
    articles and books followed by secondary sources, including
    unpublished theses.

                                                            UWI-T

Anguilla

1183   WESTLAKE, DONALD E.
            Under an English heaven / Donald E. Westlake. - New York :
        Simon and Schuster, 1972. - 278p.
            Bibliography: p.265-268

        Lists newspaper and magazine titles with the broad dates
    relevant to the Anguilla secession movement and British inter-
    vention, as well as journal articles, with a few books and public
    documents also listed separately.

                                                            UWI-T

Belize

1184   BIANCHI, WILLIAM J.
       Belize : the controversy between Guatemala and Great
Britain over the territory of British Honduras in Central
America / William J. Bianchi. - New York : Las Americas
Publishing Company, 1959. - 142p.
       Bibliography: p.138-142

       Entries which are arranged alphabetically by author,
include treaties between Great Britain and Spain and Great Britain
and Guatemala as well as other material on the controversy, and
general descriptive works on Belize.

                                                        UWI-T

1185   FABELA, ISIDRO
       Belice, defensa de los derechos, de México / Isidro
Fabela. - México : Editorial Mundo Libre, 1944. - 2, 1, [7]-
423p., 1 leaf
       Bibliography: p.399-404.

                                                          LC

Grenada

1186   SINGHAM, A.W.
       The hero and the crowd in a colonial polity / by A.W.
Singham. - New Haven : Yale University Press, 1968. - xiv,
389p.
       Bibliography: p.362-371

       In addition to an alphabetical author listing of general
works includes a separate list of reports, public documents and
newspapers subdivided by country of origin with 24 items from
Grenada and shorter listings for Great Britain, Trinidad and
Tobago and the West Indies.

                                                        UWI-T

Guyana

1187   CABRERA SIFONTES, HORACIO
       Guyana Esequiba / Horacio Cabrera Sifontes. - Caracas :
[s.n.], 1970. - 139p.
       Bibliography: p.137-139

                                                          UG

1188   CUMMINGS, LESLIE PETER
       Bibliography on boundaries, boundary problems in the
Guianas / Leslie Peter Cummings. - [Turkeyen, Guyana] :
University of Guyana, [1969?]. - 7 leaves

Section 1 of his bibliography on the Guianas

Includes mainly articles and reports located in libraries
in London; location marks are included for each item listed under
title with authors and/or other reference information such as
publisher or journal title.

UWI-T

1189   SIMMS, PETER
       Trouble in Guyana : an account of people, personalities
       and politics as they were in British Guiana / Peter Simms. -
       London : George Allen and Unwin, 1966. - 198p.
       Bibliography: p.188-193

       Books and journal articles arranged alphabetically by
       author are followed by official reports and party publications
       in separate sequences.

UWI-T

1190   Stanford University. The Hoover Institution on War, Revolution
       and Peace
       Revolution and structural change in Latin America : a
       bibliography on ideology, development and the radical left
       (1930-1965) / by Ronald H. Chilcote. - Stanford, Calif. : The
       Hoover Institution on War, Revolution and Peace, Stanford
       University, 1970. - (Hoover Institution bibliographical
       series ; no.40)
            Vol.1 : Argentina-Colombia. - 668p.
                     British Guiana. - p.431-450
                     Caribbean. - p.451-462

       151 references to books, pamphlets, articles and other
       papers on Guyana representing "a fairly exhaustive collection of
       materials published by leaders of the PPP, the PNC and the UF"
       (political parties). 66 references to leftist materials on the
       Caribbean islands provide less comprehensive coverage - mainly
       articles in journals published outside the region. A separate
       list of periodicals is provided in each case.

UWI-T

1191   STEPHENSON, YVONNE V.
       A select bibliography on public administration in Guyana /
       Yvonne V. Stephenson. - 18p.
       In The state of the art in publishing and library systems
       with special reference to documentation relevant to public
       administration in Guyana / [paper presented by] Yvonne V.
       Stephenson [for] Seminar on Developing a Public Administration
       Information Network for Latin America and the Caribbean ...,
       Bridgetown, Barbados, November 1 to 3, 1978. - [S.l.] : Centro
       Latino Americano de Administración para el Desarrollo (CLAD),
       [1978]

Alphabetical author listing of papers, addresses and
official publications.

UWI-T

1192 THOMAS, MARY BARTA
      Guyana : a bibliography on national development / Mary
      Barta Thomas. - Monticello, Ill. : Council of Planning Librar-
      ians, 1976. - 49p. - (Council of Planning Librarians. Exchange
      bibliography ; no.1076)
      Mimeographed

LC

1193 VILLIERS, J.A.J. DE
      Chronological list of printed works bearing upon the
      boundary arbitration between British Guiana and Venezuela /
      J.A.J. de Villiers. - London : [s.n.], 1897. - 11 leaves
      Copy in the British Library has MS additions and
      corrections.

BL

Archival and Manuscript Materials
1194 STEPHENSON, YVONNE V.
      A summary inventory of the records in the archives of
      British Guiana : Appendix A / Yvonne V. Stephenson. - 2p.
      In The state of the art in publishing and library systems
      with special reference to documentation relevant to public
      administration in Guyana / [paper presented by] Yvonne V.
      Stephenson [for] Seminar on Developing a Public Administration
      Information Network for Latin America and the Caribbean ...,
      Bridgetown, Barbados, November 1 to 3, 1978. - [S.l.] : Centro
      Latino Americano de Administración para el Desarrollo (CLAD),
      [1978]

UWI-T

Indexes
1195 Great Britain, Foreign Office
      British Guiana boundary : arbitration with the United
      States of Venezuela ; the case on behalf of the government of
      Her Britannic Majesty. - (Appendix ... The counter-case ...
      Appendix ... Argument ... Index to cases, counter-cases and
      printed arguments) / Foreign Office. - London : [s.n.], 1898. -
      12v.

BL

Jamaica

1196 Jamaica. Committee to Examine the Structure and Organisation
      of Local Government
      Report on the reform of local government in Jamaica /
      Committee to Examine the Structure ... Local Government. -
      Kingston, Jamaica : [s.n.], 1974. - 22p.

Mimeographed
Chairman : G.E. Mills
Bibliography: p.115-116

17 references to items cited in the text with brief
additional list citing relevant reports on Jamaica and other
West Indian territories.

UWI-J

Trinidad and Tobago

1197 JACOBS, W. RICHARD
        Butler versus the King : riots and sedition in 1937 /
     edited by W. Richard Jacobs ; comments by George Weekes, Joe
     Young. - Port of Spain, Trinidad : Key Caribbean Publications,
     [c1976]. - 254p.
        Bibliography: p.252-254

        103 items including transcripts of Crown-Copyright records
     from the Public Record Office, notes of Butler's meetings,
     letters from Butler to the Acting Colonial Secretary and Acting
     Governor, handbills, subscription lists, etc.

UWI-T

1198 MALIK, YOGENDRA K.
        East Indians in Trinidad : a study in minority politics /
     Yogendra K. Malik. - London : Oxford University Press for the
     Institute of Race Relations, 1971. - xv, 199p.
        Bibliography: p.175-185

        Lists official documents and government publications
     followed by unpublished material and political party publications
     as well as books and articles from journals and newspapers.

UWI-T

1199 MILLETTE, JAMES
        The genesis of crown colony government : Trinidad, 1873-
     1810 / James Millette. - Curepe, Trinidad : Moko Enterprises,
     1970. - xviii, 295p.
        Bibliography: p.268-286

        Arranged by type of source and alphabetically by author
     within appropriate sections. Includes correspondence and other
     manuscript sources, contemporary pamphlets, periodicals and
     newspapers as well as modern printed works.

UWI-T

1200 Skirmishes, riots, labour disturbances, inquiry commission(s).
     - [S.l. : s.n.], [196-?]. - 1 leaf
        Typescript

Twenty brief references to reports on disturbances with an introductory note on Trinidad and Tobago.

TCL

1201 Trinidad and Tobago. Central Library
List of books and other material on politics in Trinidad and Tobago : 1962 to the present / Central Library. - [Port of Spain, Trinidad] : Central Library West Indian Reference [Section], 1971. - 3 leaves
Typescript

Listing of 14 books and pamphlets in Dewey Classification order plus 9 periodical and newspaper titles with frequency and place of publication as well as references to 22 information files under such headings as black power; courts martial 1970; disturbances 1970; elections, general - 1966 and 1971, and under the names of local political parties - PNM, Tapia House Group, DLP, UNIP, etc.

TCL

1202 Trinidad and Tobago. Central Library
List of books on Chaguaramas in the West Indian Section / Central Library. - [Port of Spain, Trinidad : Central Library], 1968. - 1 leaf
Typescript

Seven references to reports, speeches and official documents pertaining to the naval base leased to the U.S. at Chaguaramas in Trinidad.

TCL

1203 Trinidad and Tobago. Ministry of Planning and Development. Library
The Public Service / Ministry of Planning and Development Library. - [Port of Spain, Trinidad : Ministry of Planning and Development Library], 1979. - 4 leaves

Comprises 48 items available in the library. Chronologically arranged, the bibliography comprises general reports, classification and compensation plans, training reports on specific departments, U.N. reports and speeches.

MF-T

POPULATION

1204   EDMONSTON, BARRY
        Population research in Latin America and the Caribbean : a
reference bibliography / Barry Edmonston. - Ann Arbor, Mich. :
University Microfilms International for the Internation Studies
Program and the Latin American Studies Program, Cornell
University, 1979
                                        Choice, vol.18, no.10
                                              June 1981, p.1386

1205   KUCZYNSKI, R.R.
        Demographic survey of the British colonial empire / by
R.R. Kuczynski. - London : Oxford University Press, 1953. - 3v.
        Vol.III :   West Indian and American territories. - 497p.
        Bibliography: p.477-493

        Subdivided into several sections by country or group of
territories.   Includes mainly official reports and laws for the
former colonial territories of the West Indies.   Includes Cayman,
Turks and Caicos Islands and Virgin Islands as well as British
Honduras, the Windwards, Leewards and the larger now independent
territories.
                                                         UWI-T

1206   ROBERTS, GEORGE W.
        Fertility and mating in four West Indian populations :
Trinidad and Tobago, Barbados, St. Vincent, Jamaica / G.W.
Roberts. - [Mona], Jamaica : Institute of Social and Economic
Research, University of the West Indies, 1975. - 341p.
        Bibliography: p.329-333

        Seventy-four references to reports, journal articles and
books arranged alphabetically by author.
                                                         UWI-T

1207   TEKSE, KALMAN
        A study of fertility in Jamaica / Kalman Tekse. -
[Kingston], Jamaica : Demography and Vital Statistics Section,
Department of Statistics, [1968]. - vi, 27p.
        Bibliography: p.26-27

        24 references mainly to journal articles and government
reports arranged alphabetically by author.
                                                         UWI-T

1208   United Nations.   Statistical Office
        Bibliography of recent official demographic statistics /
Statistical Office. - New York : [s.n.], 1954. - 80p. -
(Statistical papers, series M, 18 ; ST/STAT/SER. M/18)

Reprinted from: Demographic Yearbook 1953.

Lists "official publications containing census and other demographic statistics for each area of the world." The bibliography is supplemented by bibliographies in the 1954 and 1955 editions of the Demographic Yearbook. Includes listings for the Bahama Islands, Bermuda and the British West Indies as a group as well as listings for individual islands and groups such as the Leewards and Windwards.

LC

1209 United States. Library of Congress. Census Library Project
General censuses and vital statistics in the Americas : an annotated bibliography of the historical censuses and current vital statistics of the 21 American republics, the American sections of the British Commonwealth of Nations, the American colonies of Denmark, France and the Netherlands, and the American territories and possessions of the United States / prepared under the supervision of Irene B. Tauber. - Washington, D.C. : U.S. Government Printing Office, 1943. - ix, 151p.

"Includes information for British, Danish, French and Dutch colonies in the Western Hemisphere" - Blaine Etheridge Catalogue.

LC

1210 University of Puerto Rico. Institute of Caribbean Studies
Politics and population in the Caribbean / Aaron Segal with the assistance of Kent C. Earnhardt. - Rio Piedras, Puerto Rico : Institute of Caribbean Studies, University of Puerto Rico, 1969. - [3], 158, [55]p. - (Special study ; no.7)
Bibliography: p.[159-205]

247 references, some annotated, arranged alphabetically by author under countries or groups of islands and covering all the islands of the Caribbean as well as Guyana, Surinam and French Antilles. Includes dissertations, theses, books, reports and journal articles. A general list of 100 references not specifically on the Caribbean follows. Author and subject indexes are provided.

UWI-T

1211 University of Texas. Department of Sociology. Population Research Center
International population census bibliography : Latin America and the Caribbean / Population Research Center, University of Texas. - Austin, Tex. : Bureau of Business Research, University of Texas, 1965. - 1 v. (various pagings). - (Census bibliography; no.1)

This is the first in a planned series on census reports.
Citations are obtained for the most part by inspection of census
publications. The holdings of the Library of Congress, Bureau of
the Census Library and the New York Public Library have been
checked. Locations are given and arrangement is alphabetical by
country or groups of islands, e.g., Windward Islands, and chronological within each section. Includes some brief explanatory
notes.

UWI-T

Barbados

1212　University of the West Indies (Cave Hill). Institute of Social
　　　and Economic Research (Eastern Caribbean)
　　　　　The population of Barbados : a select bibliography /
　　　[compiled by Joycelin Massiah]. - Cave Hill, Barbados :
　　　Institute of Social and Economic Research, U.W.I., 1974. - 8
　　　leaves. - (Occasional bibliography series ; no.2)

　　　　　Arranged by form of material with sections for books,
　　　pamphlets, papers, theses, articles, official documents and
　　　periodical titles.

UWI-T

Jamaica

1213　EYRE, LAURENCE ALAN
　　　　　Geographic aspects of population dynamics in Jamaica / L.
　　　Alan Eyre. - Boca Raton, Fla. : Florida Atlantic University
　　　Press, 1972. - xiv, 172p.
　　　　　Bibliography: p.159-172

　　　　　Over 100 references to works cited in the text, mainly on
　　　Jamaica. Arranged in three main sections : (1) Books, (2)
　　　Published Articles and Reports, (3) Proceedings, Theses and
　　　Unpublished Papers.

UWI-T

1214　TEKSE, KALMAN
　　　　　Population and vital statistics, Jamaica, 1832-1964 : a
　　　historical perspective / [by Kalman Tekse]. - [Kingston,
　　　Jamaica] : Department of Statistics, [1974]. - 340p.
　　　　　Bibliography: p.306-340

　　　　　Over 300 references in alphabetical author order to
　　　reports, journal articles, statistical research papers and books
　　　with relevant information followed by listings of "publications
　　　of the Population Censuses of Jamaica" and annual reports of the
　　　Registrar General's Department.

UWI-T

Trinidad and Tobago

1215   HAREWOOD, JACK
        The population of Trinidad and Tobago / by Jack Harewood ;
   prepared for [the] Committee of the International Co-ordination
   of Research in Demography (C.I.C.R.E.D.). - [S.l. : s.n.],
   1975. - xvii, 237p. - (CICRED series)
        At head of title: 1974, World Population Year
        Bibliography: p.233-237

        References grouped by chapters and arranged alphabetically
   by author in such sections as population growth, distribution and
   internal migration, fertility and mating.
                                                           UWI-T

1216   Selected titles for a bibliography of research on the
   population characteristics of Trinidad and Tobago. - [S.l. :
   s.n.], [197-?]. - 2 leaves
        Typescript

        Arranged alphabetically by author. Mainly publications of
   the Statistical Office of Trinidad and Tobago and the Institute
   of Social and Economic Research of the University of the West
   Indies.
                                                           UWI-T

PSYCHOLOGY

1217   BRODBER, E.
        Social psychology in the Caribbean : a bibliography and
   some comments on lacunae and areas of saturation / by E.
   Brodber. - [S.l. : s.n.], 1972. - 33p.
        Mimeographed

                                                           IDRC

1218   BRODBER, ERNA
        Social psychology in the English-speaking Caribbean : a
   bibliography and some comments / Erna Brodber. - p.398-417
        In Social and economic studies. - Vol.23, no.3 (1974)

        Arranged under subject headings : Socialisation, Inter-
   action and Tests, Experiments and Theories. Sources of bibliographic information are also listed.
                                                           UWI-T

RACE RELATIONS

1219   Community Relations Commission
          Race relations in Britain : a select bibliography /
       Community Relations Commission. - 4th ed. - London : The
       Commission, 1974. - 29p.
                                                                UWI-T

1220   Community Relations Commission
          Race relations in Britain : a select bibliography /
       Community Relations Commission. - 5th ed. - London : The
       Commission, 1975. - 29p.

          Items arranged under headings : Education, Employment,
       Housing, Immigrants and Community Studies, Immigration, Police
       and the Immigrant Community, Prejudice and Discrimination, Race
       Relations, Social Services, Statistics, Youth, Bibliographies,
       Periodicals and Journals. Many items deal with West Indians.
                                                                UWI-T

1221   Community Relations Commission
          Race relations in Britain : a select bibliography /
       Community Relations Commission. - 6th ed. - London : The
       Commission, 1976. - 24p.
                                                          Ref.no.664
                                                          Item no.22

1222   Community Relations Commission
          Race relations in Britain : a select bibliography with
       emphasis on Commonwealth immigrants / Community Relations
       Commission. - 3rd ed. - London : Community Relations Commission,
       1973. - 23p.
                                                          Ref.no.664
                                                          Item no.19

1223   Community Relations Commission
          Race relations in Britain : selected bibliography with
       emphasis on Commonwealth immigrants / Community Relations
       Commission. - 2nd ed. - London : Community Relations
       Commission, 1971. - 19p.
                                                          Ref.no.664
                                                          Item no.18

1224   Lambeth Libraries
          Black Britons : a select bibliography on race / compiled
       by John Buchanan. - London : London Borough of Lambeth, 1972.
       - 24, [1]p.

Entries in the first two sections are arranged under
headings :   Black People in Britain, Race Relations. The other
sections are devoted to the history, arts and politics of Africa,
Indo-Pakistan and Bangladesh and the West Indies, which comprises
81 entries.

UWI-T

1224a LEVINE, ROBERT M.
Race and ethnic relations in Latin America and the
Caribbean : an historical dictionary and bibliography /
Robert M. Levine. - Metuchen, N.J. ; London : Scarecrow Press,
1980. - vii, 252p.
Selected bibliography : p.151-243

1,342 entries arranged geographically. Sections include
the General Caribbean (84 items), Jamaica (76 items), Trinidad-
Tobago (34 items), Other British West Indies including the
Bahamas and Barbados (67 items), Central America (with a few
items on British Honduras), South America with a section devoted
to British Guiana/Guyana (33 items).

UWI-T

1225 TOMLINSON, SALLY
Race and education in Britain, 1960-77 : an overview of
the literature / Sally Tomlinson. - p.3-33
<u>In</u> Sage race relations abstracts. - Vol.2, no.4 (Nov. 1977)
Bibliography: p.22-33

Bibliographic essay discusses relevant publications under
section headings such as background and language, performance
and achievement, intelligence and behaviour, identity and
aspirations. The bibliography consists of books, pamphlets,
periodical articles and theses and includes items on the education
of West Indian children as well as the mental health and race
relations problems of this immigrant group.

UWI-T

1226 University of Sussex. Centre for Multi-racial Studies
Items concerning race relations from Caribbean newspapers,
March-December 1969 / Centre for Multi-racial Studies. -
[Brighton, England] : Centre for Multi-racial Studies,
University of Sussex, 1972. - (various pagings)

Benjamin

1227 WATERS, HAZEL
Guide to the literature on race relations in Britain,
1970-75 / Hazel Waters. - p.97-105
<u>In</u> Sage race relations abstracts. - Vol.1, no.2 (Mar. 1976)

Bibliographic essay providing comprehensive coverage of material published since 1970. Includes background reading, history and personal narrative, housing, immigration, law and police, prejudice and discrimination.

UWI-T

REGIONAL CO-OPERATION AND INTEGRATION

1228   AXLINE, W. ANDREW
Caribbean integration : the politics of regionalism / W. Andrew Axline. - London : Francis Pinter ; New York : Nicholas Publishing Company, 1979. - xx, 233p.
Bibliography: p.207-229

Arranged under headings : Integration and Development, Political Economy of the Caribbean, Caribbean Integration. The 177 items in the last two sections comprise books, journal articles, papers from conference proceedings and Caribbean Community Secretariat publications.

UWI-T

1229   BOROMÉ, JOSEPH A.
British West Indian Federation : development and dénouement ; a bibliography, 1959 through 1962 / Joseph A. Boromé. - p.8-10
In Bulletin of bibliography. - Vol.24, no.1 (May-Aug. 1963)

Sections for bibliographies, British and West Indian official publications are followed by books and articles, all in chronological order.

UWI-T

1230   BOROMÉ, JOSEPH A.
British West Indian Federation through 1958 : a bibliography / Joseph A. Boromé. - p.31-36
In Bulletin of bibliography. - Vol.23, no.2 (May-Aug. 1960)

Subdivided into British official and unofficial sources with a chronological arrangement within each section. Books and journal articles are listed together.

UWI-T

1231   Commonwealth Caribbean Regional Secretariat
Carifta and the new Caribbean / Commonwealth Caribbean Regional Secretariat. - [Georgetown, Guyana : Commonwealth Caribbean Regional Secretariat], [1971]. - vi, 143, [30]p.
Bibliography: Appendix VIII. - p.31-32

"A short reading list on Commonwealth Caribbean Regional
Cooperation." 34 references to books, pamphlets and journal
articles published in the fifties, sixties and early seventies.
UWI-T

1232 Commonwealth Caribbean Regional Secretariat
       From CARIFTA to Caribbean Community / Commonwealth
       Caribbean Regional Secretariat. - [Georgetown, Guyana :
       Commonwealth Caribbean Regional Secretariat], [1972]. - 180p.
       Bibliography: p.169-179

       166 items arranged alphabetically by author covering
regional integration, economic and industrial development, trade
and commerce, and politics and government. Items include journal
articles, Commonwealth Caribbean Regional Secretariat publications and U.W.I. publications. The majority of the material
listed was published in the West Indies.
UWI-T

1233 CRASSWELLER, ROBERT D.
       The Caribbean community : changing societies and U.S.
       policy / Robert D. Crassweller. - London : Pall Mall Press for
       the Council on Foreign Relations, 1972. - x, 470p.
       Bibliography: p.439-455

       Treats the wider Caribbean area including Central America
in essay notes under such headings as The Caribbean environment,
aid matters, economic and development matters, The Commonwealth
Caribbean regionalism, integration and functional cooperation.
Excludes official publications and archival materials.
UWI-T

1234 EASTON, DAVID K.
       A bibliography on the Federation of the British West
       Indies / David K. Easton. - p.1-14
       In Current Caribbean bibliography. - Vol.5 (1955)

       Bibliography is in three sections: - (1) Documents of
Official Commissions (2) Documents of British Caribbean Associations and (3) Books and Other Monographs. Items, the majority of
which were published in the 1940's and 1950's, are annotated.
UWI-T

1235 EASTON, DAVID K.
       Bibliography [on West Indian Federation] / prepared by
       David K. Easton. - p.253-256
       In The Caribbean : contemporary trends / edited by A.
       Curtis Wilgus. - Gainesville, [Fla.] : University of Florida
       Press, 1953. - (Series one ; v.3)

307

A selective listing divided into three sections : - (1)
Reports of Government Agencies, (2) Reports of the Conferences
of Private and Semi—government Organizations, (3) Books.

UWI-T

1236 ETIENNE, FLORY
La Commission des Caraïbes / Flory Etienne. - Paris : M.
Lavergne, imprimeur, 1952. - 192p.
Label mounted over imprint on cover: Paris : Receuil Sirey
Bibliography: p.183-190

UWI-J

1237 Footsteps to federation : bibliographical notes. - p.257-258
In Caribbean. - Vol.10 (May 1957)

Annotated list of 13 reports and conference papers on
aspects of closer association between the West Indian territories.

UWI-T

1238 GEISER, HANS J.
Legal problems of Caribbean integration : a study on the
legal aspects of CARICOM / by Hans J. Geiser, Pamela Alleyne
and Carroll Gajraj. - St. Augustine, Trinidad and Tobago :
Institute of International Relations, 1976. - 275p.
Bibliography: p.177-182

Listing is divided into basic texts and treaties,
collections of documents, official reports, papers and speeches,
newspapers, books and articles.

UWI-T

1239 Institute of Jamaica. West India Reference Library
Caribbean economic integration : short reading list /
prepared by Rosalie Williams. - [Kingston, Jamaica] : Institute
of Jamaica, West India Reference Library, 1970. - 5p.
Mimeographed

Two general headings only - Carifta and Economic Integration - each subdivided into books and periodicals.

UWI-J

1240 Institute of Jamaica. West India Reference Library
A list of books on West Indian federation / compiled by
the West India Reference Library ... Kingston, Jamaica :
Institute of Jamaica, 1957. - [1], 12p.
Mimeographed

"Attempts to trace the development of the federal concept
in the Caribbean."

UWI-T

1241   Institute of Jamaica. West India Reference Library
         A list of books on West Indian federation / [compiled by
         the West India Reference Library]. - 2nd ed. / by Anne
         Benewick. - [Kingston, Jamaica] : Institute of Jamaica, West
         India Reference Library, 1962. - 47p.
         Mimeographed

         Includes sections on the Federal movement to 1947, the
West Indies Federation 1947-1962 and a list of relevant periodicals. Author and subject indexes and one or more of three
library locations in Jamaica are provided.

                                                            UWI-T

1242   MILNE, R. STEPHEN
         Impulses and obstacles to Caribbean political integration
         / R. Stephen Milne. - p.291-316
         In International studies quarterly. - Vol.18 (Sept. 1974)
         Bibliography: p.314-316

         Alphabetical author list of references mainly on regional
integration both economic and political.

                                                            UWI-T

1243   MORDECAI, JOHN
         The West Indies ; the federal negotiations / John
         Mordecai ; epilogue by W. Arthur Lewis. - London : George
         Allen and Unwin, 1968. - 484p.
         Bibliography: p.470-476

         Under official sources are listed separately the papers
emanating from U.K., U.S., W.I. Federal, Jamaica and Trinidad
and Tobago governments as well as pre-federal organizations.
Articles, books and pamphlets are arranged in author order
followed by periodical and newspaper titles with relevant
information.

                                                            UWI-T

1244   POOLE, BERNARD L.
         The Caribbean Commission : background of cooperation in
         the West Indies / Bernard L. Poole. - Columbia, S.C. :
         University of South Carolina Press, 1951. - xix, 303p.
         Bibliography: p.277-288

         Lists documents by source followed by monographs and
special studies, books and articles in periodicals, newspapers
and unpublished material covering the former territories of
France, the U.S., Great Britain and the Netherlands.

                                                            UWI-T

1245   PROCTOR, J.H.
       Federalism in the West Indies / J.H. Proctor
       In Federalism in the Commonwealth : a bibliographical
commentary / edited by W.S. Livingston. - London : Cassell for
the Hansard Society, [1963]

                                                        UWI-J

1246   University of Guyana. Library
       A bibliography on the West Indies Federation / by Yvonne
Stephenson. - Georgetown : University of Guyana Library, 1972.
- 34 leaves. - (University of Guyana library series ; no.6)
       Mimeographed

       Prepared as a guide for students of the University of
Guyana. Items which include books, pamphlets, government docu-
ments and periodical articles located in the University of
Guyana Library are alphabetically arranged by author.

                                                        UWI-T

1247   University of the West Indies (St. Augustine). Library
       Caribbean Community : a list of references to the litera-
ture held in the Library ... . - St. Augustine, Trinidad :
Library, University of the West Indies, [1979]. - 7p.
       Mimeographed

       Arranged by author in broad subject groups such as
Caribbean integration, Carifta documents, Caricom documents,
guides and handbooks, articles and monographs. Includes one
reference to pre-federal literature on a customs union.

                                                        UWI-T

1248   West Indies (Federation). Federal Information Service.
       Reference Library
       List of books on aspects of W.I. Federation ... / Federal
Information Service Reference Library. - [Port of Spain,
Trinidad : Federal Information Service Reference Library],
[1961]. - 3p. on 2 leaves
       Mimeographed

       Lists bibliographies, reports and general works.

                                                        UWI-T

1249   West Indies (Federation). Federal Information Service.
       Reference Library
       A select list of literature on the West Indies Federation
since 1957 / compiled by M. McConnie ... . - [Port of Spain,
Trinidad : Federal Information Service Reference Library],
1961. - 5 leaves
       Mimeographed

Includes several references to journal articles and
government reports as well as books. A list of the principal
periodicals and newspapers published in the West Indies is also
provided.

UWI-T

RELIGION

1249a University of the West Indies (Cave Hill). Main Library
        The church in the Caribbean : a select bibliography /
       compiled by Jean A. Callender. - Cave Hill, Barbados: Main
       Library, University of the West Indies, 1981. - 24p.

        224 items. Alphabetical author arrangement covering :
       General (95 entries), Barbados (53 entries), Belize (3 entries),
       Guyana (9 entries), Jamaica (21 entries), Leeward & Windward
       Islands (9 entries), Trinidad & Tobago (11 entries).

UWI-T

1250 Catholic Association for International Peace. Inter-American
       Committee
        Catholic life in the West Indies / by Richard Pattee and
       the Inter-American Committee ; a report of the Inter-American
       Committee. - Washington, D.C. : The Catholic Association for
       International Peace, 1946. - 64p. - (Catholic Association for
       International Peace pamphlet ; no.37)
        Bibliography: p.60-64

UWI-J

1251 Christian Action for Development in the Caribbean.
       Documentation Service
        Selected bibliography of established religions in the
       Caribbean / CADEC Documentation Service. - Bridgetown,
       Barbados : CADEC, [1978]. - 4p.
        Mimeographed

        34 entries ; no annotations.

UWI-B

1252 DAHLIN, TERRY
        Caribbean religion : a survey and bibliography / Terry
       Dahlin and Reed Nelson. - p.339-354
        In Windward, Leeward and Main : Caribbean studies and
       library resources ; Final report and working papers of the
       Twenty-fourth Seminar on the Acquisition of Latin American
       Library Materials. - Madison, Wisc. : SALALM Secretariat, 1980

Bibliography: p.346-352

Items are arranged alphabetically by author under
headings : (a) Bibliographies, (b) Books, (c) Periodical Articles.
UWI-T

1253 DAHLIN, THERRIN C.
The Catholic left in Latin America : a comprehensive
bibliography / Therrin C. Dahlin, Gary P. Gillum and Mark L.
Grover. - Boston : G.K. Hall, 1981. - xlvi, 410p. - (A
Reference publication in Latin American studies)

The section on the Caribbean (p.217-222) includes a few
references on the English-speaking Caribbean. Author and title
indexes are provided.
LC

1254 PARDEE, CELESTE
Distribution of religions in the West Indies / Celeste
Pardee. - [College Station, Tex.] : Texas A and M University,
1975. - 45p.
Mimeographed
Bibliography: p.40-43

57 entries.
CADEC-B

1255 PIERSON, ROSCOE M.
West Indian church history : a finding list of printed
materials relating to the history of the church in the English-
speaking Caribbean / compiled by Roscoe M. Pierson. -
Lexington, Ky. : Lexington Theological Seminary Library, 1967.
- 34p.

Preliminary alphabetical listing of works compiled from a
number of bibliographies. Most of the volumes listed were not
seen by the author. None of the serial publications of the
various missionary societies are listed.
UWI-J

1256 SIMPSON, GEORGE EATON
Religious cults of the Caribbean : Trinidad, Jamaica and
Haiti / George Eaton Simpson. - Rio Piedras, Puerto Rico :
Institute of Caribbean Studies, University of Puerto Rico,
1970. - 308p.
Bibliography: p.289-303

Arranged by country or region with separate sections on
Jamaica and Trinidad. Includes references to the Ras Tafari and
Shango.
UWI-T

1257   SMITH, GEORGE WILFRED
        Conquests of Christ in the West Indies : a short history of
        evangelical missions / George Wilfred Smith. - Browns Town, St.
        Ann, Jamaica : Printed at the Evangelical Bookroom, [1939]
        Bibliography: p.126-128

                                                        Ref.no.5
                                              1937-1942, p.1742

1258   Trinidad and Tobago. Central Library
        A list of books on African religions and Christianity ;
        with locations / Central Library. - [Port of Spain, Trinidad :
        Central Library], [196-?]. - 3 leaves, 1p.
        Typescript

        Alphabetical author listing of works mainly of relevance
to the church in the West Indies. Separate one page listing of
periodical articles. Includes locations for both the Central
Library and the Trinidad Public Library, West Indian Branch.

                                                              TCL

1259   Trinidad and Tobago. Central Library
        List of books on religion in the West Indies / Central
        Library. - [Port of Spain, Trinidad] : Central Library ,
        [19-?]. - 5 leaves, 1p.
        Typescript

        Includes full annotations for 27 books and pamphlets and
a separate listing of 6 periodical articles.

                                                              TCL

Jamaica

1260   BARRETT, LEONARD E.
        The Rastafarians : the dreadlocks of Jamaica / Leonard E.
        Barrett. - Kingston : Sangster's Book Stores Ltd. in asso-
        ciation with Heinemann, 1977. - xiv, 257p.
        Bibliography: p.251-254

        67 references arranged alphabetically by author. Includes
journal and newspaper articles and pamphlets as well as books,
many of them published in the 19th and early 20th century.

                                                            UWI-T

1261   CASHMORE, ERNEST
        Rastaman : the Rastafarian movement in England / Ernest
        Cashmore. - London : Allen and Unwin, 1979. - ix, 261p.
        Bibliography: p.249-257

Includes items on the Rastafarian movement and other
religious cults, race relations, reggae. A section devoted to
music comprises 12 items, most of which are recordings by Bob
Marley.

UWI-T

1262   CHEVANNES, BARRY
The literature of Rastafari / Barry Chevannes. - p.239-262
In Social and economic studies. - Vol.26, no.2 (June 1977)

A bibliographic essay followed by a listing of 40 items
referred to in the text.

UWI-T

1263   Commonwealth Institute. Library and Resource Centre
Jamaica : the Rastafari movement / compiled by Roger
Hughes. - London : Commonwealth Institute Library and Resource
Centre, 1979. - 4 leaves

26 items arranged alphabetically by author. Includes
periodical articles.

UWI-T

1264   HUGHES, ROGER
Jamaica : the Rastafarian movement ; a bibliographic
essay / Roger Hughes. - p.104, 106-109
In Assistant librarian. - Vol.72, nos.7-8 (July/Aug. 1979)

Surveys some of the more important books, pamphlets and
periodical articles included in Ref.no.1263.

BL

1265   New York. Missionary Research Library
Listings of the Missionary Research Library's holdings on
missions in Jamaica. - New York : Missionary Research Library,
1965. - 9p. - (Occasional bulletin from the Missionary
Research Library ; vol.16, no.10, Oct. 1965)

Ref.no.75
Item no.253

1266   NOYCE, JOHN L.
The Rastafarians in Britain and Jamaica : a bibliography /
compiled by John L. Noyce. - Brighton : Noyce, 1978. - 7p.

Alphabetical author arrangement in two sections - The
Rastafarians in Jamaica (41 items) and The Rastafarians in
Britain (18 items). Items which comprise books and articles in
periodicals include several on reggae music.

UWI-T

1267 OWENS, J.V.
          Literature on the Rastafari : 1955–1974 ; a review / J.V.
      Owens. – p.86–105, 113–114
          In Savacou. – Vol.11–12 (Sept. 1975)

          A bibliographic essay with a list of 14 references.
                                                              UWI-T

1268 A Preliminary Rastafari bibliography. – p.56–58
          In Caribbean quarterly. – Vol.24, nos.3–4 (Sept.–Dec. 1978)

          An alphabetical author listing of 133 items (books and
      articles) drawing on the works of Joyce Gordon (Ref.no.1269) and
      Roger Hughes (Ref.no.1263).
                                                              UWI-T

1269 University of the West Indies (Mona). Library
          Bibliography on Rastafari – 1955–1976 / [compiled by
      Joyce Gordon]. – [Mona, Jamaica : Library, University of the
      West Indies], 1976. – 5 leaves
          Typescript

          Divided into four sections for books, periodical articles,
      Rastas' own literature and papers, reports and unpublished items.
      This list was later used in the compilation published in
      Caribbean Quarterly (Ref.no.1268).
                                                              UWI-J

Trinidad and Tobago

1270 SIMPSON, GEORGE EATON
          The shango cult in Trinidad / George Eaton Simpson. – [Rio
      Piedras, Puerto Rico] : Institute of Caribbean Studies,
      University of Puerto Rico, 1965. – 140p.
          Bibliography: p.131–136

          Arranged alphabetically by author and by date of publi-
      cation under each author.
                                                              UWI-T

SCIENCE

1271 Jamaica. Scientific Research Council
          Annual report ... / Scientific Research Council. – 1st
      (1961)- . – Kingston, Jamaica : [Scientific Research Council],
      1961-
          Annual

From the fourth report (to Mar. 1964) lists of unpublished
reports as well as published work based on research projects
conducted in the divisions of the Council are included. The
latter include Agro-industry, Mineral Resources, Industrial
Development and Food Science and Nutrition Divisions.

UWI-T

1272   Recent publications on the Caribbean area
       In Caribbean journal of science. - Vol.1, no.1 (Feb.
       1962)
       Quarterly

       Lists of new work in natural sciences relevant to the
Caribbean compiled by regular correspondents whose initials appear
at the end of the relevant section in each issue. Includes such
sections as geography, geology, zoology, ornithology, marine
biology and meteorology and climatology. All listings include
monographs and serial articles in alphabetical author order.
Scope is the wider Caribbean area.

UWI-T

1273   Some recent theses in science and technology
       In West Indian science and technology. - Vol.1, no.1 (1976)

       Title varies and the section has appeared in two of three
issues to date; author and title listing of theses and dissertations from the University of the West Indies campuses.

UWI-T

1274   United States. National Oceanographic Data Center
       Cooperative Investigation of the Caribbean and Adjacent
       Regions (CICAR) / National Oceanographic Data Center. -
       Washington, D.C. : U.S. National Oceanographic Data Center,
       1970-1972. - 3v.
       Vol.1 : Bibliography on meteorology, climatology and
       physical/chemical oceanography. - 1970. - 2pts. - 614p.
       Vol.2 : Bibliography on marine biology. - 1971. - 243p.
       Vol.3 : Bibliography on marine geology and geophysics. -
       1972. - 238p.

       Fourteen cooperating countries (including the U.S.,
U.S.S.R., U.K., Netherlands, Mexico, Jamaica, Trinidad and other
Caribbean countries) make up the Cooperative Investigation group
- CICAR. The first volume provides over 3,000 references, many
with abstracts. The second and third volumes cover over 14,000
references.

UWI-T

1275 University of the West Indies. Trinidad Regional Virus
      Laboratory
            Titles and summaries of papers authored in part or in
      whole by staff members of the Trinidad Regional Virus
      Laboratory, 1953-64 : Part I. - Titles and summaries of papers
      relating to Trinidad Regional Virus Laboratory activities by
      non TRVL personnel 1953-1964 : Part II. - [Port of Spain,
      Trinidad] : Trinidad Regional Virus Laboratory, 1965
            Part I. - 23p. - Part II. - 7p.

            Chronological listings of scientific research papers
      mainly on virology and related studies conducted in Trinidad and
      published in such journals as the American Journal of Tropical
      Medicine and Hygiene, West Indian Medical Journal, Journal of the
      Agricultural Society of Trinidad and Tobago, Journal of Medical
      Entomology and American Journal of Veterinary Research.
      Summaries are given but there is no index.

                                                              UWI-T

1276 University of the West Indies (St. Augustine). Department of
      Mechanical Engineering
            List of theses, publications, reports and brief descriptions
      of current work on solar energy and related subjects / Depart-
      ment of Mechanical Engineering. - St. Augustine : [Department
      of Mechanical Engineering, U.W.I.], 1972. - 2p.
            Mimeographed

            Listing of nine items represents work done by members of
      the department.

                                                              UWI-T

                         SLAVERY AND SLAVE TRADE

1277 Brown University. John Carter Brown Library
            Africans in colonial Americas : an exhibition of books
      and prints opened at the annual meeting of the Associates of
      the John Carter Brown Library, May 1, 1970. - Providence,
      R.I. : [John Carter Brown Library, Brown University], 1970. -
      21p.
            Mimeographed

            68 fully annotated entries arranged under headings :
      African Presence, Slave Trade, Conditions of Servitude,
      Narratives of Slavery, Revolt against Servitude, Amelioration of
      Slavery and Conversion of Negroes, Abolitionist Impulse, African
      Culture in the Americas, Wall Panels (i.e., prints and groups of
      prints).

                                                              UWI-J

                                317

1278   CRATON, MICHAEL
        Sinews of empire : a short history of British slavery /
by Michael Craton. - New York : Anchor Press/Doubleday, 1974. -
xxii, 413p.
        Bibliography: p.385-398
        Also published: London : Temple Smith

        "Survey of the scholarship to date on slavery with valuable
interpretations by the author." Listing is under such headings
as guides and bibliographies, documents - printed collections,
general sources and colonial sources, followed by general works
in alphabetical author order.
                                                        UWI-T

1278a DRESCHER, SEYMOUR
        Econocide : British slavery in the era of abolition /
Seymour Drescher. - Pittsburgh, Pa. : University of Pittsburgh
Press, 1977. - 279p.
        Bibliography: p.261-271

        Separate alphabetical listings of manuscript sources,
official and semi-official documents and newspapers followed by
an extensive list of other works mainly on the history of slavery
and the slave trade.
                                                        UWI-T

1279   GASTON, L. CLIFTON
        Negro slavery and race relations in Latin America and the
Caribbean to 1900 : a select bibliography of available sources
/ L. Clifton Gaston. - New Orleans, La. : Latin American
Library, Tulane University, [197-?]. - 35 leaves
        Mimeographed

        419 items arranged alphabetically by author under three
sections : (1) Books and Monographs, (2) Essays from Multi-
authored Compendia, (3) Periodical Articles. Includes several
entries on the British West Indian colonies, including theses.
                                                        UWI-T

1280   GREEN, WILLIAM A.
        British slave emancipation : the sugar colonies and the
great experiment 1830-1865 / William A. Green. - Oxford :
Clarendon Press, 1976. - x, 449p.
        Bibliography: p.416-438

        Several references on social and economic conditions in
the West Indian territories, subdivided into primary (manuscripts,
newspapers and periodicals, contemporary books and pamphlets) and
secondary works in alphabetical author order.
                                                        UWI-T

1281   JAKOBSSON, STIV
          Am I not a man and your brother? : British missions and
       the abolition of the slave trade and slavery in West Africa
       and the West Indies 1786-1838 / Stiv Jakobsson. - [Uppsala,
       Sweden] : Gleerup, 1972. - 661p. - (Studia missionalia
       Upsaliensia ; 17)
          Bibliography: p.594-619

          Includes references to Methodist and other Christian
       missions as well as anti-slavery and slavery in the West Indies.
                                                                UWI-T

1282   PORTER, DALE H.
          The abolition of the slave trade in England, 1784-1807 /
       Dale H. Porter. - [S.l.] : Archon Books, 1970. - xii, 162p.
          Bibliography: p.146-157

          Manuscript and published sources listed separately,
       including several parliamentary papers in chronological order;
       monographs and journal articles in alphabetical author order.
                                                                UWI-T

1283   PRICE, RICHARD
          Maroon societies : rebel slave communities in the
       Americas / edited by Richard Price. - New York : Doubleday,
       1973. - vii, 429p.
          Bibliography: p.404-416

          Includes references to slave revolts in the West Indies
       especially on maroons in Jamaica and the Guianas arranged
       alphabetically by author.
                                                                UWI-T

1284   WILLIAMS, ERIC
          Capitalism and slavery / Eric Williams. - London : Andre
       Deutsch, 1964. - 285p.
          Bibliography: p.262-270

          A bibliographic essay arranged first by sources citing
       specific library and archival collections for manuscripts and
       other primary sources, followed by secondary sources subdivided
       into contemporary and modern. Discusses and evaluates each work
       cited.
                                                                UWI-T

Bermuda

1285   PACKWOOD, CYRIL OUTERBRIDGE
          Chained on the rock : slavery in Bermuda / Cyril Outer-
       bridge Packwood. – New York : Eliseo Torres, 1975. – xii, 226p.
          Bibliography: p.220-222

          Lists published and unpublished primary sources followed
       by books on Bermuda and articles from journals.
                                                                UWI-T

Jamaica

1286   HIGMAN, B.W.
          Slave population and economy in Jamaica, 1807-1834 / B.W.
       Higman. – London : Cambridge University Press, 1976. – vii,
       327p.
          Bibliography: p.311-323

          Arranged by form – manuscripts, official publications,
       maps, etc. – with other primary and secondary source material
       arranged alphabetically by author.
                                                                UWI-T

                    SOCIAL AND ECONOMIC CONDITIONS

1287   ALLEN, DEVERE
          Caribbean : laboratory of world co-operation / Devere
       Allen. – New York : League for Industrial Democracy, 1943. –
       40p.
             On cover: L.I.D. pamphlet series
             Bibliography: p.38-40

                                                                  LC

1288   Bibliographie [sur l'immigration dans les sociétés
       caribéenes]. – p.169-182
             In Actes du XLIIe Congrès International des Américanistes,
       Paris, 2-9 September, 1976. – Paris : Société des Américanistes,
       1977. – Vol.1

                                                          Ref.no.18
                                                              1979

1289   Caribbean Commission
          The Caribbean islands and the war : a record of progress
       in facing stern realities / Caribbean Commission. – Washington,

D.C. : U.S. Government Printing Office, 1943. - v, 85p. -
(U.S. Department of State publication ; no.2023)
     Bibliographical note: p.63-64

LC

1290   EISNER, GISELA
         Jamaica, 1830-1930 : a study in economic growth / by
     Gisela Eisner. - [Manchester, England] : Manchester University
     Press, 1961. - xxiii, 399p.
         Bibliography: p.381-390

         Extensive listings of statistical sources, parliamentary
     and non-parliamentary papers arranged chronologically for govern-
     ment documents and alphabetically by author within four broad
     period divisions for monographs. Book references cover all the
     West Indian islands with some emphasis on Jamaica.

UWI-T

1291   ERICKSEN, E. GORDON
         The West Indies population problem : dimensions for action
     / E. Gordon Ericksen. - Lawrence, Kan. : University of Kansas,
     1962. - 194p. - (The University of Kansas publications.
     Social science studies ; 1962)
         Selected bibliography: p.177-190

         Divided into three sections : (1) Books, (2) Articles,
     (3) Public Documents and Reports. Includes items on population,
     sociology, agriculture, migration, economics, history.

IIR-T

1292   HAWKINS, IRENE
         The changing face of the Caribbean / Irene Hawkins. -
     [Bridgetown], Barbados : Cedar Press, 1976. - xi, 271p.
         Bibliography: p.238-246

         36 selected references in alphabetical author order
     relating to notes on the text followed by general background
     reading suggestions focusing chiefly on social and economic
     conditions including regional integration and finally a listing
     of important statistical sources by country.

UWI-T

1293   HENRY, ZIN
         Labour relations and industrial conflict in Commonwealth
     Caribbean countries / Zin Henry. - [Port of Spain], Trinidad :
     Columbus Publishers, 1972. - xii, 283p.
         Bibliography: p.278-283

Lists books and journal articles separately from government documents and publications, each arranged alphabetically by author or government. Includes references on trade unions and on such leaders as Marcus Garvey and Captain Cipriani.

UWI-T

1294 HEWITT, ARTHUR REGINALD
West Indian immigrants in Great Britain / Arthur Reginald Hewitt. - London : Library Association, 1955. - 5p. - (Library Association. Special subject lists ; no.1)

50 references.

BL

1295 Indexes to reports of commissioners, 1832-1847 : West Indies and Mauritius (labour). - [S.l. : s.n.], 1847. - 187p.

7,500 references.

Ref.no.4
Vol.3, p.3373

1296 MANNERS, R.A.
Remittances and the unit of analysis in anthropological research / R.A. Manners. - p.193-195
In Southwestern journal of anthropology. - Vol.21 (Autumn 1965)

Ref.no.5
1966, p.292

1297 MINTZ, SIDNEY W.
An anthropological approach to the Afro-American past : a Caribbean perspective / Sidney W. Mintz and Richard Price. - Philadelphia, Pa. : Institute for the Study of Human Issues, 1976. - iii, 64p.
Bibliography: p.51-64

162 items include material about the social and economic conditions of the English, French and Dutch Caribbean with emphasis on such subjects as slavery, acculturation and family structure.

UWI-T

1298 O'LOUGHLIN, CARLEEN
Economic and political change in the Leeward and Windward Islands / Carleen O'Loughlin. - New Haven : Yale University Press, 1968. - 260p. - (Caribbean series ; no.10)
Bibliography: p.251-254

Lists government publications for the smaller islands of
the Eastern Caribbean including reports on closer union and on
Eastern Caribbean federation as well as books, articles and
monographs in a separate alphabetical sequence by author.

                                                  UWI-T

1299   PHILPOTT, STUART B.
           West Indian migration : the Montserrat case / Stuart B.
       Philpott. - London : Athlone Press, 1973. - 210p. - (London
       School of Economics monographs on social anthropology ; no.47)
           Bibliography: p.200-205

           Works cited arranged in alphabetical author order.
       Includes books, journal articles and some newspapers.

                                                  UWI-T

1300   Selected bibliography on immigrants and immigration with
       emphasis on West Indian immigrants. - p.10-15
           In Emergency librarian. - Vol.3 (Sept. 1975)

           Annotated.

                                                  Ref.no.5
                                            Aug. 1976, p.206

1301   SENIOR, CLARENCE
           A report on Jamaican migration to Great Britain / Clarence
       Senior and Douglas Manley. - Kingston : Government Printer,
       1955. - ii, 67p.
           Bibliography: p.63-67

           61 items listed include a few on migration from the West
       Indies and West Indians in Britain.

                                                  UWI-T

1302   United States. Department of State. Division of Library and
       Reference Services
           Economic studies of under-developed countries, Latin
       America and the Caribbean / Division of Library and Reference
       Services, Department of State. - [Washington, D.C.] : Division
       of Library and Reference Services, Department of State, 1950.
       - 90 leaves. - (Bibliography ; no.52)
           Cover title

           750 references.

                                                  LC

1303   University of the West Indies (St. Augustine). Institute of
       Social and Economic Research
           Migrant groups in the Caribbean : a topical essay and
       introductory review of the literature ; prepared for a research
       guide to Central America and the Caribbean / by Marianne

Ramesar. - St. Augustine, Trinidad : Institute of Social and
Economic Research, University of the West Indies, 1978. - 23p.
References: p.18-23

Bibliographic essay in two sections : (1) General Studies
on Migration and (2) Studies of Particular Migrant Groups, viz.,
East Indians, Portuguese, Free Africans, Chinese, Europeans,
Javanese and Lebanese. It is followed by a list of 72 references
arranged in similar sections. Predominantly journal articles.

UWI-T

1304 WILLIAMS, ERIC
The negro in the Caribbean / Eric Williams. - Washington,
D.C. : The Associates in Negro Folk Education, 1942. - 199p.
Also published in 1969 : Negro Universities Press and in
1971 : Haskell House Publishers
Bibliography: p.110-117

This select bibliography is in four sections : (A)
Official Reports subdivided into (a) British Islands, (b) American
Islands, (B) Books, (C) Pamphlets, (D) Articles

UWI-T

Barbados

1305 GREENFIELD, SYDNEY M.
English rustics in black skin : a study of modern family
forms in a pre-industrial society / Sydney M. Greenfield. -
New Haven : College and University Press, [c1966]. - 208p.
Bibliography: p.199-202

Ref.no.5
1967, p.23

1306 HANDLER, J.S.
Aspects of slave life in Barbados : music and its cultural
context / J.S. Handler. - p.5-46
In Caribbean studies. - Vol.11, no.4 (Jan. 1972)
Bibliography: p.41-46

Alphabetical author arrangement of 99 items dealing mainly
with the social and economic conditions (including slavery) of
Barbados and the West Indies as a whole.

UWI-T

Belize

1307 BOLLAND, O. NIGEL
       The formation of a colonial society : Belize, from conquest
    to crown colony / O. Nigel Bolland. - Baltimore, Md. : Johns
    Hopkins University Press, 1977. - xiv, 240p.
       Bibliography: p.225-234

       Lists manuscript and printed sources, the latter subdivided
    into books, articles and unpublished theses. Includes both
    contemporary works and modern secondary sources, especially
    articles on slavery, Black Caribs and the Mayas in British
    Honduras.

                                                        UWI-T

1308 BOLLAND, NIGEL
       Land in Belize 1765-1871 / Nigel Bolland and Assad Shoman.
    - [Mona], Jamaica : Institute of Social and Economic Research,
    University of the West Indies, 1977. - 142p. - (Law and society
    in the Caribbean ; no.6)
       Bibliography: p.138-140

       50 references mainly on land use, agricultural policy and
    other aspects of social and economic conditions especially in the
    former colony of British Honduras.

                                                        UWI-T

Guyana

1309 ADAMSON, ALAN H.
       Sugar without slaves : the political economy of British
    Guiana, 1838-1904 / Alan H. Adamson. - New Haven : Yale
    University Press, 1972. - 315p. - (Caribbean series ; no.13)
       Bibliography: p.299-307

       Arranged in general groupings according to form with
    monographs arranged alphabetically by author.

                                                        UWI-T

1310 DAVID, WILFRED L.
       The economic development of Guyana, 1953-1964 / Wilfred L.
    David. - Oxford : Clarendon Press, 1969. - xxi, 399p.
       Bibliography: p.379-387

       Lists the names of government departments and other bodies
    regularly issuing reports followed by specific reports on the
    Guyana economy alphabetically by author or title and other
    publications such as journal articles. Includes general works on
    economic development as a whole in a final section.

                                                        UWI-T

1311 DESPRES, LEO A.
        Cultural pluralism and nationalist politics in British
        Guiana / Leo A. Despres ; with a foreword by M.G. Smith. –
        Chicago : Rand McNally, 1967. – xxx, 310p. – (Rand McNally
        studies in political change)
            Bibliography: p.293–299

        Lists books, articles, periodicals and reports separately
    and alphabetically by author within each group. Includes
    references to racial groups in Guyana and the West Indies as a
    whole.

                                                                UWI-T

1312 GLASGOW, ROY ARTHUR
        Guyana : race and politics among Africans and East Indians
        / Roy Arthur Glasgow. – The Hague : Martinus Nijhoff, 1977. –
        153p. – (Studies in social life ; 14)
            Bibliography: p.147–153

        Arranged by form in seven sections including books,
    publications of government, learned societies and other organi-
    zations, periodical articles, essays and articles in collections,
    unpublished papers and theses, newspapers. Items listed range
    over several subjects tangential to the text.

                                                                UWI-T

1313 JAYAWARDENA, CHANDRA
        Conflict and solidarity in a Guianese plantation / Chandra
        Jayawardena. – [London] : University of London, The Athlone
        Press, 1963. – 159p. – (Monographs on social anthropology ;
        no.25)
            Bibliography: p.151–154

        Includes references to coolie immigrants and special
    reports on Guyana.

                                                                UWI-T

1314 MANDLE, JAY R.
        The plantation economy : population and economic change in
        Guyana 1838–1960 / Jay R. Mandle. – Philadelphia : Temple
        University Press, 1973. – xv, 170p.
            Bibliography: p.159–166

        129 references to books, journal articles and several
    government reports and papers arranged alphabetically by author.
    Topics covered include sugar and rice industries, economy,
    agriculture, population.

                                                                UWI-T

Jamaica

1315 CAMPBELL, MAVIS CHRISTINE
        The dynamics of change in a slave society : a socio-
political history of the free coloreds of Jamaica, 1800-1865 /
Mavis Christine Campbell. - Rutherford, [N.J.] : Fairleigh
Dickinson University Press, 1976. - 393p.
        Bibliography: p.372-386

        Arranged by type of source - original correspondence,
contemporary and earlier works, newspapers and modern works in
alphabetical author order, some with brief critical notes.
                                                        UWI-T

1316 GERLING, WALTER
        Wirtschaftsentwicklung und Landschaftswandel auf den
westindischen Inseln Jamaika, Haiti und Puerto Rico ; Beitrag
zu spanischen, franzöischen, englischen und amerikanischen
kolonisations Methoden in Westindien / Walter Gerling. -
Freiburg i.Ba. : C. Sintermann, 1938. - 262p. - (Ver öffent-
lichungen des Instituts fur Amerika forschung an der
Universität Würzburg. - (Neue Folge der "Studien über Amerika
und Spanien" ; 1)
        Bibliography: p.41-262.
                                                        UWI-J

1317 KUPER, ADAM
        Changing Jamaica / Adam Kuper. - London : Routledge and
Kegan Paul, 1976. - 163p.
        Bibliography: p.156-160

        Alphabetical author listing of books, articles and signed
reports with a separate brief section for unsigned official
reports.
                                                        UWI-T

1318 PALMER, RANSFORD W.
        The Jamaican economy / Ransford W. Palmer. - New York :
Praeger, [1968]. - xvi, 185p. - (Praeger special studies in
international economics and development)
        Bibliography: p.179-185

        Lists reports and official documents separately from
books, followed by articles and periodicals.
                                                        UWI-T

1319 WRIGHT, RICHARDSON LITTLE
        Revels in Jamaica, 1682-1838 ; plays and players of a
century, tumblers and conjurers, musical refugees and solitary
showmen, dinners, balls and cockfights, darky mummers and

other memories of high times and merry hearts / Richardson
Little Wright. - New York : Dodd, Mead, 1937. - xiiip., 1 leaf,
378p.
       Bibliography: p.339-357

       Bibliography arranged in sections corresponding to the
chapters of the book consists mainly of items on the social and
economic conditions of Jamaica, but includes some historical and
descriptive works.

                                                UWI-T

Trinidad and Tobago

1320   BRERETON, BRIDGET
       Race relations in colonial Trinidad, 1870-1900 / Bridget
Brereton. - London : Cambridge University Press, 1979. - ix,
251p.
       Bibliography: p.238-243

       Items arranged under sections : (a) Primary Sources,
which include manuscripts, parliamentary papers, local commissions,
Trinidad newspapers, contemporary books and articles, and (b)
Secondary Sources, comprising books, articles and unpublished
theses and papers.

                                                  UWI-T

1321   KLASS, MORTON
       East Indians in Trinidad : a study of cultural persistence
/ Morton Klass. - New York : Columbia University Press, 1961. -
265p.
       Bibliography: p.251-256

       Arranged alphabetically by author with date of publication
highlighted. Includes journal articles and a few unpublished
papers.

                                                  UWI-T

1322   LA GUERRE, JOHN GAFFAR
       Calcutta to Caroni : the East Indians of Trinidad ;
studies / edited by John Gaffar La Guerre. - London : Longman
Caribbean, 1974. - xix, 111p.
       Bibliography: p.108-111

       Select listing in five sequences covering (1) books, (2)
articles, periodicals and pamphlets, (3) theses and unpublished
work, (4) weeklies, monthlies, newsletters and (5) reports and
official documents.

                                                  UWI-T

1323 University of Puerto Rico. Institute of Caribbean Studies
       The East Indian indenture in Trinidad / by Judith Ann
   Weller. - Rio Piedras, Puerto Rico : Institute of Caribbean
   Studies, University of Puerto Rico, 1968. - xxii, 172p. -
   (Caribbean monograph series ; no.4)
       Bibliography: p.169-172

       Lists books in alphabetical author order followed by some
   public documents available locally and two newspaper titles.
                                                              UWI-T

1324 WOOD, DONALD
       Trinidad in transition : the years after slavery / Donald
   Wood. - London : Oxford University Press for the Institute of
   Race Relations, 1968. - x, 318p.
       Bibliography: p.306-310

       Lists 19 local newspaper titles followed by books,
   articles and pamphlets mainly on Trinidad in alphabetical author
   order. Includes references to the history of ethnic groups in
   Trinidad.
                                                              UWI-T

                    SOCIAL AND ECONOMIC DEVELOPMENT

1325 BECKFORD, GEORGE L.
       Persistent poverty : under-development in the plantation
   economies of the Third World / George L. Beckford. - New York
   : Oxford University Press, 1972. - xxvii, 303p.
       Bibliography: p.287-296

       Alphabetical author listing of books, journal articles
   and conference papers including some references to plantation
   systems, agriculture, land use and the sugar industry in the
   economy of the Caribbean region as part of the Third World.
                                                              UWI-T

1326 BRYDEN, JOHN M.
       Tourism and development : a case study of the Commonwealth
   Caribbean / John M. Bryden. - Cambridge : University Press,
   1973. - xii, 236p.
       Bibliography: p.222-227

       Lists in one sequence, alphabetically by author (or "where
   no author is given, under the sponsoring organisation or
   publisher") books, journal articles, theses, speeches, government reports and serial titles, including conference proceedings
   and other official or semi-official publications in series.
                                                              UWI-T

1327   Caribbean Commission. Central Secretariat
            The promotion of industrial development in the Caribbean /
       Caribbean Commission Central Secretariat. - Port of Spain,
       Trinidad : Caribbean Commission, 1952. - 172p.
            Bibliography: p.167-172

            Lists relevant Commission and Colonial Development and
       Welfare Organization publications as well as legislation under
       the several member territories followed by development plans for
       each and general listing of U.N. reports. Includes miscellaneous
       items on industrialization.

                                                                 UWI-T

1328   Caribbean Organization. Library
            Bibliography of development plans / Caribbean Organization
       Library. - Puerto Rico : Central Secretariat, Caribbean
       Organization, 1963. - 9p.
            Mimeographed

            Arranged by country and includes the countries served by
       the Organization.

                                                                 UWI-T

1329   Economic and social development in the Caribbean : selected
       holdings of the Library, Institute of Social and Economic
       Research, UWI, Mona, Jamaica
            In IDRC Library Bulletin, vol.4, no.8 (30 Apr. 1975). -
       78p.

            A special issue of the Bulletin devoted to selections from
       ISER lists of additions between 1968 and 1974. Items listed
       primarily on development in the Caribbean area, Latin America and
       the Third World. Classified arrangement with broad subject
       headings with author, subject and title indexes. Classification
       numbers are included. Covers subjects such as population, labour,
       education, commerce, culture, agriculture, industries, regional,
       urban and rural planning, history and geography.

                                                                 UWI-T

1330   GIRLING, R.K.
            Technology and dependent development in Jamaica : a case
       study / R.K. Girling. - p.169-189
            In Social and economic studies. - Vol.26, no.2 (June 1977)
            References: p.186-189

            69 references to journal articles, books and a few
       unpublished items cited in the text.

                                                                 UWI-T

1331   JEFFERSON, OWEN
       Caribbean economic problems : reading list / Owen
       Jefferson. - p.159-171
       In Caribbean economy : dependence and backwardness / edited
       by George L. Beckford. - Mona, Jamaica : Institute of Social
       and Economic Research, University of the West Indies, 1975

       A basic and introductory list of readings used for an
       undergraduate course on Caribbean political economy. Subdivided
       into several sections including sector studies (agriculture,
       tourism, industrialization, etc.), and problem areas and policy
       issues such as income distribution, fiscal policy, foreign
       investment and economic planning.

                                                                UWI-T

1331a United Nations. Economic Commission for Latin America.
       Office for the Caribbean
       Bibliography : Planning / prepared by United Nations
       Economic Commission for Latin America Office for the Caribbean.
       - Port of Spain, Trinidad and Tobago : Office for the
       Caribbean, U.N. Economic Commission for Latin America, 1982. -
       iv, 40p.

       95 entries covering topics such as planning in the agri-
       cultural, economic, educational, food/nutrition, industrial,
       manpower spheres, national, regional and physical planning.
       Abstracts and locations are given. Author, geographic location,
       subject and title indexes provided. Includes material on non-
       English-speaking territories.

                                                                UWI-T

1331b United Nations. Economic Commission for Latin America.
       Office for the Caribbean. Caribbean Documentation Centre
       Select bibliography on coastal area development and
       environmental, physical and regional planning in the Caribbean
       region / Caribbean Documentation Centre, United Nations ECLA
       Office for the Caribbean. - [S.l.]: Caribbean Documentation
       Centre, United Nations ECLA Office for the Caribbean, 1980. -
       9p. - (CEPAL,CARIB 80/10)

       100 entries arranged alphabetically by author within
       subject groupings : Coastal Area Development, Environmental
       Planning, Marine Resources, Physical and Regional Planning,
       Ports and Harbours. Includes journal articles, government publi-
       cations, publications of international organizations including
       those of the United Nations. Locations are provided.

                                                                UWI-T

Guyana

1332 Guyana. Ministry of Education and Social Development
         Ministry of Education and Social Development reports. -
      [S.l. : s.n.], [1977]. - 4p.
         Mimeographed

                                                                    UG

1333 HINDS, YVONNE
         Industrial development in Guyana : a preliminary biblio-
      graphy / compiled by Yvonne Hinds and C. Knee. - Georgetown :
      National Science Research Council, 1978. - 10p.
         Mimeographed

                                                          Ref.no.73
                                                          1978, p.3

1334 ODLE, MAURICE A.
         The evolution of public expenditure : (the case of a
      structurally dependent economy : Guyana) / Maurice A. Odle. -
      [Mona], Jamaica : Institute of Social and Economic Research,
      University of the West Indies, 1976. - xvi, 271p.
         Bibliography: p.257-266

         157 references to reports and official publications of
      Guyana government agencies and bodies, and to studies related to
      the Guyana economy in monographs and journals followed by a more
      general list of works quoted in the text.

                                                                UWI-T

1335 University of Wisconsin. Land Tenure Center. Library
         Rural development in Venezuela and the Guianas : a
      bibliography of materials dealing with Venezuela and the
      Guianas in the Land Tenure Center Library. - Madison, Wis. :
      [Land Tenure Center Library, University of Wisconsin], 1972. -
      67p. - (Training and methods series ; 20)

                                                                 LTCL

Jamaica

1336 CLARKE, COLIN G.
         Kingston, Jamaica : urban development and social change,
      1692-1962 / Colin G. Clarke. - Berkeley : University of
      California Press, 1975. - xi, 270p. - (American Geographical
      Society research series ; no.27)
         Bibliography: p.257-266

         Simple alphabetical author arrangement of extensive list
      of books, articles, theses and reports mainly on Jamaica with a
      few items on the West Indies as a whole.

                                                                UWI-T

1337   GIRVAN, NORMAN
         Foreign capital and economic under-development in Jamaica
     / Norman Girvan. - [Mona], Jamaica : Institute of Social and
     Economic Research, University of the West Indies, 1971. - xvii,
     [1], 282p.
         Bibliography: p.269-278

         Alphabetical author listing of books, papers and journal
     articles with a short section on statistical sources.
                                                          UWI-T

1338   JEFFERSON, OWEN
         The post-war economic development of Jamaica / Owen
     Jefferson. - [Mona], Jamaica : Institute of Social and Economic
     Research, University of the West Indies, 1972. - xv, 302p.
         Bibliography: p.287-297

         Lists reports of commissions of enquiry followed by
     government serial titles and other government publications
     relevant to the Jamaican economy. Includes two lists of relevant
     secondary materials, mainly journal articles on the Jamaican
     economy in the penultimate, and on general problems of economic
     development in the final section.
                                                          UWI-T

1339   WALSH, B. THOMAS
         Economic development and population control : a fifty-year
     projection for Jamaica / B. Thomas Walsh. - New York :
     Praeger, 1971. - xiii, 134p. - (Praeger special studies in
     international economics and development)
         Bibliography: p.125-134

         Arranged alphabetically by author.
                                                          UWI-T

1340   WIDDICOMBE, STACEY H.
         The performance of industrial development corporations :
     the case of Jamaica / Stacey H. Widdicombe, Jr. - New York :
     Praeger, 1972. - xxvi, 418p. - (Praeger special studies in
     international economics and development)
         Bibliography: p.409-418

         Lists Jamaica IDC reports and publications and other
     official reports and publications on finance, industry and
     development in Jamaica with more general books and periodical
     articles separately listed in alphabetical author order.
                                                          UWI-T

St. Lucia

1341   WEISBROD, BURTON A.
       Disease and economic development : the impact of parasitic
       diseases in St. Lucia / Burton A. Weisbrod et al. - [Madison,
       Wis.] : University of Wisconsin Press, 1973. - xvii, 218p.
       Bibliography: p.197-213

       Over 150 references to works on health, economics and
   specific tropical diseases followed by 30 items on St. Lucia and
   the West Indies (p.208-210).

                                                               UWI-T

Trinidad and Tobago

1342   Trinidad and Tobago. Ministry of Planning and Development.
       Library
       Chaguaramas : development plans / Ministry of Planning
       and Development. - [Port of Spain, Trinidad] : Ministry of
       Planning and Development, [197-?]. - 1p.

       Nine items. Prepared for a proposed bibliography of
   Trinidad and Tobago.

                                                               MF-T

SOCIAL SCIENCES

1343   BRUNN, STANLEY
       Urbanization in developing countries : an international
       bibliography / by Stanley Brunn. - East Lansing : Latin
       American Studies Center, Michigan State University, 1971. -
       xviii, 693p. - (Latin American Studies Center research report ;
       no.8)

       Includes a separate section on the West Indies.

                                                                 LC

1344   California State University. Latin American Studies Center
       Black Latin America : a bibliography / Latin American
       Studies Center, California State University. - Los Angeles :
       Latin American Studies Center, California State University,
       1977. - 73p. - (Latin America bibliography series ; no.5)

The bibliography is based on a course on Black Latin
America and it was developed in anticipation of the first
congress of black culture in the Americas in Cali, Colombia.
Although intended to cover all fields in the social sciences and
the humanities, coverage of the former is fuller. Arranged in
broad geographical sections subdivided by country. Includes
sections on Jamaica (40 refs.), Trinidad and Tobago (22 refs.),
British West Indies (84 refs.), and Caribbean general (40 refs.)
which are subdivided into books and articles, the latter
including sections of books. Listings concentrate on works
available in the U.S.

UWI-J

1345 CRAHAN, MARGARET E.
        Africa and the Caribbean : the legacies of a link / edited
      by Margaret E. Crahan and Franklin W. Knight. - Baltimore ;
      London : The Johns Hopkins University Press, 1979. - xii,
      159p. - (Johns Hopkins studies in Atlantic history and culture)
        Select bibliography: p.146-157

        Includes monographs and periodical articles on the English-
speaking territories. Items cover culture, folklore, religion,
slavery and slave trade, language and the African influence.

UWI-T

1345a ELLIS, MAUREEN YVONNE
        Family structure, fertility and family planning programs
      in the West Indies : a bibliography essay / Maureen Yvonne
      Ellis. - [S.l. : s.n.], 1972. - vi, 101 leaves
        Bibliography: p.91-101

        A thesis presented to the Faculty of the Graduate School
of Cornell University for the degree of Master of Arts. Surveys
all the major studies for the English speaking Caribbean
"including foundation, government and private organization
reports." Bibliography of 120 items arranged alphabetically by
author.

UWI-T

1346 FRUCHT, RICHARD
        Black society in the New World / edited ... by Richard
      Frucht. - New York : Random House, 1971. - xi, 403p.
        Bibliography: p.394-403

        Arranged according to the subject sections into which the
book is divided and then alphabetically by author. Subjects
include slavery, plantations, black peasantry, race and class
relations, family and interpersonal relations, religion and
black power. Each section includes more general works as well as
some specifically on the Caribbean.

UWI-T

1347   LOWENTHAL, DAVID
        West Indian societies / David Lowenthal. - London : Oxford
University Press for the Institute of Race Relations, London,
in collaboration with the American Geographical Society, New
York, 1972. - viii, 385p.
        Bibliography: p.324-373

        Lists newspapers and periodicals dealing mainly with the
West Indies by title with publisher, frequency, date of publication and location followed by references to books, articles,
theses and reports in a single alphabetical sequence by author.
Chapters in the main work cover topics such as history, social
structure, ethnic groups, emigration, racial and national
identity.

                                                              UWI-T

1348   Research Institute for the Study of Man
        A selected bibliography on culture and society in the
Caribbean / Research Institute for the Study of Man. - [New
York : Research Institute for the Study of Man], 1964. - 52p.
        Mimeographed

        The bibliography covers a wide range of subjects
including archaeology, ethnohistory, language studies, demography,
religion, magic, socio-economic and socio-political patterns.
Items are arranged alphabetically by author within subject groups.
                                                              UWI-T

1349   ROSE, E.J.B.
        Colour and citizenship : a report on British race relations
/ E.J.B. Rose and others. - London : Oxford University Press
for the Institute of Race Relations, 1969. - 815p.
        Bibliography: p.797-804

        Books and articles listed separately from official
publications, the former arranged alphabetically by author and
the latter by title.

                                                              UWI-T

1350   Royal Institute of Linguistics and Anthropology
        Inventory of Caribbean studies : an overview of social
research on the Caribbean conducted by Antillean, Dutch and
Surinamese scholars in the period 1945-1973 with an index of
Caribbean specialists and a bibliography / [compiled by René
Mevis ; translated by Michael Hoyle]. - Leiden : Caribbean
Department, Royal Institute of Linguistics and Anthropology,
[1974]. - 181p.
        Bibliography: p.148-178

Oriented mainly towards the Netherlands Antilles but includes research on some English-speaking territories especially Guyana and Jamaica. Alphabetical author listing in chronological sequence for each and a separate list of unpublished graduate theses by Antillean, Dutch and Surinamese students.

UWI-T

1350a Royal Institute of Linguistics and Anthropology
       Inventory of Caribbean studies : an overview of social
       scientific publications on the Caribbean by Antillean, Dutch
       and Surinamese authors in the period 1945-1978/79 / Theo M.P.
       Oltheten. - Leiden, Netherlands : Royal Institute of Linguistics
       and Anthropology, 1979. - 280p.

       Continuation of Ref.no.1350. Author alphabetical listing
of publications mainly on the Netherlands Antilles and Surinam but
includes some entries on the Caribbean in general with items on
Guyana, Jamaica, Barbados, and Trinidad and Tobago.

UWI-T

1351   United States. Department of State. Office of External
       Research
       American republics : a list of current social science
       research by private scholars and academic centers / Office of
       External Research, Department of State. - Washington, D.C. :
       Office of External Research, Department of State, 1968. -
       104p. - (External research list ; no.227)

       The last of an annual series of lists published for 18
years to disseminate information on "research in progress [and
completed] dealing with foreign areas and international affairs."
Compiled from information submitted by scholars and research
centers in the U.S. and including annotations. Arranged by
subject and individual countries. Coverage includes British
Honduras, Guyana, Jamaica, Trinidad and Tobago and the West
Indies generally.

UWI-T

1352   University of Sussex. Institute of Development Studies
       Village studies : data analysis and bibliography /
       compiled at the Institute of Development Studies, University
       of Sussex by Mick Moore, John Connell and Claire M. Lambert.
       - London : Mansell, 1978
       Vol.2 : Africa, Middle East and North Africa, Asia
       (excluding India), Pacific Islands, Latin America, West
       Indies and the Caribbean, 1950-1975. - 348p.

       Information on studies of single villages in the form of
an annotated bibliography. Studies on social science and land
use with social anthropology as one of the largest categories.

Titles listed alphabetically by author/institution with topics,
author and institution indexes.

UWI-T

1353   University of the West Indies (Cave Hill). Institute of
        Social and Economic Research (Eastern Caribbean)
            A bibliography of the Commonwealth Caribbean peasantry,
        1838-1974 / compiled by Trevor G. Marshall. - Cave Hill,
        Barbados : Institute of Social and Economic Research (Eastern
        Caribbean), University of the West Indies, 1975. - 47 leaves.
        - (Occasional bibliography series ; no.3)

            A reference guide to research on the subject this is part
        of a larger project on a history of Caribbean peasantry since
        1838. Listings under economic, sociological and historical
        categories in alphabetical author order under territory subdivi-
        sions. Includes contributions from the U.W.I., St. Augustine
        library, the Barbados Public Library and the Public Archives of
        Barbados.

UWI-T

1354   University of the West Indies (Mona). Department of Social
        and Preventive Medicine. Family Planning/Epidemiology Unit
            West Indian family planning bibliography (1954-1974) /
        U.W.I. Department of Social and Preventive Medicine. - Mona,
        Jamaica : Family Planning/Epidemiology Unit, Department of
        Social and Preventive Medicine, U.W.I., 1976. - iii, [1], 75p.
            Mimeographed

            A listing of 350 references. Arranged under sections :
        Social, Psychological and Cultural, Organizational, Political,
        Evaluation of Programme, Clinical, Communication, Education,
        Demography, Economics, Medical Care and Family Planning,
        Conferences and Reports, Student Group Projects - Social and
        Preventive Medicine. Includes many journal articles and theses.
        Author index and locations provided. Areas covered are Jamaica,
        Barbados, Guyana, Trinidad and the general Caribbean with a few
        items on British Honduras, the Bahamas and the non-English-
        speaking Caribbean.

UWI-T

1355   University of the West Indies (Mona). Institute of Social
        and Economic Research
            An annotated bibliography of social work : research papers,
        1963-1972 / Erna Brodber. - [Mona, Jamaica] : ISER, 1976. -
        26p.
            Mimeographed

A chronological listing of 139 research papers prepared by
social welfare students at the University in fulfillment of the
requirements for the certificate in social work. Arrangement is
alphabetical within each year and symbols are used to indicate
the general area of social welfare concern in each case.

UWI-J

1356 University of the West Indies (St. Augustine). Department of
      Sociology
      Caribbean social structure : selected bibliography /
      Department of Sociology, U.W.I. - [St. Augustine, Trinidad :
      Department of Sociology, The University of the West Indies],
      1970. - 24p.

      Prepared for use by undergraduates at U.W.I. Alphabetical
author listing by subject. Includes many journal articles.

UWI-T

1357 University of the West Indies (St. Augustine). Institute of
      Social and Economic Research
      A bibliography of publications and inventory of reports
      and studies relating to human resources in the Commonwealth
      Caribbean : Stage 1 - Material located in Trinidad and
      Tobago / by Marianne Ramesar. - St. Augustine, Trinidad :
      Institute of Social and Economic Research, University of the
      West Indies, 1978. - 68p.
      Mimeographed

      Arranged under broad subject groupings such as economic
development, statistics, manpower and employment, education and
training, migration and brain drain and by countries within each
of these groups with locations spanning 10 collections in
Trinidad and Tobago.

UWI-T

1358 University of the West Indies (St. Augustine). Institute of
      Social and Economic Research
      A select bibliography of publications and studies
      relating to human resources in the Commonwealth Caribbean :
      material available in Trinidad and Tobago / compiled by
      Marianne Ramesar. - St. Augustine, Trinidad : Institute of
      Social and Economic Research, University of the West Indies,
      1981. - xiv, 127p. - (Human resources ; 3)

      755 items arranged under chapter headings subdivided into
geographical categories : Manpower and Employment, Including
Unemployment, Industrial Relations, Trade Unions, Social
Security, Attitude to Work, Career Aspirations and Discrimination
in Employment, Education and Training, Population, Social Organization and Welfare, Migration and Urbanisation, Economic
Development and Income Distribution, Industrial and Agricultural

Development and Employment, The Character of Labour Force Data.
Locations span 10 collections in Trinidad and Tobago.

UWI-T

1359   University of the West Indies (St. Augustine). Library
           The family in the Caribbean : a list of references to
       literature held in the Library, U.W.I., St. Augustine. - St.
       Augustine, Trinidad : Library, The University of the West
       Indies, 1979. - 6p.

           53 items arranged under subject headings - General, The
       East Indian Family, Family Life Education, Family Planning,
       Mating Patterns, Population Studies. Periodical articles and
       conference proceedings are included.

UWI-T

Indexes
1360   AIRS : index to the Daily Gleaner / West India Reference
       Library, Institute of Jamaica. - October-December, 1975- . -
       [Kingston, Jamaica] : West India Reference Library, Institute
       of Jamaica, 1976-
           Quarterly

           Concentrates on information pertaining to important social,
       economic and political affairs in the Caribbean. Entries include
       date, page and column number, Caribbean geographic code,
       identification tag for type of article, title, subject headings
       and keywords in context.

UWI-T

1361   Association of Caribbean University, Research and Institutional
       Libraries (ACURIL). Indexing Committee (English-speaking area)
           CARINDEX : Social sciences / ACURIL Indexing Committee. -
       Vol.1, no.1 (1977)- . - St. Augustine, Trinidad : ACURIL
       Indexing Committee (English-speaking area), 1977-
           Bi-annual

           An outgrowth of Evelyn's West Indian Social Sciences Index
       (Ref.no.1363), this is a subject guide to Caribbean periodical
       literature in the social sciences with an author index. Issues
       subsequent to the first cover most of the region's current social
       science periodicals and some newspapers (including one daily -
       the Trinidad Guardian). A few titles are indexed cover to cover
       while many others are done on a selective basis through coopera-
       tive regional effort coordinated by an editorial committee in
       Trinidad. Two-column entries per page using Library of Congress
       subject headings expanded or modified as necessary.

UWI-T

1362   Association of Caribbean University, Research and Institu-
       tional Libraries (ACURIL). Indexing Committee (English-
       speaking area)
           CARINDEX : social sciences; special issue, 1978 ; an
       index to book reviews in selected Caribbean periodicals /
       compiled by Kaye Larbi. - St. Augustine, Trinidad : ACURIL
       Indexing Committee (English-speaking area), 1978. - v, 72p.
           Index to 14 periodicals

           Concentrates on periodicals not normally covered by
       standard indexing services, although other journals are included.
       Arranged alphabetically by author of the book reviewed or in the
       case of a periodical by title. Each item gives the title of book
       reviewed, name of reviewer and title of journal in which the
       review appears, with full bibliographic details. Covers 1942 to
       1977.
                                                                   UWI-T

1363   EVELYN, SHIRLEY
           West Indian social sciences index : an index to Moko, New
       World Quarterly, Savacou, Tapia, 1963-1972 / prepared by
       Shirley Evelyn with an introduction by Gordon Rohlehr. - St.
       Augustine, Trinidad : [The author], 1974. - ix, 117p.

           An author and subject index to four "little" magazines/
       newspapers and their occasional publications appearing in the
       period specified.
                                                                   UWI-T

1364   Naciones Unidas. CEPAL/CLADES
           Cladindex : resúmenes de documentos CEPAL/ILPES 1970/1976
       / CEPAL/CLADES. - Vol.1, No.1 (1977)- . - Santiago de Chile :
       CEPAL/CLADES, Naciones Unidas, 1978-
           Bi-annual
           Part 1 : Abstracts. - Part 2 : Indexes
           From vol.3, no.1 (1980) continued by: Cepalindex

           The listing and abstracts are intended to cover all the
       publications of ECLA and English-speaking Caribbean territories
       are included in its scope. Indexes are provided by descriptor,
       author, institution, title, UN symbol, series, conference, and
       by country.
                                                                   UWI-T

1365   United Nations. Economic Commission for Latin America. Office
       for the Caribbean. Caribbean Development and Cooperation
       Committee
           CARISPLAN abstracts / Caribbean Development and Cooperation
       Committee. - No.1 (1980)- . - Port of Spain, Trinidad : CDCC,
       1980-
           Bi-annual

Computer-produced listing of documents produced by the Office relating to planning and development in the Caribbean. Entries for subsequent issues are supplied by national planning agencies in member states of the CDCC "organized in categories that represent the purpose for which the document was written". Indexes are provided by author, institution, conference, UN symbol, subject and country.

UWI-T

1366   University of the West Indies (Mona). Institute of Social and Economic Research
Social and economic studies : author and keyword index ; volumes 1-26, 1953-1977 / compiled by Reivé Robb as part of the DOERS project. - Mona, [Jamaica] : Institute of Social and Economic Research, U.W.I., 1980. - 280p.

Consists of a single author and keyword index arranged alphabetically. Produced by computer, it will be updated by annual indexes and future cumulations. The index is part of a bigger project which includes the establishment of a Data Bank and Documentation Centre, undertaken by the Institute to improve its research and documentation facilities.

UWI-T

1367   University of the West Indies (Mona). Institute of Social and Economic Research
Social and economic studies author index 1953-1957 / Fred Nunes. - Kingston : Institute of Social and Economic Research, University of the West Indies, 1979. - 98p. - (Working paper ; no.23)

In addition to the alphabetical author index entries, there are sections covering book reviews and review articles and special issues. The sections dealing with special issues are arranged firstly by titles of issues under broad subject headings and then by contents of issue under broad subject headings.

UWI-T

Periodicals and Serials
1368   Committee on Latin America
Latin American economic and social serials / Committee on Latin America. - London : Bingley, 1969. - 189p.

Arranged in groups by geographic area including individual Caribbean territories and groups such as Windward Islands, with UK library holdings indicated. Alphabetical title arrangement in each area listing is supplemented by a title index.

UWI-T

1369   FERGUSON, CYNTHIA T.
          Periodicals in social science : a classified guide to
       periodicals available in the University of the West Indies
       Library and the Institute of Social and Economic Research
       Library / compiled by Cynthia T. Ferguson. - Kingston :
       [s.n.], 1972. - 9p.
          Mimeographed

          Commissioned by Sangster's University Bookshop Ltd.
                                                         Ref.no.80

Guyana

1370   Guyana. Public Free Library
          Family life and child rearing in Guyana / Public Free
       Library. - Georgetown : Public Free Library, 1971. - 2 leaves
          Typescript

          Compiled in response to an enquiry. Includes books and
       periodical articles.
                                                              NLG

1371   MITCHELL, WILLIAM B.
          Area handbook for Guyana / William B. Mitchell and others ;
       prepared for the American University by Johnson Research
       Associates. - Washington, D.C. : U.S. Government Printing
       Office, 1969. - xiv, 378p. - (DA Pam 550-82)
          Bibliography: p.351-367

          Entries are grouped under four major subject headings -
       Social, Political, Economic and National Security; each section
       is further subdivided into recommended and other sources each
       arranged alphabetically by author.
                                                            UWI-T

1372   Social science bibliography of the Linden area. - p.127-129
          In Guyana journal of sociology. - Vol.1, no.1 (Oct. 1975)
                                                              NLG

Jamaica

1373   GILMORE, WILLIAM C.
          Towards a bibliography on Jamaican social problems /
       William C. Gilmore. - [Cave Hill, Barbados] : Faculty of Law,
       University of the West Indies, [1974]. - 2, 5p.
          Mimeographed

99 entries comprising books, monographs, unpublished material and journal articles, mainly from Social and Economic Studies.

UWI-B

1374   KAPLAN, IRVING
        Area handbook for Jamaica / Irving Kaplan and others ... ; prepared by Foreign Area Studies (FAS) of the American University. - Washington, D.C. : U.S. Government Printing Office, 1976. - xii, 332p. - (DA Pam 550-177)
        Bibliography: p.287-313

        Entries are grouped under four major subject headings : Social, Political, Economic, and National Security. Alphabetical author arrangement within each section.

UWI-T

1375   SMITH, M.G.
        A framework for Caribbean studies / by M.G. Smith. - Mona, [Jamaica] : The Extra Mural Department, University of the West Indies, [195-?]. - 70p. - (Caribbean affairs)
        Bibliography: p.66-70

        Arranged alphabetically by author it includes a few items on social structure and organization in Jamaica.

UWI-T

Trinidad and Tobago

1376   BLACK, JAN KNIPPERS
        Area handbook for Trinidad and Tobago / Jan Knippers Black, Howard I. Blutstein, Kathryn Therese Johnston [and] David S. McMorris ; [prepared by Foreign Area Studies (FAS) of the American University]. - Washington, D.C. : U.S. Government Printing Office, 1979. - xiv, 304p.
        Bibliography: p.261-301

        Extensive alphabetical author listings in four sections. Works on the social, political and economic and national security aspects of Trinidad and Tobago.

UWI-T

1377   LEVIN, DANIEL
        Susu and investment in Trinidad : a pilot survey of the rotating credit association / Daniel Levin. - Hockessin, Del. : [The author], 1973. - 96p.
        Photocopy of mimeographed paper
        Bibliography: p.85-96

Listings arranged alphabetically by author in two sections - methodology references on sou-sou and credit associations, and field references giving background information on the society studied. Includes unpublished theses and several journal articles on Trinidad and the West Indies social and economic patterns.

UWI-T

SOCIOLOGY

Grenada

1378 Bibliography on Grenada : works of sociological interest. - p.69-70
In Caribbean quarterly. - Vol.20, no.1 (Mar. 1974)

29 items arranged alphabetically by author.

UWI-T

SPIRITUALISM

1379 ZARETSKY, IRVING I.
Spirit possession and spirit mediumship in Africa and Afro-America : an annotated bibliography / Irving I. Zaretsky and Cynthia Shambaugh. - New York : Garland Publishers, 1978. - xxii, 443p. - (Garland reference library of social sciences; v.56)

This annotated bibliography presents a comprehensive guide to source material on the spirit cults of Africa and Afro-America. In addition to the over 2,000 citations, indices classify cited materials by subject, ethnic group, political unit, and geographical region. A list of periodicals investigated enables future researchers to avoid needless duplication of the efforts of the authors.

LC

STATISTICS

1380   MORAIS, ALLAN I.
        Useful sources of Caribbean statistics / Allan I. Morais. -
        p.7-9, 24
        In Caribbean Commission monthly information bulletin. -
        Vol.7, no.1 (Aug. 1953)

                                                        Ref.no.92
                                                Vol.1, Item 1.0193

1381   United Nations. Economic Commission for Latin America. Office
        for the Caribbean
        A directory of major statistical publications / Office for
        the Caribbean, ECLA. - Port of Spain, Trinidad and Tobago :
        Economic Commission for Latin America Office for the Caribbean,
        1981. - 23p. - (CEPAL/CARIB 81/2)

            Arranged by subjects : Agriculture, Forestry and Fishing,
        Demographic and Social Statistics, External Trade - Imports and
        Exports, Finance, Industrial Statistics - Mining, Manufacturing
        and Construction, National Accounts and Balance of Payments,
        Prices, Transport, Storage and Communication, Tourism, and within
        these alphabetically by country. Includes French and Spanish-
        speaking Caribbean.

                                                            UWI-T

1382   United Nations. Economic Commission for Latin America. Office
        for the Caribbean
        Economic activity - 1976 - in Caribbean countries /
        prepared by Economic Affairs Officers ... ECLA Office for the
        Caribbean. - [Port of Spain, Trinidad] : ECLA Office for the
        Caribbean, [1977]. - (various pagings)

            Includes a three-page "selected list of statistical
        publications and sources" arranged by country covering all the
        member countries of the Caribbean Development and Cooperation
        Committee (CDCC) for which the ECLA Office serves as Secretariat.
                                                            UWI-T

Trinidad and Tobago

1382a   Trinidad and Tobago. Ministry of Finance. Library
        Sources of statistical information : Trinidad and Tobago /
        P. Raymond. - Port of Spain, Trinidad and Tobago : Ministry of
        Finance, 1980. - 20p.

Alphabetical title list of 194 government publications.
Includes items on agriculture, censuses, education, revenue and
expenditure, gross domestic product, travel, labour force, manpower, national income, overseas trade, tourism, and industry.

UWI-T

1383   Trinidad and Tobago. Ministry of Planning and Development.
       Library
              Sources of statistical information / Ministry of Planning
       and Development Library. - [Port of Spain, Trinidad] : Ministry
       of Planning and Development Library, 1979. - 20p.
              Mimeographed

              Mainly Central Statistical Office publications with some
       Central Bank statistical publications and other items containing
       important statistics.

MF-T

TOURISM

1384   Institute of Jamaica
              Tourism : a reading list compiled from the collection of
       the West India Reference Library / by A. Silvera. - Kingston :
       Institute of Jamaica, 1974. - 28p.
              Typescript

NLJ

1385   PÉREZ, LOUIS A.
              Underdevelopment and dependency : tourism in the West
       Indies / Louis A. Pérez. - [El Paso, Tex.] : Center for Inter-
       American Studies, University of Texas at El Paso, 1975. - 47p.
              Bibliography: p.43-47

              Arranged in three sections each alphabetically by author,
       as follows : (i) Unpublished Materials, (ii) Published Materials
       : Books (iii) Published Materials : Articles.

UWI-T

1386   Trinidad and Tobago. Ministry of Planning and Development
              Bibliography of tourism (selected Caribbean studies and
       other works) / compiled by Haven Allahar. - Port of Spain :
       Ministry of Planning and Development, 1975. - 11p.

MF-T

Trinidad and Tobago

1387   Trinidad and Tobago. Ministry of Planning and Development.
        Library
            Tourism / compiled by Patricia Raymond. - [Port of Spain :
        Ministry of Planning and Development], [197-?]. - 3p.
            Mimeographed

            23 items. Prepared for a proposed bibliography of Trinidad
        and Tobago.

                                                                    MF-T

1388   Trinidad and Tobago. Ministry of Planning and Development.
        Library
            Tourism/hotel development/hotel training laws / Patricia
        Raymond. - [Port of Spain, Trinidad] : Ministry of Planning and
        Development Library, [197-?]. - 1p.
            Mimeographed

            9 items. Prepared for a proposed bibliography of Trinidad
        and Tobago.

                                                                    MF-T

TRANSPORTATION

1389   University of California. Department of Geography
            Air transport in the Lesser Antilles / Peter W. Rees ;
        report on field work ... ; James J. Parsons, principal investi-
        gator. - Berkeley : University of California, 1964. - 185p.
            Bibliography: p.181-185

            Selected references to books and reports, journal articles
        and statistical sources.

                                                                    UWI-T

VOLCANOES

1390   HOVEY, EDMUND OTIS
            Bibliography of literature of the West Indian eruptions,
        published in the United States / Edmund Otis Hovey. - p.562-566
            In Bulletin of the Geological Society of America. - Vol.15
        (1903)

            Includes articles on West Indian volcanoes generally and
        St. Vincent in particular.

                                                                    UWI-T

WOMEN

1391 A bibliography of regional resource materials. - p.181-208
        In Caribbean resource book : by, for and about women in
      their efforts to achieve the objectives of the International
      Women's Year World Plan of Action / [compiled by] the Women's
      Bureau of Jamaica, the Extra Mural Department of the University
      of the West Indies and the International Women's Tribune Centre
      (New York). - [Bridgetown, Barbados : Extra Mural Department,
      U.W.I.], [1978]
        Cover title: Caribbean resource book focusing on women in
      development

        Full references to books, journals, articles, films and
      other media divided into sections on development, education,
      labour and unemployment, health and family life, religion and
      church, and status of women - politics and legislation and
      statistics.
                                                              UWI-T

1391a BUVINIĆ, MAYRA
        Women and world development : an annotated bibliography /
      Mayra Buvinić, Cheri S. Adams, Gabrielle S. Edgcomb and
      Maritta Koch-Weser. - Washington, D.C. : Overseas Development
      Council, 1976. - 162p.

        "Provides sources on the effects of socioeconomic develop-
      ment and cultural change on women and women's reactions to these
      changes throughout the world. Presented in nine subject categories
      and by geographic regions within each category. The work contains
      a substantial amount of references to Latin America and the
      Caribbean."
                                                Ref.no.15, no.39, 1977
                                                            Item no.1

1392 HENRY, FRANCIS
        The status of women in Caribbean societies : an overview of
      their economic and sexual roles / Francis Henry and Pamela
      Wilson. - p.165-198
        In Social and economic studies. - Vol.24, no.2 (1975)
        References: p.195-198

        59 items arranged alphabetically by author mainly dealing
      with the family in the Caribbean.
                                                              UWI-T

1392a Inter-American Institute of Agricultural Sciences (IICA).
      Committee for Rural Women and Development

Rural women : a Caribbean bibliography with special
reference to Jamaica / Committee for Rural Women and Development, IICA. – San José [Costa Rica] : Inter-American Institute
of Agricultural Sciences, 1980. – vi, 29p. – (Series on agricultural information and documentation ; no.8)
Cover title: Bibliography on the Latin American and
Caribbean rural woman, Vol.1)

Arranged in three sections : Women and Development, Rural
Women in Jamaica, Jamaican Women. Comprises 142 annotated items
including monographs, periodical articles, and theses. The
majority of publications listed are in the National Library,
Institute of Jamaica, the University of the West Indies (Mona),
the United Nations Library in Kingston, and the Jamaica Women's
Bureau.

UWI-T

1393   STUART, BERTIE A. COHEN
Women in the Caribbean : a bibliography / compiled and
annotated by Bertie A. Cohen Stuart. – Leiden, Netherlands :
Department of Caribbean Studies, Royal Institute of Linguistics
and Anthropology, 1979. – 163p.

Includes material from the English-speaking Caribbean,
including Guyana, the Bahamas and Bermuda. All items are
annotated. Arrangement is by subject : Family and Household,
Cultural Factors, Education, Economic Factors, and Politics and
Law. Some sections are devoted to bibliographies, introductory
works, bibliographies of individual women, and a list of women's
organizations. Author index and index according to categories
provided.

UWI-T

1394   Trinidad and Tobago. Central Library
List of books and articles which give information on
women's role in society with special reference to the West
Indies / Central Library. – [Port of Spain, Trinidad] : West
Indian Reference Section, Central Library of Trinidad and
Tobago, 1974. – 2 leaves
Typescript

16 references mainly to articles in journals and newspapers published in the seventies.

TCL

1395   University of the West Indies (Cave Hill). Institute of
Social and Economic Research (Eastern Caribbean)
Women in the Caribbean : an annotated bibliography ; a
guide to material available in Barbados / compiled by Joycelin
Massiah with the assistance of Audine Wilkinson [and] Norma
Shorey. – Cave Hill, Barbados : Institute of Social and

Economic Research (Eastern Caribbean), University of the West
Indies, 1979. - xviii, 133p. - (Occasional bibliography
series ; no.5)

The 408 items related to English-speaking and non-English-
speaking territories are divided into eleven categories, subdivided by individual territory or groups of territories. Sources
include books, chapters in books, articles, unpublished theses,
pamphlets, official documents, newspaper articles and official
addresses. There is an author index and a list of periodicals.

UWI-T

1396 University of the West Indies (St. Augustine). Library
      List of references on women in the Caribbean / Library,
      U.W.I. - St. Augustine, Trinidad : Library, University of the
      West Indies, [1978]. - 4 leaves
      Typescript

45 references to books, reports and journal articles in
alphabetical author order; some are briefly annotated.

UWI-T

YOUTH AND ADOLESCENCE

1397 Caribbean Regional Centre for Advanced Studies in Youth Work
      Bibliography for youth leadership training programmes /
      Caribbean Regional Centre for Advanced Studies in Youth Work.
      - [Georgetown, Guyana] : Caribbean Regional Centre for Advanced
      Studies in Youth Work, [1975]. - 40 leaves
      Mimeographed

Listings under subjects such as communication, family life
education, leadership, psychology of adolescence and social
psychology.

UG

1398 PHILLIPS, A.S.
      Adolescence in Jamaica / A.S. Phillips. - Kingston :
      Jamaica Publishing House, 1973. - viii, 148p.
      Bibliography: p.137-142

Arranged alphabetically by author, listing of books and
articles includes some unpublished studies submitted for the
certificate or diploma in education of the University of the West
Indies.

UWI-T

1399   RUBIN, VERA
        We wish to be looked upon : a study of the aspirations of
      youth in a developing society / Vera Rubin and Marisa
      Zavalloni. - New York : Teachers College Press, Columbia
      University, 1969. - vi, 251p.
        Bibliography: p.243-249

        Arranged by author. Includes several references to
      journal articles on social studies in the Caribbean with some
      emphasis on Trinidad (the locale of the study), Guyana and
      Jamaica.

                                                                UWI-T

                                ZOOLOGY

1400   ALLEN, ROBERT PORTER
        Birds of the Caribbean / Robert Porter Allen. - London :
      Thames and Hudson, 1962. - 256p.
        Bibliography: p.249-253

        Arranged alphabetically by author, this listing includes
      several references to journal articles.

                                                                UWI-T

1401   LACK, DAVID
        Island biology ; illustrated by the land birds of Jamaica
      / David Lack. - Oxford : Blackwell, 1976. - xvi, 445p. -
      (Studies in ecology ; vol.3)
        Bibliography: p.411-418

        Arranged alphabetically by author, the list includes
      mainly journal articles on bird life in Jamaica and the Lesser
      Antilles including Tobago, Dominica, St. Lucia, St. Vincent and
      Barbados.

                                                                UWI-T

1402   RIMOLI, RENATO O.
        Bibliografía de los moluscos vivientes y extintos del área
      del Caribe / Renato O. Rimoli. - p.179-193
        In Anuario científico. - Vol.2, no.2 (1977)

        Alphabetical author arrangement.

                                                              Ref.no.18
                                                                  1979

1403   University of the West Indies (Mona). Department of Zoology
        The biology, ecology, exploitation and management of
   Caribbean reef fishes : scientific report of the U.W.I.
   Fisheries Ecology Research Project, Port Royal Marine Labora-
   tory, Jamaica, 1969–1973 / by V.C. Billings née Grant and J.
   Munro. – Kingston, Jamaica : Zoology Department, U.W.I., 1974
        Part 5e : The biology, ecology and bionomics of Caribbean
   reef fishes : Pomadasyidae (Grunts). – 128 leaves. – (Research
   report from the Zoology Department, University of the West
   Indies ; no.3)
        Bibliography: p.120–128

        Alphabetical author listing of monographs and articles.
                                                         UWI–T

Guyana

1404   Guyana. Ministry of National Development and Agriculture
        Bibliography of all entomological publications / Ministry
   of National Development and Agriculture. – Georgetown :
   Ministry of National Development and Agriculture, 1973
                                                  Ref.no.495
                                                  Item no.1030

Jamaica

1405   CALDWELL, DAVID K.
        Marine and fresh water fishes of Jamaica / by David K.
   Caldwell. – Kingston, Jamaica : Institute of Jamaica, 1966. –
   120p. – (Bulletin of the Institute of Jamaica. Science series;
   no.17)
        Bibliography: p.108–119

        Arranged alphabetically by author.
                                                         UWI–T

Trinidad and Tobago

1406   University of the West Indies (St. Augustine). Department of
   Zoology
        An annotated bibliography to the fauna (excluding insects)
   of Trinidad and Tobago 1817–1977 / Peter R. Bacon. – St.
   Augustine, Trinidad : Department of Zoology, the University of
   the West Indies, 1978. – 117p. – (Department of Zoology.
   Occasional papers ; no.1)

559 "references ... to observations or research carried out
in Trinidad and Tobago or to work on animals collected in these
islands." Annotations indicate scope and content of each reference
with a taxonomic and ecological bias. Includes references to
papers not available in Trinidad and Tobago but no library
locations provided. Arranged alphabetically by authors with an
index by species.

UWI-T

Name Index

All references are to item numbers in the bibliography.

Asterisks are used to identify journal titles in which listed bibliographies appear.

Aarons, J., 387
Abonnenc, E., 331
Abraham, E.A.V., 981
Abrahams, Roger D., 711
Academy of Natural Sciences, Philadelphia, 749
ACURIL, see Association of Caribbean University and Research Libraries. Association of Caribbean University Research and Institutional Libraries. Asociación de Bibliotecas Universitarias y de Investigación del Caribe
Adams, Cheri S., 1391a
Adamson, Alan H., 1309
Adonias, I., 388
Afro-American Studies, Department of. University of Wisconsin, Milwaukee, 677, 781
Agency for International Development. United States, 459, 461, 492, 496, 508
Agency for International Development. Mission to Guyana. United States, 372
Agricultural Experiment Station. University of Maryland, 888
Agricultural Extension. Department of. University of the West Indies. St. Augustine, 453

Agriculture, Department of. Guyana, 502
Agriculture, Faculty of. University of the West Indies. St. Augustine, 453-457, 472, 473, 487, 488
Agriculture, Ministry of. Guyana, 887
Agriculture and Fisheries, Ministry of. Jamaica, 506
Agriculture and Lands, Ministry of. Jamaica, 507
Agriculture, Lands and Fisheries, Ministry of. Trinidad and Tobago, 509, 730
Agriculture, Office of. United States AID, 492
Agriculture Library, Department of. United States, 468
Agriculture, Nutrition, Fisheries and Forestry, Committee on. Caribbean Research Council. Caribbean Commission, 725, 874
AGRINTER, see Sistema Interamericano de Información para las Ciencias Agrícolas
AIBDA, see Asociación Interamericana de Bibliotecarios y Documentalistas Agrícolas
AID, see Agency for International Development

AIRS: index to the Daily Gleaner, 1360
Alcala, V.O., 637
Alcock, Miranda, 460, 485
Alderman, Ralph H., 306
Allahar, Haven, 1386
Allen, Devere, 1287
Allen, Robert Porter, 1400
Alleyne, Alvona, 416, 1052, 1110
Alleyne, Michael H., 644
Alleyne, Pamela, 1238
Allis, Jeanette Braunsberg, 1059, 1060
Allsopp, Dorothy Y.B., 845
Almanzar, Alcedo, 1143
Alonzo, Shirley, 727
Altbach, Philip G., 634, 635
*American Anthropology, 679
American Antiquarian Society, 232, 401
*American Antiquarian Society. Proceedings, 232, 401
*American Antiquity, 518
American Council of Learned Societies, 223
American Folklore Society, 711, 718
American Geographical Society. New York, 25, 234, 1347
American Geological Institute, 745
American Historical Association, 772
American Journal of Tropical Medicine and Hygiene, 1275
American Journal of Veterinary Research, 1275
American Library Association, 223
American University, 1371, 1374, 1376
*The Americas, Academy of American Franciscan History, 271
Anderson, Teresa, 482
Andersons, Edgars, 863
Andic, F.M., 172
Andrews, Charles McLean, 800, 801
Anglo-American Caribbean Commission, 144, 611

Anglo-American Caribbean Commission, see also Caribbean Commission. Caribbean Organization
Anikina, E.B., 423
*Annals of the Carnegie Museum, 582
Annan, Gertrude, 829
*Annual Report of the American Historical Association, 394
Antigua Public Library, 285a
*Anuario científico, 513, 1402
Archives Department. Barbados, 294, 1353
Archives Department. Barbados, see also Archives, Department of. Barbados
Archives, Department of. Barbados, 174
Archives of British Guiana, 1194
Archives of Simancas. Valladolid, 813
Archives of the Indies. Seville, 813, 834, 865
Armstrong, Hamilton Fish, 903
Army, Department of the. United States, 141
Arthur B. Spingarn Collection. Howard University Library, 39
Arts and General Studies, Faculty of. University of the West Indies. Mona, 150, 151
Arts and General Studies, Faculty of. University of the West Indies. St. Augustine, 152
Arts Council Collection of Modern Literary Manuscripts. Stratford, 552
Asein, Samuel O., 1094
Asenjo, Conrado F., 459a
Ash, Lee, 1138
Asociación de Bibliotecas Universitarias y de Investigación del Caribe, 1, 2, 3
Asociación de Bibliotecas Universitarias y de Investigación del Caribe, see also Association of Caribbean University and Research Libraries. Association of Caribbean University Research and Institutional Libraries

Asociación Interamericana de
Bibliotecarias y Documenta-
listas Agrícolas, 484
*Assistant Librarian, 1264
Associated Colleges of the Mid-
west, 515
Association of Caribbean Universities and Research
Institutes, 777
Association of Caribbean Univer-
sity and Research Libraries,
445, 607, 636, 891, 1037,
1051
Association of Caribbean University and Research Libraries,
see also Asociación de
Bibliotecas Universitarias y
de Investigación del Caribe.
Association of Caribbean
University Research and
Institutional Libraries
Association of Caribbean Univer-
sity, Research and Institu-
tional Libraries, 1361, 1362
Association of Caribbean Univer-
sity Research and Institu-
tional Libraries, see also
Asociación de Bibliotecas
Universitarias y de Investi-
gación del Caribe. Associa-
tion of Caribbean University
and Research Libraries
Asturias, Francisco, 847
Atlanta University, 1082
Augelli, John P., 739
A.W.B. Long Collection. Univer-
sity of Guyana Library, 378
Axline, W. Andrew, 1228

Baa, Enid M., 261, 262
Bacon, Peter R., 1406
Bahadur, Gloria, 1053
Bahamian Reference Collection.
College of the Bahamas
Library, 288, 289
Baker, Edward C., 831, 832
Baker, M., 389
Bandara, S.B., 1073
Bank of Guyana, 624
Baptist Missionary Society, 802
Barbados General Agricultural
Society, 844

Barbados Museum and Historical
Society, 838
Barbados Museum and Historical
Society Bulletin, 846
Barbados Museum and Historical
Society Journal, see
Journal of the Barbados
Museum and Historical
Society
Barbados Public Library, 26, 72,
175, 292, 837, 838, 842, 843,
1353
*Barbados Sugar Industry Review, 884
Barham, A., 78
Barker, Glenys H., 461, 504
Barnes, R.F., 470
Barnes, Sandra, 154
Barratt, P.J.H., 287
Barrett, Leonard E., 1260
Barron, C.N., 754
Barrow, Lois, 1030
Bath, Sérgio, 297
Baugh, Edward, 1031, 1091
Baxter, Ivy, 398
Bayitch, S.A., 145
Baynes, E.W., 957
*The Beacon, 1080
Beck, Jane C., 78a
Beckford, George L., 1325
Beckwith, Martha Warren, 722
*Behaviour Science Research, 672
Bell, Herbert C., 804
Bell, T.W., 729
Belmonte, B.E.J.C., 982
Benewick, Anne, 1241
Benjamin, J., 341
Benjamin, Wilhelmina, A., 865
Benjamin, Wilhelmina, A., see also
McDowell, Wilhelmina
Bennett, Hazel E., 636, 651
Bermuda Archives, 849
Bermuda Book Store, 313
The Bermuda Library. Bermuda,
312, 849
Best, L., 617
Besterman, Theodore, 4
B.G. Philatelic Journal, 1147, 1148
Bianchi, William J., 1184
*Bibliographic Index, 5
Bibliography, Division of.
Library of Congress, 144, 308,
374-376

*Bibliography and index of geology, 743
*Bibliography, Documentation, Terminology, 430
Biblioteca José Antonio Echeverria. Casa de las Américas, 89
Biblioteca Nacional. Madrid, 865
Billings, V.C., 1403
Bim, 1080, 1089, 1091, 1118, 1119
Biological Sciences, Department of. University of the West Indies. St. Augustine, 470
Bishopp, D.W., 1141
Bisessar, S., 498
Black, Clinton V., 860
Black, Jan Knippers, 1376
*Black Images, 1078, 1094
*Black Lines, 715
Bliss Institute. Belize, 298, 299, 301
Bliss Institute. Belize, see also British Honduras Library Service. British Honduras National Library Service. National Collection. Belize. National Library Service
Blizzard, Flora, 667
Bloomfield, Valerie, 80, 235, 263, 699, 1154
Blume, Helmut, 81, 732–734
Blutstein, I., 1376
Bodleian Library. Oxford, 773, 1174
Boerboom, J.H.A., 581
Bolland, O. Nigel, 1307, 1308
*Books, 1042
Boromé, Joseph A., 1229, 1230
Boston College Library, 27, 717
Boston Public Library, 28
Bolton, J., 390
Boultbee, Paul G., 288, 289
Bowin, C.O., 744
Boxill, Anthony, 1074
Bradley, Leo H., 299, 301–302
Brathwaite, Chelston W.D., 460
Brathwaite, Edward Kamau, 82, 399, 420, 1095, 1112
Brereton, Bridget, 1320
Brewster, Havelock, 605
Brewster, Maria, 630

Brierley, John S., 494
British Council of Churches, 660
British Development Division in the Caribbean. Barbados, 35, 751, 962, 1011, 1011a, 1020
British Guiana Bibliography Committee, 333
*British Guiana Directory and Almanac, 332
*British Guiana Medical Annual, 1130
British Guiana Philatelic Journal, see B. G. Philatelic Journal
British Guiana Public Free Library, 334, 335
British Guiana Public Free Library, see also Guyana Public Free Library. Guyana National Library. Guyana Public Library
British Honduras Library Service, 300, 301
British Honduras Library Service, see also Bliss Institute. Belize. British Honduras National Library Service. National Collection. Belize. National Library Service. Belize
British Honduras National Library Service, 302
British Honduras National Library Service, see also Bliss Institute. Belize. British Honduras Library Service. National Collection. Belize. National Library Service. Belize
British Institute of International and Comparative Law, 932
British Library, 228
British Library, see also British Museum
British Museum, 54, 55, 236, 237, 773, 800, 827, 835, 1174
British Museum, see also British Library
British Museum Library, 54, 55
British Virgin Islands Public Library, 320, 322–232
Brodber, Erna, 1217, 1218, 1355

Brooklyn Public Library, 29
Browman, Gwyneth, 105
Brown, Adlith, 605
Brown, Ann Duncan, 144
Brown, C.R., 937
Brown, J., 281
Brown, Lloyd W., 1066
Brown University, 83, 1277
Brunn, Stanley, 1343
Bryant, Robyn, 273
Bryden, John M., 1326
Buchanan, John, 1224
Building Research Station. DSIR, 869
Bullbrook, J.A., 520
Bullen, Ripley P., 517
*Bulletin of Bibliography, 314, 315, 1229, 1230
*Bulletin of the Association for Commonwealth Literature and Language Studies, 1033
*Bulletin of the Geological Society of America, 1390
*Bulletin of the Institute of Historical Research, 814
*Bulletin of the Library Association of Barbados, 238
Bureaux, see Foreign and Domestic Commerce. Latin America and the Caribbean etc.
Burnham, Alan, 424
Burns, A.C., 960
Bushong, Allen D., 264, 272
Buvinič, Mayra, 1391a
Byrne, R., 570

Cabrera Sifontes, Horacio, 1187
CADEC, see Christian Action for Development in the Caribbean
CAGRINDEX, 485
Caldwell, David K., 1405
California State University. Los Angeles, 84, 1344
Callender, Jean A., 148a, 285b, 293a, 1249a
Camacho, M.V., 958
Cameron, Norman E., 336, 534, 1108
Campbell, Elizabeth, 238
Campbell, H., 535
Campbell, Mavis Christine, 1315

Campbell, Tony, 295
Campbell-Platt, Kiran, 660
Canadian International Development Agency, 751
Canning House Library. Hispanic and Luso Brazilian Council, 192
Canning House Library. Hispanic Council, 38
Cant, R.V., 753
Canton, E. Berthe, 875, 1034
CARDI, see Caribbean Agricultural Research and Development Institute
Cardona, María Elena Argüello de, 1, 2
*Caribbean, 1237
Caribbean Agricultural Research and Development Institute, 461
Caribbean Commission, 70, 85, 86, 111, 170, 583, 637, 725, 874, 875, 1159, 1244, 1289, 1327, 1380
Caribbean Commission, see also Anglo-American Caribbean Commission. Caribbean Organization
Caribbean Commission Library, 875
*Caribbean Commission Monthly Information Bulletin, 111, 170, 1380
Caribbean Community, 68, 177, 178, 606, 619-621, 1247
Caribbean Community Secretariat, 68, 177, 178, 606, 619-621
Caribbean Community Secretariat Library, 68, 178, 619-621
Caribbean Community Secretariat Library, see also Information and Documentation Section. Caribbean Community Secretariat
Caribbean Development and Cooperation Committee. United Nations Economic Commission for Latin America, 1365, 1381
Caribbean Development Bank Library. Barbados, 179

Caribbean Documentation Centre.
  Office for the Caribbean.
  Economic Commission for Latin
  America, 1331b
Caribbean Economic Development
  Corporation. San Juan, 71,
  252
Caribbean Festival of Arts, 89,
  1043
Caribbean Festival of Arts, see
  also Caribbean Festival of
  Creative Arts
Caribbean Festival of Creative
  Arts, 1040
Caribbean Festival of Creative
  Arts, see also Caribbean
  Festival of Arts
Caribbean Free Trade Association,
  1247
*Caribbean Historical Review, 798
Caribbean Industrial Research
  Institute, 462, 745
*Caribbean Journal of Education,
  912, 913
*Caribbean Journal of Science,
  746, 1272
Caribbean Organization, 70, 87,
  180, 249, 709, 1328
Caribbean Organization Library,
  180, 249, 709, 1328
Caribbean Organization, see also
  Anglo-American Caribbean
  Commission. Caribbean
  Commission
*Caribbean Quarterly, 231, 259,
  1119, 1268, 1378
Caribbean Regional Centre for
  Advanced Studies in Youth
  Work. Guyana, 164, 1397
Caribbean Regional Library, 71,
  88, 164, 181, 182, 252
Caribbean Research Centre. St.
  Lucia, 919
Caribbean Research Council.
  Caribbean Commission, 725,
  874
Caribbean Research Institute.
  College of the Virgin
  Islands, 7
*Caribbean Review, 128, 778

*Caribbean Studies, 69, 259, 268,
  269, 590, 833, 900, 914, 922,
  1306
Caribbean Studies, Department of.
  Royal Institute of Linguistics
  and Anthropology. Leiden,
  1393
Caricom, see Caribbean Community
Caricom Bibliography, 68
*Caricom Bulletin, 606
Carifesta, see Caribbean Festival
  of Arts
Carifesta Literary Committee, 82
Carifta, see Caribbean Free Trade
  Association
CARINDEX, 1361
CARIRI, see Caribbean Industrial
  Research Institute
*CARISPLAN abstracts, 1365
Carmichael, Gertrude, 867, 868
Carnegie Free Library. Trinidad,
  425, 435, 523, 1075
Carnegie Institute. Pittsburgh,
  572
Carnegie Institution of Washing-
  ton, 800, 801, 804, 815
Carnegie, Jeniphier B., 1061
Carrington, Lawrence D., 910, 925
Carson, Edward A., 836
Cartey, Wilfred, 1095
Cartographic Division. Lands
  Department. Guyana, 393
Casa de las Américas, 89
Cashmore, Ernest, 1261
Catholic Association for Inter-
  national Peace, 1250
CDCC, see Caribbean Development
  and Cooperation Committee
Census Library, Bureau of the.
  United States, 1211
Center for African and African-
  American Studies. Atlanta
  University, 1082
Center for Applied Linguistics.
  Eric Clearinghouse for
  Linguistics, 917
Center for Inter-American
  Relations, New York, 1038,
  1056
Center for Latin American Studies.
  Tulane University, 275a

Center for Latin American Studies. University of Florida, 116, 1051

Central American Field Program. Associated Colleges of the Midwest, 515

Central Bank. Barbados, 173

Central Bank of Trinidad and Tobago, 629, 630, 1383

Central Bank Research Library. Trinidad and Tobago, 630

Central Experiment Station Library. Ministry of Agriculture, Lands and Fisheries. Trinidad and Tobago, 509

Central Library of St. Lucia, 421, 422

Central Library of Trinidad and Tobago, 67, 76, 77, 138-140, 198-200, 253, 254, 433-439, 446, 450, 539, 554, 560, 576, 646, 647, 675, 706, 712, 713, 723, 724, 879, 1057, 1058, 1069, 1083-1088, 1115, 1119, 1175, 1201, 1202, 1258, 1259, 1394

Central Secretariat. Caribbean Commission, 85, 86, 583, 1327

Central Statistical Office. Trinidad and Tobago, 442, 443, 1216, 1383

Centre de Recherches Caraïbes. Université de Montréal. Martinique, 510, 673

Centre for Developing Area Studies. McGill University, 273, 274

Centre for Information and Advice for Educational Disadvantage, 643

Centre for Multi-racial Studies. University of Sussex, 1226

Centre for Multi-racial Studies. University of Sussex. Barbados, 61

Centre for Multi-racial Studies. University of the West Indies/University of Sussex, 219

Centro Interamericano de Documentación e Información. Agrícola (CIDIA) Instituto Interamericano de Ciencias Agrícolas, 483

Centro Latinoamericano de Documentación Económica y Social (CLADES), 1364

CEPAL/CLADES. Naciones Unidas, 1364

Cepal Index, see Cladindex

Chaffee, Wilber A., 768

Chamber of Commerce. Barbados, 844

Chambers, Audrey, 415, 416

Chandler, Michael J., 838-840, 846

Chang, Henry C., 7

Chapman, T., 463, 464

Charles, Dorothy, 5

Chesney, H.A.D., 503

Chevrette, Valerie, 522

Chevannes, Barry, 1262

Chilcote, Ronald H., 1190

*Choice, 113, 354

Chow, J.E., 1130

Christian Action for Development in the Caribbean, 183, 1251

Christiani, Joan, 524, 545

CICAR, see Cooperative Investigation of the Caribbean and Adjacent Regions

CICRED, see Committee of the International Co-ordination of Research in Demography

CIDA, see Canadian International Development Agency

CIDIA, see Centro Interamericano de Documentación e Información Agrícola

CLADES, see Centro Latinoamericano de Documentación Económica y Social

Cladindex, 1364

Clarke, Colin G., 1336

Clegern, Wayne, M., 90

Clermont, Norman, 510

Cline, Herman, 18

CODECA, see Caribbean Economic Development Corporation

Cole, George Watson, 314, 315, 571

Colindale Newspaper Library.
British Library, 228
College Library. University of
California. Los Angeles, 134
College of the Bahamas Library,
288, 289
College of the Virgin Islands.
St. Thomas, 7, 203
College of the Virgin Islands
Library. St. Thomas, 57
Collins, B.A.N., 1155
Collins, Carol, 378, 381
Collins, Claire, 379, 382
Collymore, Frank, 1091
Colón, Francisco Sevillano, 843
Colonial Development and Welfare,
1327
*Colonial Geology and Mineral
Resources, 765
Colonial Office. Great Britain,
36, 220, 242, 284, 290, 316,
325, 329, 343, 403, 419, 428,
429, 807, 828, 935, 1159
Colonial Office Library. Great
Britain, 36, 220, 242
Columbus Memorial Library.
Washington, D.C., 9
COMCARC, see Commonwealth
Caribbean Resource Centre
Comisión Económica para America
Latina (CEPAL). Naciones
Unidas, 1364
Comissiong, Barbara, 18, 445,
472, 473, 1035, 1036
Comitas, Lambros, 91, 92, 1164
Committee for Rural Women and
Development. Inter-American
Institute of Agricultural
Sciences, 1392a
Committee of the International
Co-ordination of Research in
Demography (CICRED), 1215
Committee on Latin America.
London, 830, 1092, 1368
Committee to examine the Struc-
ture and Organization of
Local Government. Jamaica,
1196
Commonwealth Agricultural
Bureaux, 465

Commonwealth Bureau of Agricul-
tural Economics, 451
Commonwealth Bureau of Soils,
490, 491, 500, 501
Commonwealth Caribbean Regional
Secretariat, 1231, 1232
Commonwealth Caribbean Resource
Centre. Barbados, 265, 845
Commonwealth Institute. London,
93-99, 184-187, 337, 400,
1093, 1109, 1263
Commonwealth Institute Library.
London, 98, 400
Commonwealth Institute Library,
see also Commonwealth Insti-
tute Library and Resource
Centre. London
Commonwealth Institute Library and
Resource Centre. London, 99,
184-187, 1109, 1263
Commonwealth Institute Library and
Resource Centre, see also
Commonwealth Institute Library
Commonwealth Legal Advisory
Service. British Institute of
International and Comparative
Law, 932
Commonwealth Relations Commission,
101
Commonwealth Secretariat. London,
250
Communications, School of.
Temple University, 592
Community and Race Relations Unit.
British Council of Churches,
660
Community Relations Commission.
London, 239, 240, 638, 1219-
1223
Connell, John, 1352
Conservation and Cultural Affairs,
Department of. United States
Virgin Islands, 204, 252
Cooper, Alan, 575
Cooperative Investigation of the
Caribbean and Adjacent Regions
(CICAR), 1274
Coote, C.H., 390
Cordeiro, Daniel Raposo, 8, 18

Cornell University. Ithaca. New
    York, 327, 1204, 1345a
Cornforth, I.S., 493
Cosminsky, Sheila, 1119a
Council of Planning Librarians,
    870, 1039, 1192
Council on Foreign Relations,
    902, 903, 905, 906
Cova, Arabia Teresa, 3
Cowlishaw, S.J., 486, 488
Cox, Barbara C., 260
Cox, Edward Godfrey, 597
Cracknell, Basil E., 324
Crahan, Margaret E., 1345
Craig, Dennis R., 911-913
Craig, Susan, 1153
Crassweller, Robert D., 1233
Craton, Michael, 834, 856, 1278
*CRC Journal, 703
CRESALC, see Regional Committee
    on Family Life and Sex Educa-
    tion for Latin America and
    the Caribbean
Creyke, Peter, 888
Cronon, E. David, 537
Cross, Malcolm, 661
Crouse, Nellis M., 768a
Cruickshank, J. Graham, 293
Cummings, Leslie Peter, 741, 1188
Cumper, G.E., 1139
Cundall, Frank, 30-32, 100, 401,
    405, 413, 1156
Curaçao Public Library, 188
*Current Caribbean Bibliography,
    70, 71, 1034, 1234
Cuthbert, Zinka, 659

Dahlin, Terry, 1252
Dahlin, Therrin, C., 1253
Dalton, L.C., 984, 985
Daly, Stephanie, 1025, 1026
*Dangava, 863
Daniels, Marietta, 1157
Davenport, Frances G., 800
David, Wilfred L., 1310
Davidson, William V., 669a
Davis, Lenwood G., 538
Davis, Stephen, 702
Day, Allison, 101
Deal, Carl, 18, 266, 267
De Lattre, Rae, 404
De Leeuw, Hendrik, 603

*Demographic Yearbook, 1208
Departments, see Agriculture,
    Archives, Economics etc.
Derbyshire, D.C., 683
Despres, Leo A., 1311
Devaux, Robert, J., 422
Development Planning Team. Guyana
    Ministry of Economic Develop-
    ment, 625
Dill, Thomas Melville, 971
Dillard, J.L., 914
Dillett, A.A., 300
Divisions, see Bibliography,
    Libraries and Museums, etc.
Dixon, C.G., 755
DOERS. Institute of Social and
    Economic Research. University
    of the West Indies. Mona,
    1366
Donohoe, William Arlington, 848
Dossick, Jesse J., 268, 269
Dow, Henry, 426
Drescher, Seymour, 1278a
DSIR, see Scientific and Indus-
    trial Research, Department of
Duchesne-Fournet, Jean, 339
Duke, E.M., 986
Duncan, Joy, 105
Dunn, Patricia Y., 1037
Durrant, Fay, 595, 956, 1158
Du Simitière, Pierre Eugene, 810
Dwyer, F.X., 933
Dyrud, John, 934

Earnhardt, Kent C., 1210
Earnshaw, W., 951
Easton, David K., 102, 1234, 1235
ECLA, see Economic Commission for
    Latin America
Economic Commission for Latin
    America. United Nations,
    1331a, 1331b, 1364, 1365,
    1381, 1382
Economic Development, Ministry
    of. Guyana, 625
Economic Studies and Planning
    Division. Industrial Develop-
    ment Corporation, 892
Economics, Department of.
    University of the West Indies.
    Mona, 886

Economics, Department of.
University of the West
Indies. St. Augustine, 617
Edgcomb, Gabrielle S., 1391a
Edmonston, Barry, 1204
Education and Social Development,
Ministry of. Guyana, 1332
Education, School of. University
of the West Indies. Mona,
651
Education, School of. University
of the West Indies. St.
Augustine, 705
Education, School of. University
of the West Indies, see also
Institute of Education.
University of the West Indies
Education, Social Development and
Culture, Ministry of.
Guyana, 653
Education Library, Ministry of.
Jamaica, 655, 656
*Educational Journal of Trinidad
and Tobago, 659
Edwards, David, 505
Edwards, Francis, 103
Edwards, Viv, 915, 916
Eigenmann, C.H., 572
Eisner, Gisela, 1290
Elcock, Theresa, 150
Elkin, Judith, 1054
Ellis, Maureen Yvonne, 1345a
*Emergency Librarian, 1300
Emmanuel, Patrick A., 1178
Employers' Consultative Associa-
tion of Trinidad and Tobago,
1014
Encinas, Joyce, 1030
Energy and Energy-based Indus-
tries Library, Ministry of.
Trinidad and Tobago, 202
Engber, Marjorie, 1038
Engeldinger, Eugene A., 540
Engineering, Faculty of.
University of the West Indies.
St. Augustine, 882
English, Department of. Univer-
sity of the West Indies. St.
Augustine, 707, 1049
Ennever, Olive, 1126, 1127
*Erdkunde, 732, 733

ERIC Clearinghouse for Linguis-
tics, 917
Ericksen, E. Gordon, 1291
Erickson, Elizabeth B., 508
Erickson, Frank A., 508
Erskine, R.H., 987
Espinet, Shirley, 445, 472
Espinet, Shirley, see also
Evelyn, Shirley
Etienne, Flory, 1236
Evans, Mary M., 802
Evelyn, Shirley, 473, 1363
Evelyn, Shirley, see also
Espinet, Shirley
*Excerpta Botanica, 581
Extra Mural Department. University
of the West Indies, 1110
Extra-Mural Department. Univer-
sity of the West Indies.
Cave Hill, 1391
Extra-Mural Department. Univer-
sity of the West Indies.
Mona, 1071, 1375
Extra-Mural Department, see also
Extra-Mural Studies, Depart-
ment of
Extra-Mural Studies, Department
of. University College of
the West Indies, 1070
Extra-Mural Studies, Department
of. University of the West
Indies. Mona, 248
Extra-Mural Studies, Department
of. University of the West
Indies. St. Augustine, 1072
Extra-Mural Studies, Department
of. University of the West
Indies. St. Lucia, 420
Extra-Mural Studies Unit.
University of the West Indies.
St. Augustine, 1089, 1091
Eyre, Alan, 1213

Fabela, Isidro, 1185
Faculties, see Agriculture, Arts
and General Studies, etc.
Fairbanks, Carol, 540
Fairbridge, Rhodes, W., 749
Family Planning/Epidemiology Unit.
University of the West Indies.
Mona, 1354

FAO, see Food and Agriculture
    Organization
*Farm Journal of Guyana, 498
Farrier, Francis Quamina, 541
Fauquenoy, Marguerite, 340
Federal Information Service
    Reference Library. West
    Indies Federation, 257, 1248,
    1249
Feeney, V. Joan, 1039
Furguson, Cynthia T., 1369
*Field Letters of the West Indies,
    385
Figueredo, Alfredo E., 673
Finance, Ministry of. Trinidad
    and Tobago, 1382a
Finance Library, Ministry of.
    Trinidad and Tobago, 1382a
Fink, L.K., 752
Fisher, Herbert H., 465a
Fisheries Department. Guyana
    Ministry of Agriculture, 887
Fisk University Library. Nash-
    ville. Tennessee, 33
Fitzpatrick, John C., 820
Fletcher, Beryl N., 1126, 1127
Flint, John E., 131
Florida Technological University
    Library, 34
Florida University, see Univer-
    sity of Florida
Floyd, Barry, 402
*Focus, 1080
Folk Research Centre. St. Lucia,
    919
*Folklore, 716
Food and Agriculture Organization.
    United Nations, 241, 476
Forbes, A.G., 975
Ford, Worthington Chauncey, 820
Foreign and Commonwealth Office.
    Great Britain, 35, 37, 291,
    305, 445
Foreign and Commonwealth Office
    Library. Great Britain, 37,
    445
Foreign and Domestic Commerce,
    Bureau of. United States,
    584
Foreign Area Materials Center.
    New York State, 122

Foreign Area Studies (FAS).
    American University, 1374,
    1376
Foreign Office. Great Britain,
    390, 391, 1195
Forestry Department. Guyana.
    726
Forestry Division Library.
    Ministry of Agriculture, Lands
    and Fisheries. Trinidad and
    Tobago, 730
Foster, Harry La Tourette, 598
Foster, Phillips, 888
Foundation for Scientific Research
    in Surinam and the Nether-
    lands, 1140
Fournier, A., 341
Fox, Elton C., 542
Franklin, Conrade Bismark, 427
Frazier, E. Franklin, 611
Frewer, Louis B., 824
Frucht, Richard, 1346
Fuller, C., 45
Furtado, W.A., 952, 992-994

Gajraj, Carroll, 1238
Garner, Olivia, 342
Gaston, L. Clifton, 1279
Gates, Brian, 103a
Geiser, Hans J., 1238
*Gentleman's magazine, 245
Geoabstracts. University of East
    Anglia, 763
Geography, Department of. McGill
    University, 477, 760
Geography, Department of. Univer-
    sity of California. Berkeley,
    1389
Geography Department. University
    of the West Indies. Mona,
    737, 738
Geological Reference File.
    American Geological Institute,
    745
Geological Society of America,
    762
Geological Survey. Guyana, 754,
    759
Geological Survey, Ministry of.
    Guyana, 758

Geological Survey Department
   Library. Guyana, 755, 761
George, H.K., 755
Georgetown University, 1170
Gerling, Walter, 1316
Gibbs, A., 756, 757
Gibson, K., 928
Giglioli, G., 1128
Gillis, 570
Gillum, Gary P., 1253
Gilmore, William C., 1373
Girling, R,K., 1330
Girvan, Norman, 876, 877, 886,
   1337
Glasgow, Roy Arthur, 1312
Glassner, Martin Ira, 900
Glazier, Stephen D., 673, 674
Gocking, William, 22, 225, 825
Goeje, C.H. de, 929
Goldstraw, Billie, 1052
Goldstraw, Billie, see also Gold-
   straw, Irma E.
Goldstraw, Irma E., 543
Gomes, P.I., 877
Gonsalves, Ralph E., 1179
Gonzales, Anson John., 1113,
   1114, 1117
González-Blanco, Pedro, 303
Goodland, J.R., 573
Goodwin, R. Christopher, 511
Gordon, Arnold, 1146
Gordon, Joyce, 1269
Gordon, K., 503
Gordon, N. Montgomery, 867
Goveia, Elsa V., 769, 792
Government, Department of.
   University of the West
   Indies. Mona, 1158
Government Printing Office.
   Jamaica, 412
Goslinga, Marian, 128
Gower, Charlotte D., 671
Graham, Edward H., 582
Graham-Perkins, C.H., 996, 997
Grain Legume Research Programme.
   Faculty of Agriculture.
   University of the West
   Indies. St. Augustine, 470
Granberry, J., 518
Grant, C.H., 304
Gray, Reginald, 972

Great Britain. Ministry ...,
   see under name of Ministry
Green, Carol, 544
Green, William A., 1280
Greene, J.E., 1151, 1160
Greenfield, Sydney M., 1305
Gregory, Winifred, 223
Griffin, Charles C., 770
Griffin, Ernest C., 270
Griffin, Grace Gardner, 771
Griffith, W. Brandon, 995
Griffiths, Gareth, 1062
Griller, Nancy L., 906
Groot, Silvia W. de, 345
Gropp, Arthur E., 9-11, 385
Grover, Mark L., 1253
Gunther, Jean, 906
Guyana. Department ... Ministry
   ..., see under name of
   Department
*Guyana Journal of Sociology,
   1372
*Guyana Library Association
   Bulletin, 395, 396
*Guyana Medical Science Library
   Bulletin, 568, 1131
Guyana National Archives, 852a
Guyana National Library, 12, 13,
   73, 105, 106, 259, 545, 684,
   930, 1053, 1096, 1098-1100,
   1104, 1107
Guyana National Library, see also
   British Guiana Public Free
   Library. Guyana Public Free
   Library. Guyana Public
   Library
Guyana National Science Research
   Council, 495
Guyana Public Free Library, 14,
   190, 191, 342, 346-351, 521,
   546, 626, 685-687, 719, 1040,
   1105, 1129, 1137, 1370
Guyana Public Free Library.
   MacKenzie, 352
Guyana Public Free Library, see
   also British Guiana Public
   Free Library. Guyana
   National Library. Guyana
   Public Library
Guyana Public Library, 524

Guyana Public Library, see also
   British Guiana Public Free
   Library. Guyana National
   Library. Guyana Public Free
   Library
Guyana Public Service Associa-
   tion, 871
Guyana Rice Board, 499
Guyana University, see Univer-
   sity of Guyana
Guyanese National Bibliography,
   73

Hadwen, Peter, 751
Hallewell, Lawrence, 107, 221,
   1092
Halstead, John P., 1161
Hamner, Robert D., 547-548
Hammett, Sir Clifford J., 963,
   970, 973, 974, 976, 1002,
   1007, 1011
*Handbook of Jamaica, 413, 764
*Handbook of Latin American
   Studies, 15
Handler, Jerome S., 841, 1306
Hanham, H.J., 772
Hanke, Lewis, 15, 110, 111
Hannay, Annie M., 468
Hannays, Irma, 607, 891
Harewood, Jack, 1215
Haring, Clarence Henry, 773
Harrigan, Norwell, 321
Harris, L.J., 1076
Harris, William W., 598
Harrison, Ira E., 1119a
Harrison, John P., 822
Harrison, Sir John, 1141
Harrison, W., 570
Harry, Lloyd S., 727
Hart, Estellita, 640
Hart, Richard, 112
Harvard University, 608, 1145
Harvard University Law School,
   608
Harvard University Library, 1145
Hawkins, Irene, 1292
Hazlewood, Arthur, 609, 610
Headicar, B.M., 45
Health, Ministry of. Trinidad &
   Tobago, 561-563, 1121-1125
Hearne, John, 1033

Heiliger, Edward M., 1162
Hellman, Florence S., 144, 308,
   374, 376
Helmreich, William B., 549
Henderson, T.H., 453-455
Henriques, Fernando, 1052
Henry, Francis, 1392
Henry, Maureen, 154
Henry, Zin, 1293
Herdeck, Donald, 525
Herrera, E., 463, 464, 489
Herstein, Sheila R., 309a
Hewitt, Arthur Reginald, 233,
   1024, 1294
Higman, B.W., 1286
Hill, Errol, 704, 1106, 1111, 1116
Hill, Janet, 1055
Hill, W.C., 775
Hills, Theo L., 274
Hinds, Suzette, 411
Hinds, Yvonne, 1333
*Hispania, 129
*Hispanic American Periodicals
   Index, 260
Hispanic and Luso Brazilian
   Council. London, 192
Hispanic Council. London, 38
Hispanic Foundation. Library of
   Congress, 20
Hiss, Philip Hanson, 353
Historical Association. London,
   780
Historical Exhibition Working
   Party. West Indies Festival
   of Arts, 797
Historical Records Survey.
   Pennsylvania, 810
Historical Society of Trinidad &
   Tobago, 56, 867, 868
History, Department of. Univer-
   sity of the West Indies, 831,
   838
The Hoover Institution on War,
   Revolution and Peace, 1190
House of Commons. Great Britain,
   104, 344
House of Commons Library. Great
   Britain, 394
Hovey, Edmund Otis, 1390
Howard University, 39, 611
Howard University Library.
   Washington, D.C., 39

Huggard, Walter Clarence, 1023
Hughes, Roger, 1263, 1264
Humanidades y Educación, Facultad
de. Universidad Católica
"Andrés Bello," 678
Hunte, Diane, 528
Hurault, J., 331
Hurwitz, E.F., 113, 354

ICTA, see Imperial College of
Tropical Agriculture
*IDRC Library Bulletin, 1329
IICA, see Inter-American Insti-
tute for Cooperation on
Agriculture
IICA-CIDIA, see Instituto Inter-
americano de Ciencias Agrí-
cŏlas. Centro Interameri-
cano de Documentación e
Información Agrícŏla
Imperial College of Tropical
Agriculture, 65, 452, 455,
463, 464, 466, 472, 473,
489, 874, 883
Imperial College of Tropical
Agriculture, see also
Agriculture, Faculty of.
University of the West
Indies
Indexing Committee. Association
of Caribbean University,
Research and Institutional
Libraries, 1361, 1362
Industrial Development Corpora-
tion. Trinidad and Tobago,
201, 880, 891-893
Information, Ministry of.
Guyana, 384
Information and Culture, Ministry
of. Guyana, 566, 1096, 1097
Information and Documentation
Section. Caribbean Community
Secretariat, 177
Information and Documentation
Section. Caribbean Community
Secretariat, see also Carib-
bean Community Secretariat
Library
Information Center on Children's
Cultures. U.S. Committee for
UNICEF, 1056

Ingram, Kenneth Everard, 226, 811,
861
Institut des Hautes Etudes de
l'Amérique Latine, 735
Institut Latinskoi Amerik.
Moscow, 423
Institute for the Study of Human
Issues. Philadelphia, 512,
711, 1297
Institute of Advanced Legal
Studies. University of
London, 942
Institute of Caribbean Studies.
University of Puerto Rico,
69, 172, 262, 833, 1210,
1256, 1270, 1323
Institute of Caribbean Studies.
University of Puerto Rico,
see also Instituto de Estudios
del Caribe. Universidad de
Puerto Rico
Institute of Commonwealth Studies.
University of London, 208,
233, 263, 277, 445
Institute of Commonwealth Studies.
University of Oxford, 609, 610
Institute of Commonwealth Studies
Library. University of
London, 208, 1177
Institute of Development Studies.
University of Guyana, 877
Institute of Development Studies.
University of Sussex, 1352
Institute of Education. Univer-
sity of London, 59, 60
Institute of Education. Univer-
sity of the West Indies.
Mona, 410
Institute of Education. Univer-
sity of the West Indies, see
also Education, School of.
University of the West Indies
Institute of Education Documen-
tation Centre. University
of the West Indies. Mona,
649, 650
Institute of Historical Research.
University of London, 774
Institute of International Rela-
tions. University of the West
Indies. St. Augustine, 1238

Institute of Jamaica, 16, 30-32,
40-42, 74-76, 193, 194, 229,
230, 404-406, 411, 413, 550,
551, 696, 769, 790, 795, 858,
918, 925, 1073, 1077, 1156,
1239-1241, 1360, 1384, 1392a,
1405
Institute of Jamaica, see also
National Library of Jamaica
Institute of Jamaica Library,
30-32, 40, 41, 413, 790
Institute of Jamaica Library, see
also West India Reference
Library
Institute of Latin American
Studies. University of
London, 107, 278, 826
Institute of Latin American
Studies. University of
Texas. Austin, 247
Institute of Marine Science.
University of Miami. Coral
Gables, 752
Institute of Musicology. Univer-
sity of Uppsala, 700
Institute of Race Relations.
London, 662, 1055, 1198,
1347, 1349
Institute of Race Relations
Library. London, 662
Institute of Social and Economic
Research. University College
of the West Indies. Mona,
1139
Institute of Social & Economic
Research. University of the
West Indies, 1216
Institute of Social & Economic
Research. Eastern Caribbean.
University of the West
Indies. Cave Hill, 148, 212,
469, 478, 947a, 948, 1178,
1212, 1353, 1395
Institute of Social and Economic
Research. University of the
West Indies. Mona, 78, 214,
505, 789, 857, 872, 877, 885,
890, 1139, 1151-1153, 1179,
1180, 1206, 1308, 1329, 1331,
1334, 1337, 1338, 1355, 1366,
1367

Institute of Social and Economic
Research, University of the
West Indies. St. Augustine,
1303, 1357, 1358
Institute of Social and Economic
Research Library. University
of the West Indies. Mona,
1369
Instituto Braseileiro de
Bibliografia e Documentação.
Rio de Janeiro, 357
Instituto de Estudios del Caribe.
Universidad de Puerto Rico,
612
Instituto de Estudios del Caribe.
Universidad de Puerto Rico,
see also Institute of Carib-
bean Studies. University of
Puerto Rico
Instituto de Investigaciones
Históricas, 678
Instituto Interamericano de
Ciencias Agrícolas (IICA),
483
Instituto Interamericano de
Ciencas Agricólas, see also
Inter-American Institute for
Co-operation on Agriculture.
Inter-American Institute of
Agricultural Sciences
Instituto Panamericano de
Geografía e Historia, 282,
769, 842
Inter-American Committee.
Catholic Association for
International Peace, 1250
Inter-American Institute for Co-
operation on Agriculture, 460
Inter-American Institute for Co-
operation on Agriculture, see
also Instituto Interamericano
de Ciencas Agrícolas
Inter-American Institute of Agri-
cultural Sciences, 504,
1392a
Inter-American Institute of Agri-
cultural Sciences, see also
Instituto Interamericano de
Ciencas Agrícolas. Inter-
American Institute for Co-
operation on Agriculture

*Inter-American Library Relations, 434
Inter-American University. Puerto Rico, 49
Internation Studies Program. Cornell University, 1204
*International and Comparative Law Quarterly, 932
International Bank for Reconstruction and Development, see World Bank
International Council for Educational Development, 635
*International Journal of the Sociology of Language, 910, 911
International Monetary Fund, 43
*International Studies Quarterly, 1242
International Women's Tribune Centre. New York, 1391
Island Record Office. Jamaica, 860
Island Resources Foundation. United States. Virgin Islands, 823

Jackson, Irene V., 1133
Jacobs, Fred Rue, 552
Jacobs, P.M., 774
Jacobs, W. Richard, 1197
Jahn, Janheinz, 1041
Jakobsson, Stiv, 1281
Jamaica (Government), 803
Jamaica. Ministry ..., see under name of Ministry
Jamaica Archives, 860, 862
Jamaica Independence Festival Committee, 406
Jamaica Industrial Development Corporation, 889, 1340
Jamaica Information Service, 862
Jamaica Library Association, 149, 1029
*Jamaica Library Association Bulletin, 415, 416
Jamaica Library Service, 74, 406, 407, 628, 873, 1029, 1043, 1044, 1067, 1068, 1112
Jamaica National Bibliography, 76
Jamaica Women's Bureau, 1392

James, Louis, 1042
Jameson, K.P., 496
Jarrett, J.R., 966
Jayawardena, Chandra, 1313
Jefferson, A., 926
Jefferson, Owen, 1331, 1338
Jenkins, Valerie, 949
Jesse, Charles, 420
John Carter Brown Library. Brown University, 1277
John Rylands University Library. Manchester, 44
Johnson, Anita, 230
Johnston, Kathryn Therese, 1376
Joint Bank-Fund Library, 43
Jones, C.K., 20
Jones, Johanna, 1045
Jones, Joseph Jay, 1045
Jordan, Alma, 18, 430, 473, 1028a, 1029
Jordan, Anne H., 146a
Joseph, Ben, 5
*Journal of Broadcasting, 589
*Journal of Child Psychology and Psychiatry, 666
*Journal of Commonwealth Literature, 548, 1052, 1073, 1089
*Journal of Geophysical Research, 744
*Journal of Librarianship, 235, 699
*Journal of Medical Entomology, 1275
*Journal of Negro History, 676
*Journal of the Agricultural Society of Trinidad & Tobago, 463, 464, 486, 489, 1275
*Journal of the Barbados Museum and Historical Society, 293, 296, 845, 846
Jung Bahadur Singh Collection, 693

Kabdebo, Thomas George, 688
*Kairi, 558
Kallicharan, V.L., 495
Kaplan, Irving, 1374
Kapp, Kit S., 414
Kelly, David H., 635
Kempadoo, Peter, 721
Kendall, Aubyn, 522a
Kennard, C.P., 499
Kennedy, James R., 122
Kerst, Erna W., 870*

Khan, E.J.A., 502
Khudoley, K.M., 762
Kidder, Frederick E., 271, 272, 526
Kinghorn, Marion, 763
Kingston and St. Andrew Parish Library. Jamaica Library Service, 1044
Klass, Morton, 1321
Knee, C.D., 495, 1333
Knight, Annette, 154
Knight, Franklin W., 1345
Koch-Weser, Maritta, 1391a
Koeman, C., 392
Koninklijke Akademie van Weten-schappen, 929
Koster, C.J., 830
Kraal, J.F., 114
Kraus-Thomson Organization Ltd., 222
Kreslins, Janis A., 902, 906
Kuczynski, R.R., 1205
Kulhawik, Leonard R., 417
Kuper, Adam, 1317
*Kyk-Over-Al, 368, 1047, 1080, 1089a

Lack, David, 1401
La Flamme, Alan G., 672
La Guerre, John Gaffar, 553, 1322
Lall, Kissoon O.M., 393
Lamb, F. Bruce, 725a
Lambert, Claire M., 1352
Lambeth Libraries. London, 1224
Lambeth Palace Library. London, 812
Land Tenure Center. University of Wisconsin. Madison, 481, 482, 623, 1335
Land Tenure Center Library. University of Wisconsin. Madison, 481, 482, 1335
Lands and Surveys Department. Guyana, 341, 393
Lands and Surveys Department. Trinidad & Tobago, 448
Langer, William L., 903
Larbi, Kaye, 594, 668, 1362
Latin America and Caribbean, Bureau of. U.S. AID, 459, 508

Latin American Collection. University of Texas Library. Austin, 209
Latin American Library. Tulane University. 1279
*Latin American Research Review, 264
Latin American Studies Center. California State University. Los Angeles, 84, 1344
Latin American Studies Center. Michigan State University, 306, 1343
Latin American Studies Program. Cornell University, 1204
Lauerhass, Ludwig, 641
Laurent, Sharon, 462
Law, Faculty of. University of the West Indies. Cave Hill, 943a, 950, 962, 973, 976, 1000, 1002, 1007, 1011, 1011a, 1020, 1028, 1373
Law, Faculty of. University of the West Indies. Mona, 949
Law Library, Faculty of. University of the West Indies. Cave Hill, 210, 211, 595, 934, 943-947, 956, 962, 963, 969, 970, 973, 974, 976, 1002, 1007, 1011, 1011a, 1020, 1028
Law, School of. University of Miami, 145
Law Library. Trinidad and Tobago High Court, 953, 1027
Lawrence David, 663
Lawrence, Yvonne T., 996
Le Clerc, Charles, 115
Ledin, R. Bruce, 467
Lee, William Rastrick, 999
Leffal, Dolores C., 676
Legal Affairs, Ministry of. St. Vincent, 1011a
Le Gendre, E., 1017
Leigh, Audrey, 551
Lent, John A., 231, 587-592
Levin, Daniel, 1377
Levine, Robert M., 1224a
Levy, Catherine, 1163
Levy, Claude, 116
Lewin, Evans, 52, 53, 130
Lewin, P.E., 775
Lewis, P. Cecil, 964, 1003

Lewis, Rupert, 1158
Lexington Theological Seminary
   Library, 1255
Libraries and Museums, Bureau of.
   United States Virgin Islands,
   57, 579
Libraries & Museums, Division of.
   U.S. Virgin Islands, 252
Libraries and Museums, Division of.
   U.S. Virgin Islands, see also
   Libraries and Museums, Bureau
   of. Libraries, Museums and
   Archaeological Services,
   Bureau of. Public Libraries and
   Cultural Affairs, Bureau of
Libraries and Reference Services,
   Division of. United States
   Department of State, 616
Libraries, Museums & Archaeo-
   logical Services, Bureau of.
   U.S. Virgin Islands, 204
Libraries, Museums & Archaeolo-
   gical Services, Bureau of.
   U.S. Virgin Islands, see also
   Libraries and Museums, Bureau
   of. Libraries & Museums,
   Division of. Public
   Libraries and Cultural
   Affairs, Bureau of
Library and Reference Services,
   Division of. Department of
   State. United States, 1302
Library Association of Trinidad
   & Tobago, 1030, 1075
Library Association Youth
   Libraries Group. Great
   Britain, 1054
Library Company of Philadelphia,
   810
Library of Congress. United
   States, 9, 15, 20, 143, 144,
   246a, 285, 308, 373-376,
   408, 820, 1209, 1211
Lincoln, Waldo, 232
Lincoln, Wayne, 253
Lines, Jorge A., 515
Literature Sub-Committee.
   National History and Arts
   Council. Guyana, 1097
*Literary Half-Yearly, 1065
Liverpool, Hollis Urban Lester,
   705

Livestock Science, Department of.
   University of the West
   Indies. St. Augustine, 486,
   488
Lloyd Library. Cincinnati, 577
London, Hetty, 395
London School of Economics.
   University of London, 1299
London School of Economics.
   University of London, see
   also London School of Eco-
   nomics and Political Science
London School of Economics and
   Political Science. University
   of London, 45
London School of Economics and
   Political Science. University
   of London, see also London
   School of Economics
London University, see University
   of London
Long, A.W.B., 386
Long, Anton V., 857
Long Collection. University of
   Guyana Library, 368, 386
López, Manuel D., 554a
Lounsbury, Ralph G., 821
Lovejoy Library. University of
   Southern Illinois, 146
Lowenthal, David, 117, 1164,
   1347
Lunan, J., 998
Luso-Brazilian Council. London,
   38
Luso-Brazilian Council. London,
   see also Hispanic and Luso-
   Brazilian Council
Lutchman, Harold A., 871

McConnie, M., 1249
McDonald, J.R., 759
McDowell, Robert Eugene, 1103
MacDowell, Wilhelmina A., 442
McDowell, Wilhelmina, see also
   Benjamin, Wilhelmina
McGill University, 118, 273, 274,
   477, 760
McGlynn, Eileen A., 515a
Mackenzie, Donald R., 870
McLennan Library. McGill
   University, 118
McMorris, David S., 1376

McWatt, Mark, 1052
Maczewski, Johannes, 734
Madan, Raj, 664
Mahabir, Sandra, 455
Malik, Yogendra K., 1198
Malm, Krister, 700
Malone, Sir Clement, 977
Mandle, Jay R., 1314
Manley, Douglas, 1301
Manners, R.A., 1296
Manross, W.W., 812
Manuscripts, Department of.
    British Museum, 236
Manuscripts, Division of.
    Library of Congress, 820
Marie, J.M., 478
Marsala, Vincent John, 858
Marshall, Ashley Roy, 967
Marshall, Trevor G., 1353
Marshall, Woodville K., 776, 777
Martin, Tony, 555
Marx, Robert F., 859
Massachusetts Institute of
    Technology, 748
Massiah, Joycelin, 1212, 1395
Mathews, Thomas G., 172, 612,
    778
Matley, C.A., 764
Mattson, Peter H., 746, 747
Maxwell, Leslie F., 936
Maxwell, W. Harold, 937
Mayers, Phyllis, 285a
Mechanical Engineering, Depart-
    ment of. University of the
    West Indies. St. Augustine,
    882, 1276
Medical Department. Guyana,
    1128
Medical Library. Trinidad and
    Tobago Ministry of Health,
    561-563, 1121-1125
Meek, C.K., 938
Meliczek, Hans, 622
Mellown, Elgin W., 556
Menezes, Mary Noel, 689, 853
Merani, Amin, 273
Merrill, Gordon C., 282
Merriman, J., 349
Merriman, Stella E., 524
Methodist Church. Barbados, 844
Mevis, René, 1350
Meyerhoff, A.A., 762

Miami University, see University
    of Miami
Michigan State University, 306,
    1343
Miller, Benjamin Leroy, 1142
Millette, James, 1199
Milne, A. Taylor, 766, 767
Milne, R. Stephen, 1149, 1242
Ministries, see Agriculture,
    Education etc.
Minkel, Clarence W., 270, 306
Minot, James, 999
Mintz, Sidney W., 119, 512, 1297
Missionary Research Society.
    New York, 1265
Mitchell, Sir Harold, 120, 1165,
    1166
Mitchell, William B., 1371
MLA International bibliography of
    books and articles on the
    modern languages and litera-
    tures, 1063
Mobile Microfilm Unit. UNESCO,
    842, 843
Mock Yen, Alma, 248
Modern Language Association of
    America, 1063
Moneague Teachers' College.
    Jamaica, 410
Monteiro, Palmyra V.M., 247
Montserrat Public Library, 418
Moore, Mick, 1352
Moore Collection. Centre for
    Multi-racial Studies.
    Barbados, 61
Morais, Allan, 583, 1380
Morales Carrión, Arturo, 779
Moravian Church. Barbados, 844
Mordecai, John, 1243
Morne Educational Complex
    Library. St. Lucia, 919
Morrell, W.P., 780
Morse, Jim, 1134
Morton, Julia F., 577a
Mosquito Control Service.
    Medical Department. Guyana,
    1128
Moss, Sylvia, 940, 945
Munro, J.L., 1403
Munroe, Trevor, 1158, 1180
Murray, David John, 1167
Murray, Rudy G., 1078

Music Library Association.
Puerto Rico, 1135

Naciones Unidas, 1364
Nardin, J.C., 852
National Archives. Trinidad and
Tobago, 539, 554
National Archives. United
States, 821
National Archives and Records
Service. United States, 822
The National Bibliography of
Barbados, 72
National Book League. London,
93, 95, 121, 599, 1046, 1054,
1169
National Collection. Belize,
298-302
National Collection. Belize, see
also Bliss Institute.
Belize. British Honduras
Library Service. British
Honduras National Library
Service. National Library
Service. Belize
National Development and Agri-
culture, Ministry of.
Guyana, 503, 1404
National History and Arts
Council. Ministry of Infor-
mation and Culture. Guyana,
566, 1096, 1097
National Investment Company.
Jamaica, 221a
National Library. Madrid, 813,
865
National Library of Guyana, see
Guyana National Library
National Library of Jamaica,
40-42, 1392a
National Library of Jamaica,
see also Institute of Jamaica
National Library of Paris, 813
National Library Service.
Belize, 298, 299
National Library Service.
Belize, see also Bliss Insti-
tute. British Honduras
Library Service. British
Honduras National Library
Service. National
Collection. Belize

National Maritime Museum.
London, 827
National Oceanographic Data
Center. Washington, 1274
National Research Council.
U.S.A., 223
National Science Research Council.
Guyana, 727, 1333
Natural Sciences, Faculty of.
University of the West Indies.
Mona, 737, 738
Nelson, Reed, 1252
Netherlands Universities Founda-
tion for International
Cooperation, 1168
New, William H., 1064
New York Botanical Garden Library,
578
New York Public Library, 46-48,
176, 1211
*New York Public Library Bulletin,
46
Newson, Linda A., 516
Newton, A.P., 767
Newton, Velma E., 939, 940, 942a,
943a-946, 947a, 956
Neymeyer, Robert J., 79, 123
Nielsen, Edward C., 1170
*Nieuwe West-Indische Gids, 157-163
Nijhoff, M., 355
N.M. Williams Memorial Ethno-
logical Collection, 27
Nodal, Roberto, 677, 781, 919a
Norman Manley Law School Library.
Jamaica, 195
Norton, Anne, V., 734, 737
Nouvion, V. de, 356
Noyce, John Leonard, 307, 1266
Nunes, Fred, 1367
Nystrom, Bradley, 634

*Occasional Bulletin from the
Missionary Research Library,
1265
Odle, Maurice A., 1334
Office for the Caribbean.
Economic Commission for
Latin America, 1331a, 1331b,
1365, 1381, 1382
Office of External Research.
United States Department of
State, 1351

Office of Intelligence Research, U.S. Department of State, 616
Office of the Prime Minister. Trinidad and Tobago, 449
Okpaluba, Chuks, 872
O'Leary, Timothy J., 690
Olivera, Ruth R., 275a
Oliviera de Araujo Haugse, Vera Lucía, 641
Oltheten, M.P., 1350a
O'Loughlin, Carleen, 1298
Oltheten, M.P., 1350a
Organisation des Nations Unies par l'Education, la Science et Culture, 736
Organisation des Nations Unies par l'Education, la Science et Culture, see also United Nations Educational Scientific and Cultural Organization
Ormerod, D.A., 1076
Orvedal, Arnold C., 492
Osgood, Cornelius, 691
Overseas Development, Ministry of. Great Britain, 189, 326, 901
Overseas Development, Ministry of. Great Britain, see also Overseas Development Administration. Great Britain
Overseas Development Administration. Great Britain, 35, 291, 305
Overseas Development Administration. Great Britain, see also Ministry of Overseas Development. Great Britain
Overseas Development Library, Ministry of. Great Britain, 189, 901
Owens, J.V., 1267
Oxford University, see University of Oxford

Packwood, Cyril Outerbridge, 1285
Padrón, Francisco Morales, 813
Pagney, Pierre, 735
Palace Library. Madrid, 813, 865
Palmer, Margaret, 319

Palmer, Ransford, W., 613, 1318
Pan-American Institute of Geography and History, 270
Pan American Institute of Geography and History, see also Instituto Panamericano de Geografía e Historia
Pantel, A. Gus, 511, 513
Pantin, Maritza, 472, 528
Pardee, Celeste, 1254
Pares, Richard, 782, 814
Parker, Betty June, 641a
Parker, David W., 804
Parker, Franklin D., 641a
Parmer, Charles B., 600
Parsons, Elsie Worthington (Clews), 710, 718
Parsons, James J., 1389
Pasea, G.A., 989
Patchett, Keith William, 941, 949, 967
Pattee, Richard, 1250
Paulin, Charles O., 815
Penfold, P.A., 243
Penn, E.R., 320
Penn, Verna E., 320, 322, 323
Pérez, Louis A., 1385
Phillips, A., 1398
Phillips, P.L., 394
Phillips, Peter, 904
Philpott, Stuart B., 1299
Piedracueva, Haydée, 18
Pierson, Roscoe M., 1255
Planning and Development, Ministry of. Trinidad and Tobago, 615, 631-633, 657, 731, 881, 894-898, 1203, 1342, 1383, 1386-1388
Planning and Development Library, Ministry of. Trinidad and Tobago, 615, 631-633, 897, 898, 1203, 1342, 1383, 1387, 1388
P.N.M. Publishing Company, 539
Pollak-Eltz, Angelina, 678
Pollard, E.R., 1141
Poole, Bernard L., 1244
Population Censuses of Jamaica, 1214
Population Research Center. University of Texas. Austin, 1211

Porcari, Serafino, 1161
Porter, Dale H., 1282
Posnett, Norman W., 291, 305, 326
Poston, Susan L., 642
Pottinger, L.C., 221a
Power, J.L., 244
Price, Richard, 512, 679, 1283, 1297
Pridmore, F., 1144
Primus, Wilma Judith, 920, 927
Printed Books, Department of. British Museum, 237
Proctor, J.H., 1245
Proudfoot, Mary, 124
Pryce, Ken, 594
Public Free Library. British Guiana, see British Guiana. Public Free Library
Public Free Library. Guyana, see Guyana Public Free Library
Public Libraries and Cultural Affairs, Bureau of. United States Virgin Islands, 261
Public Libraries and Cultural Affairs, Bureau of. United States Virgin Islands, see also Libraries and Museums, Bureau of. Libraries and Museums, Division of. Libraries, Museums and Archaeological Services, Bureau of
Public Record Office. Bahamas, 836
Public Record Office. Great Britain, 243, 773, 801, 805-808, 823, 835, 836, 852a, 865, 1174, 1197
Pugh, R.B., 808
Purushothaman, M., 643
Putnam, P.C., 748

Quamina, Lynda, 668
Questel, Victor, 557, 558

Race Relations Board. London, 240
Radio Education Unit. Department of Extra-Mural Studies. University of the West

Indies. Mona, 248
Rae, J.S., 965, 1001
Ragatz, Janet Evans, 126
Ragatz, Lowell Joseph, 125-127, 245, 783-788, 816-818
Raghubeer, E., 653
Ramchand, Kenneth, 1052, 1079
Ramesar, Marianne, 1303, 1357, 1358
Ramsahoye, F.H.W., 979
Raymond, Patricia, 615, 657, 731, 881, 895, 896, 898, 1382a, 1387, 1388
Raymond, Ursula, 16
Rebel, Thomas P., 878
*Les Receuils du CERAG, 909
Redpath Library. McGill University, 166
Rees, Peter W., 1389
Regional Committee on Family Life and Sex Education for Latin America and the Caribbean (CRESALC), 643
Registrar General's Department. Jamaica, 860
Reid, Dorcas Worsley, 129
Reilly, Philip M., 291, 305, 326
Reinecke, John E., 921
Reis, C., 1018
Research and Publications Fund Committee. University of the West Indies, 940, 1061
Research Institute for the Study of Man. New York, 91, 92, 196, 1348
Research Institute for the Study of Man Library. New York, 196
*Revista/Review Interamericana, 511, 639, 1136
*Revue Française d'Histoire d'Outre Mer, 852
Rhodes House Library. University of Oxford, 824, 865
Richards, Horace Gardiner, 749
Richards, Judith E., 17
Ricketts, W.R., 1148
Riley, Alleyne, 378
Rimoli, Renato O., 1402
Robb, Reivē, 1366
Roberts, George W., 1206
Roberts, Henry L., 905, 906

Roberts, Joan, 253
Roberts, Walter Adolphe, 601
Robertson, Amy, 651
Rodney, Walter, 789
Rodway, James, 358, 852a
Roessingh, M.P.H., 855
Roman, Simon, 742
Roopchand, T., 359
Rose, E.J.B., 1349
Rose, F.G., 1130
Roth, Vincent, 333, 360
Roth, Walter Edmund, 381, 692
Roth Collection. University of
    Guyana Library, 379, 381
Rouse, Irving, 514
Royal Agricultural and Commercial
    Society of British Guiana,
    361-366
Royal Colonial Institute, see
    Royal Empire Society.
    London. Royal Commonwealth
    Society. London
Royal Commonwealth Society.
    London, 50, 51, 131, 197, 527
Royal Commonwealth Society
    Library. London, 50, 197,
    527
Royal Commonwealth Society
    Library, see also Royal
    Empire Society Library
Royal Empire Society. London,
    52, 53, 130, 224
Royal Empire Society Library.
    London, 52, 53
Royal Empire Society Library.
    London, see also Royal
    Commonwealth Society Library
Royal Historical Society. Great
    Britain, 772
*Royal Historical Society of
    London Transactions, 782
Royal Institute of International
    Affairs. London, 369
Royal Institute of Linguistics
    and Anthropology. Leiden,
    1350, 1350a, 1393
Rubin, Joan, 922
Rubin, Vera, 1399
Rundel, Philip W., 579
Runnymede Trust. London, 660
Rutten, Louis, M.R., 750

Rutter, M., 666
Ryan, Mary L., 906

Sabin, Joseph, 132, 137
Sabin, R., 331
*Sage Race Relations Abstracts,
    915, 1225, 1227
St. Croix Landmarks Society, 171
St. Thomas Public Library, 57
SALALM, see Seminar on the
    Acquisition of Latin American
    Library Materials
Salmon, James, E.M., 1005, 1006
Sander, Reinhard W., 1080, 1089,
    1089a, 1091
Sanders, Ron, 593
Sangster, Donald B., 877
Sani, Ruta Mara, 1081
Saroop, Hayman Cecil, 670
Saunders, D. Gail, 836
*Savacou, 1267
Schmid, Janeiro B., 1120
Schomburg, Arthur A., 33
Schomburg Center for Research in
    Black Culture. New York
    Public Library, 176
Schomburg Collection. New York
    Public Library, 48
*School Librarian, 101
Schools, see Education, Law, etc.
Schulze, Adolf, 367
Scientific and Industrial
    Research, Department of.
    Great Britain, 869
Scientific Association of
    Trinidad, 427
Scientific Research Council.
    Jamaica, 1271
Scobie, Edward, 665
SCONUL Latin American Group, see
    Standing Committee on National
    and University Libraries
    Latin American Group
Scottish Record Office. Great
    Britain, 809, 865
Segal, Aaron, 1210
Seismic Research Unit. University
    of the West Indies. St.
    Augustine, 745, 751
Sellers, John R., 246a

Seminar on Developing a Public
    Administration Information
    Network for Latin America
    and the Caribbean, 1191,
    1194
Seminar on the Acquisition of
    Latin American Library
    Materials, 17, 18, 22, 80,
    154, 225, 630, 793, 825,
    1110, 1252
Semper, D.H., 960
Senate Sub-committee for
    Linguistics. University of
    the West Indies, 924, 925
Senior, Clarence, 1301
Serbin, Andrés, 1150
Sewlal, Enos, 431, 866
Seymour, A.J., 368, 1089a, 1096
Shahabuddeen, M., 980
Shambaugh, Cynthia, 1379
Sharples, O.E., 990
Shepherd, Phyllis, 1105
Sheppard, Jill, 669
Sherlock, Philip M., 405
Sherriff, P.M.C., 978, 1010
Shillingford, J.D., 327
Shillingford, Jennifer, 327
Shillingford, Leona, 327
Shilstone, E.M., 296
Shinebourne, John, 378, 645
Shoman, Assad, 1308
Shorey, Norma, 1395
Silvera, A., 550, 1384
Simmonds, Jessica, see also
    Wellum, Jessica, 432
Simms, Peter, 1189
Simpson, Donald H., 53, 527
Simpson, George Eaton, 1256, 1270
Sims, Janet L., 538
Sims, Michael, 275
Singewald, Joseph, 1142
Singh, K.B., 693, 720
Singh, Paul G., 1172
Singham, A.W., 1163, 1186
Sinha, N.K.P., 760
Sistema Interamericano de
    Información para las Ciencias
    Agrícolas (AGRINTER), 483
Sivanandan, A., 662
Sjögren, Bengt, 602
Slader, C.H. Yorke, 995
Slavin, Suzy, 118

Smith, Ann Thirkell, 451
Smith, George Wilfred, 1257
Smith, John Russel, 133
Smith, M.G., 1375
Smith, Raymond T., 369
*Social and Economic Studies, 259,
    605, 777, 904, 1149, 1155,
    1160, 1218, 1262, 1330, 1373,
    1392
Social and Preventive Medicine,
    Department of. University of
    the West Indies. Mona, 1126,
    1127, 1354
Social Sciences, Faculty of.
    University of the West Indies.
    St. Augustine, 617
Sociology, Department of. Univer-
    sity of Texas. Austin, 1211
Sociology, Department of. Univer-
    sity of the West Indies. St.
    Augustine, 1356
Soil Science, Department of.
    University of the West Indies.
    St. Augustine, 493
Solomon, Mervyn M., 629
Soodeen, Rawwida, 460
*Southeastern Latin Americanist,
    417
Southern Illinois University, see
    University of Southern
    Illinois
*Southwestern Journal of Anthro-
    pology, 1296
Spackman, Ann, 1173
Spano, Angelo F., 740
Spingarn, Arthur B., see Arthur
    B. Spingarn
Spurdle, Frederick G., 1174
Stancil, Carol F., 134
Standing Committee on National
    and University Libraries
    Latin American Group, 107
Stanford University, 1190
Stanton, Robert J., 559
Starkey, Otis P., 135
State, Department of. United
    States, 142, 616, 1302, 1351
Statistical Office. United
    Nations, 1208
Statistics, Department of.
    Jamaica, 1207, 1214

Steele, Beverley, 330
Steer, Edgar S., 506, 507
Stephens Book Department, 539, 554
Stephenson, Wenda, 396
Stephenson, Yvonne V., 379, 382, 383, 1191, 1194, 1246
Stevens, H., 136
Stevens, Henry, 54, 55
Stevenson, Robert Murrel, 1135
Steward, Julien H., 694
Stoelting, Winifred L., 1082
Stone, Carl, 1152
Stuart, Bertie A. Cohen, 1393
*Studies in Black Literature, 1066
Sugar Producers' Association. Barbados, 884
Sussex University, see University of Sussex
Suter, H.H., 765
Szwed, John F., 711

Tarriff Commission. United States, 585
Tauber, Irene B., 1209
Taylor, Douglas MacRae, 680, 923
Technical Information Service. Caribbean Industrial Research Institute, 745
Tekse, Kalman, 1207, 1214
Temple University, 592
Texas A and M University, 1254
Texas University, see University of Texas
Thomas, Leila, 1112
Thomas, Mary Barta, 1192
Thompson, Donald, 1136
Thompson, John Eric, 519, 682
Thompson, Lawrence S., 137
Thorpe, Marjorie, 1036
Tiele, P.A., 370
Tillinghast, William H., 1145
Tobago Regional Library. Central Library of Trinidad and Tobago, 139
Tomlinson, Sally, 1225
Tooley, Ronald Vere, 246, 286, 328
Toomey, Alice F., 19
Trade, Industry, Agriculture and Tourism, Ministry of. St.

Lucia, 622
*Trinidad, 1080
Trinidad and Tobago Gazette, 444
Trinidad and Tobago High Court, 953
Trinidad and Tobago Historical Society, see Historical Society of Trinidad and Tobago
Trinidad and Tobago Independence Celebrations [Committee], 440
Trinidad and Tobago Ministry ..., see under name of Ministry
Trinidad and Tobago National Bibliography, 77
*Trinidad and Tobago Review, 1032
*Trinidad and Tobago Yearbook, 426, 427
Trinidad Public Library, 67, 539, 866, 1258
Trinidad Regional Virus Laboratory University of the West Indies, 1275
*Tropical Agriculture, 458, 485-487
Troyna, B.S., 703
Tucker, Terry, 317, 849
Tulane University, 56a, 275a, 1279
Tulane University Library, 56a
Tweedy, Mary Johnson, 604
*Twentieth Century Literature, 1076
Twining, Mary Arnold, 714, 715
Tyson, Carolyn, 823
Tyson, George F., 819, 823

UCWI, see University of the West Indies
Udal, John Symonds, 716
Ulibarri, George S., 822
UNESCO, see United National Educational Scientific and Cultural Organization
Union of Cultural Clubs. British Guiana, 371
Union Géographique Internationale, 736
United Nations, 241, 751, 736, 842, 843, 1208, 1331a, 1331b, 1364, 1365, 1381, 1382, 1392a

United Nations Educational
Scientific and Cultural
Organization, 241, 842, 843
United Nations Educational
Scientific and Cultural
Organization, see also
Organisation des Nations
Unies par l'Education, la
Science et Culture
United Nations Library. Kingston,
1392a
United States Committee for
UNICEF. New York, 1056
United States Department ...,
see under name of Department
United States. Library of
Congress, see Library of
Congress
Universal Negro Improvement
Association. Kingston, 555
Universidad Católica "Andrés
Bello". Caracas, 678
Universidad de Puerto Rico, 612
Universidad de Puerto Rico, see
also University of Puerto
Rico
Université de Montreal.
Martinique, 510, 673
Université Libre de Bruxelles,
941
University Centre. Univer-
sity of the West Indies.
Montserrat, 418
University Centre Library.
University of the West
Indies. Antigua, 63
University College of the West
Indies. Mona, 769, 844,
1070, 1139
University College of the West
Indies, see also University
of the West Indies
University of California.
Berkeley, 1389
University of California. Los
Angeles, 134
University of Florida. Gaines-
ville, 58, 116, 205, 1051
*University of Florida Agricul-
tural Experiment Station
Bulletin, 467

University of Florida Libraries,
58, 1051
University of Florida Research
Library, 205
University of Guelph, 667
University of Guelph Library, 667
University of Guyana, 21, 206,
207, 358, 377-383, 386, 397,
564, 575, 627, 645, 648, 653,
654, 695, 720, 721, 741, 853,
877, 907, 924, 928, 1090,
1172, 1176, 1188, 1246
University of Guyana Library, 21,
206, 207, 377-383, 397, 564,
627, 645, 648, 653, 654, 695,
720, 721, 853, 907, 924, 928,
1090, 1176, 1246
University of London, 45, 59,
60, 107, 208, 233, 263, 277,
278, 445, 774, 826, 942,
1177, 1299
University of Maryland, 888
University of Miami. Coral
Gables, 145, 752
University of Oxford, 609, 610,
824, 865
University of Puerto Rico, 69,
172, 262, 833, 1210, 1256,
1270, 1323
University of Puerto Rico, see
also Universidad de Puerto
Rico
University of Southern Illinois,
146
University of Sussex, 61, 219,
1226, 1352
University of Texas. Austin, 62,
146a, 209, 247, 920, 1211
University of Texas. The General
Libraries, 146a
University of Texas Library.
Austin, 62, 209, 920
University of the West Indies,
63, 418, 420, 460, 565, 831,
838, 924, 925, 940, 1059,
1061, 1216, 1232, 1273,
1275, 1398
University of the West Indies, see
also University College of
the West Indies

University of the West Indies.
Cave Hill, 64, 148, 148a,
210-213, 219, 285b, 293a,
469, 478, 595, 777, 791, 934,
942a, 943-948, 950, 956,
962, 963, 969, 970, 973, 974,
976, 1000, 1002, 1007, 1011,
1011a, 1020, 1028, 1178,
1212, 1249a, 1353, 1373,
1391, 1395

University of the West Indies.
Mona, 22, 74, 78, 149-151,
153, 214, 215, 225, 248,
279, 280, 406, 409, 410, 505,
617, 649-651, 737, 738, 831,
838, 857, 872, 877, 885, 886,
890, 926, 949, 961, 1048,
1071, 1073, 1126, 1127, 1139,
1151-1153, 1158, 1163, 1179,
1180, 1206, 1329, 1331, 1334,
1337, 1338, 1354, 1355, 1366,
1367, 1369, 1375, 1392a, 1403

University of the West Indies.
St. Augustine, 23, 24, 65,
77, 152, 154, 155, 216-218,
283, 453-458, 470-473, 479,
480, 485-488, 493, 497, 565,
596, 617, 618, 639, 652,
658, 668, 698, 701, 705,
707, 708, 745, 794, 882, 883,
890, 899, 927, 1049, 1050,
1072, 1091, 1238, 1247,
1276, 1303, 1353, 1356-1359,
1396, 1406

University of the West Indies
Faculty of Law Library. Cave
Hill, 210, 211, 595, 934,
943-947, 956, 962, 963, 969,
970, 973, 974, 976, 1002,
1007, 1011, 1011a, 1020,
1028

University of the West Indies
Library. Cave Hill, 63, 64,
148a, 213, 285b, 293a, 791,
956, 1249a

University of the West Indies
Library. Mona, 22, 74, 153,
215, 225, 226, 279, 280,
406, 409, 769, 790, 793,
825, 926, 961, 1048, 1073,
1163, 1269, 1369, 1392a

University of the West Indies
Library. St. Augustine, 23,
24, 65, 77, 154, 155, 216-
218, 283, 458, 471-473, 479,
480, 485, 497, 565, 596, 618,
639, 652, 658, 668, 698, 701,
708, 745, 794, 883, 899, 927,
1050, 1247, 1353, 1359, 1396

University of Uppsala, 700

University of Wisconsin. Madison,
481, 482, 623, 1335

University of Wisconsin. Milwaukee, 677, 781

UWI, see University of the West
Indies

Vanderwal, Ronald L., 795
Van Ee, Patricia, 246a
Varlack, Pearl, 321
Vaughn, Robert V., 156
Vernon, L.G., 300
VILINET, see Virgin Islands
Library and Information Net-
work
Villiers, J.A.J. de, 1193
Vinson, James, 529-531
Virgin Islands Library and
Information Network, 203
*Voices, 1080
Von Scholten Collection. St.
Thomas Public Library, 57

Waddell, David Alan Gilmour, 309,
796
Wagenaar, Hummelinck P., 157-163
Walcott, Derek, 1095
Walkley, Jane, 1065
Wallace, Elisabeth, 1181
Wallace, J. Allen, 740
Walne, Peter, 826
Walrond, Cheryl, 164
Walsh, B. Thomas, 1339
Walvin, James, 856
War Office. Great Britain, 244
Warden, David Baillie, 165
Wardle, D.B., 827, 828
Warwick, Ronald, 1093
Waters, Hazel, 1227
Watson, Gayle, 18
Watson, Karl S., 1051
Watts, David, 580

Weather Bureau. United States,
740, 742
Weisbrod, Burton, 1341
Welch, I.A., 728
Weller, Judith Ann, 1323
Wellum, Jessica, see also
Simmonds, Jessica
Welt-Wirtschafts-Archiv
Bibliothek. Hamburg, 108,
109
Wenner-Gren Foundation for
Anthropological Research,
680
West, Robert Cooper, 739
West, Stanley L., 256
West India Committee. London,
66
West India Reference Library.
Institute of Jamaica, 16,
42, 75, 76, 193, 194, 229,
230, 404, 406, 411, 550, 551,
696, 918, 1073, 1077, 1239-
1241, 1360, 1384
West Indian Branch. Trinidad
Public Library, 1258
West Indian Collection. Barbados
Public Library, 175
West Indian Collection. Univer-
sity of the West Indies
Library. Cave Hill, 64
*West Indian Law Journal, 939
West Indian Legislation Indexing
Project. Faculty of Law
Library. University of the
West Indies. Cave Hill, 962,
963, 969, 970, 973, 974, 976,
1000, 1002, 1007, 1011, 1020,
1028
West Indian Medical Journal,
1275
West Indian Reference Collection.
Central Library of Trinidad
and Tobago, 646, 712
West Indian Reference Section.
Carnegie Free Library, 536
West Indian Reference Section.
Central Library of Trinidad
and Tobago, 199, 200, 253,
254, 560, 576, 647, 706, 713,
723, 724, 879, 1069, 1086,
1087, 1115, 1119, 1175, 1394

*West Indian Science and Tech-
nology, 1273
West Indies. Federation, 227,
257, 1248, 1249
West Indies Festival of Arts,
797
*West Indische Gids, 114
Westerman, J.H., 569, 1140
Westlake, Donald E., 1183
Westminster City Libraries.
London, 168
Whim Greathouse Collection, 171
White, Janet, 651
Whitten, Norman E., 169
Widdicombe, Stacey H., 889, 1340
Wilkinson, Audine, 148, 285b,
469, 1395
Wilkinson, Henry Campbell, 318,
850
Will, Henry Austin, 1181
William Bryant Foundation, 34
Williams, D., 566
Williams, Daniel T., 567
Williams, Don, 702
Williams, Eric, 170, 611, 798,
799, 864, 1284, 1304
Williams, Fay M., 996, 997
Williams, James, 931
Williams, Joseph John, 697, 717
Williams, N.M., see N.M. Williams
Memorial Ethnological
Collection
Williams, R.L., 885, 890
Williams, Rosalie, 75, 696, 1077,
1239
Williams, W.E., 950
Wilson, Charles Morrow, 170a
Wilson, P.N., 489
Wilson, Pamela, 1392
WINBAN, see Windward Islands
Banana Research Scheme
Windward Islands Banana Research
Scheme, 474, 475
Winter, E.E., 1141
*WLWE Newsletter, 1074
Wood, Donald, 1324
Woman's Bureau of Jamaica, 1391
Woodward, Ralph Lee, 309a
Woolbert, Robert Gale, 908
Woolrich, B.M.A., 310
Work, Monroe, 6, 681

Working Party on Library Holdings
    of Commonwealth Literature.
    Commonwealth Institute.
    London, 1093
World Agricultural Economics and
    Rural Sociology Abstracts,
    451
World Bank, 43
*World Literature Written in
    English, 556, 1036, 1080,
    1089a
Worthy Park Sugar Estate, 856
Wren, Maureen, 568, 1131
Wright, Philip, 229
Wright, Rae, 1037
Wright, Richardson Little, 1319
Wroth, Lawrence C., 829
Wulff, Erika, 171
Wust, Georg, 1146

*Yearbook of Caribbean Research,
    86
Yusuf, Zarina, 425

Zaretsky, Irving I., 1379
Zavalloni, Marisa, 1399
Zetzekorn, William David, 311
Zimmerman, Irene K., 172, 258
Zoology, Department of. Univer-
    sity of the West Indies.
    Mona, 1403
Zoology, Department of. Univer-
    sity of the West Indies. St.
    Augustine, 1406
Zubatsky, David S., 278
Zuvekas, Clarence, 459

Subject Index

Acculturation, 1297
Administration, legal, see Legal
 administration
Administration, public, see
 Public administration
Adolescence, see Youth
Adams, Sir Grantley Herbert,
 526, 527
Adult education, see Education
 adult
African diaspora, see Blacks
Africans, 1303, see also Blacks
Agard, Clifford, 525
Agrarian reform, see Land Reform
Agricultural economics, 453, 454,
 457, 476-482, 494
 Barbados, 477
 Dominica, 478
 Guyana, 477, 495
Agricultural education, see
 Education, agricultural
Agricultural extension, 453, 454
 Guyana, 495
 Jamaica, 508
Agricultural marketing, 476
 Jamaica, 738
Agricultural planning, 1331a
Agricultural statistics, see
 Statistics - agriculture
Agriculture, 63, 86, 87, 105,
 451-459, 609, 610, 614, 617,
 739, 1291, 1329, 1331
 Antigua, 451, 459
 Bahamas, 291
 Barbados, 293a, 451, 459
 Belize, 305, 459, 1308
 British Virgin Islands, 459

Cayman Islands, 459
Dominica, 324, 326, 451, 459
Grenada, 451, 459, 494
Guyana, 341, 372, 382, 495-
 497, 575, 625, 1314
Jamaica, 451, 504-508, 738,
 888
Leeward Islands, 451
Montserrat, 451, 459
St. Kitts-Nevis-Anguilla, 459
St. Lucia, 451, 459
St. Vincent, 451, 459
Trinidad and Tobago, 451,
 509, 1382a
Turks and Caicos Islands, 459
Windward Islands, 451
Agriculture, tropical, 65, 455,
 458
 Indexes, 65
Agro-industries, 1271
Agronomy, 490
Alcoholism, 594
 Jamaica, 1132
Ali, Jamal, see Agard, Clifford
Alladin, M.P., 525, 528
Allen, Oswald, 528
Allfrey, Phyllis Shand, 525, 1059
Als, Michael, 525, 528
Amerindian languages, 923
Amerindians, 82, 679, 680, 734
 Guyana, 341, 350, 378, 688,
 689, 692, 694
Anguilla, see Leeward Islands and
 St. Kitts-Nevis-Anguilla,
 see also under specific
 subjects
Anguilla secession, 1183

Animal health, Animal husbandry,
    Animal nutrition, Animal
    physiology, Animal produc-
    tion, see Animal science
Animal science, 457, 486, 487,
    489
    Belize, 305
    Dominica, 326
    Guyana, 495
        see also Dairy science,
        Livestock science
Anthologies, 1032, 1045, 1051,
    1052, 1074, 1090
Anthony, Michael, 523, 525, 528,
    530, 1059, 1061, 1079
Anthropology, 78, 113, 123, 510-
    514, 516, 533, 671, 675,
    Bahamas, 672, 834
    Belize, 515, 515a, 680
    Guyana, 353, 694
    Dominica, 532
    Jamaica, 511
    Trinidad and Tobago, 437, 516
Anthropology, physical, 510, 511,
    513
    social, 1352
Anthropometry, 510
Antigua, 49, 225, 284-286, see
    also Leeward Islands and
    under specific subjects
Aquatic sciences
    Guyana, 495
Arawak languages, 918
    Guyana, 929
Arawaks, 675
    Guyana, 694
Archaeology, 56, 79, 123, 517,
    520, 522, 671, 1348
    Bahamas, 518, 834
    Belize, 309a, 519, 522a
    Guyana, 341, 691
    Jamaica, 859
    Trinidad and Tobago, 437, 520
Architecture
    Guyana, 521
    Jamaica, 186
Archibald, Douglas, 525, 528,
    529, 1040
Archives, 17, 766, 767, 775,
    797, 803, 804, 815
    Anguilla, 831
    Antigua, 831

Bahamas, 836
Barbados, 838-840, 844
Barbuda, 831
Bermuda, 312, 317, 813
British Virgin Islands, 831,
    851
Dominica, 813, 832, 833
Grenada, 832, 833, 852
Grenadines, 832
Guyana, 855, 1194
Jamaica, 862
Leeward Islands, 831
Montserrat, 831
Nevis, 831
St. Kitts, 831
St. Lucia, 420, 832, 833
St. Vincent, 832, 833
Trinidad, 813
Trinidad and Tobago, 440, 866
Windward Islands, 813, 832, 833,
    see also History –
    Archival and manuscript
    material
Archives, ecclesiastical
    Barbados, 838, 844, 845
    Jamaica, 860
    Windward Islands, 833
Aroids, 461, 473
Arrowroot, 473
Art, 170
    Barbados, 293a
    Belize, 522a
    Periodicals and serials, 1092
    Pre-Columbian, 522
Arthur, William S., 525
Arts, 79, 99, 1224
    Antigua, 285b
    Barbuda, 285b
    Jamaica, 186, 398, 402 see
        see also Creative arts,
        Fine arts, Folk arts
Ashby, Osborne, 525, 528
Ashtine, Eaulin, 525, 528
Associated States, see West Indies
    Associated States
Author bibliography, see Bibliog-
    raphy, individual and
    biography, collective
Autobiography
    Trinidad and Tobago, 1113
Avocado, 462
Bahama Islands, see Bahamas

Bahamas, 25, 43, 49, 51-53, 97,
113, 125, 141, 287-291
see also under specific
subjects
Banana, 457, 462, 465, 471, 472,
474, 475
Banana industry, 468, 471, 478
Banking
Trinidad and Tobago, 629
Baptist Missionary Society
Papers, 802
Baptists, 802
Barbados, 23, 28, 49, 51-53, 72,
81, 113, 135, 141, 292, 293
see also under specific
subjects
Barbados cherry, see Cherry, West
Indian
Barbados Sugar Industry Review
Indexes, 884
Barbuda, 285a, 285b
see also Leeward Islands and
under specific subjects
Barrett, C. Lindsay, 525
Barrow, Errol Walton, 526
Bartica. Guyana, 359
Baugh, Edward Alston Cecil, 525
Bauxite industry
Guyana, 876, 886, 1141
Jamaica, 876, 886
Beans, 465
Beaubrun, Michael H., 562
Belize, 43, 50-52, 141, 185,
297-311, 682
see also British Honduras and
under specific subjects
Bennet, Alvin G., 525
Bennett, Louise, 525, 1049, 1059,
1064
Bermuda, 25, 29, 43, 51-53, 97,
125, 134, 312-318
see also under specific
subjects
Bermuda triangle, 134
Bibliographic essays, see Essays,
bibliographic
Bim
Indexes, 1089, 1091
Biogeography, 738

Biography, 118, 128, 184, 775,
1039, 1044, 1047
Guyana, 334, 336
St. Lucia, 420
Biography, collective, 523-531
Tobago, 435
Trinidad and Tobago, 437, 1113
Biography, individual, 532-568
Biology, 569
Bahamas, 570
Bermuda, 571
Guyana, 572-575
Trinidad and Tobago, 576
see also Botany, Natural
History, Zoology
Biology, marine, 1272, 1274
Bird, Vere Cornwall, 526
Birds
Trinidad and Tobago, 187
see also Ornithology
Black, Clinton, 525
Black arts movement. United
States, 1039
Black Caribs, see Caribs, black
Black culture, 676, 677, 1277,
1344, 1345
Black history, 33
"Black Irish"
Jamaica, 697
Black literature, 33, 48, 681,
1039, 1046
see also Literature
Black peasantry, see Peasantry,
black
Black power, 1039, 1346
Trinidad and Tobago, 1201
Blacks, 82, 512, 681, 685
Great Britain, 915, 1224
Guyana, 685
Jamaica, 697
see also Africans,
Ethnic groups
Blaize, Herbert A., 526
Book reviews, see Criticism
Border disputes, see Boundary
disputes
Botany, 577-579
Barbados, 580
Belize, 305
Dominica, 326
Guyana, 581, 582
see also Flora, Natural
history

Botany, medical, 577a
Boundary disputes
    Belize, 299, 1184, 1185
    Guyana, 854, 1187, 1188, 1193
        Indexes, 1195
Brain drain, 1357
Braithwaite, E.R., 525, 1040,
    1059
Bramble, William, 526
Brassicas, 463
Brathwaite, Edward Kamau, 523–
    525, 531, 1040, 1049, 1059,
    1061, 1064
British Caribbean Court of
    Appeal, 955
British Guiana, 52, 53, 103, 125,
    126, 225, 331–335, 339, 340,
    343–345, 353, 355–358, 360,
    362, 364, 366–371, 373–376,
    378, 379, 381
    see also Guyana
British Honduras, 125, 297, 300–
    302, 306, 308, 309, 310
    see also Belize
British Virgin Islands, 320, 321
    see also under specific
    subjects
Brown, Lennox, 525
Brown, Wayne, 523, 525
Buccaneers, 100, 103, 773
Burnham, Linden Forbes Sampson,
    526
Business, see Commerce
Bustamante, Sir William Alexander
    Clarke, 526, 527
Butler, T.U.B., 1197
Cacao, see Cocoa
Caicos Islands, see Turks and
    Caicos Islands
Calypso, 169, 699, 701, 708,
    1136
    Trinidad, 707
Cambridge, Arnold, 525, 528
Cameron, Norman E., 525, 534,
    1040
Campbell, George, 525, 1059
Campbell, John, 525
Cannabis
    Jamaica, 1132
Carberry, H.D., 525, 1059

Carew, Jan, 523–525, 527, 1040,
    1041, 1059
Carib languages, 918
Caribbean Commission, 788, 1236,
    1244
Caribbean Community, 1238, 1247
    Treaties, 1238
Caribbean Free Trade Association,
    1231, 1239
Caribbean studies projects.
    University of the West Indies,
    150–152
Caribs, 675, 679, 683
    Dominica, 324, 532
Caribs, Black, 680
    Belize, 669a, 1136, 1307
Caricom, see Caribbean Community
Carifta, see Caribbean Free Trade
    Association
Carnival, 169, 533, 701, 708
    Trinidad and Tobago, 187,
        704–706, 708
Carter, Martin, 523, 525, 531,
    1040, 1041, 1049, 1059, 1064
Cartey, Wilfred, 525
Casimir, Joseph Raphael Ralph, 525
Cassava, 461
Castor oil, 463
Catholics, 1250, 1253
Cayman Islands, 25
    see also under specific
    subjects
Censuses, 221, 1208, 1209, 1211
    Jamaica, 1214
    Trinidad and Tobago, 1382a
        see also Population,
        Vital statistics
Central government, see Govern-
    ment, central
Chaguaramas. Trinidad, 1202,
    1342
Challenger Expedition. Bermuda,
    571
Charles, Bertram, 525
Charles, Faustin, 525
Cherry, Barbados, see Cherry, West
    Indian
Cherry, West Indian, 459a, 467
Chinese, 1303
Christian Missions, see Missions,
    Christian

Church
    Baptist, see Baptists
    Catholic, see Catholics
    Church archives, see
        Archives, ecclesiastical
Church history, 812, 1255, 1258
Churches
    Jamaica, 31
Ciboney, 675
Cipriani, Arthur Andrew, 525,
    527, 1293
Citrus, 465, 472
Citrus industry
    Dominica, 885
Civil rights, 947a
Civil service, see Public service
Clarke, A.M., 525, 528, 1040, 1059
Clarke, Austin C., 525, 530,
    1040, 1059, 1064, 1079
Climate, 81, 492, 732-735
    Belize, 740
    Guyana, 742, 760
        see also Climatology,
        Geography
Climatology, 732, 1272, 1274
    Dominica, 326
    Jamaica, 738
        see also Climate,
        Environmental sciences,
        Geography
Cobham, Gilles, L., 525, 528
Cocoa, 457, 465, 466
Cocoa industry
    Dominica, 885
Coconut, 465
Coffee
    Jamaica, 890
Coffee industry, 45
    Jamaica, 890
Collymore, Frank, 525, 531, 1040,
    1041, 1059, 1064
Colonial history, see History,
    colonial
Colonial office papers, 801, 804
Commerce, 583-585, 612, 1232,
    1329
    Barbados, 293a
    Guyana, 625
    Trinidad and Tobago, 201
Commissions of enquiry, 124, 594,
    1320
    Indexes, 104, 445

Jamaica, 1338
    Sugar industry, 469
    Trinidad and Tobago, 431, 445,
        864, 1200, 1320
Common Market. Caribbean, 105,
    619-621
Communication, 586-592, 1397
    Anguilla, 587, 590
    Antigua, 587, 590
    Bahamas, 587, 589, 591
    Barbados, 586, 587, 590, 591
    Belize, 309a
    Bermuda, 587, 589, 590, 591
    Dominica, 587, 590
    Grenada, 587, 590, 591
    Guyana, 341, 586, 593
    Jamaica, 586, 587, 589-591
    Leeward Islands, 589, 591
    Montserrat, 587, 590
    Nevis, 587, 590
    St. Kitts, 587, 590
    St. Lucia, 587, 590
    St. Vincent, 587, 590
    Trinidad, 586
    Trinidad and Tobago, 587,
        589-591
    Windward Islands, 589
Community development
    Guyana, 1335
Community relations, 239
Comparative education, see Educa-
    tion, comparative
Conservation, 569, 1140
Constantine, Learie, 525, 527
Constitution
    Guyana, 346
Constitutional history, see
    History, constitutional
Construction, 86
Consumption economics, 610
Cookery, 154, 711
    Jamaica, 186
Coolie immigrants, see Immigrants,
    coolie
Cooperation, regional, see
    Regional cooperation and
    integration
Cooperative Republic of Guyana,
    see Guyana
Cooperatives, 615, 631
    Guyana, 626, 627
    Trinidad and Tobago, 615, 631

Corruption, 594
Cotton, 463
Coulthard, Gabriel, 525
Couronians
    Tobago, 863
Court of Appeal, Jamaica, 954,
    955
Courts martial
    Trinidad and Tobago, 1201
Court of Appeal, 954, 955
Creative arts, 79
    Jamaica, 398
        see also Arts, Fine Arts
Credit unions
    Trinidad and Tobago, 1377
Creole languages, 909-915, 919-
    923, 927
    Dominica, 910, 921
    Grenada, 921
    Guyana, 930
    St. Lucia, 910, 919, 921
    Trinidad, 921
Creoles
    Jamaica, 399
Cricket
    Trinidad and Tobago, 187
Criminology, 594
    Jamaica, 595
Criticism, 99, 420, 1031, 1032,
    1037, 1039, 1045, 1047-1049,
    1052, 1059-1065, 1074, 1089,
    1091, 1094, 1095
    Indexes, 1089, 1091, 1362
Crop husbandry, see Crop science
Crop science, 453, 454, 457, 460-
    475
    Belize, 305
    Dominica, 326
    Guyana, 456a, 495, 498, 499
    Jamaica, 506
    Trinidad and Tobago, 465a
Crowley, Daniel J., 525, 533
Cult music, 699
    Trinidad and Tobago, 1136
Cults, folk, see Folk cults
Cults, religious, see Religious
    cults
Cultural pluralism, 169
Culture, 79, 102, 106, 154, 525,
    664, 788, 1329
    Barbados, 293a
    Belize, 305, 306

Dominica, 326
Guyana, 334, 693, 719, 920
Jamaica, 398, 402
Trinidad and Tobago, 705
Women, 1393
Culture, black, see Black culture
Culture, folk, see Folk culture
Cundall, Frank, 525
Curriculum development, 651
    see also Education
Customs union, 1247
Da Costa, Jean Constantine, 525
Daily Gleaner
    Indexes, 1360
Dairy husbandry, see Dairy science
Dairy science, 457, 488, 489
    see also Animal science,
    Livestock science
Dance, 148a, 699, 701, 711, 1039,
    1136
    Jamaica, 1136
    Trinidad and Tobago, 187, 596
        see also Folk dance
Daniel, Edith, 525, 528
Dasheen, 464
    see also Aroids
Dathorne, O.R., 525, 530, 1040,
    1059
De Boissiere, Ralph, 525, 528,
    1041, 1059
De Coteau, Delano, see Malik,
    Abdul
Delinquency, 594
De Lisser, Herbert George, 525,
    1040, 1059, 1079
Democratic Labour Party. Trinidad
    and Tobago, 1201
Demography, see Population
Dentistry
    Guyana, 1131
Description and travel, 42, 46,
    79, 93, 128, 144, 153, 597-
    602, 676, 783, 1044
    Belize, 847
    Bermuda, 604
    Guyana, 341, 362, 599
    Jamaica, 599
    Leeward Islands, 603
    St. Lucia, 420
    Trinidad and Tobago, 437
    Windward Islands, 603
        see also Geography

Development, community, see
  Community development
Development, rural, see Rural
  development
Development plans, 1327, 1328
Deviant behaviour, 594
Dialect languages, 309a, 911,
  912, 915, 921, 924-926
  see also Creole languages,
  Patois language, Pidgin
  languages
Dialect languages, negro, 917
Dialectology, 169
Disabled, education of, 651
Discography, see Phonodiscs
Discrimination, racial, see
  Racial discrimination
Diseases, communicable
  Guyana, 1131
    see also under specific
    diseases
Diseases, tropical, 1341
  St. Lucia, 1341
    see also under specific
    diseases
Dissertations, doctoral, 57, 261,
  262, 264, 266-272, 274-280
  Agriculture, 453, 454, 461
  Bahamas, 268
  Belize, 309a, 768
  East Indians, 668
  Economics, 774
  Education, 641a, 652, 774
  Ethnic groups, 664
  Geology, 763
  Guyana, 768
  History, 768, 774, 777
  Jamaica, 268, 417, 763, 768
  Law, 774
  Literature, 1064
  Performing arts, 1136
  Population, 1210
  Science, 1273
  Sociology, 774
  Trinidad and Tobago, 268
    see also Theses
Dixon, McDonald, 525
DLP, see Democratic Labour Party
Doctoral dissertations, see
  Dissertations, doctoral
D'Oliveira, Evadne, 525

Dominica, 49, 324-327
  see also Windward Islands and
  under specific subjects
Drama, 148a, 525, 1031, 1032,
  1034, 1039, 1044, 1047, 1048,
  1050, 1052, 1066-1072, 1083,
  1085
  Barbados, 293a, 1035
  Grenada, 1035, 1036
  Guyana, 336, 362, 721, 1035,
    1102, 1105, 1106
  Indexes, 1089, 1091
  Jamaica, 1035, 1111
  Montserrat, 1036
  Trinidad, 1035
  Trinidad and Tobago, 187, 440,
    1036, 1113, 1115, 1116
Drayton, Geoffrey, 525, 1059
Dress, 711
Drug abuse, 594
Du Simitière papers, 810
East Indian indenture, 1323
East Indians, 668, 695, 1303,
  1359
  Culture, 668, 693
  Economics, 668
  Guyana, 670, 687, 691, 693,
    695, 720
  History, 668
  Jamaica, 670
  Literature, 668, 1102
  Politics, 668
  Sociology, 668
  Trinidad, 1321-1323
  Trinidad and Tobago, 670, 698,
    1198
    see also Hindus
Eastern Caribbean Federation,
  1298
Ecology
  Guyana, 341, 573
  Plant, 579
    Guyana, 575
Economic conditions, 42, 78a, 119,
  144, 613, 676, 734, 739, 818,
  1161, 1168, 1280, 1287-1304,
  1306, 1325
  Antigua, 285b
  Barbados, 293a, 837, 1306
  Barbuda, 285b
  Belize, 1307, 1308

Guyana, 353, 369, 980, 1309–
1314, 1334
Jamaica, 889, 1315–1319
Leeward Islands, 283
St. Lucia, 622
Trinidad and Tobago, 201,
1197, 1320–1324
Economic development, 81, 610,
1232, 1233, 1325–1331, 1336,
1357, 1358, 1391a
Dominica, 885
Guyana, 341, 1310, 1333,
1334, 1335
Jamaica, 1336–1340
St. Lucia, 1341
Trinidad and Tobago, 1342
see also Industrial
development
Economic geography, see Geo-
graphy, economic
Economic history, see History,
economic
Economic integration, see
Integration, economic
Economic planning, 1331, 1331a
Economic statistics, see
Statistics, economic
Economics, 45, 63, 78, 93, 106,
113, 119, 123, 127, 128, 145,
184, 605–621, 632, 788,
1158, 1159, 1165, 1228, 1291
Barbados, 613
Belize, 305, 306, 309, 309a,
311
Dominica, 326
Guyana, 185, 372, 382, 495,
613, 624–627, 1371
Indexes, 619–621
Jamaica, 186, 402, 404, 609,
613, 628, 1374
Periodicals and serials,
1368
Trinidad and Tobago, 187,
613, 629–633, 1376
Women, 1393
Economics, consumption, see
Consumption economics
Economics, production, see
Production economics
Economics, transport, see
Transport economics
Education, 45, 59, 60, 87, 105,

106, 123, 184, 634–652, 662,
664, 676, 916, 1220–1223,
1225, 1329, 1357, 1358
Barbados, 293a, 837
Belize, 641
Guyana, 185, 341, 346, 362,
372, 495, 625, 635, 641,
642, 653, 654, 1332
Jamaica, 404, 410, 641, 642
Indexes, 655, 656
Trinidad and Tobago, 187, 641,
642, 657, 658, 1382a
Indexes, 659
Women, 1391, 1393
see also Curriculum
development
Education, adult
Trinidad and Tobago, 657
Education, agricultural, 495, 645,
646
Education, comparative, 60
Education, family life, see
Family life education
Education, higher, 634, 635
Education, home economics, 646
Education, industrial, 645, 646
Education, medical, 645
Education, secondary
Trinidad, 647
Trinidad and Tobago, 705
Education, technical, 645, 646
Guyana, 654
Trinidad and Tobago, 657
Education, vocational, 645
Trinidad and Tobago, 632
Educational planning, 1331a
Edwards, Walter, 928
Eggplant, 463, 472
Elder, J.D., 525
Elections, 1154, 1158
Anguilla, 1178
Antigua, 1178
Barbados, 1178
Dominica, 1178
Grenada, 1178
Guyana, 1151
Montserrat, 1178
Nevis, 1178
St. Kitts, 1178
St. Lucia, 1178
St. Vincent, 1178
Trinidad and Tobago, 1201

Employment, 614, 660, 664, 1219–
    1223, 1357, 1358
    Trinidad and Tobago, 632
    Women, 1391
Emtage, James, B., 525, 1059
Endicott, Stephen, see Roberts,
    Walter Adolphe
Energy, 1139
Engineering, 86
Entomology
    Guyana, 1404
        see also Zoology
Environmental planning, 1331b
Environmental sciences
    Bahamas, 291
    Dominica, 327
        see also Climatology,
        Geography
Escoffery, Gloria, 525, 1059
Eseoghene, see Barrett, C.
    Lindsay
Essays, 1034, 1049
    Guyana, 362
Essays, bibliographic, 102, 110,
    111, 113, 127, 172, 221, 612,
    787, 799
    Biography, 526, 553
    Biology, 569
    Economics, 612
    Education, 640
    Ethnomusicology, 699
    Family planning, 1345a
    Federation, 1245
    Fertility, 1345a
    Folklore, 716
    Grenada, 852
    Guyana, 354, 852a
    History, 769, 776–778, 787,
        792, 796, 798, 814, 852,
        864
    Language and linguistics, 915
    Law, 934, 943a
    Literature, 1081, 1097, 1108
    Medicine, 1120, 1130
    Migration, 1303
    Natural resources, 1138
    Politics and government,
        1157, 1162
    Race relations, 1225, 1227
    Rastafarians, 1262, 1264,
        1267

Regional co-operation, 1233
    Slavery, 1284
    Social sciences, 1345a
    Trinidad and Tobago, 430, 431
Ethics, legal
    see Legal ethics
Ethnic groups, 79, 510, 660–668,
    916, 1054, 1224, 1224a, 1226,
    1303, 1311, 1347
    Barbados, 293a, 669
    Canada, 667
    Great Britain, 660, 662–666,
        1220, 1279, 1294, 1301
    Guyana, 354, 369, 661, 670
        684, 687, 691, 719, 852a,
        1311, 1312
    Jamaica, 399, 670
    Trinidad, 661, 1321–1324
    Trinidad and Tobago, 431, 670
        see also under specific
        ethnic groups
Ethnicity, 1149
    Guyana, 1149, 1150
Ethnography, 671, 1348
    Bahamas, 672
    Guyana, 694
    Trinidad and Tobago, 673–675
Ethnology, 48, 676–681
    Bahamas, 672
    Belize, 682
    Guyana, 345, 350, 354, 683–
        695, 720
    Jamaica, 677
Ethnomusicology, 533, 699–701
    Jamaica, 702, 703
    Trinidad and Tobago, 704–708
Europeans, 82, 1303
Extension, agricultural, see
    Agricultural extension
Family life, 594, 664, 1346,
    1370
    Women, 1391–1393
Family life education, 644, 1126,
    1359, 1397
Family planning, 1126, 1354,
    1354a, 1359
    Barbados, 1354
    Belize, 1354
    Guyana, 1354
    Jamaica, 1354
    Trinidad, 1354

Farming, small scale
    Barbados, 480
    Jamaica, 505
    Trinidad, 480
Farrier, Francis Quamina, 525,
    541, 1040
Fauna, 81, 98, 569, 734
    Belize, 309a, 311
    Bermuda, 315
    Guyana, 350, 572, 574
    Jamaica, 402
    Trinidad and Tobago, 437,
        576, 1406
        see also Natural
        history, Zoology
Fauna, marine, 571
Federal Supreme Court of the
    West Indies, 955
Federalism, see Federation
Federation, 1235, 1237, 1240,
    1241, 1245
    see also Integration,
    regional, Regional coopera-
    tion
Federation, Eastern Caribbean,
    see Eastern Caribbean
    Federation
Federation, West Indies, see
    West Indies Federation
Fertility, 1345a
    Trinidad and Tobago, 1215
Fertilizers, 493
Fibre crops, 463
Fiction, 103a, 139, 184, 525,
    638, 1031, 1032, 1038, 1039,
    1044, 1047, 1048, 1052,
    1073-1088, 1164
    Barbados, 1036
    Dominica, 1036
    Guyana, 1096, 1102, 1107
    Indexes, 1089, 1091, 1118
    Jamaica, 186, 1109
    St. Kitts, 1036
    Trinidad and Tobago, 187,
        434, 436, 440, 1036,
        1114, 1115, 1117
        Indexes, 1118
        see also Novels, Short
        stories
Figueroa, John, 525, 531, 1059

Filariasis
    Guyana, 1128, 1131
Films, 103a, 235, 240
    Jamaica, 404
    Trinidad and Tobago, 449
        see also Non-book
        materials
Finance, 45, 605
    Guyana, 372
    Jamaica, 1340
Finance, public, see Public
    finance
Fine arts
    Guyana, 362
        see also Arts, Creative
        arts
Fiscal policy, 605, 1331
    Trinidad and Tobago, 629
Fisheries, 86, 879, 881
    Guyana, 495, 572, 887
    Jamaica, 506, 1405
    Trinidad and Tobago, 894
Flora, 81, 98, 569, 577, 579,
    734
    Belize, 309a, 311
    Bermuda, 315
    Guyana, 350, 574, 582
    Jamaica, 186, 402
    Kartabo Region. Guyana, 582
    Trinidad and Tobago, 437, 576
        see also Botany, Natural
        history
Flora, Marine, 571
Folk arts
    Jamaica, 398
Folk cults
    Guyana, 720
Folk culture, 711
Folk dance
    Trinidad and Tobago, 437
Folk literature, 1034, 1048
Folk medicine, 78a, 1119a
Folk music, 681, 699
    Jamaica, 1136
        see also Folk songs
Folk songs, 701, 1134
    Belize, 1136
    Black Caribs, 1136
    Trinidad and Tobago, 437

Folk tales, 139, 169, 710, 1050
    Andros Island. Bahamas, 718
    Trinidad and Tobago, 437,
       723, 724
Folklore, 63, 78, 78a, 103a, 169,
    533, 681, 709-717, 1044,
    1345
    Barbados, 293a
    Bahamas, 718
    Guyana, 719-721
    Jamaica, 722
    Trinidad and Tobago, 723-724
Food, 1139, 1331a
Food science, 1271
Food technology, 454
Forde, A.N., 525, 1040, 1059
Foreign exchange
    Trinidad and Tobago, 629
Foreign policy, 902, 904, 907,
    1175
    Anguilla, 906
    Belize, 902, 906
    Guyana, 902, 906, 908
    Jamaica, 900, 902, 906
    Leeward Islands, 906
    Trinidad and Tobago, 900,
      906
    Windward Islands, 906
Foreign relations, see Foreign
    policy
Forest resources, 1139
Forestry, 86, 579, 725, 725a
    Bahamas, 291, 725a
    Barbados, 725
    Belize, 185, 305, 725, 725a
    Dominica, 326
    Guyana, 341, 725-728
    Jamaica, 725a
    Leeward Islands, 725
    Trinidad and Tobago, 725,
      725a, 729-731
    Windward Islands, 725
Freeport. Bahamas, 287
Fruit processing, 467
Fulham papers, 812
Ganja, see Cannabis
Garvey, Amy, 555
Garvey, Marcus Josiah, 527, 537,
    538, 542, 549-551, 555, 567,
    1041, 1293

Genetics, 510
Geochemistry
    Jamaica, 763
Geography, 98, 184, 638, 732-739,
    1272, 1329
    Barbados, 738
    Belize, 309a, 311, 740
    Dominica, 327, 738
    Guyana, 336, 345, 353, 495,
      741, 742
    Jamaica, 186, 738
    Leeward Islands, 293
    Trinidad, 738
    Trinidad and Tobago, 431
      see also Climate,
      Climatology, Description
      and travel, Environmental
      sciences
Geography, economic
    Jamaica, 738
Geography, physical, 117
    Jamaica, 402, 738
Geography, political, 81
Geography, soil, 492
Geography, urban
    Jamaica, 738
Geology, 144, 492, 743-752, 1146,
    1272
    Anguilla, 745
    Antigua, 745
    Bahamas, 753
    Barbados, 745
    Bermuda, 315
    Cayman Islands, 744, 763
    Dominica, 745
    Grenada, 745
    Guyana, 341, 728, 754-760
      Indexes, 761
    Indexes, 743
    Jamaica, 744, 747, 762-764
    Leeward Islands, 745
    Mazuruni-Puruni. Guyana, 757
    Montserrat, 745
    Oko-Blue Mountains. Guyana,
      756
    St. Kitts-Nevis, 745
    St. Lucia, 745
    St. Vincent, 745
    Trinidad, 747, 765
    Windward Islands, 745

Geology, marine, 1274
  Jamaica, 763
Geomorphology, 492
Geophysics, 751, 1146, 1274
Geoscience
  Belize, 305
  Dominica, 326
Geothermics, 751
Geriatrics
  Guyana, 1131
Giglioli, George, 566, 568
Gilkes, Michael, 525
Giuseppi, Neville, 525
Giuseppi, Undine, 525
Gomes, Albert, 525
Gonzalez, Anson, 525, 1059
Gonzalez, Maria, 523, 525
Goveia, Elsa, 523
Government, 78, 93, 98, 106,
  123, 128, 138, 144, 609, 900,
  1154-1182, 1232
  Anguilla, 1183
  Barbados, 837, 1174
  Belize, 1184
  Dominica, 327
  Grenada, 1186
  Guyana, 369, 980, 1150,
    1187-1195
  Jamaica, 1174, 1196
  Leeward Islands, 1174
  Trinidad and Tobago, 1197-
    1203
    see also Politics, Self-
    Government
Government, central
  Guyana, 346
Government, local
  Barbados, 1172
  Guyana, 346, 1172
  Jamaica, 1172, 1196
  Trinidad and Tobago, 1172
Government publications, 16, 58,
  90, 112, 117, 135, 138, 174,
  189, 210, 211, 215, 220-227,
  255, 256, 594, 611, 725,
  745, 934, 943a, 1120-1123,
  1154, 1159, 1166, 1171-1173,
  1180-1183, 1186, 1205, 1207,
  1229, 1234, 1235, 1238,
  1278a, 1290, 1291, 1293,
  1298, 1304, 1326, 1349,
  1382a, 1395

Antigua, 285b
  Serials, 225
Bahamas, 287-289
Barbados, 174, 225, 294, 613,
  842-844, 1172, 1212
  Serials, 225
Barbuda, 285b
Belize, 304, 309a, 1181
Bermuda, 318, 849
British Virgin Islands, 321-
  323
Grenada, 1186
Guyana, 225, 346, 369, 372,
  383, 384, 593, 613, 661,
  754, 758, 759, 761, 886,
  1151, 1172, 1189, 1191,
  1310-1312, 1314, 1332,
  1334
  Serials, 225, 346
Jamaica, 74, 221a, 225, 399,
  411, 412, 505, 613, 857,
  858, 886, 889, 1172,
  1181, 1214, 1243, 1286,
  1317, 1318, 1338, 1340
  Serials, 225, 411
St. Lucia
  Serials, 225
Serials, 70, 222, 223, 226,
  637, 830
Trinidad and Tobago, 225, 253,
  434, 436, 439, 441-445,
  613, 630, 657, 661, 1153,
  1172, 1181, 1186, 1198,
  1202, 1243, 1322, 1323
  Indexes, 445, 630
  Serials, 225, 442-444
West Indies Federation, 1243,
  1246
    see also Parliamentary
    papers
Grange, Peter, see Nicole,
  Christopher
Grassland husbandry, 457, 486,
  488, 489
Gray, Cecil Roderick, 525
Grenada, 329, 330
    see also Windward Islands and
    under specific subjects
Groundnuts, 463, 465
Gullah, 919a

Guyana, 21, 43, 49–51, 73, 106,
    141, 185, 336–338, 341, 342,
    346–352, 354, 357, 359, 361,
    363, 372, 377, 380, 382, 383,
    626
    see also British Guiana and
    under specific subjects
Gynaecology
    Guyana, 1131
Harris, Theodore Wilson, see
    Harris, Wilson
Harris, Wilson, 524, 525, 530,
    531, 564, 1040, 1049, 1059,
    1061, 1064, 1079
Health, 105, 106, 662, 664, 1126,
    1127
    Barbados, 293a
    Guyana, 341, 372, 625
    Women, 1391
Health, animal, see Animal
    science
Health, public, see Public
    health
Hearne, John, 523–525, 530, 1040,
    1041, 1059, 1064, 1079
Hendriks, A.L., 525, 531, 1059
Herbert, C.L., 525, 1059
Hercules, Frank, 525, 1059
Hill, Errol, 523, 525, 529, 1040,
    1041
Hillary, Samuel, 525
Hindus
    Trinidad and Tobago, 698
        see also East Indians
History, 23, 42, 46, 47, 57, 63,
    79, 93, 113, 117, 127, 130,
    131, 138, 144, 153, 154, 170,
    184, 278, 664, 676, 766–799,
    834, 980, 1044, 1161, 1224,
    1291, 1329, 1347
    Archival and manuscript
        material, 800–829, 831–
        833, 835, 836, 838–844,
        851, 852–855, 860–862,
        865, 866
    Anguilla, 831, see also
        History – Leeward Islands
    Antigua, 285b, 814, 831, see
        also History – Leeward
        Islands
    Bahamas, 802, 824, 834–836

Barbados, 781, 814, 837–846
Barbuda, 285b, 831, see also
    History – Leeward Islands
Belize, 185, 303, 309, 311,
    802, 824, 847, 848
Bermuda, 824, 849, 850
British Virgin Islands, 831,
    851
Dominica, 832, 833
Esequibo Colony. British
    Guiana, 1187
Grenada, 832, 833, 852
Grenadines, 832
Guyana, 185, 333, 334, 336,
    341, 345, 350, 354, 360,
    362, 369, 692, 781, 824,
    852a–855, 980
Indexes, 867, 868
Jamaica, 31, 401, 402, 404,
    802, 814, 856–862
Leeward Islands, 283, 831
Montserrat, 831, see also
    History – Leeward Islands
Nevis, 831, see also History –
    Leeward Islands
Periodicals and serials, 830
Reference works, 770
St. Kitts, 814, 831, see also
    History – Leeward Islands
St. Lucia, 832, 833
St. Vincent, 832, 833
Tobago, 863, see also History
    – Trinidad and Tobago
Trinidad, 520, 802
Trinidad and Tobago, 187, 431,
    437, 440, 781, 864–868,
    1320, 1324
Windward Islands, 832, 833
    see also Black history
History, colonial, 784–788, 812
History, constitutional, 775, 777,
    1159, 1173, 1182
    Guyana, 382
History, economic, 612, 775, 777
History, political, 777
History, social, 777
History, teaching of, 790
Hochoy, Sir Solomon, 526
Hodge, Merle, 525, 1059
Home economics, 105, 638
Hopkinson, Slade, 525, 1040, 1059

Hotel industry, 896
    Trinidad and Tobago, 895,
        896, 1388
House of Commons sessional
    papers, 816
House of Lords sessional papers,
    817
Housing, 87, 660, 662, 664, 869,
    870, 1220-1223
    Belize, 869
    Bermuda, 869
    Guyana, 869
Human resources, 1357, 1358
Humanities, 8, 79, 122, 123,
    1344
Hutchinson, Lionel, 525, 1059
Hydrogeology, 751
Hydrography, 1145, 1146
Hydro-power
    Guyana, 341
Immigrants
    Canada, 667, 1300
    Great Britain, 662-666, 1220-
        1223, 1294, 1301
Immigrants, coolie
    Guyana, 1313
Immigration, 1288, 1347
    Canada, 1300
    Great Britain, 660, 662, 664-
        666, 1200-1223, 1227,
        1301
Income, national, see National
    income
Income distribution, 614, 1331,
    1358
Indenture, East Indian, see
    East Indian indenture
Independence movements, 799
    see also Self-government
Industrial court. Trinidad and
    Tobago, 1014
Industrial development, 617, 880,
    1168, 1232, 1327, 1331, 1358
    Dominica, 885
    Guyana, 372, 1333
    Jamaica, 738, 889, 1271,
        1340
    Trinidad and Tobago, 201
        see also Economic
        development

Industrial education, see
    Education, industrial
Industrial law, see Labour law
Industrial planning, 1331a
Industrial relations, 594, 871,
    872, 1293, 1358
    Barbados, 871
    Guyana, 871, 872
    Jamaica, 871-873
    Trinidad, 871
    Trinidad and Tobago, 632, 872
    West Indies Associated States,
        871
        see also Trade unionism
Industry, 105, 154, 613, 874-
    883, 1329
    Barbados, 293a
    Dominica, 885
    Guyana, 625, 886, 887
    Jamaica, 888-890, 1340
    Trinidad and Tobago, 731,
        891-899, 1382a, 1388
        see also under specific
        industries
Ingram, Kenneth, E.N., 525
Integration, economic, 1239, 1242,
    1247
Integration, political, see
    Integration, regional
Integration, regional, 1233-1249
    see also Federation, Regional
    cooperation
International relations, 900-908,
    1157
Invader, Lord, 526
Investment, foreign, 1331
Iremonger, Lucille, 525
Island-Carib language
    Dominica, 923
    St. Vincent, 923
Jagan, Cheddi, 526
Jamaica, 25, 27, 30-32, 40, 43,
    44, 51-53, 74-76, 89, 97,
    113, 119, 141, 186, 193, 225,
    398-410, 423, see also under
    specific subjects
Jamaica gun court, 594
James, C.L.R., 523, 525, 530, 553,
    1040, 1059
John, Errol, 525, 1040, 1041
Jokes, 711

Jones, Evan, 525
Joshua, Ebenezer, 526
Journal of the Barbados Museum
    and Historical Society
    Indexes, 845, 846
Journals of the House of Assembly
    of Bermuda
    Indexes, 971
Kali Mai Puja. Guyana, 720
Keane, Ellsworth McG., 525
Kempadoo, Peter, 525, 1040, 1059
Khan, Ismith, 525, 1059
Kissoon, Freddie, 525
Kyk-Over-Al
    Indexes, 1089a
Labour, 609, 610, 1295, 1329
    Women, 1391
Labour disturbances, 431
    Trinidad and Tobago, 1197,
        1200
        see also Social
        disturbances
Labour law, 594
    Guyana, 872
    Jamaica, 872
    Trinidad and Tobago, 632,
        872, 1014
Labour relations, see Industrial
    relations
Ladoo, Harold Sonny, 525, 1059
Lamming, George, 523-525, 527,
    530, 1040, 1041, 1049, 1059,
    1061, 1064, 1079
Land reform, 622, 623
    Dominica, 326
Land tenure, 614, 622
    Dominica, 326
    St. Lucia, 622
Land use, 477, 492, 494, 739,
    1325, 1352
    Belize, 1308
Language, 79, 93, 128, 711, 909-
    927, 1345, 1348
    Antigua, 912, 918, 921
    Barbados, 293a, 918, 921
    Belize, 309a, 910, 918, 921
    Cayman Islands, 912
    Dominica, 910, 912, 921
    Grenada, 912, 921
    Guyana, 334, 350, 694, 910,
        912, 918, 921, 928-931

Jamaica, 186, 404, 910, 912-
    913, 918, 921, 1109
    Makucki Indians. Guyana, 931
    Periodicals and serials, 1092
    Reference works, 919
    St. Lucia, 910, 912, 918, 919, 921
    Trinidad and Tobago, 910, 912,
        918, 921
        see also Linguistics
Language, teaching of, 911-913
Languages, see under specific
    languages, see also Dialect
    languages
La Rose, John, 525
Lauchmonen, see Kempadoo, Peter
Law, 66, 145, 195, 210, 211, 221,
    783, 829, 932-950
    Anguilla, 962, see also Law -
        St. Kitts-Nevis-Anguilla
        Indexes, 962
    Antigua
        Indexes, 963-965
    Bahamas, 287, 936, 937, 966
    Barbados, 936, 937
        Indexes, 967-969
    Barbuda
        Indexes, 963, 965
    Belize, 936
        Indexes, 970
    Bermuda, 937
        Indexes, 971, 972
    British Virgin Islands
        Indexes, 973
    Cayman Islands, 936
    Dominica
        Indexes, 974, 975
    Grenada
        Indexes, 976-978
    Grenadines
        Indexes, 1011a
    Guyana, 362, 936, 937, 979-
        980
        Indexes, 954, 955, 981-
            990
    Indexes, 951-965, 967-978,
        981-1003, 1007-1028
    Jamaica, 404, 936, 937, 954,
        955
        Indexes, 991-999
    Leeward Islands, 936, 954,
        955
        Indexes, 957-961

Montserrat
   Indexes, 1000
   Periodicals and Serials, 937
St. Kitts-Nevis-Anguilla
   Indexes, 1001-1003
St. Lucia, 937, 1004-1006
   Indexes, 1007-1010
St. Vincent
   Indexes, 942a, 978, 1011,
      1011a
Trinidad, 1019
Trinidad and Tobago, 442,
   936, 937
   Indexes, 954, 955, 1012-
      1027
Turks and Caicos Islands,
   936
   Indexes, 1028
West Indies Associated
   States
   Indexes, 954, 955
Windward Islands, 936, 937
   Indexes, 954, 955
Women, 1391, 1393
Law reports of British Guiana
   Indexes, 988
Lebanese, 1303
Leeward Islands, 43, 51, 52, 53,
   81, 113, 281-283, see also
   under specific islands and
   subjects
Leftist movement
   Guyana, 1190
Legal administration, 594
Legal ethics, 942a
Legends
   Guyana, 719
Legumes, 463, 472
Lettuce, 464, 472
Lewis, Enid Kirton, 525
Librarianship
   Trinidad and Tobago, 433,
      1030
Libraries, 184
Libraries, special
   Trinidad and Tobago, 255
Library cooperation, 1029
Linden. Guyana, 359
Lindo, Archie, 525

Linguistics, 78, 79, 909-927
   Dominica, 532
   Guyana, 345, 694, 928
      see also Language
Literary criticism, see Criticism
Literature, 42, 63, 79, 93, 95,
   99, 117, 123, 128, 138, 139,
   170, 525, 676, 1031-1052
   Barbados, 1051, 1095
   Bermuda, 318
   Cayman Islands, 1051
   Dominica, 1051
   Guyana, 185, 333, 334, 362,
      1051, 1096-1108
   History, 1045, 1047, 1048
   Indexes, 1089-1091, 1118
   Jamaica, 186, 404, 1051,
      1109-1112
   Leeward Islands, 283
   Periodicals and serials, 1037,
      1044, 1050-1052, 1079,
      1092, 1093, 1113
      Indexes, 1089, 1089a,
         1091
   References works, 1037
   St. Lucia, 1051
   Trinidad and Tobago, 187, 431,
      433, 437, 440, 1051,
      1113-1119
      see also Black literature
Literature, black, see Black
   literature
Literature, children's, 95, 139,
   1050, 1053-1058, 1084
   Guyana, 1104
   Trinidad and Tobago, 1114
Literature, oral, see Oral
   literature
Livestock science, 453, 454, 457,
   486-489
   Jamaica, 506
      see also Animal science,
      Dairy science
Local government, see Government,
   local
Lovelace, Earl W., 523, 525, 530,
   1040, 1059
Lucie-Smith, Edward, 525, 531,
   1059, 1064
McDermot, Thomas Henry, 525, 1059
McDonald, Ian, 525, 1059
McFarlane, Basil, 525, 1059

McFarlane, John Ebenezer Clare,
    525, 1041, 1059
McKay, Claude, 523, 525, 527,
    540, 544, 554a, 1041, 1059,
    1064, 1079
McTair, Roger, 1059
McNeill, Anthony, 525, 1059
Magic, 1348
Maingot, Rodney, 563
Mais, Roger, 523, 525, 527, 1040,
    1041, 1059, 1061, 1064, 1079
Maize, 463, 465
Malaria
    Guyana, 1128
Malik, Abdul, 525, 1059
Mangoes, 462, 472
Manley, Norman Washington, 526,
    527
Manpower, 1358
    Trinidad and Tobago, 632,
        1382a
Manpower planning, 1331a
Manufacturing, see Industry and
    under specific industries
Manuscripts, 42, 50, 112, 126,
    766, 767, 773, 779, 783, 799,
    810, 811, 819, 820, 823-826,
    839, 1137, 1167, 1174, 1182,
    1278a, 1280, 1282, 1284
    Barbados, 28, 580, 669, 838,
        839, 841-843, 845
    Belize, 50, 1307
    Bermuda, 50, 317, 318, 849
    Guyana, 50, 341, 378, 381,
        689, 852a
    Jamaica, 27, 74, 75, 399,
        856, 857, 1286
    Trinidad and Tobago, 56,
        1199, 1320
        see also History -
        Archival and manuscript
        material
Maps, 16, 17, 25, 42, 50, 83,
    103, 167, 184, 220, 234, 236,
    237, 242-247, 797, 813
    Antigua, 286
    Bahamas, 247, 288, 289
    Barbados, 28, 295, 296
    Belize, 247
    Berbice. Guyana, 392
    Bequia, 246

Bermuda, 319
British Virgin Islands, 320
Demerara. Guyana, 392
Dominica, 326, 328
Essequibo. Guyana, 392
Grenada, 328
Guyana, 247, 353, 361, 378,
    387-394, 758, 759
Jamaica, 30, 74, 75, 186,
    247, 404, 413, 414, 1286
Montserrat, 418
Nevis, 246
Orinoco-Essequibo region.
    Guyana, 389
Roraima. Guyana, 388
St. Kitts, 246
St. Lucia, 246
St. Vincent, 246
Tobago, 447, see also Maps -
    Trinidad and Tobago
Tortola. British Virgin
    Islands, 320
Trinidad and Tobago, 424, 440,
    447, 448
Turks and Caicos Islands, 247
    see also Non-book
    materials
Maps, soil
    Barbados, 241
    Guyana, 241
    Jamaica, 241
    Trinidad and Tobago, 241
Maps, survey
    Guyana, 341, 758, 759
Margetson, George Reginald, 525,
    1041
Marijuana, see Cannabis
Marine biology, see Biology,
    marine
Marine geology, see Geology,
    marine
Marketing, agricultural, see
    Agricultural marketing
Marley, Bob, 703, 1261
Maroons
    Guyana, 1283
    Jamaica, 31, 696, 1283
Marson, Una M., 525, 1059
Matura, Mustapha, 529
Mass communication, see Communi-
    cation

Mass media, see Communication
Mathematics
    Guyana, 336
Mating, 1359
    Trinidad and Tobago, 1215
Mayas,
    Belize, 299, 311, 682, 1307
Mazaruni. Guyana, 341
Medical education, see Education,
    medical
Medicinal plants, see Botany,
    medical
Medicine, 86, 562, 783, 1119a–
    1127
    Guyana, 566, 568, 1128–1131
    Jamaica, 1132
    Periodicals and serials,
        1120
    Trinidad and Tobago, 561
        see also Diseases and
        under specific aspects
        and diseases
Medicine, folk, see Folk
    medicine
Medicine, social and preventive,
    86, 1126–1127, 1354
    Jamaica, 1126, 1127, 1132
Mendes, Alfred, 525, 1041, 1059
Metal working industry.
    Trinidad and Tobago, 893
Meteorology, 1272, 1274
Migrants, 925
Migration, 79, 612, 935, 1291,
    1299, 1303, 1357, 1358
    Great Britain, 1301
    Trinidad and Tobago, 632
Migration, internal
    Trinidad and Tobago, 1215
Millets, 463
Mineral resources
    Guyana, 758, 759, 1142
    Jamaica, 1271
Miners
    Guyana, 341
Mining
    Guyana, 625, 755
Missions, Christian, 1257, 1281
    Guyana, 334, 353, 367
    Jamaica, 1265
    Methodist, 1281
Mittelholzer, Edgar, 523, 525,
    530, 546, 1040, 1041, 1059,

    1061, 1064, 1079
Moko
    Indexes, 1363
Molluscs, 1402
Monetary policy, see Fiscal
    policy
Montserrat, 283, 418
        see also Leeward Islands
        and under specific sub-
        jects
Morant Bay rebellion. Jamaica,
    862, 1156
Morris, John, see Hearne, John
Morris, Mervyn, 525, 1059
Music, 99, 148a, 184, 638, 699–
    701, 711, 1044, 1133–1136
    Barbados, 293a
    Bahamas, 1136
    Belize, 185, 1136
    Guyana, 721, 1137
    History, 1135
    Jamaica, 186, 404, 702, 703,
        1136, 1261
    Periodicals and serials, 1092
    Trinidad and Tobago, 187
        433, 700, 1136
        see also Folk songs
        433, 700, 1136
        see also Folksongs
Music, cult, see Cult music
Music, folk, see Folk music
Music, religious, see Religious
    music
Music scores
    Guyana, 1137
Naipaul, Shiva, 525, 530, 1059
Naipaul, Vidia, 523, 525, 530,
    547, 548, 1040, 1041, 1049,
    1059, 1061
National income, 609, 610
    Trinidad and Tobago, 1382a
National planning, 1331a
National security
    Guyana, 1371
    Jamaica, 1374
    Trinidad and Tobago, 1376
Nationalism, 1158, 1347
Nationalism, Afro-American,
    1039
Natural history, 66
    Bahamas, 570, 834
    Dominica, 324

Guyana, 692
Jamaica, 31
Trinidad, 516
    see also Botany, Fauna,
    Flora, Zoology
Natural resources, 144, 1138–
1140
Belize, 305
Guyana, 1141, 1142
Leeward Islands, 283
Marine, 1331b
Trinidad and Tobago, 441
Negroes, see Blacks
Nettleford, Rex Milton, 525
Nevis, see St. Kitts–Nevis–
Anguilla
see also under specific
subjects
New World Quarterly
Indexes, 1363
Newspapers, 57, 70, 117, 120,
228–233, 252, 255, 586, 711,
783, 787, 830–832, 838, 841,
1037, 1166, 1180, 1186,
1238, 1249, 1278a, 1280,
1347
Bahamas, 231
Barbados, 231, 252, 842–844
Belize, 311
Bermuda, 231, 232, 318, 849
British Virgin Islands, 231
Cayman Islands, 231
Dominica, 327
Grenada, 1186
Guyana, 385, 386, 397
Indexes, 1360, 1361, 1363
Jamaica, 30, 229, 231, 401,
    402, 404, 857, 858
    Indexes, 1360
Leeward Islands, 231
Montserrat, 418
St. Lucia, 420, 422
Trinidad and Tobago, 231,
    253, 431, 446, 450, 704,
    115 1153, 1186, 1201, 1320,
    1324
    Indexes, 1361, 1363
Turks Islands, 231
Windward Islands, 231
Nicole, Christopher, 523, 525,
530, 1040, 1059

Non-book materials, 33, 42, 50,
57, 96, 97, 234–248, 699,
702, 825
Barbados, 295, 296
Guyana, 337, 361, 387–394,
693
Jamaica, 413, 414
Trinidad and Tobago, 440
Novels, 1034, 1050, 1073, 1075,
1078, 1081, 1088
Barbados, 1035
Dominica, 1035
Guyana, 362, 1035
Jamaica, 1035
Tobago, 1035
Trinidad, 1035
Trinidad and Tobago, 1113
    see also Fiction
Numismatics, 1143, 1144
Nutrition, 1271
Guyana, 1129
Obeah, 78a, 678, 716, 717
Jamaica, 717
Oceanography, 81, 1145, 1146,
1274
Okra, 472
Oral literature
Trinidad and Tobago, 707
Ornamentals, 472
Ornithology, 1272, 1401
    see also Birds, Zoology
Ottley, Carlton Robert, 525
Paleobotany, 579
Palmer, C. Everard, 525, 1059,
1079
Pangola grass, 465, 488
Papaya, 465, 472
Parliaments, 1176
Parliamentary papers. Great
Britain, 100, 104, 816, 817,
841, 1290
    Indexes, 104
Trinidad and Tobago, 442,
1320
Patterson, Orlando, 525, 1040,
1059, 1064
Patois language
St. Lucia, 919
Pawan, J. Lennox, 561
Pawpaw, see Papaya
Peasantry, black, 1346

Penology, 594
People's National Congress.
  Guyana, 1190
People's National Movement.
  Trinidad and Tobago, 1201
People's Progressive Party.
  Guyana, 1190
Peppers, 472
Periodicals and Serials, 42, 70,
  90, 117, 120, 191, 215, 223,
  249-258, 586, 711, 1164,
  1166, 1190, 1249, 1347, 1395
  Bahamas, 251, 256, 288, 289,
    830, 1092
  Barbados, 251, 252, 256, 830,
    1092, 1093
    Indexes, 845, 846, 884
  Belize, 252, 830
  Bermuda, 251, 830, 1092
  British Virgin Islands, 252
  Cayman Islands, 830
  Dominica, 252, 256
  Guyana, 251, 252, 256, 395-
    397, 830, 1092, 1093
    Indexes, 24, 65, 118, 845,
      846, 884, 1059, 1089,
      1091, 1361-1363, 1366,
      1367
  Jamaica, 74, 75, 250-252,
    401, 402, 404, 415, 416,
    830, 857, 1092, 1093,
    1110, 1338
  Leeward Islands, 830
  St. Kitts, 252
  St. Lucia, 252, 256, 1092,
    1093
  St. Vincent, 252, 1093
  Trinidad and Tobago, 251,
    256, 431, 433, 436, 442,
    450, 630, 712, 830,
    1092, 1093, 1113, 1199,
    1201
  Windward Islands, 830
Petroleum industry
  Trinidad and Tobago, 876,
    898, 899
Philately
  Guyana, 1147
    Indexes, 1148
Philosophy
  Guyana, 333, 362

Phonodiscs, 103a, 699, 711,
  1134
  Jamaica, 702, 1261
  Montserrat, 418
  Trinidad and Tobago, 187
    see also Discography,
    Non-book materials
Phonograph records, see Phono-
  discs
Photographs
  Guyana, 361
    see also Non-book
    materials
Physical geography, see Geography
  physical
Physical planning, 1331a, 1331b
  Trinidad and Tobago, 1342
Physiology, animal, see Animal
  science
Phytogeography
  Guyana, 575
Pidgin languages, 912, 913, 920,
  921, 927
Pigeon pea, 457, 470
Pigs, 489, see also Livestock
  science
Pilgrim, Frank, 525
Pineapple, 472
Planning, see Agricultural
  planning, Economic planning,
  etc.
Plant ecology, see Ecology, plant
Plant pathology, 460, 465, 470
Plantain, 462
Plantation system, 153, 612, 888,
  1325, 1346
Plants, medicinal, see Botany,
  medical
Plants, poisonous, see Poisonous
  plants
Plays, see Drama
PNC, see People's National
  Congress
PNM, see People's National
  Movement
Poetry, 148a, 184, 525, 1031,
  1032, 1034, 1038, 1044,
  1047, 1048, 1050, 1094,
  1164
  Antigua, 1036
  Barbados, 1036, 1095

Dominica, 1036
Grenada, 1036
Guyana, 336, 362, 1102, 1108
    Indexes, 1089-1091, 1118
Jamaica, 186, 1109, 1112
Montserrat, 1036
St. Kitts, 1036
St. Vincent, 1036
Trinidad and Tobago, 187,
    440, 1036, 1113, 1115,
    1119
    Indexes, 1118
Poisonous plants, 465a
Police, 594, 1220
Political development, 81
    see also Politics
Political disturbances, 1156
    Trinidad and Tobago, 1197,
    1201
        see also Social disturb-
        ances
Political geography, see
    Geography, political
Political history, see History,
    political
Political parties, 1154, 1177,
    1180
    Guyana, 1189, 1190
    Trinidad and Tobago, 1198,
    1201
Political sociology, see
    Sociology, political
Politics, 45, 78, 93, 98, 106,
    113, 123, 128, 130, 131, 138,
    144, 145, 154, 184, 285b,
    613, 614, 664, 676, 788,
    900, 1154-1182, 1224, 1228,
    1232
    Anguilla, 1183
    Barbados, 293a, 837
    Belize, 185, 306, 309, 311
    Dominica, 327
    Grenada, 1186
    Guyana, 333, 354, 369, 852a,
        1149-1151, 1169, 1187-
        1194, 1371
        Indexes, 1195
    Jamaica, 402, 1152, 1169,
        1374
    Trinidad and Tobago, 187,
        1169, 1197-1203, 1376

Women, 1391, 1393
    see also Government
Pollution
    Jamaica, 763
Population, 609, 610, 734, 1204-
    1211, 1291, 1329, 1348, 1358,
    1359
    Barbados, 1212
    Guyana, 1314
    Jamaica, 1213, 1214
    Trinidad and Tobago, 1215,
    1216
        see also Censuses, Vital
        statistics
Population statistics, see
    Statistics, population
Pork-knockers
    Guyana, 341
Port Royal. Jamaica, 859
Portuguese, 1303
Potato, Irish, 461, 473
Potato, sweet, 461, 464, 473
Poultry, 489, see also Livestock
    science
PPP, see People's Progressive
    Party
Press, 783, see also Communica-
    tion
Press freedom, 587, 592
Price, George Cadle, 526
Prints, 50, 83, 167, 841, 1277
    Guyana, 361, 381
    Jamaica, 404
Privy Council, 955, 987, 996,
    997
Production economics, 605
Productivity, 614
    Jamaica, 628
Prose, 148a
Prostitution, 594
Psychology, 1397
    Guyana, 333
Psychology, social, 1217, 1218,
    1397
Public administration, 214, 1155,
    1171, 1179
    Guyana, 346, 1191, 1194
    Jamaica, 402
Public finance
    Trinidad and Tobago, 629

Public health, see Medicine,
    social and preventive
Public service
    Trinidad and Tobago, 1203
        see also Public adminis-
        tration
Public utilities
    Guyana, 625
Questel, Victor D., 525, 1059
Rabies
    Trinidad and Tobago, 561
Race, 1347
Race relations, 947a, 1158,
    1224a, 1226, 1279, 1346
    Bahamas, 1224a
    Barbados, 1224a
    Belize, 1224a
    Great Britain, 660, 663, 664,
        1219-1225, 1227, 1261,
        1349
    Guyana, 661, 1150, 1151,
        1224a
    Jamaica, 1224a
    Trinidad, 661
    Trinidad and Tobago, 1224a,
        1320
Racial discrimination, 1220-
    1223, 1227
Racism, 664
Radio scripts, 248
    Jamaica, 398
Raleigh, Sir Walter, 854
Rastafarians, 1262, 1267-1269
    Great Britain, 1261, 1266
    Jamaica, 1256, 1260, 1263,
        1264, 1266
Reckord, Barry, 525, 529
Records, see Phonodiscs
Redcam, Tom, see McDermot,
    Thomas Henry
Redhead, Wilfred, 525, 1040
"Redlegs"
    Barbados, 669
Reference works, 146, 638, 1174
    Atlases, 167
    Directories, 118, 589
    Jamaica
        Almanacs, 401
    Trinidad and Tobago
        Almanacs, 427
        Yearbooks, 1113

    Yearbooks, 120, 1166
Reggae, 699, 702, 703, 1261, 1266
Regional cooperation, 106, 606,
    900, 1228-1249, 1292
    see also Federation, Integra-
    tion, regional
Regional planning, 1329, 1331a,
    1331b
Regionalism, see Regional
    cooperation
Reid, Vic, 523-525, 530, 1040,
    1041, 1059, 1061, 1064
Religion, 63, 79, 103a, 106, 676,
    711, 783, 802, 812, 1249a-
    1259, 1345, 1346, 1348
    Barbados, 293a, 1249a
    Belize, 1249a
    Guyana, 333, 362
    Jamaica, 1249a, 1260-1269
    Leeward Islands, 1249a
    Trinidad and Tobago, 149a, 1270
    Windward Islands, 1249a
    Women, 1391
Religious cults, 169, 678
    Jamaica, 1256
    Trinidad, 1265
        see also specific cults
Religious music, 699, 1133
Resources, mineral, see Mineral
    resources
Resources, water, see Water
    resources
Reviews, see Criticism
Rhone, Trevor D., 525
Rhys, Jean, 523, 525, 530, 552,
    556, 559, 1040, 1059, 1061,
    1064
Rice, 464, 465
Rice industry
    Guyana, 498, 499, 1314
Riots, see Social disturbances
Roach, Eric, 525, 1040, 1059
Roberts, Walter Adolphe, 525, 526,
    1059, 1079
Rock steady, 699
Rodway, James A., 525
Rogers, De Wilton, 525
Root crops, 461, 473
Roy, Namba, 525, 527, 1059
Rum industry, 875
    Jamaica, 875

Rural development
  Guyana, 1335
  Jamaica, 1392a
Rural planning, 1329
Rural sociology, see Sociology,
  rural
Sadeek, Sheik Mohamed, 525, 1040,
  1059
St. Christopher, see St. Kitts-
  Nevis-Anguilla
St. Kitts-Nevis-Anguilla, 283
  see also Leeward Islands and
  under specific subjects
St. Lucia, 225, 419-421
  see also Windward Islands and
  under specific subjects
St. Omer, Garth, 525, 1040,
  1059
St. Vincent, see Windward
  Islands and under specific
  subjects
Salkey, Andrew, 523, 525, 530,
  1040, 1041, 1059, 1061, 1064,
  1079
San Fernando. Trinidad, 425
Sancho, Thomas Anson, 525
Savacou
  Indexes, 1363
Schomburgh, Robert, 574
Science, 86, 788, 1271-1276
  Guyana, 336, 353
  Jamaica, 404
Science, applied
  Guyana, 362
Science, pure
  Guyana, 333, 362
Scott, Dennis, 525, 1059
Sealy, Clifford, 525
Secondary education, see Educa-
  tion, secondary
Self-government, 798
  see also Government,
  Independence movements
Selvon, Samuel, 523, 525, 530,
  1040, 1041, 1049, 1059, 1061
Seymour, A.J., 525, 531, 545,
  1040, 1041, 1059, 1064
Shakers, 678
Shango, 678
  Trinidad and Tobago, 1136,
    1256, 1270

Sherlock, Philip, 524, 525, 1059
Short stories, 1050, 1080
  Antigua, 1036
  Grenada, 1036
  Guyana, 362
  Montserrat, 1036
  Trinidad and Tobago, 1113
    see also Fiction
Shouters, 678
Simpson, Louis, 525, 1059, 1064
Ska, 699
Slave revolts, 1283
Slave trade, 103, 127, 792, 816,
  817, 1277-1284, 1345
Slavery, 44, 48, 66, 100, 127,
  153, 167, 783, 792, 798, 799,
  816, 817, 925, 1167, 1277-
  1284, 1297, 1306, 1345, 1346
  Barbados, 293a, 1306
  Belize, 1307
  Bermuda, 1285
  Jamaica, 31, 44, 1286
  Laws, 998
Smith, M.G., 525, 1059
Social and Economic Studies
  Indexes, 259, 1366, 1367
Social and preventive medicine,
  see Medicine, social and
  preventive
Social anthropology, see Anthro-
  pology, social
Social conditions, 42, 98a, 144,
  512, 594, 664, 1161, 1168,
  1280, 1287-1304, 1306
  Antigua, 285b
  Barbados, 293a, 837, 1305,
    1306
  Barbuda, 285b
  Belize, 1307, 1308
  Blacks, 681
  Dominica, 324
  Guyana, 369, 661, 980, 1309-
    1314
  Jamaica, 402, 1315-1319
  Leeward Islands, 283
  St. Lucia, 622
  Trinidad, 661
  Trinidad and Tobago, 1197,
    1320-1324
Social development, 1325-1331,
  1336, 1391a
  Guyana, 1332, 1335

Jamaica, 1336–1340
St. Lucia, 1341
Trinidad and Tobago, 441,
    1342
Social disturbances, 1156
Trinidad and Tobago, 431,
    1197, 1200, 1201
    see also Labour distur-
    bances, Political
    disturbances
Social protest, 1039
Social history, see History,
    social
Social psychology, 594
Social sciences, 8, 24, 79, 86,
    113, 122, 123, 278, 664, 788,
    1044, 1343–1359, 1399
Barbados, 1350a
Belize, 309, 311
Guyana, 333, 336, 1350,
    1350a, 1370–1372
Indexes, 1360–1367
Jamaica, 1350, 1350a, 1373–
    1375
Linden. Guyana, 1372
Periodicals and serials,
    1368, 1369
Indexes, 1360–1363, 1366,
    1367
Trinidad and Tobago, 437,
    1350a, 1376, 1377
Social services, 594
Great Britain, 1220–1223
Social statistics, see
    Statistics, social
Social welfare, 1358
Social work
    Student project reports,
    1355
Sociolinguistics, 922
Sociology, 78, 119, 184, 1158,
    1291, 1297, 1346, 1347,
    1356
Barbados, 1305
Grenada, 1378
Guyana, 362
Jamaica, 404, 1375
Trinidad and Tobago, 187
Sociology, political, 1149
Guyana, 1149–1151
Jamaica, 1152

Trinidad and Tobago, 1153
Sociology, rural
Guyana, 495
Soil geography, see Geography,
    soil
Soil maps, see Maps, soil
Soil science, 453, 454, 457, 490–
    493
Antigua, 492
Bahamas, 492
Barbados, 492
Barbuda, 492
Belize, 305, 492
Carriacou, 492
Cayman Islands, 492
Dominica, 326, 492
Grenadines, 492
Guyana, 341, 492, 500–503,
    728
Jamaica, 492
St. Lucia, 492
St. Vincent, 492
Trinidad and Tobago, 492
Turks and Caicos Islands, 492
Solar energy, 882
Sorghum, 463
Sou-sou
Trinidad and Tobago, 1377
Southwell, Caleb Azariah Paul,
    526
Spiritualism, 1379
Sport
Barbados, 293a
Belize, 309a
Trinidad and Tobago, 437
Stamp collecting, see Philately
Statistics, 1292, 1357, 1380–
    1383
Agriculture, 1381, 1382a
Education, 1382a
Fisheries, 1381
Forestry, 1381
Guyana, 625
Industry, 1381, 1382a
Jamaica, 1337
Manpower, 1382a
Tourism, 1381, 1382a
Trade, 583, 613, 1381
Trinidad and Tobago, 1382a,
    1383
Women, 1391

Statistics, economic, 1381, 1382a
Statistics, population, 613, 1208, 1381
  Jamaica, 1214
Statistics, social, 1381
Statistics, vital, see Vital statistics
Steelband, 699, 701, 708
Stewart, John, 1059
Student project reports. ICTA/ UWI, 150-152, 454, 455, 457, 458, 461, 488, 651, 738, 882, 1354, 1355, 1398
  Agriculture, 454, 455, 457, 458
  Crop science, 461
  Education, 651, 1398
  Engineering, 882
  Geography, 738
  Livestock science, 488
  Social and preventive medicine, 1354
  Solar energy, 882
Sugar industry, 66, 153, 469, 479, 612, 874, 897, 1325
  Antigua, 874
  Barbados, 874, 884
  Guyana, 874, 1314
  Jamaica, 874, 888
  Leeward Islands, 874
  Periodicals and serials Indexes, 884
  Trinidad and Tobago, 874, 897
Sugar industry review. Barbados Indexes, 884
Sugar technology, 456, 469, 874
Sugar-cane, 457, 465, 874
Sugar-cane wax, 883
Suicide, 594
Supreme court. Jamaica, 996, 997
Supreme court. Trinidad and Tobago, 1013
Supreme court of British Guiana, 985, 986, 990
Supreme courts, 954, 955
Survey maps, see Maps, survey
Susu, see Sou-sou
Tannia, 464, 465

Tape recordings, 103a, 248
  Guyana, 720, 721, 928
    see also Non-book materials
Tapia
  Indexes, 1363
Tapia House Group. Trinidad and Tobago, 1201
Taxation, 605, 608, 880
  Bahamas, 608
  Barbados, 608
  Bermuda, 608
  Guyana, 608
  Jamaica, 608
  Trinidad, 608
Taylor, Douglas, 532
Taylor, Stanley, 525, 1079
Technical education, see Education, technical
Technology, 86, 877
  Trinidad and Tobago, 201
Technology, food, see Food technology
Technology, sugar, see Sugar technology
Telemaque, Harold M., 525, 1040, 1041, 1059
Theatre
  Trinidad, 1136
Theses, 17, 57, 65, 118, 147, 214, 261-263, 265, 273, 274, 275a, 276, 277, 279, 280, 594
  Agriculture, 453-455, 457-459, 461, 463, 464, 472, 477, 488, 489, 494, 498
  Anthropology, 510
  Archaeology, 517
  Bahamas, 774
  Barbados, 774, 1212
  Belize, 304, 309a, 774, 1307
  Bermuda, 774
  Botany, 580
  Communication, 589
  East Indians, 698
  Economic development, 1326
  Economics, 774
  Education, 645, 650, 651, 774, 1225
  Engineering, 1276
  Ethnic groups, 661, 664, 1225
  Ethnomusicology, 707

Garvey, Marcus Josiah, 537
Geology, 746, 751, 760
  Guyana, 760, 774, 1312
  History, 774, 857
  Jamaica, 399, 774, 857, 1213,
    1336, 1392a
  Language and linguistics,
    915
  Law, 595, 774, 934, 940
  Leeward Islands, 774
  Literature, 1061, 1064
  Medicine, 1354
  Performing arts, 1136
  Petroleum industry, 899
  Politics and government, 774,
    1153, 1180, 1182
  Population, 1210, 1212, 1213
  St. Kitts, 774
  Science, 1273
  Slavery, 1279
  Social and economic condi-
    tions, 1307, 1312, 1320,
    1322
  Social and economic develop-
    ment, 1336
  Social sciences, 1347, 1350,
    1354, 1377
  Sociology, 774, 1153
  Solar energy, 882, 1276
  Technology, 882
  Trinidad and Tobago, 774,
    1153, 1320, 1322, 1377
  Windward Islands, 774
  Women, 1392a, 1395
    see also Dissertations,
    doctoral
Thomas, G.C., 525, 1059
Tobacco, 464
Tobago, 427, 428, 431
  see also Trinidad and Tobago
  and under specific subjects
Tomatoes, 464, 472
Topography, 734
Tortola. British Virgin
  Islands, 320
Tourism, 79, 105, 617, 1326,
  1331, 1384-1386
  Barbados, 293a
  Jamaica, 738
  Trinidad and Tobago, 895,
    1382a, 1387, 1388

Trade, 87, 154, 612, 1232
  Guyana, 625
  Jamaica, 738
  Trinidad and Tobago, 1382a
Trade, external, 605
Trade statistics, see Statistics -
  trade
Trade unionism, 871
  Barbados, 871
  Guyana, 871, 872
  Jamaica, 871-873
  Trinidad and Tobago, 871,
    872, 1382a
  West Indies Associated States,
    871
    see also Industrial
    relations
Trade unions, 1158, 1177, 1293
Transport economics, 609, 633
  Trinidad and Tobago, 633
Transportation, 633, 1389
  Barbados, 293a
  Guyana, 372, 625
Travel, see Description and
  travel
Trinidad, 424, 429, 431, 436
  see also Trinidad and Tobago
  and under specific subjects
Trinidad and Tobago, 23, 43, 51-
  53, 77, 81, 113, 141, 187,
  225, 423, 424, 426-441, 449
  see also under specific
  subjects
Trinidad Guardian
  Indexes, 1361
Trinidad law reports
  Indexes, 1027
Trinidad Theatre Workshop, 557
Tropical agriculture, see
  Agriculture, tropical
Tropical Agriculture Indexes, 65
Tropical diseases, see Diseases,
  tropical
Turks Islands, 290, see also
  Turks and Caicos Islands
Turks and Caicos Islands, 97
  see also under specific
  subjects
Turtle industry, 878
  Bahamas, 878
  Bermuda, 878
UF, see United front

Unemployment, see Employment
Unions, credit, see Credit
    unions
UNIP, see United Independence
    Party
United Front. Guyana, 1190
United Independence Party.
    Trinidad and Tobago, 1201
Urban development, 676
Urban geography, see Geography,
    urban
Urban planning, 1329
Urbanization, 1343, 1358
Vampire bat
    Trinidad and Tobago, 561
Van Sertima, Ivan, 525
Vegetation, 579
    Guyana, 581, 760
Vernon, Edward, 820
Virology, 1275
Virtue, Vivian, 525, 1059
Vital statistics, 1209
    see also Censuses, Popula-
    tion
Vocational education, see
    Education, vocational
Vocational training, see
    Education, vocational
Volcanoes, 1390
    St. Vincent, 1390
Voodoo, 678
Wager, Sir Charles, 820
Waite-Smith, Cicely, 525, 1040
Walcott, Derek, 523, 525, 529,
    531, 543, 547a, 557, 558,
    1040, 1041, 1049, 1059,
    1061
Walcott, Roderick, 525, 1040,
    1041
Water resources, 751, 1139
    Dominica, 326
Water riots
    Trinidad, 1156
Weeds, 465a
    Guyana, 465a
    Jamaica, 465a
    Trinidad and Tobago, 465a
West India Committee Papers,
    804
West Indian cherry, see Cherry,
    West Indian

West Indian Reports
    Indexes, 953-955
West Indies Associated States,
    1173
West Indies Federation, 24, 117,
    258, 900, 1170, 1173, 1229,
    1230, 1234, 1235, 1237, 1240,
    1241, 1243, 1246, 1248, 1249
Wickham, John, 525
Williams, Dennis, 525, 1040,
    1059, 1064
Williams, Eric Eustace, 523, 525,
    526, 536, 539, 554, 560, 565
Wilson, Jeanne, 525
Windward Islands, 43, 51-53, 81,
    113
    see also under individual
    islands and specific subjects
Witchcraft, 717
Women, 212, 1391-1396
    Jamaica, 1392a
Women writers, 1036, 1098
Wynter, Sylvia, 524, 525, 1041,
    1059
Yam, 461, 462, 464, 465, 473
Yellow fever
    Guyana, 1128
York, Andrew, see Nicole,
    Christopher
Youth, 594, 1126, 1127, 1220,
    1397-1399
    Guyana, 1399
    Jamaica, 1399
    Trinidad, 1399
Youth leadership, 1397
Zoology, 1272, 1400-1403
    Guyana, 360, 1404
    Jamaica, 1405
    Trinidad and Tobago, 1406
        see also Biology,
        Entomology, Fauna,
        Natural history